# Zimbabwe's Trajectory:

## Stepping Forward or Sliding Back?

# Zimbabwe's Trajectory:

## Stepping Forward or Sliding Back?

Edited by

# Eldred V. Masunungure

Published by
Weaver Press, Box A1922, Avondale, Harare. 2020
<www.weaverpresszimbabwe.com>
and
The Mass Public Opinion Institute (MPOI), Box 8360, Harare, 2020

Typeset by Weaver Press
Cover by Danes Design, Zimbabwe
Printed by Bidvest, South Africa

The publishers note that any opinions and views expressed in this
publication are the responsibility of the individual authors and that they do
not necessarily subscribe to the views of the contributors.

ISBN: 978-1-77922-376-0  (p/b)
ISBN: 978-1-77922-377-7 (PDF)
ISBN: 978-1-77922-378-4 (ePub)

# Contents

# List of Tables and Figures

## Tables

## Figures

# Notes on Contributors

**ANYWAY CHINGWETE** holds a Master's degree in Population Studies and an Honours degree in Economics from the University of Zimbabwe. She has trained in survey methodology, research analysis and poverty in Africa and currently works for the Institute for Justice and Reconciliation in Cape Town as the Project Manager on the Afrobarometer Project. She has contributed regularly to the Afrobarometer publication database since 2005, and sits on the management committee of the Institute for Democracy, Citizenship and Public Policy in Africa, based at the University of Cape Town.

**RICHMAN KOKERA** is a Lecturer in the Department of Psychology at the University of Zimbabwe, and is a former Research Officer at the Mass Public Opinion Institute.

**JONATHAN KUGARAKURIPI** is a Research Officer at MPOI. He holds an Honours degree in Psychology from the University of Zimbabwe and has a particular interest in political psychology research.

**GREG LININGTON** is a lawyer and lecturer in the Department of Political and Administrative Studies at the University of Zimbabwe. He holds two Masters degrees, one in Constitutional Law (UNISA) and another in Public International Law (London). His research interests include investigating constitutional amendment theories and the interpretation and enforcement of provisions in the Declaration of Rights. He has written a book on Zimbabwe's Constitutional Law, as well as articles and book chapters on aspects of constitutional law.

**ALOIS MADHEKENI** is a democracy and governance expert who specialises in power politics and governance in southern Africa. He has taught local government courses at the University of Zimbabwe and is currently the co-ordinator of the community development programme of Silveira House Jesuit Social Justice and Development Centre. He holds a PhD in multilevel government law and policy from the University of the Western Cape.

ELDRED V. MASUNUNGURE is a Political Science and Public Administration graduate of the University of Zimbabwe and Dalhousie University (Canada) and teaches Public Policy and Political Theory courses at both undergraduate and post-graduate levels in the Department of Political and Administrative Studies at the University of Zimbabwe. He has published widely, including editing *Defying the Winds of Change: Zimbabwe's 2008 Elections* (2009) and co-editing *Zimbabwe: Mired in Transition* (2012). He is the Director of the Harare-based Mass Public Opinion Institute, where he is the Principal Investigator of the Afrobarometer Project.

NATASHA MATAIRE has a Masters degree in International Relations from the University of Zimbabwe and is a former teaching assistant at the Department of Political and Administrative Studies. She has experience in elections-related research at an NGO in Harare. Other areas of research include human rights, international political economy and foreign affairs. She is a regular contributor to the Black and White Youth Movement in Africa, an NGO that seeks to elevate African youth regardless of race. She is preparing to embark on her PhD studies in 2021.

LAWRENCE MHANDARA holds a PhD in Peace Studies and is a senior lecturer in the Department of Political and Administrative Studies at the University of Zimbabwe. His research covers politics, security and conflict issues. His latest publication, 'The Great Lakes Region Security Complex: Lessons for the African Solutions for Peace and Security Approach', was published in the Institute of Peace and Security Studies' Journal of African-Centred Solutions to Peace and Security.

TABANI MOYO is the Director of the Media Institute of Southern Africa (MISA) Zimbabwe. Prior to his appointment, he served as MISA's Programmes Officer, doubling as the Branding Manager for the network Regional Office. He has wide experience in the print media, communications and advertising industries. He holds a Masters in Business Adminstration (ESAMI, Tanzania), a Postgraduate Diploma in Marketing Management (Chartered Institute of Marketing, London), and is studying towards a DBA at the University of KwaZulu-Natal.

SIMANGELE MOYO-NYEDE is a Research Officer with the Mass Public Opinion Institute. She holds an MSc in International Relations and a BSc Honours degree in Political Science, both from the University of Zimbabwe. Her research interests include women's rights and governance.

ASHTON MURWIRA holds a Phd in Peacebuilding (Durban University of Technology), and an MSc in International Relations and a BSc Honours in Political Science from the University of Zimbabwe, where he is a lecturer in the Department of Political and Administrative Studies at UZ. He lectures in courses that include Comparative Politics, International Relations and Foreign Policy. His research interests are in peace and conflict, international relations, and governance.

STEPHEN NDOMA is a researcher based in Harare. He has an MA in Public Administration and a BSc Honours in Politics and Administration from the University of Zimbabwe. He is currently employed as Principal Researcher at the Mass Public Opinion Institute where he has managed a series of projects commissioned by the Afrobarometer Network. His strength lies in research planning, execution, data analysis and dissemination of research findings

NHLANHLA NGWENYA is currently the Media Manager for OSISA and was the Director of MISA Zimbabwe until 2017, following a decade at the Media Monitoring Project Zimbabwe. He holds an MA in International Development Management (University of Bradford, UK), and a BA Honours in Linguistics, an MA in Media and Communications Studies, and a Postgraduate Diploma in Media and Communications Studies, all from the University of Zimbabwe. He is the Chairperson of the privately run online news platform Radio VOP and sits on the Management Committee of the Human Rights NGO Forum.

PEDZISAI RUHANYA is a Senior Lecturer in the Journalism and Media Studies section of the University of Zimbabwe's Department of English. He holds a BSc Honours in Sociology from the University of Zimbabwe, an MA in Human Rights from the University of Essex (UK), and a PhD in Media and Democracy from the University of Westminster (UK). He has published articles in peer-reviewed journals on media and democracy, and co-edited, with Professor Sabelo Gatsheni-Ndlovu, *The History and Political Transition of Zimbabwe – From Mugabe to Mnangagwa* (2020).

# Zimbabwe's Fragile Independence, 1980-2020

## Eldred V. Masunungure

*Independent Zimbabwe is a success. …For the most part,
Zimbabwe under Mugabe is moving forward with the tasks of
national reconstruction and development in a manner that is
heartening* (Davidow, 1983: 95, 96).

*Quintessentially, Zimbabwe, which is now one of the poorest
countries in the world and rated the second failed state after
Somalia, has gone through a series of disastrous political and
economic errors over five decades'* (Makina, 2010: 101)

*'The Zimbabwe I once loved has become a cemetery for my son's
future' said Ashley Randen, an unemployed single mother of a
12-year-old boy in Harare.*[1]

18 April 2020 marked a tumultuous four decades of political independence
from white minority rule that was personified by its intransigent leader,
Ian Douglas Smith, who was determined to exercise indefinite hegemony
over an overwhelmingly black majority. Despite its repressive predations,
the settler-colonial regime constructed one of the most robust states
and economies in sub-Saharan Africa, which the post-colonial black
government proceeded to systematically erode, apparently oblivious
of the then Tanzanian President Julius Nyerere's admonition to Robert

---

[1] 'Zim reaches tipping point as inflation is blacked out', *Zimbabwe Independent*, 9
August 2019.

Gabriel Mugabe, Zimbabwe's new Prime Minister: 'You have inherited a jewel: Keep it that way'. Today, both the state and the economy are shells of their former selves while the country's citizens have been reduced to the Fanonian 'wretched of the earth'. In early December 2019, the BBC's 'Hard Talk' was entitled: 'Zimbabwe: A giant facing economic collapse'. Indeed, for many Zimbabweans, life now approximates the Hobbesian state of nature where life is 'solitary, nasty, poor, brutish and short'.

Zimbabwe's four independent decades provide a chequered story but a pattern can be discerned. The first decade was, with the exception of the ill-fated 'moment of madness' i.e. the 1982-1987 Gukurahundi atrocities, a developmental one in its distributional benefits to the formerly disadvantaged majority population. At Independence, the country proudly stepped forward into the community of nations after one and half decades of international isolation and comprehensive, mandatory sanctions. It was a moment of jubilation though signals of predation had already begun to emerge towards the end of that decade. The second decade was a transitional one in both the socio-economic and political domains. In the latter, there was a sharp transition from a corporatist or statist economic framework of the 1980s to a liberal or market-oriented one in the 1990s. It was a decade that connected the first decade of a positive trajectory to the last two decades of serious decline leading to the birth and proliferation of civic organisations advocating for democratisation of the political agora and governance systems. In the first decade, everything that could go right went right; in the last two decades, anything that could go wrong went wrong. Today, Zimbabwe has become a fragile state.

This book casts a longitudinal perspective in an attempt to understand the principal dynamics since the country's independence in 1980. It is not and cannot be a definitive statement on Zimbabwe's post-uhuru path. In any case, an ambition to do so would probably be unattainable given its puzzling complexity, enigmatic power politics, and a seemingly schizophrenic citizenry that is simultaneously one of the most literate and one of the politically meekest populations on the African continent.[2] Indeed, anyone who claims to fully know Zimbabwe and what makes it tick is either God or plainly dishonest.

---

2   Not that Zimbabweans are congenitally submissive but this was nurtured by multiple experiences, particularly the experience of the liberation war which they are repeatedly reminded about as well as the horrendous Matabeleland atrocities. Most people, especially the older generation, do not want war or any other armed conflicts at any cost.

Fragility, in its various forms and degrees of intensity, has been the defining feature of the country's last three of the four decades and this is notwithstanding the leadership change from former (and now late) President Robert Mugabe to Emmerson Dambudzo Mnangagwa in November 2017. In fact, if anything, the fragility of Zimbabwe's political economy has deepened, another aspect of the vicious crisis the country has been trapped in since 1980. It is the country's tumultuous four independence decades of chronic fragility that is the focus of this chapter, a story of a country's descent from being the breadbasket of the region to becoming a basket case.

## Fragility and a fragile situation: Conceptual considerations

Like many Social Science concepts, fragility is a contested term with multiple definitions some of which tend to conflate fragility with failure especially when used with reference to the state. Based on their development experience in various parts of the world, several international development organisations have shared their insights and perspectives on what fragility entails. Three such definitions will suffice for our purposes.

The Organisation for Economic Co-operation and Development (OECD) states that there cannot be a 'one-size fits all' definition of the term because fragility differs from one state to the other:

> Pockets of fragility may occur at a subnational level, making it hard to keep the fragile states terminology. The States of Fragility report 2015 marks a change towards defining dimensions of fragility: violence, justice, institutions, economic foundations and resilience. Thus, the OECD breaks down the drivers of fragility for each country and reveals different patterns of vulnerability instead of trying to stringently define fragility.[3]

The International Monetary Fund offers a more comprehensive definition:

> ... fragile states have characteristics that substantially impair their economic and social performance and these include weak governance, limited administrative capacity, chronic humanitarian crises, persistent social tensions, and often, violence or the legacy of armed conflict and civil war. In these countries the poor quality of policies, institutions and governance substantially impairs economic

---

3   FSDR/DEVINVEST (2016).

performance, the delivery of basic social services and the efficacy of donor assistance. ... They also have considerable negative spill-over effects on economic growth in neighbouring countries.[4]

Menocal and Othieno, after observing that there is no authoritative definition of fragility, point out that it is characterised by:

> ... the presence of weak institutions and governance systems and a fundamental lack of... state capacity and/or political will to fulfil essential state functions, especially in terms of providing basic services to the poor... *At its core, fragility is a deeply political phenomenon*, even if this is something that donors are sometimes reluctant to acknowledge explicitly (Menocal and Othieno, 2008: 1-2, my emphasis).

Applying the above definitions, it is beyond dispute that Zimbabwe's fragility is embedded in its political system – the governance institutions, processes and associated leadership – whose malign ramifications have affected virtually all the other facets of society. Indeed, it is tempting to agree with those who have characterised the country as a failed state, a characterisation that this chapter does not endorse. Instead, we argue that Zimbabwe is a *fragile* state, not a *failed* one, noting, however, that the country is ever at risk of failing.

Bratton and Masunungure, and following Brinkerhoff, argue that states fail 'when they lose all three of the following attributes: (a) a monopoly on the legitimate use of force (b) the capacity to provide basic public services and (c) recognition of state sovereignty abroad' (2009 7, 2). The point is that some aspects of the state apparatus may exhibit failure or breakdown while other parts continue to function, some even robustly. It is, for instance, difficult to identify any territorial part of Zimbabwe that would constitute an 'ungoverned space' in the sense visible in countries such as Somalia, Afghanistan, South Sudan, Mali, Yemen and Syria. As the two authors assert, 'a decline in state capacity is rarely an all-or-nothing occurrence as implied in the binary category of state failure. More often, institutional unravelling is a matter of degree' (2009, 8).

The notion of state failure came under increasing attack from both academics and development practitioners to the extent that from 2014, the Failed States Index (FSI) published by the United States Fund for Peace (FFP) and the American magazine *Foreign Affairs* abandoned the

---

4   Ibid.

terminology in favour of the term 'Fragile States Index'. An early attack on the terminology of failed states came from Claire Leigh of the Overseas Development Institute (ODI) who rejected the concept complaining that:

> ... the label 'failed state' implies no degree of success or failure, no sense of decline or progress. Failed means there is no way back. Failed means a binary division between those countries that are salvageable and those beyond redemption. It is a word reserved for marriages and exams. It does not belong in a pragmatic debate.[5]

'Fragility', the concept that replaced 'failed' states, has also not been wholly endorsed by academics and policy makers though it is seen as being more realistic and policy relevant.[6] Stewart and Brown (2010: 6) synthesise the various definitions of fragile states and offer their own three-pronged definition which sees fragile states as 'states that are failing, or in danger of failing, with respect to authority, comprehensive access to basic services, or governance legitimacy'. Their three prongs or dimensions of fragility are:

1. *Authority failures*: the state lacks the authority to protect its citizens from violence of various kinds;
2. *Service failures*: the state fails to ensure that all citizens have access to basic services; and
3. *Legitimacy failures*: the state lacks legitimacy, enjoys only limited support among the people, and is typically not democratic.

The two authors further point out that, though the three dimensions are causally connected to each other, many states are fragile in one or two dimensions, but rather few are fragile in all three. Applying the three-dimensional framework of fragility shows that Zimbabwe exhibits failure in respect of two of the three dimensions, that is, service delivery failure and legitimacy failure. To Stewart and Brown, criteria for service failure are inadequate delivery of (or access to):

(a) health services

(b) basic education

(c) water and sanitation

(d) basic transport and energy infrastructure, and

---

5 'Failed States Index belongs in the policy dustbin', *The Guardian*, 2 July 2012.
6 See for instance, 'Is ranking failed or fragile states a futile business?' *The Washington Post*, 14 July 2014.

(e)   reduction in income poverty.

With regard to legitimacy failure, Stewart and Brown identify the following characteristics:

(a)   no democracy (that is, no free, fair, and regular elections)

(b)   a strong role for the military

(c)   acquisition of power by force

(d)   suppression of the opposition

(e)   government control of the media

(f)   exclusion of significant groups of the population from power, and

(g)   absence of civil and political liberties, such as free speech and protection from arbitrary arrest (ibid.: 10).

Zimbabwe perfectly fits the description in respect of service failure. The country displays service inadequacies in all the above-listed sub-dimensions, especially from around 2000, and things have been deteriorating since then. The same is true of legitimacy; Zimbabwe exhibits failure in all the seven sub-categories that Stewart and Brown identify.

Despite the definitional clarity offered by Stewart and Brown, the very terminology of 'fragile states' has itself also met criticism in that it is viewed as overly restrictive; that it is state-centric, seeing and restricting failure to the state and its institutions. It has been argued that fragility can and often goes beyond the state and its structures to also infect the non-state domain such that it becomes inadequate to still refer to that scenario as state fragility.

To get around this problem, some literature now refers to 'fragile situations' which are characterised by human insecurity as is the case in Zimbabwe, especially in the last two decades. This also appears to be the line of thinking of the AfDB which writes that: 'As fragility does not respect state boundaries, the strategy focuses on fragile situations rather than fragile states alone ...' and that no country is immune to fragility.[7] Zimbabwe's fragile situation is confirmed by the World Bank ranking below '3' on its Country Policy and Institutional Assessment (CPIA) index. The CPIA indicators have fallen from 3.3 in 1999 to 1.6 in 2008 and

---

7   AfDB (n.d.), p. 7.

improved a decade later to 2.8 in 2017 and 2018.[8] In line with this, Menocal and Othieno (2008: 2) contend, and we agree, that: 'Above all, a fragile situation is often one characterised by a fundamental lack of effective political processes that can bring state capacities and social expectations into equilibrium' and that in such a fragile setting, 'the political settlement or social contract binding state and society together is not resilient and has become deeply undermined or contested.'

Whether the terminology used is that of 'failed states', or that of 'fragile states' or 'fragile situations', Zimbabwe features in any of the categories. However, Mugabe, the country's imperial president for 37 years, vehemently denied that Zimbabwe was anywhere near being either a failed or fragile state. For instance, at a panel discussion on fragile states at the 2017 World Economic Forum in Durban, South Africa, he was asked if corruption and bad leaders contributed to failed states and if Zimbabwe was one. To the consternation of his audience, he audaciously replied:

> Zimbabwe is the most highly developed country in Africa. After South Africa, I want to see another country as highly developed. We have over 14 universities and our literacy rate is over 90 [%] - the highest in Africa. And yet they talk about us as a fragile state.[9]

Interestingly, but to some, incredibly, the FFP fragility rating for 2019 shows Zimbabwe's situation has improved and the Fund offers its defence:

> Even though Zimbabwe continues to rank in the top 10 most fragile countries (a distinction it has held for 10 of the 14 most recent iterations of the FSI), its positive rate of change actually belies its current ranking. Despite years of undemocratic rule under Robert Mugabe, Zimbabwe has managed to recover from its crises of the early 2000s to the point of being the sixth-most improved country on the FSI over the past decade. Of course, some caution should be taken in assessing that progress given Zimbabwe's comparatively weak starting point. But it also reinforces the maxim that progress and development is inexorably a slow process (Fund for Peace, 2019: 28)

Since the publication, livelihoods have increasingly worsened and whatever optimism citizens harboured has dissipated, even amongst

---

8   Zim-MTDF (2009).
9   'Mugabe: Zim is the most highly developed country in Africa after SA' *News245*, 4 May 2017.

core regime supporters. Even at the time the FFP was writing, most Zimbabweans felt the country was going in the wrong direction as is amply attested by their opinion over time – see Figure 1. Since 2013, a growing number of Zimbabweans believed the country is on the wrong trajectory than those felt it was going in the right direction and from 2014, up to six in ten citizens lament the direction the country is taking.

Further, in a survey conducted by the Mass Public Opinion Institute (MPOI) at the end of 2018, it was reported that 'an overwhelming majority of the adult population (87%) describes the present economic condition of this country as 'fairly' or 'very bad'. Only six per cent (6%) give the economy a thumbs-up'.[10]

**Figure 1.1: Zimbabwe's Country Direction, 2012-2018**

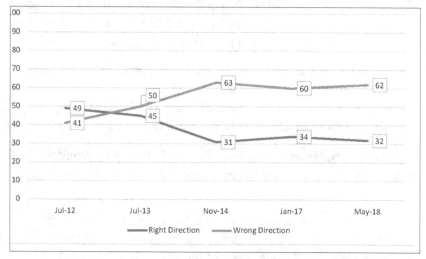

**Source: Afrobarometer survey data from 2012 to 2018.**

## Zimbabwe's defining moments on the path to fragility

To the structural legacies of fragility inherited at independence – e.g. social inequalities, apartheid-like discrimination, skewed and racially based land discrimination, were soon to be added new layers of brittleness – e.g. ethnic and regional marginalisation, politicised cleavages and polarisation as well as endemic, massive corruption – that compounded the situation. As will be demonstrated throughout the book, the new layers of fragility soon destabilised the new state and have become a permanent and intractable feature of the country's body politic. Today, no part of the

---

10  MPOI Consultancy Report, November 2018, not for circulation.

country's political economy is free from fragility.

One of the historical burdens of Zimbabwe is that it was born in war following a protracted and costly armed struggle. Elections held in February 1980 under the 1979 Lancaster House Settlement[11] saw Mugabe's ZANU-PF resoundingly sweeping to victory, ushering in a free and Black-led Zimbabwe. Initially, the country became a beacon of hope for southern Africa and Africa as a whole as it seemed to be well governed with a robust agro-based industrial economy. Mugabe won domestic and international acclaim for pronouncing and implementing a policy of racial reconciliation and was even nominated for a Nobel Peace Prize in 1980, 'credited with creating Africa's most successful multiracial state'.[12] Three years after independence, David Davidow, who was deputy head of mission at the US Embassy in Harare in 1979-1982, confidently wrote: 'Independent Zimbabwe is a success' (Davidow, 1983: 85) and that: 'For the most part, Zimbabwe under Mugabe is moving forward with the tasks of national reconstruction and development in a manner that is heartening' (Ibid.: 96).

At the time, the reconciliation policy enunciated by the President was a masterstroke in stabilising black/white relations but it was fundamentally inadequate in that it viewed the lines of cleavage narrowly as being only racial. The policy was blind to the equally salient intra-black tensions and strains that had previously led to violence within the nationalist movements. Thus, a fatal flaw of the policy was its lack of equal focus on the crying need for intra-black reconciliation, especially between the majority Shona (about 80% of the population) and the predominantly Shona ZANU party on one hand and the minority Ndebele (about 16% of the population) and their predominantly Ndebele ZAPU party on the other. This misjudgement soon proved a grave mistake as noted below.

## The Gukurahundi: A 'Moment of Madness'

Barely two years into its independence euphoria, Zimbabwe was thrown into one of its darkest – if not the darkest – episodes of its post-liberation

---

11 The Lancaster House Agreement of December 1979 and the Lancaster House Constitution (LHC) acted as the midwives to independence after the March 1980 elections where ZANU-PF won 57 of the 80 Black seats in the 100-member elective House of Assembly. PF ZAPU, the rival liberation movement under Joshua Nkomo won 20 seats and the remaining three seats were won by Bishop Muzorewa's UANC party. Twenty out of the 100 seats were reserved for Whites under the LHC.

12 'Robert Mugabe: Tyrant of Zimbabwe who presided over despoliation of the country once regarded as jewel of Africa', *The Telegraph*, 6 September 2019.

era, what has come to be called *Gukurahundi*.[13] In fact, a major source of Zimbabwe's fragility is traceable to the disturbances in western Zimbabwe. This was a vicious, chilling 'ethnic cleansing' campaign[14] whereby the Shona-dominated crack unit, the Fifth Brigade, was unleashed in Matabeleland and parts of the adjoining Midlands provinces in reaction to dissident activity in the region. The campaign began in earnest in 1982 and ended in 1987, and left behind a trail of deaths and destruction with estimates ranging from 8,000 to 20,000[15]– predominantly ZAPU supporters – who perished in the conflict. Indeed, to many observers and analysts, fear of retribution for this murderous campaign contributed to Mugabe's clinging to power for nearly four decades and had to be eased out of power by a combination of a military intervention, impeachment proceedings and massive street protests.[16]

Further, the Gukurahundi crusade had such profound implications that the late Professor Masipula Sithole actually felt that the future of democracy in Zimbabwe pivoted on the outcome of the disturbances. Writing just before the end of the conflict in 1987, he posited that: 'It is the central thesis of this chapter that … ultimately, democracy in Zimbabwe depends largely on the resolution of the conflict in Matabeleland' (1990: 471). It was also Sithole's view that Gukurahundi was not entirely unexpected but rather the continuation of the ZANU/ZAPU conflict that dated back to the nationalist and liberation struggles from the early 1960s to independence. Lending credence to this perspective, Ndlovu-Gatsheni (2011:39) asserted that: 'ZAPU and ZANU fought over authenticity and which party was more committed to the liberation of the country'. Thus, the ZANU/ZAPU conflict was a long-standing battle for supremacy that reached a decisive stage at independence with the added difference that ZANU now controlled the state and ZAPU did not and was presumably

---

13 Gukurahundi is Shona for 'the first spring rains that sweep away the chaff of the last harvest'.

14 It has variously been referred to as 'genocide', 'a violent pogrom against the rural Ndebele population of Matabeleland and Midlands' (Bratton, 2014). The North Korean, Shona-only Fifth Brigade that carried out the scorched-earth operation reported directly to Mugabe, then Head of Government and prime minister.

15 The most authoritative source of what happened is the Report prepared and published by the Catholic Commission for Justice and Peace. The Report was released in 1997 after being kept under wraps for 13 years on account of the political sensitivity of the research. According to one account, the Report 'catalogued a tale of savagery reminiscent of the worst atrocities of the Ugandan dictator, Idi Amin'.

16 Ironically, those who dislodged Mugabe, including the successor, were allegedly heavily involved in the Gukurahundi campaign.

unhappy with how things had turned out in 1980:[17]

> … with an arsenal of arms buried in various places in Matabeleland, and a cadre of young men aching to fight, ZAPU had not only the will, but also the capacity to test both Mugabe's will to rule and ZANU's capacity to survive. Post-independence dissident activity then must be seen in terms of this decisive test. It is a test that those intimately connected with the development of the liberation struggle could see coming, and that must fade away as Mugabe's will and ZANU's capacity are effectively demonstrated. (Sithole, 1990: 173).

Due to space limitations, this chapter will not probe deeply into exactly what happened, who did what and why. In any case, the Gukurahundi story is yet to be fully told, but its consequences are clearly on display. Gukurahundi has become – alongside the land problem, discussed below – Zimbabwe's 'wicked problem',[18] that is, a social problem that is complex, messy, persistent, and seemingly resistant to resolution. Moreover, both the nature of the problem and the preferred solution, are strongly contested. Gukurahundi remains an ugly scar on the country's body politic.

To this day, the Gukurahundi issue remains a profoundly emotional and deeply divisive issue, the large elephant in the room though the Mnangagwa government has made tentative efforts to address the matter.[19] Reflecting its profoundly controversial nature, Mnangagwa's efforts have themselves courted intense differences and misgivings among the Ndebele communities within civil society and between some CSOs and traditional leaders while the opposition formations have also waded in. The minimum requirement among the aggrieved pressure groups and communities is

---

17 Joshua Nkomo (1984) entitled one of the chapters, 'The Doubtful Elections', whose last sentence was: 'That the first elections in free Zimbabwe failed to reflect the people's will, is something of which I am sure'.

18 The term 'wicked problem' was coined by Rittel and Webber (1973).

19 Mnangagwa's efforts formally started in March 2019 when he met the Matabeleland Collective (a consortium of civic organisations based in Matabeleland), later called the Matabeleland Civil Society. Disagreements within it led to a breakaway Matabeleland Forum, a more radical formation. He also later met chiefs from the region. These forays have seriously divided the Ndebele community. On some of the coverage of the engagements, see: 'Matabeleland Collective collapses over Gukurahundi', *The Standard*, 9 February 2020; 'Gukurahundi: Mnangagwa squanders another opportunity to apologie', *Cite*, 15 February 2010; 'ED, Mat leaders seek Gukurahundi closure', *The Herald*, 15 February 2020; 'Government explores legally, culturally acceptable processes … ED to meet Matabeleland leaders over Gukurahundi reburials', *The Sunday News*, 23 February 2020.

that the government, more particularly the current President, must offer an unconditional public apology admitting to their culpability in the massacres.[20]

Regrettably, the nearest the government has come to such an apology is Mugabe's admission that the Gukurahundi campaign was a 'moment of madness'. To compound matters, Mnangagwa, Mugabe's successor, is one of those directly implicated in the planning and execution of what many people in and outside Matabeleland regard as a massacre and even as genocide. Since his ascendancy, Mnangagwa has made some gestures towards expressing the regime's regret by arranging meetings with diverse groups including CSOs organised under the Matabeleland Collective, religious and traditional leaders in the affected Matabeleland and Midlands provinces.[21] Compounding the grievances of the Gukurahundi period is that Perance Shiri, the commander of the Fifth Brigade which committed the atrocities, is a key Cabinet minister in the Mnangagwa government and has not, to date, uttered a word of compunction.

Post-Gukurahundi, Shona/Ndebele rapprochement remains a challenging issue despite the efforts of the National Peace and Reconciliation Commission (NPRC). This constitutional organ, which revealingly took more than four years to become established (even though its lifespan is only for a decade), was starved of an operational budget, thus exemplifying the low priority that the government places on the body. Further, the controversial omnibus Constitutional Amendment No. 2 that proposes to make more than twenty amendments to the supreme law, does not include increasing the lifespan of the NPRC beyond 2023 as has been proposed for the 60 seats reserved for women in the National Assembly.

Gukurahundi ended in 1987, a year to be remembered for different reasons. In December of that year, the two antagonistic forces represented by PF-ZAPU and ZANU-PF negotiated an elite settlement to end the Gukurahundi conflict through what they called the Unity Accord – of parties, rather than peoples – which is now etched on the national calendar

---

20  Emmerson Mnangagwa was Minister of State for National Security, 1980-88.

21  In March 2019, Mnangagwa met the clergy and civic society groups and the flagship issue raised was the need for an apology. Apology was also the topical demand when, in June 2019, he met chiefs from Matabeleland and Midlands provinces. In February 2020, he again met members of the Matabeleland Collective where, again, multiple sensitive issues were raised with a view to bringing closure to darkest chapter in Zimbabwe's posti-independence history. The grievances include exhumation and reburial of Gukurahundi victims.

as Unity Day celebrated annually on 22 December.[22] While the Unity Accord brought to an end deadly regional conflict, it also brought the country perilously close to Mugabe's ambition of creating a one-party state in Zimbabwe. Though he and his party later retreated from this long-cherished dream, the spectre of the one-party state remained to haunt the country and, crucially, political practice has mimicked that of a one-party system i.e. Zimbabwe became a *de facto* one-party state. This has been an enduring source of fragility at the political level.

At about the same time was the centralisation of executive power which the Lancaster House Constitution had shared (wisely, with hindsight) between the executive Prime Minister who was Head of Government and the ceremonial President who was the Head of State, about which political scientist Jonathan Moyo observed:

> The year 1987 also saw the political transition from the prime-ministerial executive system to an Executive Presidency brought about by the Constitution of Zimbabwe Amendment (No. 9) Act (No. 31 of 1990). The Executive Presidency, according to many observers, elevated Mugabe and clothed him with 'the omnipotent powers typically given to executive presidents in a one-party state' (Moyo, 1992: 30).

Constitutional scholar Luke Mhlaba had earlier warned that 'the salient feature of the Zimbabwean system is that (the) Seventh amendment gave the executive President much greater power than Parliament, with only notional checks' (Mhlaba, 1989: 4). This was coupled with the Presidential Powers (Temporary Measures) Act which had been enacted a year earlier which, according to Linington, basically, gave 'the President the right to legislate unilaterally' (1997: 34-35). This was one of the early signs of Zimbabwe's shrinking political space, one that has continued to contract inexorably and is indeed a key defining hallmark of Zimbabwe's current fragility. Moreover, its descent into an imperial presidency can be traced from this momentous constitutional development.

The first decade ended with economic headwinds hitting landlocked Zimbabwe, prompting the government to shift from a statist to a market-centred development paradigm. In 1990, it adopted and began implementing (albeit half-heartedly) a World Bank/IMF supported

---

22 The two parties officially merged on 22 December 1989 at the conclusion of the joint congress which also reaffirmed the unified party's commitment to seek the creation of a one-party state.

austerity measure called the Economic Structural Adjustment Programme (ESAP) which in several ways reversed many of the social developmental gains of the first independence decade. According to Barry et al. (2009: 5), the 1990s policy and implementation errors pivoting around a disappointing ESAP

> [set] the scene for the disorderly and chaotic policies of the 2000s when the economy spiralled downwards under the weight of wholesale expropriation and mismanagement of the larger farms, erosion of tax revenues and declining public services, arbitrary money-financed productive subsidies and political repression.

## The land issue – Zimbabwe's 'Wicked Problem'

Central to Zimbabwe's socio-economic and political malaise that Barry and his colleagues referred to was the politically-motivated fast-track land reform programme (FTLRP) that began at the turn of the new millennium. The consequences wrought by the chaotic and often violent land acquisition and redistribution programme have been deep, wide and far-reaching and recovery will take a long time. The heaviest and most enduring blows were delivered on the agro-based economy given the centrality of agriculture in the country's political economy whereby, as late as 2000, a quarter of the formal sector labour force was employed on commercial farms (Sachikonye, 2003). Further, according to the UNDP (2008), over half of the inputs into agriculture were supplied by the manufacturing sector, while 44% of agricultural output was sold to the manufacturing sector. Decimating this agricultural sector was the equivalent of killing the goose that lays the golden eggs. Today, there is neither the goose nor the eggs.

It must be made clear in discussing this historically rooted, deeply political and emotionally charged land issue that virtually all stakeholders on this matter – including the white commercial farmers themselves – were not viscerally opposed to land redistribution as a mechanism of addressing the grossly unequal and racially skewed land ownership. There was universal consensus on the imperative for reform but the methodology – violent[23] and chaotic to the core – was the pivotal point of contention.

Zimbabwe's land issue is as old as the founding of settler colonialism and has been the most resilient problem facing successive governments

---

23  The war veterans, who authored the fast-track land reform programme, actually called their approach, 'jambanja', a colloquial word suggesting a battle cry infused with violence and terror.

from colonial times. As in other settler societies, the land issue was the nub of political action in the country both before and after independence. Indeed, the land 'question' was the most robust mobiliser and radicaliser of black nationalism in the country, culminating in the seven-year armed liberation struggle. Needless to say, independence in 1980 led to a ferment of hope among the landless rural communities, which had been the bedrock of the liberation war that, finally, land was to be restored to the previously disadvantaged – see Table 1.1 for the highly skewed land distribution between the 4.5 million black communal farmers and their 6,000 white counterparts. This burning issue was addressed in phases, initially well-planned, but later morphing into a haphazard, disjointed exercise that became a major trigger to Zimbabwe's plunge.

**Table 1.1: Land holding by race at independence in 1980**

| Group | Population size | Size of land held (hectares) |
|---|---|---|
| White farmers | 6 000 | 15.5 million |
| Black small-scale farmers | 8 500 | 4 million |
| Black communal farmers | 4 500 000 | 16.4 million |

**Source: in Tom and Mutswanga (2015: 2)**

The first phase was a rational land policy period which hardly disrupted the agricultural sector. Thus, Jeffrey Davidow observed:

The need to turn over land to the peasants is proclaimed as an article of revolutionary faith, but the Mugabe government's land reform program moves at a careful pace dictated by a perceived need for detailed planning. Yet the number of white commercial farmers, who are the backbone of Zimbabwe's domestic and export crop producers, has actually increased since independence (1983: 95).

But the then Lancaster House Constitution included various 'sunset' clauses which, among other things, explicitly forbade any compulsory acquisition of land and only allowed for purchase on a 'willing buyer, willing seller' basis. In this phase of the land redistribution programme, the government acquired 40% of the target of eight million hectares, resettling more than 50,000 families (out of the targeted 162,000 households) on more than three million hectares (Human Rights Watch, 2002: 6). When the 'sunset' clauses expired in 1990, the government enacted the Land

Acquisition Act in 1992 that paved the way for compulsory acquisition of land with 'fair' compensation. Paradoxically, however, the 1990s decade, which had the necessary legislative instruments to expedite the process, actually witnessed a slowdown in the pace of acquisition and resettlement. HRW notes that 'fewer than 20,000 families were resettled', less than half of those resettled when there were restrictive clauses. The second phase ended in turmoil with the beginning of what Matondi (2012: 2) called radical land repossession by peasants and war veterans.

Following on the heels of huge unbudgeted gratuities and benefits to the veterans of the liberation war, and coupled with sending over 7,000 troops to the Democratic Republic of Congo, this was the harbinger of an unprecedented vicious cycle that threw the agro-based economy into a tailspin from which it still has to recover. An obituary of Mugabe captures this well:

> Within months the Zimbabwean Dollar had halved in value, the stock market had collapsed, and inflation had risen to nearly 50 per cent.
>
> In the ensuing economic chaos, unemployment rose to more than 50 per cent, and incomes fell to levels not seen since the worst days of white rule. A series of strikes brought basic services grinding to a halt; price rises precipitated food riots and demonstrations that were brutally suppressed.[24]

Tom and Mutswanga (2015) refer to this short period as the third phase (1998-2000) as the period of increasing violent, extrajudicial land occupations by war veterans and villagers. This was followed by the FTLRP that escalated in 2000 – after the government lost the February 2000 constitutional referendum – and was an appropriation of land from white farmers, this time, without compensation. The ruling party and government labelled this phase the Third Chimurenga, suggesting that it was the continuation of the unfinished liberation war. The cardinal importance of the land to the regime was aptly expressed in the catchy slogan: 'Land is the economy and the economy is land' which became the battle rallying cry for ZANU-PF especially during the 2000 parliamentary and 2002 presidential election campaigns. Both in discourse and practice, land was placed at the centre of development policy.

---

24 'Robert Mugabe, tyrant of Zimbabwe who presided over the despoliation of the country once hailed as the 'jewel of Africa' – obituary'. *The Telegraph*, 6 September 2019.

The FTLRP radically transformed and reconfigured the country's political economy on a scale never hitherto experienced in sub-Saharan Africa with up to 11 million hectares of land acquired and redistributed. Barry et al. (2009) describe a process of dispossessing landowners that was 'as disorderly and extralegal as it was disastrous for output, tax revenue and living standards'.

The destructive consequences of the FTLRP did not arise from the acquisition and re-distribution of large proportions of the formerly white-owned landowners to the black majority. This was not the cardinal issue. The crust of the problem was the re-enactment of the skewed land re-distribution within the black community where the chief beneficiaries were the new ruling oligarchy and those closely connected to the incumbent regime, many of whom became multiple farm owners, in contravention of the government's own policy. An investigation of this sensitive issue was carried out by a ZimOnline Investigations Team which reported in 2010 that:

> President Robert Mugabe, his loyalists in ZANU-PF, cabinet ministers, senior army and government officials and judges now own nearly 5 million hectares of agricultural land, including wildlife conservancies and plantation land, seized from white commercial farmers since 2000, investigations by ZimOnline have revealed.

> This means that a new well-connected black elite of about 2 200 people now control close to half of the most profitable land seized from about 4 100 commercial farmers.[25]

It may well be true that the programme benefited up to 300,000 new farmers most of whom had small-scale plots and farms ranging from 10 to 50 hectares but the elite had 'parcelled among themselves choice farms spanning from 250 hectares to as much as 4,000 hectares in the most fertile farming regions in the country, in clear violation of the government's own policy of capping farm sizes'. Mugabe and his family reportedly owned fourteen farms, 'at least 16,000 hectares in size'. The decimation of the agricultural sector and the agro-based industries wrought by the FTLRP had ramifications throughout the country's political economy, escalating a twin political and economic crisis that had started at the end of the 1990s decade. The vicious cycle of fragility was intensified and is yet to be reversed.

---

25 'Zimbabwe's new land barons', *ZimOnline*, 30 November 2010. See also, 'Mugabe and allies own 40% of land seized from white farmers – inquiry', *The Guardian*, 30 November 2010.

## The economic meltdown

The end of the second phase of the FTLRP was the beginning of the escalation of Zimbabwe's now deep and chronic instability and comprehensive fragility. A confluence of events took place around this time especially from the end of 1997, which is best symbolised by what came to be termed 'Black Friday', a financial meltdown on 14 November 1997 when the Zimbabwe dollar fell by 72% against the US dollar in just four hours of trading time. 'Black Friday' was itself precipitated by President Mugabe's economically irrational decision – motivated by political survival – to award each of the 50,000 liberation war veterans a ZS50,000 (equivalent of about US$4,000) gratuity and another Z$2,000 per month for life. The Zimbabwe dollar never recovered from each plunge until it became virtually worthless by the end of 2008 and the government was compelled to introduce the multi-currency system at the end of January 2009 just a few days before the installation of the Government of National Unity (GNU) in February 2009. In sympathy with the degraded local currency was massive hyperinflation which had the singular historical record of being the second highest in the world, second only to Hungary. The country's statistical agency was also forced to stop calculating the inflation rate for technical reasons after it breached 231 million per cent in July 2008.[26] The 1998-2008 decade was a truly and tragically lost decade. Michael Bratton expresses this poignantly:

> The period 2000-2008 ended in a full-blown economic crisis. At a time when real per capita incomes were beginning to rise in the rest of Africa and inflation was dropping in neighbouring countries, Zimbabwe was battered by the world's lowest rate of growth and highest rate of inflation. The economy contracted in every year between 1998 and 2008, shrinking by half over the whole period; by the latter year it was close to collapse. The last official report on inflation in mid-2008 pegged the rate at 231 million percent, though private economists estimated far higher levels. *All key production sectors – agricultural, industrial and manufacturing – operated at a fraction of former capacity. Consumers faced extreme shortages of staple foods, motor fuels, foreign currency and local banknotes.*

---

26 Other credible sources put it at much higher by end of 2008. According to the IMF (2009), hyperinflation peaked at an annual rate of 500 billion percent. Steve Hanke (2016) contests this figure, arguing that the 'correct number' is 'a whopping 89.7 sextillion percent.

*Electricity blackouts were a serious problem. Unemployment surpassed 80 percent. By 2009, up to half the population was dependent on international food aid.* Prisoners were dying of starvation and disease in the country's overcrowded jails. Basic social services crumpled: schools were closed countrywide and a cholera epidemic killed four thousand (2014: 84-85, my emphasis).

The emphasised parts of the Bratton quotation are meant to draw exact parallels with what is happening at the time of writing (2020), twelve years after 2008, a year that many Zimbabweans and humanitarian workers remember with deep apprehension. There is wide consensus among economists on this score. In his five-decade perspective of Zimbabwe's economic performance, Daniel Makina (2010: 106) noted the following about the 1997-2008 lost decade:

> Private-sector performance was ... constrained by an overvalued exchange rate, severe shortages of foreign exchange, a shrinking domestic market, and a variety of supply-side bottlenecks that included fuel, electric power, imported inputs and skills. At the same time, the steep decline of commercial agriculture after 2000 robbed industry of its traditional source of supply of domestic inputs while also contributing to the economy-wide shrinkage of effective demand.

It is notable that Zimbabwe's plunge was happening at precisely the time when 'Africa was rising' whereby many African countries were beginning to achieve reasonable rates of growth. For instance, Makina (ibid.) writes that: 'Zimbabwe's GDP between 1998 and 2006 declined by -37 percent while there was a cumulative gain of over 40 per cent elsewhere in Africa'.

Fast forward to the year 2020, and we see the replay of what happened in the economic crisis decade (1997-2008). The most reliable indicator of this economic regression is inflation which had breached the three-figure threshold by June 2019 when it was 176%[27] and the following month, Finance Minister Mthuli Ncube took the unprecedented and panic-ridden decision of banning the publication of annualised inflation figures until February 2020 saying since the country had introduced a new currency, there was need to wait for a year so inflation figures could be calculated on a like-by-like basis. By August 2019, the IMF estimated the inflation

---

27 Economists classify hyperinflation as rates above 50% and Zimbabwe breached this by January 2019 when the inflation rate was 57%.

rate to be 300%, making it the highest in the world. At the end of the 12-month period in February 2020, Zimstat, the national statistical agency, announced that inflation had jumped to 540%.[28] Figure 3 eloquently speaks to the hyperinflationary headwinds sweeping across the country's economy.

**Figure 1.2: Growth Rates for Zimbabwe and Sub-Saharan Africa, 1981-2018**

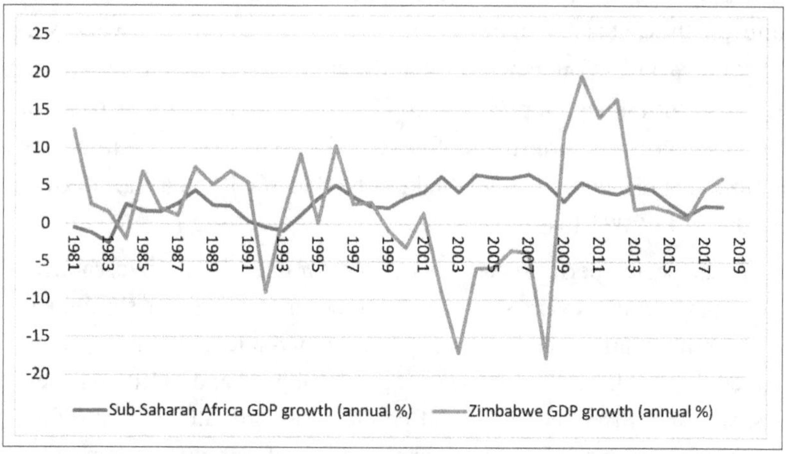

In sum, Zimbabwe remains in the throes of economic turmoil with little sign of improvement in sight; if anything, the road ahead seems longer and more imperilled. In October 2019, well before the onset of the ravaging Covid 19 virus which has threatened global and national economies, the Economic Intelligence Unit (EIU), wrote:

> We forecast that real GDP (gross domestic product) will contract by 12,9% in 2020 (following an estimated decline of 18% in 2019), as drought continues to weigh on agricultural output and energy production from hydropower, and as the ongoing currency and liquidity crisis hampers economic activity across the country. There remain significant downside risks to our medium-term outlook. Rampant inflation and plummeting productivity, a protracted drought or a significant drop in commodity prices could push the economy into a prolonged recession well beyond 2020.[29]

In its editorial, the *Zimbabwe Independent* predicted that the country was 'assured of further deterioration and a socio-economic catastrophe ahead'.

---

28  'Just in: Inflation shoots to 540%', *NewsDay*, 16 March 2020.
29  'Zim's economic outlook gloomy', *Zimbabwe Independent*, 11 October 2019.

**Figure 1.3: Inflation rate in Zimbabwe, November 2018-October 2019**

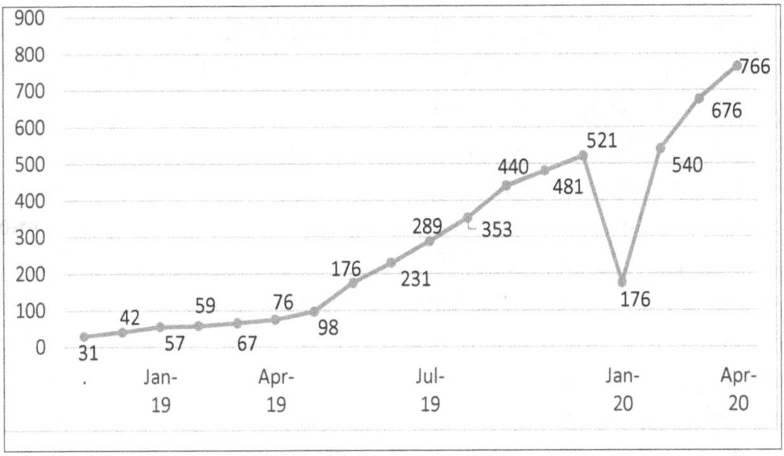

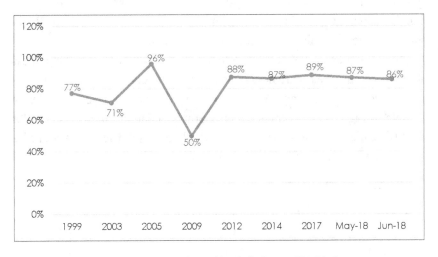

Source: 'Zimbabwe Inflation', available at: https://tradingeconomics.com/
zimbabwe/inflation-cpi

**Figure 1.4: Government performing badly on job creation || Zimbabwe |
1999-2018**

Source: Afrobarometer surveys conducted in Zimbabwe, 1999-2018.

*Respondents were asked:* How well or badly would you say the current government is handling the following matters, or haven't you heard enough to say: Creating jobs?

The economic meltdown is also illustrated starkly in the unemployment problem that has escalated every year for the last three decades. According to Afrobarometer surveys stretching over several rounds, unemployment is perceived to be the most significant problem and would have been worse had not a quarter of the population voted with their feet in search of greener pastures, even into war-torn countries like Afghanistan in a spirit of 'anywhere but Zimbabwe'. Though estimates vary widely and even wildly, formal unemployment is conservatively put at 80% but many objective economists think it is at least 90% and rising. Afrobarometer figures of those who self-report to be employed full-time range from 12% (2017) to 20% (2016). The rest of the labour force ekes out a meagre living from the huge but now saturated informal sector which is believed to constitute between 85%-90% of the economy, the second largest informal economy in the world, second only to Bolivia. Anecdotal evidence shows that this sector has now reached exhaustion point with all the social and political ramifications that this entails for those who cannot break into it.

Government has proved woefully unequal to the task of creating jobs for its citizens. Figure 4 shows the perceptions of Zimbabweans regarding the performance of their government in dealing with the chronic unemployment problem. Throughout the twenty-year period, overwhelming majorities (up to 96% in 2005) said the Government was doing 'badly/very badly' in handling the perennial problem of unemployment.

In consequence, and according to the United Nations World Happiness Report, Zimbabweans are now rated as being the third least happy citizens in the world in 2020, and have been so in the last eight years as clearly shown in Figure 5.[30] Afghanistan and South Sudan are the two countries that were the least happy and second least happy countries; both countries have been in civil conflict for several years.

## Systemic corruption

Corruption in Zimbabwe has gone beyond being endemic to being systemic to the point where little moves in the country without some corrupt act lubricating the transaction. Indeed, and sadly, corruption has become normalised. Transparency International (TI) traces the

---

30  Helen Coffey, 'Zimbabwe ranked third least country in the world', *Spotlight-Z*, 22 March 2020. According to Jeffrey Sachs, one of the report's editors, 'The World Happiness Report has proven to be an indispensable tool for policymakers looking to better understand what makes people happy and thereby to promote the wellbeing of their citizenry,' and adds that: 'Time and again we see the reasons for wellbeing include good social support networks, social trust, honest governments, safe environments and healthy lives.'

corruption story in the last 22 years when the Zimbabwe crisis started; see Table 1. 2 and Table 3 for the litany of corruption scandals stretching back to as early as 1982.

**Fig 1.5: Zimbabwe happiness index, 2013-2019**

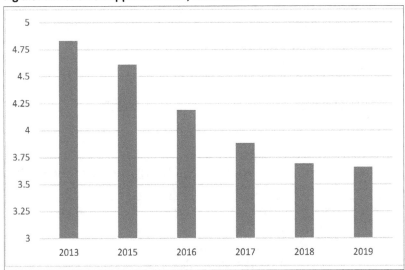

Source: UN World Happiness Report, at: http://spotlight-z.com/news/zimbabwe-ranked-third-least-happy-country-world/

**Table 1.2: Corruption Perception Indices for Zimbabwe, 1998-2019**

| Year | Corruption Perception Index | |
|---|---|---|
| | CPI Score | Rank |
| 1998 | 42 | 43 |
| 2000 | 30 | 65 |
| 2005 | 26 | 107 |
| 2008 | 18 | 166 |
| 2010 | 24 | 134 |
| 2015 | 21 | 150 |
| 2016 | 22 | 154 |
| 2017 | 22 | 157 |
| 2018 | 22 | 160 |
| 2019 | 24 | 158 |

Source: Adapted from Tizora 2009, pages 8 and 9. The Transparency International's Corruption Perceptions Index (CPI) ranks countries 'on a scale from 100 (very clean) to 0 (highly corrupt)'.

Table 1.3 shows the deteriorating levels of corruption since the new millennium. The country plunged 18 points from a CPI score of 42 to 24, having dipped to a dismal 18 in 2008. When in 2019 Zimbabwe moved only two points upwards to a score of 24 from 22 in 2018 and from a ranking of 160 in 2018 to 158 out of 180 countries in 2019, there was palpable mood of celebration in government circles prompting TI Zimbabwe to caution: 'Nothing to celebrate in Zim's improved graft'.

**Table 1.3: Corruption scandals, 1982-2014[31]**

| Period | Major Corruption Scandals |
|---|---|
| 1980s | Paweni scandal (1982), National Railways Housing Scandal (1986), Air Zimbabwe Fokker Plane Scandal worth $100 million (1987), Zisco Steel Blast Furnace Scandal (1987), Willowgate Scandal (1988), ZRP Santana Scandal (1989) |
| 1990s | War Victims Compensation Scandal (1994), GMB Grain Scandal (1995), VIP Housing Scandal (1996), Boka Banking Scandal (1998), ZESA YTL Soltran Scandal (1998), Harare City Council Refuse Tender Scandal (1998), Housing Loan Scandal (1999), Noczim Scandal (1999), DRC timber and diamond UN reported scandals (1999), GMB Scandal (1999), Ministry of Water and Rural Development Chinese tender scandal (1999), |
| 2000 to 2014 | Harare Airport Scandal (2001), Pillaging and milking of Ziscosteel (2005-8), Pillaging of diamonds in Chiadzwa (2006-present),[32] The Airport Road Scandal (2008-2014), The perpetual milking of Zimbabwe and the pillaging of the central bank under Gideon Gono. |

Though corruption is now ubiquitous in the country, it is believed to be largely perpetrated by members of the ruling ZANU-PF party and their allies in the security sector as well as government officials. Business cartels

---

31  Source: Compiled from Yamamoto, 2015.

32  Speaking to the state-controlled Zimbabwe Broadcasting Corporation at his 92nd birthday party, President Mugabe alleged that the Treasury had lost up to US$15 billion due to looting and pillaging at the Chiadzwa diamond fields.

have now joined the gravy train giving rise to allegations of state capture. In 2016, TIZ estimated that this costs the economy US$1 billion annually. Many believe this was a gross understatement and this is bolstered by the February 2016 confession of then President Robert Mugabe who publicly conceded the massiveness of the scourge in respect of the diamond mining sector alone:

> We have not received much from the diamond industry at all. I don't think we have exceeded $2 billion, yet we think more than $15 billion has been earned ... Lots of smuggling and swindling has taken place and the companies that have been mining, I want to say, robbed us of our wealth.[33]

What could be going on in other mining sectors such as platinum and gold? Tendai Biti, the vice-president of the main opposition MDC Alliance and chairman of the parliamentary Public Accounts Committee (PAC) often refers to the level of corruption as 'industrial scale' corruption.

Two months after Mugabe's revelation, then Vice-President Emmerson Mnangagwa (now president) announced that a forensic audit of the seven diamond mining companies operating in the Chiadzwa diamonds field in eastern Zimbabwe – said to be one of the world's largest deposits – would be carried out to ascertain what happened. That was the end of the story as nothing has come out of this investigation even after Mnangagwa became the country's president in November 2017. Instead, in 2016, Mugabe unilaterally took over the diamond fields and put them under the state-owned Zimbabwe Diamond Mining Company. The next development was two years later when Mugabe – now out of power and with Parliament probing the allegation – denying that there was any such looting and now arguing, rather incredibly, that the figure lacked any factual basis: 'It was just a figure. I was given that by some officials, that figure had been circulating around, but really it was not confirmed; it was just a story and there was that figure involved.'[34] After Mnangagwa came to power, one of the biggest companies, Anjin – a Chinese company – had its mining licence restored in unclear circumstances.

Mnangagwa, Mugabe's successor, made fighting corruption one of the key policy planks of his so-called 'new' dispensation. 'Corruption remains the major source of some of the problems we face as a country and its

---

33 'Miners Robbed Us, Says President', *The Herald*, 4 March 2016 (my emphasis).
34 'US15 billion missing diamonds revenue missing story false, Mugabe' *Zimbabwe Independent*, 13 April 2018.

retarding impact on national development cannot be over-emphasized. ... *My government will have zero tolerance towards corruption*.[35] Less than two years after assuming power and making this vow, he candidly lamented, like his predecessor, the gravity and intractability of corruption in the country.

> *Corruption is deep rooted.* I thought by making a pronouncement that 'let us fight corruption' it will go away. No. It's not like that. To fight corruption, you need the police to investigate but there are elements of corruption in the police. Once you get past the corruption in the police, the National Prosecution Authority has to prosecute, but there are also elements of corruption in the NPA. Then the case must go to court and there are also elements that are corrupt in the judiciary. *So the fight is so wide and deep.*[36]

Corruption has become Zimbabwe's most intractable problem whose ramifications are felt throughout the political economy of the country. In sum, the fundamental problem with corruption is that, once it sets in, at whatever level, it sticks. Indeed, it becomes well-nigh impossible to fight deeply-rooted corruption for the simple reason that it fights back, often successfully. Thus, in their cynically provocative book, Bueno de Mesquita and Smith (2011) entitle one of their chapters, 'If Corruption Empowers, then Absolute Corruption Empowers Absolutely'. Anyone who endeavours to fight embedded corruption in the country will need heavy armoury. But it is not the only big problem facing the country. The others include politicised polarisation and associated political intolerance.

## Polarisation and political intolerance

As can be deduced from the discussion so far, there are multiple reasons for Zimbabwe's fragility ranging from historical structural legacies like the seemingly intractable land question to perennially disputed elections. These have contributed to the country's polarisation which is fast morphing into hyperpolarisation.

Zimbabwe has a deeply divided past which precedes independence. However, the line of division has shifted from one historical period to another. In the colonial period, the cleavages were along racial lines,

---

35 'Zimbabwe's Mnangagwa promises zero tolerance in corruption fight', *Reuters*, 20 December 2017.

36 'Editorial Comment: Everyone must join fight against corruption', *The Sunday News*, 21 July 2019. (My emphasis).

prompting Richard Gray to entitle his 1960 book *The Two Nations* to capture the entrenched, racially defined divide between blacks and whites. At independence, Davidow also remarked that, 'Zimbabwe's most pressing problems are political, or more precisely ethnic: how the majority Shonas – 80 percent of the population – handle relations with the country's two minority ethnic groups, the Matabeles and the whites' (1983: 96).

After independence, the line of cleavage shifted from race to other cleavages such as ethnicity, region, social class – i.e. wealth[37] and poverty – but the principal one, now along partisan lines, deepened at the turn of the millennium, and it stubbornly remains this way. Divisive politics based on divisive ideologies remains the largest contributor to the comprehensive fragility in the country, and these divisions have only intensified since the July 2018 elections, although the partisan polarisation goes back to the formation of a vibrant opposition party, the MDC under Morgan Tsvangirai in September 1999, and has been a hallmark of all elections since. In 2002, then South African President Thabo Mbeki appointed a Judicial Observer Mission to observe Zimbabwe's March 2002 elections and the report observed that:

> The elections in Zimbabwe, more than anything else, have been characterised by a very high level of polarisation between the two of the five presidential candidates, Robert Mugabe and Morgan Tsvangirai and between members of their respective political parties, ZANU-PF and MDC. The origin of their respective political parties, their political outlook, election manifestos, slogans and culture diverge fundamentally' (Government of South Africa, 2002: 24).

Sixteen years later, the same level of polarisation, if not deeper, was observed by the Commission of Inquiry appointed by president

---

37  There are claims that up to 40% of the land compulsorily acquired from white farmers was given to the black elite in the party, government and the military. ZimOnline's Investigations Team , for instance, found that:'President Robert Mugabe, his loyalists in ZANU-PF, cabinet ministers, senior army and government officials and judges now own nearly 5 million hectares of agricultural land, including wildlife conservancies and plantation land, seized from white commercial farmers since 2000, investigations by ZimOnline have revealed. This means that a new well-connected black elite of about 2,200 people now control close to half of the most profitable land seized from about 4,100 commercial farmers. ... Government documents and investigations show that Mugabe and his top allies control nearly 40 percent of the 14 million hectares of land seized from white-owned farms, which if put together are the size of Slovakia, with a population of 5.4 million people.' ('Zimbabwe's new land barons' *ZimOnline*, 30 November 2010.)

Mnangagwa to probe into the 1 August 2018 post-election violence. The Commission, headed by former South African president Kgalema Motlanthe reported that: 'The Commission was struck by the deep polarisation between the country's two main political parties, ZANU-PF and MDC Alliance' (Government of Zimbabwe, 2018: 43).

After the 2018 elections, and on the basis of the pre-election surveys conducted, Bratton and Masunungure (2018: 12) noted that 'elections in Zimbabwe involve different campaigns with divergent messages directed at two distinct electorates', that 'the two electorates reflect divergent political cultures' and that 'Zimbabwe's profound levels of partisan polarization lead not only the Southern Africa region, but also the continent'. Indeed, the authors contend that: 'An argument can be made that party identification – that is, with either a ruling or opposition party – runs so deep that it now constitutes an important social identity'(ibid.: 10) and that, 'partisan polarization in Zimbabwe, already deep, has increased over time' (ibid.: 11).

The polarisation has extended to all spheres of social and political life including the media. The *Daily News* hit the nail on the head when, surprisingly, it recently became the target of the MDC-Alliance attacks. In a hard-hitting editorial, the paper responded to what it described as 'this pernicious polarisation':

> It's a sad reality that Zimbabwe's fortunes have been plunging on many fronts for the past four decades. Unfortunately, one of the things that should have fallen for good by now, but which is stubbornly defying this gravitational pull, is the toxic nature of our politics. In this polarised climate, the boneheads and windbags on both sides of Zimbabwe's political divide – egged on by their ignorant minions, mainly on social media – continue to sow seeds of anarchy between and within the country's two main political parties, a phenomenon that is spreading beyond the political sphere into all societal relations.
>
> The result of all this: everything in the country, including those that relate to the most inane of issues, is now given a political label, and also looked at from a fatal 'us' versus 'them' perspective.[38]

Where there is polarisation, almost invariably you find intolerance in its political and other forms. In fact, polarisation and intolerance often

---

38 '*Daily News* won't be bullied by nincompoops within the MDC', *Daily News*, 14 May 2020.

march together. To the Inter-Parliamentary Union (2009):

> ...political intolerance is engendered by a willingness to restrict the rights of a disliked person or group based on their differing views. It represents a threat to democracy since it discriminates against and may even silence certain parts of the population. Intolerance creates a conformist culture and a closed society, which narrows citizens' perceptions of politics and shapes their subsequent behaviour.

Since the 1980s, political intolerance has been a defining feature throughout Mugabe's authoritarian governance and his long-time political apprentice, Mnangagwa has followed suit albeit with less deftness. The Gukurahundi was the first large-scale manifestation of this, unfolding soon after independence. Since then, politically-motivated intolerance has characterised every election and escalated dramatically following the formation of the MDC which represented the first potent opposition which posed an existential threat to the ruling ZANU-PF. Political intolerance, often allied to violence and intimidation, ebbs and flows depending on the intensity of the competition in a game of power politics. Political opponents are invariably treated as enemies of the state rather than competitors for power. This is a spillover from the days of the liberation struggle when Mugabe chillingly defined ZANU's *modus operandi*:

> The ZANU axe must continue to fall upon the necks of rebels when we find it no longer possible to persuade them into the harmony that binds us all (Moore, 1990: 201).

The legacy of the armed struggle was a socio-psychology of death, terror, fear and intolerance. This was part of Zimbabwe's political inheritance and it had a bearing on post-independence governance once the victorious militants got into power. It is now generally accepted that the method one uses to climb to the top is the same method one will use to remain there. Similarly, the methods used in the liberation struggle to attain power became the same methods deployed to govern and maintain power. An early observer of this tendency was the Economist Intelligence Unit when it commented in 1983 that 'the political experience learnt in fighting a seven-year guerrilla war is leading to increasingly repressive measures and an increasing authoritarianism' (Chikwanha-Dzenga et al., 2001: 3). The authoritarianism of the era of Ian Smith Rhodesia and the liberation war authoritarianism were reproduced in post-colonial Zimbabwe. In sum, at the heart of post-colonial authoritarianism is political polarisation as well as political intolerance both of which exhibit their ugly heads in election seasons and often with deadly consequences. Norma Kriger is one observer who captured in the early 2000s the unchanging modus operandi of ZANU-PF's style of governance and that this had not changed in the two decades of elections her study covered and wondered why analysts had missed this tendency and thought the party was on the path to democracy:

> Despite their profoundly different contexts, the four general elections since 1980 expose startling similarities in the ruling party's discourse and coercive mechanisms. Opponents were cast as reactionary enemies of the state, often – in 1990, 1995, and 2000 – as mere puppets of the whites. The leaders mobilized unemployed youth, mostly males, and sometimes women, to attack opposition supporters and their property, and threatened voters with loss of jobs, houses and food relief and a return to war if they supported the opposition (Kriger, 2005: 31)

The political intolerance of the ruling party was on full display during the Gukurahundi campaign. At various points in time and in various parts of the Matabeleland region, prominent ZANU-PF politicians bluntly read the 'riots act' to the hapless Ndebele people. A sample of such warnings, some of them chilling and vicious, suffices for illustrative purposes. For instance, in April 1983 Robert Mugabe as the Prime Minister stated that:

> Where men and women provide food for dissidents, when we get there we eradicate them. We don't differentiate when we fight, because we can't tell who is a dissident and who is not... (In Ndlovu-Gatsheni, 2003, citing Lawyers' Committee for Human Rights, 1986: 38).

A year later, Mugabe went further, comparing ZAPU leader Joshua Nkomo to a cobra: 'ZAPU and its leader, Dr Joshua Nkomo, are like a cobra in a house. The only way to deal effectively with a snake is to strike and destroy its head' (Nkomo, 1984: 2).

In April 1983, in an address to a gathering of Ndebele-speaking people in Matabeleland North, the then Minister of State Security and now Zimbabwe's president, went spiritual in his cold warning: 'Blessed are they, who will follow the path of the government laws, for their days on earth shall be increased. But woe unto those who will choose the path of collaboration with dissidents for we will certainly shorten their stay on earth' (Ndlovu-Gatsheni, 2003, citing 'Minister defends Five Brigade, *The Chronicle*, 5 April 1983).

Another culprit was Enos Nkala, the Minister of Home Affairs. He did not mince his words when it came to the intentions of the violent campaign in Matabeleland and the Midlands. He once stated that:

> We want to wipe out the ZAPU leadership. You've only seen the warning lights. We haven't yet reached full blast... the murderous organisation and its murderous leadership must be hit so hard that it doesn't feel obliged to do the things it has been doing (Enos Nkala, cited in Lawyers' Committee for Human Rights, 1986: 52).

After white Zimbabweans appeared to have spurned Mugabe's reconciliation effort, he did not mince his words on those he felt were unrepentant. Addressing a post-election rally, he thundered: 'We are working with those whites who want to work with us. But the rest will have to find a new home. We will kill those snakes among us. We will smash them completely' (the italicised was said in Shona).[39]

Intimidation and intolerance towards the opposition was not confined to the first decade but has been a feature of ZANU-PF throughout its rule. In March 2000, just seven months after the formation of the MDC and less than three months before the June 2000, President Mugabe read the riot act to the opposition party when he warned: 'Those who try to cause disunity among our people must watch out because death will befall them.'[40] A month later, Mugabe focused his ire directly to the opposition party leader, Morgan Tsvangirai warning him that he was playing with fire which would consume him: 'Let him not start the fire which may engulf him!'[41] Then barely three weeks before the 24-25 June 2000 elections Defence Minister Moven Mahachi, made one of the most chilling warnings when he reportedly to his campaign audience: 'we will move door to door, killing like we did to Chiminya [Tsvangirai's electoral agent who was brutally murdered by a CIO agent and a liberation war veteran]. I am the minister responsible for defence therefore I am capable of killing'.[42]

Since the MDC's formation, the political environment has dramatically worsened, defined as it has been by chronic and widespread intolerance

---

39 'Robert Mugabe: Robert the Brute', *Zimbabwe Independent*, 22 February 2004.
40 Kriger, 2005: 27.
41 Ibid.
42 Ibid.

in politics and beyond. In important ways, ZANU-PF and the MDC have been like oil and water, 'never the twain shall meet'. At the turn of the millennium, Mugabe articulated this position in virulent and uncompromising terms at the peak of the FTLRPs:

> The MDC should never be judged or characterized by its black trade union face; by its youthful student face; by its salaried black suburban junior professionals; never by its rough and violent high-density lumpen elements. It is much deeper than these human superficies; for it is immovably and implacably moored in the colonial yesteryear and embraces wittingly or unwittingly the repulsive ideology of return to white settler rule. MDC is as old and as strong as the forces that control it; that converges on it and control it; that drive and direct; indeed that support, sponsor and spot it. It is a counter-revolutionary Trojan horse contrived and nurtured by the very inimical forces that enslaved and oppressed our people yesterday (Mugabe, 2001: 88)

This intolerance manifests itself in several ways and at various levels e.g. the political discourse as well the coercion that Kriger portrays so vividly in her article. What she said fifteen years ago is as valid now as it was then. Hate speech, worsened with the advent of social media, inciting violence during campaigns, suppression – through all forms of restrictive legislations like the infamous (and now repealed) POSA and the soon-to-be repealed AIPPA – of rights and freedoms e.g. of expression, assembly, and association became part of the political culture of doing political business.[43] This discourse of violence and intimidation runs through the four decades of independence.

In their perceptive discussion of the durability of what they called 'revolutionary regimes', Levitsky and Way (2013: 7) argued that their staying power rests, among other factors, on their destruction of independent power centres, that is, 'institutions or social classes whose power, resources, or legitimacy can serve as a basis for mobilising opposition to the regime'. The ZANU-PF party-military regime was moulded in the crucible of radical national liberation struggles for political

---

43 Notable also is that ZANU-PF, throughout its rule, has rarely been able to accept any form of responsibility for its errors of judgement. There always has to be a scapegoat. This has taken many forms: the white racist apartheid regime of South Africa before 1994, the white imperialists, regime change agents, Britain, (our former colonial power), etc. and often the argument is abusive and reductionist.

independence and true to the analysis by the aforementioned authors, the regime has gone a long way in emasculating independent counter-centres of power, including those that are constitutionally enshrined like the judiciary, electoral commission, anti-corruption bodies, parliament, the army and the police. This emasculation continued even after the leadership change in November 2017 and despite the assurances of Mnangagwa in his inaugural address on 24 November where he promised that: 'My Government will work towards ensuring that the pillars of the State assuring democracy in our land are strengthened and respected'.[44] The evisceration of these institutions of countervailing power – including those outside the state like the independent media, civic associations, etc, is all meant for Machiavellian reasons to maintain and expand regime power and diminish that of the opponents. Levitsky and Way then posit the proposition that: 'Regimes that do not destroy alternative centres of power prove less durable' (ibid.: 8).

The rival PF-ZAPU was the first to be targeted during the Gukurahundi atrocities. The overarching objective was to eliminate not only extant competitors but also, and more importantly, the structural bases of future opposition. The white agrarian elites were also viciously targeted in the early 2000s when they invested (or were perceived to be investing) their political resources in the new opposition party, the MDC, which had partly contributed to the humiliating defeat of the ZANU-PF government in the February 2000 referendum on the government's constitutional draft. In fact, both the white farmers with the alleged support of the 'white judiciary' became targets of attack with most of the remaining white judges, including the Chief Justice, being hounded into retirement to pave the way for regime-friendly black judges. By the early 2000s, the judiciary was virtually the only island of institutional autonomy in defence of citizen rights and liberties, but its independence was liquidated in the name of decolonising and Africanising the 'white judiciary'.

From its inception as the Electoral Supervisory Commission to its transformation into the Zimbabwe Electoral Commission, the party-military regime has been determined to systematically undermine their autonomy. Thus, public trust in such institutions has diminished as shown in Figure 6 – Chapters 3 and 6 discuss some of these issues.

---

44 'President Mnangagwa's inauguration speech in full', *The Chronicle*, 25 November 2017.

**Figure 1.6: Trust in Zimbabwe Electoral Commission | 2009-2018**

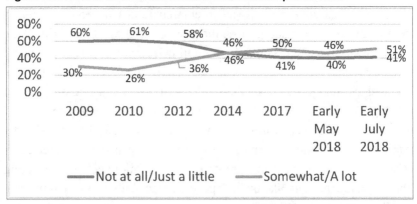

*Respondents were asked:* How much do you trust each of the following, or haven't you heard enough about them to say? (% who said 'not at all/just a little' or 'somewhat/a lot').

Figure 1.6 shows the little public trust in the country's electoral management body and it shows that the only time the trust in ZEC breached the 50% mark was in July 2018. The same pattern applies in respect of the other institutions like the police and the army. In respect of these two, the regime's strategy has been to populate them with former liberation war fighters, especially the command element of these coercive structures. These institutions have been remade in the image of the regime thus destroying the checks and balances granted in the supreme law of the country. The security sector has been heavily politicised while civilian institutions have been militarised. This is despite the fact that Sections 208, 211 and 218 of Zimbabwe's Constitution, which govern the operations of security services, forbid them from participating in partisan politics or interfering in electoral affairs. This brings us to the towering role of the security sector – especially the military – in the politics of the country, including in the determination of who will reside at State House, the official residence of the President.

## The party-military symbiosis

Perhaps the most significant political fact about post-independence Zimbabwe is that it has been and remains under a coalition of the ruling ZANU-PF party, the military in particular and the security sector in general, generally referred to as the *securocracy*. The party is the 56-year-old ZANU-PF under the enigmatic Mugabe, party leader for 40 years (from 1977-2017) and national leader for 37 years (1980 to 2017). In short, what is commonly referred to as the ZANU-PF regime, is in fact the ruling party and the military. The latter deriving from the liberation war when, as the armed wing of the liberation movement, it was often the arbiter in what Sithole (1979) identified as the 'struggles within the struggle', which were a defining feature of the liberation movement. Post-independence, the armed forces continued to act – covertly in the first two decades but more openly in the last twenty years – as the uniformed wing of the ruling ZANU-PF party. During the latter period, the military chiefs viewed their fate and that of the country as inextricably tied, like an umbilical cord, to that of ZANU-PF. Writing on the durability of what they termed 'revolutionary regimes' of which ZANU-PF is one, Levitsky and Way (ibid.: 10), citing Amos Perlmutter, observe that in the period after the capture of power 'revolutionary commanders view themselves as 'partner(s) in the revolutionary movement' and tend to be 'unswervingly loyal to the revolution and its dogmas'.

Further, and revealingly, the veterans of the armed liberation struggle i.e. the war veterans, regard themselves as the 'stockholders' rather than 'stakeholders' of the party. At a practical level, this means the military, just as it was the arbiter during the war, sees itself as an arbiter over who is qualified to stay in State House. The January 2002 'straightjacket' declaration by security chiefs led by General Vitalis Zvinavashe, the Commander of the Defence Forces (CDF), emphasised their stance:

> We wish to make it very clear to all Zimbabwean citizens that the security organizations will only stand in support of those political leaders that will pursue Zimbabwean values, traditions and beliefs for which thousands of lives were lost, in pursuit of Zimbabwe's hard won independence, sovereignty, territorial integrity and national interests. To this end, let it be known that the highest office on the land is a 'straight jacket' whose occupant is expected to observe the objectives of the liberation struggle. We will therefore not accept, let alone support or salute anyone with a different agenda that threatens the very existence of our sovereignty, our country and our people' (Statement by the Zimbabwe Defence Forces Commander, Vitalis Zvinavashe, Harare, 9 January 2002).

This statement was the turning point, the defining moment in the country's civil-military relations as the military moved from subtle to overt military intrusion in civilian politics. They would not allow ZANU-

PF to lose or allow the opposition to win; it was as clear as crystal as confirmed by Brigadier-General Douglas Nyikayaramba in his chilling warning to opposition MDC leader Morgan Tsvangirai, nine years after the Zvinavashe statement.

> Tsvangirai doesn't pose a political threat in any way in Zimbabwe, but is a major security threat. He takes instructions from foreigners who seek to effect illegal regime change in Zimbabwe. This is what has invited the security forces to be involved because we want to ensure we protect our national security interests.... Daydreamers who want to reverse the gains of our liberation struggle will continue daydreaming. They can go to hell . . . *they will never rule this country.* We cannot keep quiet. We will continue speaking and as the security forces, we will not sit back and watch things going wrong.[45]

Essentially, ZANU-PF and the military are two sides of the same coin. When ZANU-PF is in trouble, the military leaps to its rescue. Thus, the 15 November 2017 event was a military solution to the intra-ZANU PF succession-induced instability that had been brewing and had reached a crescendo in 'their' party. That instability was in turn causing turmoil and dysfunctionality in both government and state institutions and threatening the continued rule of 'their' party and the attendant access to the spoils of war. To this extent, the military intervention was not an aberration but a manifestation of the symbiotic party-military relations rooted in Zimbabwe's liberation war.

The securocratic element of Zimbabwe's party-military regime refers to the country as *'chinhu chedu'* (literally meaning 'our thing' in Shona[46]). *Chinhu* – the 'thing' i.e. Zimbabwe – belongs to those who liberated it i.e. senior leadership of the security forces of which the army is the most powerful branch. When the *'chinhu chedu'* expression is invoked, it is to fend off 'pretenders' inside and outside the party who 'did not die'

---

45 'Brigadier-General Nyikayaramba responds to Tsvangirai', *The Herald*, 22 June 2011 (emphasis added).

46 Though 'chinhu chedu' literally means 'our thing', the more powerful and emotional meaning is 'our possession'. The 'our' is not used in the collective and inclusive sense of Zimbabweans as a whole but those who actively took part in the armed liberation struggle, i.e. the former freedom fighters, now war veterans. These are the people who demanded and received from Mugabe an unbudgeted bonanza of Z$50,000 each (equivalent to US$4,000 at the time), and Z$2,000 monthly allowance each for life plus other benefits – like education and medical – for them and their families.

for Zimbabwe but want to reap where they did not sow. In other words, Zimbabwe is like a trophy, won in war or more like booty from a hunting expedition.

The practical implication of this highly charged expression is the key to ZANU-PF's staying power. Indeed, in 2014, Simon Khaya Moyo, then party Chairman, addressed a joint ZANU-PF provincial council meeting for Matabeleland South, North and Bulawayo and gloated: 'We are going to rule for a very long time. We will rule until donkeys grow horns,' he reportedly said to wild cheers.[47] Five years later, the Youth League Secretary, Pupurai Togarepi, chillingly warned the MDC Alliance, which was planning to demonstrate against the country's deteriorating living conditions: 'Zanu-PF is the ruling party of Zimbabwe, and with a very weak and out-of-sorts opposition, such as the MDC, we will rule this country until donkeys grow horns; they can only dream, but then dreams are for free'.[48]

Such is the political psychology of ZANU-PF which largely explains why the party does what it does and without any qualms. The concept of entitlement behind *chinhu chedu* drives the party's actions. Indeed, the seismic events in November 2017 leading to the deposition of Mugabe – the erstwhile defender of *chinhu* – were because he was masterminding (or suspected of engineering) the 'illegitimate' handover of *chinhu* to 'illegitimate' – and therefore undeserving or unqualified usurpers – who had not 'died for this country'. In short, the notion of *'chinhu chedu'* should be at the centre of any attempt to unravel the paradox of ZANU-PF's survival. (Some of these dynamics are more extensively treated in Chapters 4 and 8 in this book.)

## Cross-cutting issue: The supremacy of politics over economics

It has been argued, with considerable force and validity, that one of the fundamental problems that has greatly contributed to the country's prolonged quagmire is the elevation of political rationality above common economic sense; political rationality always trumps economic rationality. While this was also the case in the first two decades, it became the modus operandi after the formation of the MDC in 1999 irrespective of

---

47 'We will rule till donkeys grow horns: Zanu PF', *The Standard*, 22 June 2014.
48 '"ZANU PF Will Rule Until Donkeys Grow Horns," Pupurai Togarepi Declares', *Zimeye*, 7 August 2019.

the consequences. In fact, throughout the post-independence period and depending on the exigencies of the situation, one or the other would triumph. Roughly, one can divide the four decades according to these two rationalities as follows:

1. 1980-1990: the political and economic rationalities tended to march in tune but when push came to shove, the former won over the latter as exemplified in the Gukurahundi persecution. This period ended with the transformation from a state-led development paradigm to the adoption the Economic Structural Adjustment Programme (ESAP);

2. 2. 1991-1997: this was the ESAP era: economic rationality trumped political rationality. This was the period of the implementation of market reforms, albeit reluctantly. Nonetheless, these years witnessed the rolling back of the frontiers of the state, especially in terms of its funding and delivery of social services. However, this period ended conclusively with the war veterans' demands of their pound of flesh for fighting in the liberation war, a threat that understood the state as a milch cow. Posing a serious threat to their hold on power, Mugabe and ZANU-PF capitulated, justifying the notion that those who fought for independence should be endlessly repaid.[49] This political decision triggered the meltdown of the economy from which it still has to recover;

3. Post-1997 to early 2009: political rationality trumped economic rationality on every occasion. This was the age of partisan politics: everything played second fiddle to the imperatives of political survival in the face of an existential threat in the political domain. Most of the regime's egregious political projects took place during this period including the 'big three' i.e. the chaotic and often violent FTLRP (or Third Chimurenga), Operation Murambatsvina,[50] and Operation Mavhoterapapi.[50]

---

49 In the mid-1990s, the War Victims Compensation Fund was looted by the top political and military elites as well as war veterans who claimed huge amounts of money as compensation for the injuries and suffering experienced during the liberation war. According to press reports, disability percentages varied from 20 to 100 percent for able-bodied claimants, mostly political heavyweights in another scandal that hardly benefitted the intended beneficiaries. See particularly Mhanda (2011).

50 Operation Murambatsvina ('Operation Drive Out Trash') was a massive 'urban clean up' campaign launched by the state security apparatuses that was justified as a strategy to eradicate illegal dwellings and eliminate informal trade. It was generally perceived as a retributive political operation to punish the urban voters who had

4. 2009-2013: This was the period of the tripartite Government of National Unity (GNU) when the MDC held the all-important Ministry of Finance. And, as Figure 2 clearly shows, the decade long negative economic growth came to an abrupt end in 2008 and the country witnessed one of its fastest growth rates since independence from minus 14% in 2008 to nearly 6% in 2009 before jumping to just under 20% in 2020, unprecedented in the country's three decades. That the opposition held the purse strings, and had a different agenda, was of course a strong reason for the turn-around; but that there was a GNU at all, suddenly gave the citizens of Zimbabwe, hope and partisan politics were to some extent put aside by the ordinary citizen.

5. Post-2013 to present: political rationality trumps economic rationality, notwithstanding leadership change occasioned by the military intervention in November 2017. This is reflected in the anaemic growth already alluded to and by 2019, the economy was again in negative growth territory.

It seems clear from the above, that as far as the ruling ZANU-PF is concerned, they will sacrifice the country and its people to remain in power. In this they resemble the Rhodesian Front. After all, Mugabe and Smith shared the same attributes; both were unilateralist and intransigent political animals and masterful players of the game of power politics about which Bratton (2014) writes. Both provided narrow, reductionist, exclusive narratives and policies, a yoke under which the future will continue to labour.

## The book

The contributors to this book are both academics and practitioners. Together they cover a range of subjects that are salient in the (potential) development of the country since its independence though with more

---

overwhelmingly voted for the opposition MDC party. It had a massive social impact which attracted international attention and condemnation, prompting the United Nations to dispatch a special envoy to investigate the exercise which the UN estimated to have directly and indirectly affected about 2.4 million people across the country. In a toughly worded report in July 2005, the United Nations described Operation Murambatsvina as a 'disastrous venture' that provoked a 'humanitarian crisis of immense proportions'. The Secretary-General of the United Nations, Kofi Annan, added that 'a catastrophic injustice' had been perpetrated with 'indifference to human suffering'; see: 'U.N. Condemns Zimbabwe for Bulldozing Urban Slums', *New York Times*, 23 July 2005. Also see Bratton and Masunungure (2006).

emphasis on the period from the late 1990s which is the genesis of the country's chronic multi-dimensional and multi-layered crisis.

This first chapter has laid out some of the conceptual and empirical issues at the centre of Zimbabwe's regressing political economy. The second chapter is jointly authored by Eldred V. Masunungure and Natasha Mataire and covers the seminal political event of November 2017. It interrogates whether the 'soft coup' or military-assisted transition marked a fundamental break from the regime of Robert Mugabe. The chapter sees no basis for such a conclusion, seeing more continuity than rupture.

Chapter 3, co-authored by a team at the Mass Public Opinion Institute, focuses its empirical and analytical lens on the country's ninth parliamentary and sixth presidential elections: did they constitute a watershed? They were, after all, a seminal test. Would Mugabe's successor, Emmerson Mnangagwa deliver on his promise of 'new, open democracy' through free, fair, peaceful and credible elections? The chapter argues that while the pre-election environment and the voting process saw major improvements in the conduct of elections, the crackdown and militarisation of post-election environment shows that any hope the country may have had has been effectively dashed.

In Chapter 4, 'Zimbabwe's Predatory Ruling Elite Coalition: Continuities Beyond Mugabe' Masunungure characterises the regime in power as a ruling elite coalition comprising a triangle of power of the military, the ruling party, and business cartels. He analyses the intricate interconnected relations among the three, noting that the business cartels are a rather recent phenomenon that is anchored in the party, the military and/or the state. He also observes that the business moguls appear to have captured both the state and the party and notes the deleterious consequences of this development for national development. Masunungure concludes that as a result, Zimbabwe's authoritarian regime cannot be compared with the authoritarian but developmental states known as the Asian Tigers.

The pivotal importance of political parties in a democracy and in the democratisation process is the subject matter of Chapter 5, jointly authored by Masunungure and Stephen Ndoma. They find that one of the most significant facts about Zimbabwe is that it never was a *de jure* one-party state though, since the 1987 Unity Accord between the ruling ZANU-PF and its long-time rival, PF-ZAPU, the country has resembled a dominant one-party state. Since the formation of the main opposition Movement for Democratic Change in 1999, Zimbabwe has exhibited solid features of a two-party system, albeit an unwanted one as ZANU-PF continues to be viscerally against a functional two-party system.

Anyway Chingwete and Stephen Ndoma tackle the salience of public opinion in Chapter 6 with particular focus on the 2018 harmonised elections. Using empirical evidence from both the quantitative research (national surveys) and the qualitative focus group discussions, the chapter outlines citizens' perceptions on broadly economic and political issues pertaining to the pre and post 2018 elections era. These project a disillusioned citizenry, reeling under the daily hardship and moral discomfort of living in a troubled state. Economically, most Zimbabweans felt its government should have addressed the perennial challenges of unemployment, cash shortages and salaries or wages. On the political front, whilst only a handful welcomed the apparently more open political space obtaining during the Mnangagwa era, majorities feared the occurrence of a stolen ballot, political violence and the army's resistance to accept election results, in the event of an opposition party's election victory. Much painful still is the fact that citizens felt the post-election period in Zimbabwe was worse than the period prior to the 2018 harmonised election.

Chapter 7 by Nhlanhla Ngwenya and Tabani Moyo dissects the role of the media in Zimbabwe with special attention given to the manner in which the incumbent regime has monopolised and exploited the state media in order to advance its partisan interests and stifle the voice of the opposition as well as that of other non-state actors. This has created an unlevel playing field that has stifled the fertilisation of ideas, the freedom of the press and freedom of expression. Draconian laws and their often vicious enforcement have undergirded repression in the country and this trend is set to continue notwithstanding nominal and symbolic changes to the legal framework e.g. the upcoming disaggregation of AIPPA to three pieces of legislation: Freedom of Information Bill, Zimbabwe Media Commission Bill and the Information/ Data Protection Bill.

Chapter 8 by Pedzisai Ruhanya engages with the 'elephant in the room' i.e. the security sector in Zimbabwe. He argues that this sector, though primarily the military, has been the decisive force keeping the ruling ZANU-PF party and its former President Robert Mugabe in power, noting that it was the military who deposed him. The influence that the army has exerted over the past four decades has shaped Zimbabwe's regime into a neopatrimonial, personalistic, military oligarchy whose primary role is to keep ZANU-PF and its leadership in power. Ruhanya forcefully argues that Mugabe's fall and Mnangagwa's ascendancy have proved that whoever takes over the reins of power in Zimbabwe is unlikely to change the status quo. The regime and its many clients (including the military) have stayed intact. Ruhanya argues that the military has remained the decisive power block because of its influence on and tentacles into the political economy of the state.

In Chapter 9, Stephen Ndoma tackles the issue of national dialogue as a means to alleviating the deep polarisation in the country and the many wounds inflicted upon its victims. The author analyses the contexts in which dialogue can take place as well as factors that make or break these dialogues. The chapter is premised on what the author calls 'the compelling imperative' for national dialogue in the country. Ndoma uses the findings of Focus Group Discussions to explore public opinion about the value of national dialogue to determine if the public endorses such initiatives, and takes into account their perceptions regarding the chances of success. Ndoma also looks at the agenda and key stakeholders in the process dubbed 'Political Actors Dialogue'.

In Chapter 10, constitutional expert Greg Linington discusses the constitutional framework of Zimbabwe. He seeks to describe and analyse some of the key features of Zimbabwe's constitution. Changes made in 2013 are compared with equivalent provisions in the old constitution. The powers of the President are examined, together with the limitations imposed on those powers. The chapter discusses whether it is possible for the President to be removed from office. The structure of Parliament and the process it follows when enacting legislation is described, including the procedure for amending the constitution. It is the judiciary which receives the most attention in this chapter. The question of whether it is sufficiently independent is discussed at some length. This involves an analysis of the judicial appointment procedure as well as of the mechanism established for removing judges from office. Finally, the relationship between international law and Zimbabwe's domestic law is examined.

Chapter 11 by Alois Madhekeni discusses the elusive issue of devolution in Zimbabwe. He argues that devolution is a concept that is more admired in theory than practice noting that from Section 47 in the 1923 Constitution to Section 264 in the 2013 Constitution, devolution is provided for juridically but denied or undermined empirically. The 1979 Lancaster House Constitution (the framework for the country's independence) made no pretence of devolving power to territorial sub-units of government, while its successor, the 2013 Constitution, provides for a big bang devolution framework. Yet, in practice, this change has come to signify very little. This chapter is about the ambivalent trajectory of devolution in Zimbabwe over the last four decades. It reveals that irrespective of the juridical devolution framework, in practice, there has been more continuity than rupture. The former is reflected through a longue durée analysis of five aspects of subnational autonomy – local democracy, substantive functions, personnel administration powers, fiscal powers and limited supervision.

Chapter 12 by Lawrence Mhandara focuses an analytical lense on the region and the continent. He examines the extent to which the SADC and the AU policy on Zimbabwe has in any way changed in the post-Mugabe dispensation. The author establishes that the joint SADC-AU policy on Zimbabwe remains static. From Mugabe to Mnangagwa, the organisations have eschewed 'muscular' involvement, much to the disappointment of the opposition bloc and its domestic and foreign allies. Just as with Mugabe, emphasis remains on the notional concept of quiet diplomacy, constructive engagement and accommodation, all executed within the frameworks of multilateralism and sensitivity to African approaches.

Chapter 13 by Ashton Murwira concludes this book. It interrogates the prospects of Zimbabwe's re-engagement policy under Mnangagwa's administration arguing that re-engagement with the West has become one of the key foreign policy pillars of the administration. Mnangagwa promised to adhere to rule of law, free and fair elections, respect for human and property rights, and redress of the land question. Murwira argues that, from November 2017 to July 2018, the re-engagement policy was on track with the prospect of attaining its intended aims. Western countries were optimistic that Mnangagwa's commitment to Western liberal values and interests would change Zimbabwe's failing trajectory. The 1 August 2018 shootings and heavy-handed response to January 2019 protests, plus the obvious reluctance to implement political and security reforms have destroyed the hopes of re-engagment. Documentary evidence further indicates that Mnangagwa's promise of reform is purely rhetorical. The result has been frustration both within Zimbabwe and outside, leading to a diplomatic deadlock similar to that experienced under the Mugabe administration. Mnangagwa is not willing to reform himself out of power while the West is not prepared to re-engage with an 'un-reformed' government. Murwira concludes that re-engagement is dead in the water.

# References

AfDB (n.d.) *Addressing Fragility and Building Resilience in Africa*, 2014-2019. Abidjan: African Development Bank.

Barry, F., P. Honohan and T. McIndoe-Calder. (2009) 'Post-Colonial Ireland and Zimbabwe: Stagnation before Convergence'. Discussion Paper No. 291, The Institute for International Integration Studies.

Bratton, M. (2014) *Power Politics in Zimbabwe*. Boulder, CO: Lynne Rienner.

―――― and E.V. Masunungure (2006) 'Popular Reactions to State Repression: Operation Murambatsvina In Zimbabwe', African Affairs, 106(422), pp. 21-45.

―――― and E.V. Masunungure (2009) 'The Political Economy and Governance Context of Transition and Recovery in Zimbabwe'. Study commissioned by the World Bank, Harare.

―――― and E.V. Masunungure (2018) 'Heal the Beloved Country: Zimbabwe's Polarized Electorate'. Afrobarometer Policy Paper No. 49, September.

Bueno de Mesquita, B. and A. Smith (2011) *The Dictator's Handbook: Why Bad Behaviour is Almost Always Good Politics*. New York: Public Affairs.

Chikwanha-Dzenga, A.B, E.V. Masunungure and N. Madingira (2001) 'Democracy and National Governance in Zimbabwe: A Country Survey'. Afrobarometer Paper No. 12.

Davidow, J. (1983) 'Zimbabwe is a Success', *Foreign Policy*, 49, pp. 93-106.

FSDR/DEVINVEST (2016) 'Selected definitions and characteristics of "fragile states" by key international actors'. Geneva: ILO.

Fund for Peace (2019) *Fragile States Index Annual Report 2019*. Washington, DC: The Fund for Peace.

Government of South Africa (2002) The Judicial Observer Mission. 'Report on the 2002 Presidential Elections of Zimbabwe'.

Government of Zimbabwe (2018) 'Report of the Commission of Inquiry into the 1st of August 2018 post-election violence'. Harare: Government of Zimbabwe.

Hanke, S.H. (2016) 'Zimbabwe's Hyperinflation: The Correct Number Is 89 Sextillion Percent', *Cato at Liberty*, 3 June.

Human Rights Watch (2002) 'Fast Track Land Reform in Zimbabwe'. New York: Human Rights Watch.

IMF (2009) 'Staff Report for the 2009 Article IV Consultation.' Washington, DC: IMF.

Inter-Parliamentary Union (2009) 'International Day of Democracy 2009: Democracy and political tolerance'. Geneva: Inter-Parliamentary Union.

Kriger, N. (2005) 'ZANU (PF) Strategies in General Elections, 1980-2000: Discourse and Coercion', African Affairs, 104(414), pp. 1-34.

Lawyers' Committee for Human Rights (1986) *Zimbabwe, Wages of War: A report on human rights*. New York: Lawyers' Committee for Human Rights.

Levitsky, S. and L. Way (2013) 'The Durability of Revolutionary Regimes', *Journal of Democracy*, 24(3).

Linington, G. (1997) 'To What Extent are the Powers of the Zimbabwean President Subject to Parliamentary and Judicial Control?' *Legal Forum*, 9(2).

Makina, D. (2010) 'Historical Perspective on Zimbabwe's Economic Performance: A Tale of Five Lost Decades', *Journal of Developing Societies*, 26(1), pp. 99-123.

Masunungure, E.V. (2009) 'A Militarized Election: The 27 June Presidential Run-off', in E.V. Masunungure (ed.) *Defying the Winds of Change: Zimbabwe's 2008 Elections*. Harare: Weaver Press and the Konrad Adenauer Foundation.

Matondi, P.B. (2012) *Zimbabwe's Fast Track Land Reform*. London: Zed Books.

Menocal, A.R. and T. Othieno (2008) 'The World Bank in Fragile Situations: An Issues Paper'. Paper prepared for the conference, 'An Eye on the Future: The World Bank Group in a Changing World', Amsterdam, July 12-13.

Mhanda, W. (2011) 'The Role of War Veterans in Zimbabwe's Political and Economic Processes'. Paper presented to the SAPES Trust Policy Dialogue Forum, Harare, 7 April.

Mhlaba, L. (1989) 'Whither Parliamentary Democracy: A Look at Recent Constitutional Changes in Zimbabwe', Zimbabwe Law Review, 7, pp. 1-9.

Moore, D.B. (1990) 'The Contradictory Construction of Hegemony in

Zimbabwe: Politics, Ideology, and Class in the Formation of a New African State'. PhD thesis, University of York.

Moyo, J.N. (1992) *Voting for Democracy: Electoral Politics in Zimbabwe.* Harare: University of Zimbabwe Publications.

Mugabe, R.G. (2001) *Inside the Third Chimurenga.* Harare: Government of Zimbabwe.

Ndlovu-Gatsheni, S. (2003) 'Dynamics of the Zimbabwe Crisis in the 21st Century', *African Journal on Conflict Resolution*, 3(1), pp. 99-105.

———— (2011) 'The Zimbabwe Nation-State Project: A Historical Diagnosis of Identity and Power-Based Conflicts in a Post-Colonial State'. Discussion Paper 59. Uppsala: Nordiska Afrikainstitutet.

Nkomo, J. (1984) Nkomo: *The Story of My Life.* London: Methuen.

Rittel, H. and M. Webber (1973) 'Dilemmas in a General Theory of Planning'. *Policy Sciences.* 4(1), pp. 155-169.

Sachikonye, L.M. (2003) 'The Situation of Commercial Farm Workers after Land Reform in Zimbabwe'. A report prepared for the Farm Community Trust of Zimbabwe.

Sithole, M. (1979) *Zimbabwe: Struggles within the Struggle.* Salisbury: Rujeko Publishers.

———— (1990) 'Zimbabwe: In Search of a Stable Democracy', in L. Diamond, J. Linz and S.M. Lipset (eds), *Politics of Developing Countries: Comparing Experiences with Democracy.* Boulder, CO: Lynne Rienner.

Stewart, F. and G. Brown (2010) 'Fragile States', *CRISE Overview*, Number 3, June.

Tom, T. and P. Mutswanga. (2015) 'Zimbabwe's Fast Track Land Reform Programme (FTLRP): A Transformative Social Policy Approach to Mupfurudzi Resettlement (Shamva District, Zimbabwe)'. *IOSR Journal of Humanities and Social Science*, 20(8), pp. 51-61.

UNDP (2008) 'Comprehensive Economic Recovery in Zimbabwe – A Discussion Document'. Harare: UNDP.

Yamamoto, K. (2015) 'Mugabe's History of Corruption'. Available at https://stanleymaurojensen.blogspot.com/2015/09/mugabes-history-of-corruption.html (Accessed 14/05/19)

Zim-MDTF (2009) Draft Governance Framework. Harare: Zimbabwe Multi-Donor Trust Fund Secretariat.

# 2

# November 2017: Continuity or Rupture?

## Eldred V. Masunungure and Natasha Mataire

*'It's a new day for Zimbabwe. We are smiling,'* said Lovemore Simbeli, 19, as he sold newspapers with front-page headlines announcing Mugabe's resignation.'[1]

*'The legacies of past practice remain very much in evidence,'* (Piers Pigou, Crisis Group's senior consultant for southern Africa).[2]

*'Those who were hoping for a new trajectory under President Mnangagwa's leadership are in for a huge disappointment...'* (*NewsDay* editorial).[3]

## Introduction

It is now over two years since the 'gentle' removal of long-ruling, 93-year-old Robert Gabriel Mugabe. He was replaced by his long-time protégé, Emmerson Dambudzo Mnangagwa whose method of governance has vindicated the Dutch proverb that 'Roses fall, but the thorns remain' i.e.

---

1  'Emmerson Mnangagwa hails "new democracy" in Zimbabwe', *The Guardian*, 22 November 2017.

2  'Zimbabwe after Mugabe: Dashed hopes and economic chaos', *NewsDay*, 6 September 2019.

3  'Editorial: Zanu PF's opulence amid famine should not be surprising', *NewsDay*, 13 December 2019.

nothing fundamental has changed. Mnangagwa became the new leader of Zimbabwe and of ZANU-PF. The longevity of Mugabe's 37-year rule, and the seeming invincibility of his imperial presidency, generated and reinforced the tendency to conflate the ZANU-PF regime with his person. The November 2017 'soft coup' deflated this fallacy and simultaneously demonstrated that often, structure trumps agency, that is, established institutions override and often outlive personalities. Apart from obvious and inevitable changes in leadership style, Mnangagwa has not overhauled the entrenched ZANU-PF structure of power that his repressive predecessor had created and consolidated and which has proven that it has a life of its own beyond personalities. ZANU-PF, and the legacies of Mugabe, have endured and this largely explains the continuities rather than ruptures in the governance of the country, despite the initially much-celebrated, much-heralded leadership changes. Lovemore Simbeli (cited in the epigraph), who was smiling after the coup, is unlikely to be doing so today (January 2020). This chapter is about these continuities that define post-Mugabe Zimbabwe.

After nearly four decades of iron-fisted and deeply entrenched authoritarian rule that Zimbabweans endured with little or no resistance – which was brutally repressed where it existed – President Mugabe was eased out of power in a meticulously executed and mass-supported military operation in November 2017. For many Zimbabweans, this change signalled the end of their long agony. Indeed, Mnangagwa – who had been fired two weeks before Mugabe's removal – returned to rapturous welcome and quickly promised, among many other things, 'a new, unfolding democracy' in a new era which he labelled the 'new dispensation'. A new Zimbabwe beckoned, or so it seemed to many who believed that the heavy albatross of Mugabe's rule had been removed from their necks. However, within nine months, the same army that had been enthusiastically welcomed – and even hugged – by the public had been deployed to brutally suppress post-election protests staged by members of the same public. Then, six months later, the soldiers were again unleashed to viciously quell a mass stayaway and demonstrations that had quickly degenerated into violent protests, riots and looting.[4]

---

4   There are varying interpretations of these events, with government propaganda attributing the looting and violent riots to the main opposition MDC party and its civic society allies and therefore justifying the harsh and deadly crackdown. Some soldiers also reportedly urged on the demonstrators which suggested that they sympathised with the protesters' aims and actions. It has also alleged that ZANU-PF youths acted

## Background to Mugabe's removal

For several years before the dramatic, rapid fire events that led to the downfall of Mugabe, the ruling ZANU-PF party had been fractured into several factions that were viciously battling to succeed him. The increasingly ferocious succession struggles intensified as the president aged and his failing health deteriorated, something he denied, claiming that he was 'as fit as a fiddle'.[5] However, the once eloquent strongman began mumbling mid-sentence during speeches, and would fall asleep during meetings and public gatherings. It was becoming apparent that Zimbabwe's founding leader would not be at the helm of the party and the state for much longer but no one had the temerity to say so. And yet, his advanced age and fragile health were infecting the government and its operations and contributing to its fragility.

For his part, Mugabe stubbornly refused to name a successor and was adamant that he would contest the 2018 election; at 94 this would most likely have made him the oldest contestant for an elected presidential position in history. Incredibly, his party had endorsed this ludicrous decision, which intensified already long-running battles between two major factions that had coalesced around the so-called G40 (Generation 40) and Team Lacoste, whose leadership comprised those who had fought in the liberation struggle and could not countenance power slipping into the hands of Young Turks with no liberation war credentials. The increasingly ambitious First Lady, Grace Mugabe, was seen as godmother of the former while the then vice-president, Mnangagwa, was godfather to the latter.

In 2004, it came to light that the faction led by Mnangagwa, then Speaker of Parliament, was deftly manoeuvring to reconfigure the upper echelons of the party in what came to be known as the Tsholotsho plot.[6] Its discovery made Mugabe very angry with many of those involved fired from the party and government while others – like Mnangagwa – were demoted. The architect of the plot, Jonathan Moyo,[7] joined the

---

as agents provocateurs.

5 In an interview on his 90th birthday, Mugabe was asked about his health and claimed that, apart from cataracts and a nagging knee, he was 'as fit as a fiddle'. 'Zimbabwe army chief warns Mugabe's party that military may intervene after sackings', *The Daily Telegraph*, 13 November 2017.

6 Tsholotsho was the place in Matabeleland North where plans for the plot were to be finalised.

7 A political scientist and critic of President Mugabe and ZANU-PF, he became Mugabe's

ranks of those dismissed into the political wilderness from whence he famously lamented in 2008 that it was 'cold out there'[8] i.e. outside the ruling party. Mnangagwa, who was to have been the chief beneficiary of the 'restructured' ZANU-PF abandoned his cohorts once the plot was discovered, generating deep-seated and enduring animosity between Moyo and Mnangagwa.

The decimation of the Tsholotsho faction (later resurfacing as Lacoste) opened the door for a rival faction spearheaded by Joice Mujuru, wife to former army general, Solomon Mujuru whose machinations saw his wife rising to be one of the two vice-presidents and, at the time, outmanoeuvring Mnangagwa. Thereafter, ZANU-PF was bedevilled by combustible factionalism – allegedly devouring General Mujuru in a mysterious fire in August 2011 – which reached its apogee in two crests, the first in 2014 and the second 2017. In each case, the wave of factionalism claimed a vice-president, Mujuru in 2014 and Mnangagwa in 2017

## Towards 'Operation Restore Legacy'

For close to two decades, beginning with Vitalis Zvinavashe, then Commander of the Defence Forces (CDF), explicitly declaring that the security forces would not accept any president without liberation war credentials, the army had clearly reiterated its position. Grace Mugabe (52 at the time of the coup) had no such credentials and, by this criterion – which has never been revoked – did not qualify for the presidency; similarly, Morgan Tsvangirai was effectively disqualified by the army in 2008 (Masunungure, 2008). In fact, the emergence of the MDC in 1999, immediately posed an existential threat to the ruling party and sucked the security sector into the contestation for power. Thus, the dual process of the militarisation of politics and the politicisation of the military intensified over time culminating in Mugabe being compelled to resign. The summary dismissal of Mnangagwa on 6 November 2018 was, for the military, the straw that broke the camel's back. That something dramatic was brewing was evident from the CDF's declaration at a press conference on 13 November 2017 part of which read:

> It is with humility and a heavy heart that we come before you (the public) to pronounce the indisputable reality that there is instability

---

staunch supporter and spin doctor and was considered the foremost intellectual in ZANU-PF, in government and in the Lacoste faction.

8 'Life outside ZANU PF cold', *The Standard*, 14 June 2015.

in ZANU ...Today and as a result anxiety in the country at large. ...
We must remind those behind the current treacherous shenanigans
that when it comes to matters of protecting our revolution, the
military will not hesitate to step in. ... There is distress, trepidation
and despondency within the nation. .... The current purging,
which is clearly targeting members of the party with a liberation
background, must stop forthwith.[9]

The military's belligerent statement was in flagrant disregard of
Section 208 (2) of the Constitution which explicitly bars members of
the security forces from furthering the interests of any political party or
violating people's fundamental rights. Ironically, General Chiwenga's
opening statement quoted the Constitution as a preface and the general
was proudly waving the Constitution as he read out the above statement at
King George V1 Barracks (KG6).[10]

The military's hawkish declaration was immediately and
contemptuously dismissed by ZANU-PF with party's national
spokesperson, Simon Khaya Moyo, warning that Chiwenga's
utterances were meant to incite insurrection and violently challenge
to the constitutional order, while Moyo labelled the general's action
treasonous.[11] The ZANU-PF Youth League, led by the young, and
increasingly powerful but foolhardy Kudzanayi Chipanga, instantly
condemned the statement, declaring the league's full support for
Grace Mugabe's bid for the vice-presidency at the party's forthcoming
December 2017 National Congress as well as boldly accusing Chiwenga
of corruption. Then followed the chronology of events in what turned out
to be the 'month of long knives'.

## Timeline of a tumultuous three weeks

In narrating the events of November 2017, we recall a statement attributed
to Vladimir Lenin – founder of modern Russia: 'There are decades where
nothing happens; and there are weeks where decades happen'.

---

9   See: http://www.veritaszim.net/node/2256. The press conference was attended by
    over 100 senior military officers of the rank of Brigadier General and above or their
    equivalents in the Air Force of Zimbabwe.
10  As part of the new dispensation, the KG6 Barracks was renamed the Josiah Magama
    Tongogara Barracks, after the national liberation war hero.
11  'ZANU-PF unfazed by Chiwenga ... Raps him for treasonous statements ... Reaffirms
    primacy of politics over gun', *The Herald*, 15 November 2017.

## *4 November 2017*

First Lady Grace Mugabe was booed by youth at a Bulawayo Presidential Interface Youth Rally. Mugabe was extraordinarily angry and threatened to summarily dismiss his deputy Mnangagwa, blaming him for inciting the youth.

## *5 November 2017*

'Super Sunday Rally'– Grace Mugabe addresses an inter-denominational rally and demands that Mnangagwa be removed from both government and ZANU-PF: 'A snake is better dealt with by crushing its head.'[12]

## *6 November 2017*

Mnangagwa fired for 'consistently and persistently' exhibiting 'traits of disloyalty, disrespect, deceitfulness and unreliability.'[13] He fled into exile in South Africa.

## *13 November 2017*

KG6 'Declaration' at press conference by CDF, Constantino Chiwenga and nearly 100 army and air force generals. Cites instability in ZANU-PF and a criminal cabal around the president which obliges the military 'to take corrective measures'.

## *14 November 2017*

Troops and armoured personnel carriers deployed in the Harare streets and the police put on lockdown, especially the para-military Police Support Unit.

## *15 November 2017*

Major General Sibusiso Moyo's early morning broadcast, stating that President Mugabe and wife were under arrest but 'safe and sound'; military intervention 'not a military takeover' but targeting 'criminal elements' around the president. Intervention code-named Operation Restore Legacy.

## *18 November 2017*

Solidarity March by hundreds of thousands of celebrating

---

12 'Mnangagwa out – Grace', *NewsDay*, 6 November 2017.
13 'VP Mnangagwa fired from Govt', *The Herald*, 6 November 2017.

Zimbabweans across the social and political divide in most major cities.[14] The universal demand was that Mugabe 'must go'.

## 19 November 2017 afternoon

ZANU-PF recalls Mugabe and issued an ultimatum for him to resign by mid-day on 20 November or be impeached.

## 19 November 2017 evening

A 'caged' Mugabe addresses nation, does not resign as expected.

## 21 November 2017

The impeachment process was begun by a combined sitting of Senate and National Assembly.

The Speaker of Parliament interrupts the impeachment proceedings and reads out what turned out to be the President's historic 'voluntary' resignation. Parliamentarians across the party divides immediately broke into uproarious celebrations.

## 22 November 2017

Mnangagwa returns from self-exile.

## 24 November 2017

Mnangagwa inaugurated as the second executive President of Zimbabwe.

Thus, November 2017 was a month with potentially game-changing political events that followed each other in very quick succession. But they later turned out to be game-maintenance events.

As news filtered across the country, Zimbabweans wildly celebrated Mugabe's Waterloo moment. Fergal Keane, the BBC reporter in Harare at the material time, captured some of these momentous events. In Parliament, where the Speaker had read the resignation statement, 'the wild cheering, the thumping of tables, the dancing and singing told all of us who were present that the age of Robert Mugabe was over'. The boisterous scene was the same outside Parliament where the BBC reporter

---

14 The solidarity march, spearheaded by war veterans and supported by both main parties – i.e. ZANU-PF and the MDC-T – as well as civil society, gave the military intervention a veneer of popular legitimacy meant to project to SADC, the AU and the international community the narrative that the military operation was endorsed by the general public.

was 'enveloped by ecstatic crowds'.[15] Then Keane pondered: 'Will this spirit of unity, this freedom from fear, endure under a new dispensation? I cannot be at all certain.'

To forestall any legal challenges to the modality of this irregular assumption of power, the High Court, on the same day, declared that the army operation that facilitated Mugabe's was lawful: 'It is ordered by consent that the actions of the Zimbabwe Defence Forces (ZDF) in intervening to stop takeover of first respondent's [Robert Mugabe's] constitutional functions by those around him are constitutionally permissible and lawful.'[16]

## Mnangagwa inauguration speech: a harbinger of what was *not* to come

'It is too early to say anything definitively. We will be listening very carefully to his inauguration speech,' he added. 'That should give us some indication of the trajectory he intends to follow going forwards.' (Obert Gutu, MDC Alliance Spokesman, Quoted in *The Telegraph*, 23 November 2017)

Exactly eighteen days after he was dismissed from his post as the vice-president, Mnangagwa was sworn in as the president. The event held at the National Sports Stadium, which seats 80,000, was full to capacity. Guests included foreign diplomats: the heads of state of Botswana, Mozambique and Zambia together with former Zambian President Kenneth Kaunda were in attendance. Significantly, Rory Stewart, the United Kingdom's Minister for Africa became the first international diplomat to meet the new president.

Mnangagwa promised many things to virtually everyone. Indeed, his very first public address on his return from South Africa touched on matters that resonated with the core democratic wishes of the people. 'Today, we are witnessing the beginning of a new and unfolding democracy,'[17] he declared. To those whose hopes were for a better performing economy and jobs, he pledged: 'We want to grow our economy; we want jobs.'

Mnangagwa made similar pronouncements at his inauguration and

---

15 'Mugabe has gone,but will Zimbabwe change?' *BBC News*, 22 November, 2017.

16 'Army intervention constitutionally correct: High Court', *NewsDay*, 25 November 2017.

17 'Emmerson Mnangagwa: Zimbabwe witnessing new democracy', *Al Jazeera*, 22 November 2017.

was more expansive. He expressed a willingness to re-engage with the international community, saying Zimbabwe was now 'ready and willing for a steady re-engagement with all the nations of the world'.[18] The newly-installed president also stressed that foreign direct investment was key to resolving the country's economic crisis: 'key choices will have to be made to attract foreign direct investment to tackle high-levels of unemployment while transforming our economy'. He made it clear that in his view the land reform programme had been inevitable and 'cannot be challenged or reversed' but also committed to compensate – within the law – those whose land was taken. In addition, he promised to steer Zimbabwe towards the democratic path by delivering free and fair elections. The new president bemoaned the endemic levels of corruption that had engulfed the country and warned: 'Acts of corruption must stop forthwith. Where these occur, swift justice must be served to show each and all'. On unity, he 'humbly' appealed to all to 'let bygones be bygones' and reached out to people across the 'ethnic, racial and political' divides, following years of deep polarisation under Robert Mugabe.

To allay fears that the army would remain tangled in government affairs, Mnangagwa stated that 'All activities that the national security institutions aim to achieve must be focused on overall human security from disease, hunger, unemployment, illiteracy and extreme poverty'. In sum, his speech resonated with the people, telling them everything they wanted to hear, from the stabilisation of the economy and job creation, poverty reduction to doing away with the liquidity challenges and availing money in banks. As a defining marker of his departure from the *ancien régime*, the new president defined his forthcoming term as a 'new dispensation' in a 'second phase' of 'independence', thus presenting himself as a reformist determined to rebrand ZANU-PF, do away with toxic politics, embrace all political parties and open Zimbabwe to the rest of the world.

## A rupture that never was: Mnangagwa's lethargic attempts at breaking away from Mugabe

According to Rosenfield (2018), '... a rupture is a revolution. ... a break from what preceded it. ... the beginning of something new and a departure from the way things are.' Mnangagwa's inauguration speech had implied a complete change from the Mugabe way of managing the state. Indeed, he said that he would hit the ground running so as to repair

---

18 'President Mnangagwa's inauguration speech in full', *The Chronicle*, 25 November 2017.

the damage that Mugabe's isolationist policies had caused. A few hours after his inauguration, he met with Rory Stewart, the first British minister in twenty years to visit Zimbabwe, who expressed his own country's willingness to dialogue and mend fences at 'an absolutely critical moment in Zimbabwe's history' following 'Mugabe's ruinous rule'.[19] So successful was the dialogue between Mnangagwa and Britain that for the first time in two decades, the British government, in collaboration with the Standard Chartered Bank, provided a $100 million loan to Zimbabwe.[20] This was a far cry from Mugabe's customary anti-West rhetoric, evidenced by the notorious, 'Blair keep your England and let me keep my Zimbabwe' speech in 2002 and his threats to pull Zimbabwe out of the United Nations in 2016.

In May 2018, Zimbabwe officially applied to re-join the Commonwealth, a grouping Mugabe had angrily left in 2003. In January 2018, in another significant step towards Zimbabwe's reintegration into the international community, Mnangagwa was invited to the World Economic Forum (WEF) in Davos, Switzerland, an opportunity Mugabe had not been accorded due to the 'pariah' status the country had accrued during his tenure.[21] The WEF invitation alone was a symbolic victory for Mnangagwa as it was a sign that the global powers were eager to give him a chance, notwithstanding his dark past and his longstanding relationship with Mugabe as the latter's enforcer.

In an interview with CCTV Africa in 2015, Mnangagwa had conceded that Zimbabwe had fallen far behind in terms of development and that the government needed to swallow its pride and review some of its controversial economic policies to attract foreign investment.[22] Mugabe's Indigenisation Policy was one of such populist policies which had effectively restricted business from investing in Zimbabwe. Under the policy, investors were required to cede 51% of their investment to locals while they retained 49%. The policy was widely viewed as retrogressive, anti-investment and vulnerable to serious corruption. In line with the new president's

---

19 'Zimbabwe must reform after Mugabe, says first British minister to visit Zimbabwe in two decades', *The Daily Telegraph*, 23 November 2017. Stewart also met with leading opposition and civic society leaders.

20 'Emmerson Mnangagwa: $100 Million British Loan to Ease Zimbabwe cash Crisis', *VOA Zimbabwe*, 19 May 2018.

21 In January 2005, the US government had also labelled Zimbabwe one of the six outpost of tyranny. 'Outposts of tyranny', *Zimbabwe Situation*, 14 April 2015.

22 *Bulawayo24 News*, 15 May 2015.

'Zimbabwe is Open for Business' mantra, the Indigenisation Policy was radically amended though not repealed in March 2018 – interestingly, the diamond and platinum industries retained the policy. Otherwise, any investor was now free to incorporate, acquire or control any business and have as much shareholding as they wished. Then, in the Mid-term Fiscal Policy Statement and Supplementary Budget presented in Parliament in August 2019, the Finance Minister Mthuli Ncube announced that:

> Government, through the 2018 Finance Amendment Bill amended the Indigenisation and Empowerment Act and platinum and diamonds are now removed from the reserve list and shareholding will depend on negotiations with investors. The rest of the minerals have already been removed from the list.
>
> Subsequently, the Indigenisation and Economic Empowerment Act will be repealed and replaced by the Economic Empowerment Act, which will be consistent with the current thrust "Zimbabwe is Open for Business.[23]

In his inauguration speech, Mnangagwa had shown that he was very aware that over the years 'our domestic politics [have] become poisoned, rancorous and polarizing'[24] and that the opposition and civil society were treated with hostility and distrust while their actions closely monitored. The opposition MDC was castigated as being part of a foreign regime change agenda. Not insignificantly, Mnangagwa's installation was well attended by opposition parties and leaders including the ill and frail opposition leader, Morgan Tsvangirai and one of his deputies, Nelson Chamisa. Indeed, Mnangagwa visited Tsvangirai at his home during his last days and accorded him a belated severance package which included the government mansion that he had occupied since his days as prime minister,[25] a monthly pension and settlement of all of his medical expenses.[26] Moreover, after Tsvangirai died in February 2018, he was given a state-assisted funeral. Mugabe would not readily have made such gestures to a man he considered his mortal enemy.

---

23 'Govt to repeal indigenisation law', *The Herald*, 2 August 2019.
24 'President Mnangagwa's inauguration speech in full', *The Chronicle*, 25 November 2017.
25 Morgan Tsvangirai was Prime Minister of Zimbabwe from 2009-13, the period of the Government of National Unity.
26 'Mnangagwa Announces Mega Retirement Package for MDC Leader Tsvangirai', *PaZimbabwe*, 6 January 2018.

Another marker of Mnangagwa's apparently new outlook was that the election campaign period was unusually peaceful. To many inside and outside the country, the 2018 elections were the litmus test of good governance and a harbinger of the future. However, the elections took place in what might be called the courting phase of the new president's relationship with the citizenry and the international community. The opposition was given room to campaign freely, allowed to hold marches protesting the uneven playing field and permitted to petition the electoral management body, the Zimbabwe Electoral Commission (ZEC) for reforms. Under Mugabe, the police routinely banned such marches, arguing that they threatened national peace and security. In another major turning point, Mnangagwa welcomed foreign media and observers from the European Union, the United States and the Commonwealth. The EU, the Commonwealth and the USA[27] had been banned from monitoring Zimbabwe's elections in 2002 when relations with the Mugabe-led government soured over human rights abuses committed by the ZANU-PF regime;[28] and it was such human and property rights violations that had attracted sanctions from the Western international community.

## The Mnangagwa presidency – a continuation of the Mugabe legacy

After the inauguration speech, which was well-received domestically and internationally, many hoped Mnangagwa would drive Zimbabwe in the right direction. With hindsight, however, most would agree that they were naïve and wilfully optimistic, that indeed, a leopard such as ZANU-PF does not change its spots.

The elections on which Mnangagwa had pivoted his popular legitimacy were praised for their peaceful conduct and professional management but were condemned by many observer groups, especially the external missions, for lack of transparency and fair treatment to all contesting candidates and parties. Domestically, the main opposition party, the MDC-Alliance (MDC-A), rejected the results, disputed them in court and has adamantly refused to acknowledge Mnangagwa's legitimacy.

The military elites, continued, as under Mugabe, to interfere in the governance of public affairs with Mnangagwa seemingly unable to reign

---

27  Even one of the architects of the ZIDERA sanctions regime, Senator Jeffrey Flake, was invited to observe the elections.

28  'Zimbabwe lifts ban on election monitoring by EU and US', *The Irish Times*, 11 April 2018.

them in. Moreover, nothing came of the promised economic boom on the march to 'an upper-middle income economy country by 2030' and many would argue that with the serious fuel and power shortages, an inflation rate of 20%, the continued closure of industries, and failure to deliver on corruption, the economy is in an even worse condition than it was when Mnangagwa took over. He promised so much but has delivered so little. As reality broke through the miasma of hope, citizens reminded themselves of his past: Mnangagwa was a grandee within ZANU-PF and for more than five decades from the early 1960s, Mugabe's protégé and right-hand man, a reliable enforcer of major political 'projects' such as Gukurahundi (1982-1987) when upwards of 16,000 people were killed (CCJP and LRF 1997). and Operation Mavhoterapapi (2008) when 65 women and 413 men were killed and over 15,000 beaten or tortured.

Even after the notorious fallout leading to Mnangagwa's humiliating dismissal as vice-president on 6 November 2017,[29] Mnangagwa's inauguration speech reverberated with lavish praises for his mentor: 'To me personally, he remains a father, mentor, comrade-in-arms and my leader', the newly installed president effused. Arguably, Mnangagwa was a prisoner of his intimate past with Mugabe. It is also worth remembering that the 15 November 2017 putsch never condemned Mugabe but the 'criminal elements' that had surrounded him. Below, we see the heavy imprints of Mugabe's legacy, what clearly is a case of 'Mugabeism without Mugabe'.

## Mnangagwa's first Cabinet: continuing with the past

The make-up of a Cabinet is often a reliable indicator of the policy direction and priorities of the government leader and whether it is 'business-as-usual' or a break with the past. The first signal that Mnangagwa was bound to perpetuate – accentuate even – Mugabe's party-military regime was in the appointment of his first Cabinet. Any hopes of significant change that Zimbabweans might have harboured were dashed. Many in the opposition ranks, in civil society and in the international community had assumed that the 'new dispensation' would be reflected in the Cabinet by, for

---

29 The two long-time allies occasionally skirmished as during the Tsholotsho plot in 2004 when Mnangagwa allegedly plotted to reconfigure the ZANU-PF leadership behind Mugabe's back and was demoted for it. From mid-2017, the fallout quickly escalated with vicious personal attacks from G40 elements including the former First Lady, Grace Mugabe, who routinely savaged Mnangagwa at so-called 'youth interface rallies'.

example, incorporating non-ZANU-PF people into a coalition or national unity government as in the 2009-2013 period. Nothing in Mnangagwa's inauguration speech had suggested stasis. He had spoken of inclusivity, political tolerance and working together to rebuild the economy regardless of party affiliation which to most sounded as if he was willing to include the opposition and some non-partisan technocrats in his Cabinet as well as infuse it with more women and some young blood.

However, his appointments confirmed continuity rather than change. No opposition politicians were included on the list although they had stood with ZANU-PF in calling for Mugabe's resignation and later his impeachment. ZANU-PF made it clear that the military intervention was an internal ZANU-PF affair. Indeed, the Cabinet was dominated by ruling party old guard from the Lacoste faction as well as senior military figures who had featured prominently in Operation Restore Legacy. Indeed, the swearing-in ceremony resembled a prize-giving as Mnangagwa handed positions to his kingmakers. Major General Sibusiso Moyo, the face of the coup, was named as the Foreign Affairs Minister and Air Force Commander Perence Shiri – one-time commander of the fearsome Fifth Brigade of the Gukurahundi era – became Minister of Lands and Agriculture. War veterans' leader, Chris Mutsvangwa, who had become one of Mugabe's bitterest critics, was awarded the Ministry of Information, Media and Broadcasting Services. Patrick Chinamasa was made Finance Minister, a position he had lost when Mugabe had reshuffled the Cabinet in October 2017. Obert Mpofu who is allegedly steeped in corrupt activities[30] but who had supported the coup was made Minister of Home Affairs. Resigning from the army former Commander Constantino Chiwenga became vice-president, together with Kembo Mohadi, formerly Minister of Defence, Security and War Veterans became the second vice-president.

Thus, instead of witnessing a departure from the past, Zimbabweans witnessed the same politics of patronage that had defined Mugabe's leadership. Tendai Biti, a senior opposition MDC leader – and one who probably expected a place in the post-Mugabe sun – ruefully tweeted: 'The honeymoon is over even before it had begun. What a shame. What a missed opportunity.'

Mnangagwa's second post-election Cabinet announced in early September 2018 made several changes with some old guard 'career'

---

30  Mpofu was Minister of Mines when, according to Mugabe, the diamond sector was looted of $15 billion in revenue.

ministers being dropped while some new faces were brought in. The inclusion of controversial figures in the first Cabinet such as Mpofu, David Parirenyatwa and Supa Mandiwanzira[31] who were accused of abusing their offices had hurt Mnangagwa's image resulting in all three losing their posts. Chinamasa was also axed from the finance portfolio which was assumed by an academic and technocrat, Professor Mthuli Ncube. Olympic swimming gold medallist Kirsty Coventry was a surprise inclusion as the Minister of Youth, Sport, Arts and Recreation. However, the Cabinet also retained the same recycled old guard ministers, possibly for the sake of institutional memory and continuity.

Also, and to the bafflement of many, Mnangagwa appointed a 26-member Presidential Advisory Council (PAC), comprising of entrepreneurs, business executives, intellectuals and church leaders ostensibly to advise (on a voluntary and non-binding way) the president and the government on a wide range of sectoral issues. Part of the PACs terms of reference read: 'To proffer ideas and suggestions on key reforms and measures needed to improve the investment and business climate in the country for economic recovery and growth' in line with the Zimbabwe is 'open for business' mantra.[32] To date, PAC has been a resounding disappointment and has made little to no change to the poisonous political and parlous socio-economic condition of the country. PAC was followed by another ineffective political mechanism, the Political Actors Dialogue (POLAD) comprising those candidates who had participated in the August 2018 presidential elections. POLAD was launched by Mnangagwa in Harare in May 2019, with its creator boasting that the initiative would 'undoubtedly leave a lasting imprint on our country's political landscape and help to contribute to the turnaround of the country's socio-economic fortunes'.[33] The launch was attended by seventeen minor political parties minus the MDC-A led by Nelson Chamisa. Meantime, Mnangagwa and Chamisa have continuously accused each other of not being open to dialogue while the political, social and economic state of the country relentlessly deteriorates. Mnangagwa had, in September 2018,[34] tried to

---

31  David Parirenyatwa is a medical doctor who served as Minister of Health (2002-2009; 2013-2018). Supa Mandiwanzira is a politician and journalist who served in Mugabe's Cabinet first as Minister of Information Communication Technology and later as Minister of Information Communication Technology and Cybersecurity.

32  'AMH boss appointed to presidential advisory council', *NewsDay*, 31 January 2019.

33  'Dialogue is forever', *The Herald*, 17 May 2019.

34  Mnangagwa revealed his intentions of offering Chamisa the post during an interview

appease Chamisa by offering him the position of Leader of the Opposition even though such a position and institution did not exist anywhere in the Constitution. Chamisa contemptuously rejected the offer, insisting he had resoundingly won the electoral contest and therefore should be the giver rather than the recipient of carrots. Thus, the two parties and their leaders remain trapped in bitter confrontation, similar to that which defined Mugabe's relationship with Tsvangirai.

## Disputed elections and legitimacy issues

Contested election campaigns and disputed outcomes have become a hallmark of Zimbabwe's electoral cycle, especially after the emergence of the MDC in 1999. Until then, ZANU-PF had enjoyed unchallenged success but the 2000 Parliamentary elections heralded the beginning of a new era of stiffer competition against the once omnipotent party. All elections post-2000 – five parliamentary and four presidential contests – have all been hotly disputed with most observers – except for the SADC and AU and a few domestic observers – largely condemning them as deeply flawed, especially the 2000, 2002 and 2008 elections. Did Mnangagwa make a qualitative difference on this front? First, we should note that an election cycle is normally viewed as having three phases: the pre-election, Election Day, and post-election phases.

As other chapters have explained, the new incumbent made what appeared to be a concerted effort to distinguish his approach to the contest from his predecessor and to his credit, he did make significant positive changes to the electoral process. But they were inadequate, in part because of the enormity of the accumulated problems and issues that had to be addressed including: transparent and fair voter registration, non-partisan voter education, adequate and fair media coverage by the state-controlled media, and generally playing fair and ensuring a free ballot. With all eyes on the new government, Mnangagwa had promised to deliver a credible election. After all, much, including Mnangagwa's legitimacy was hanging on this election. The sense of illegitimacy was heavy for although Operation Restore Legacy had been ruled by the courts as lawful, there was no denying that the new interim incumbent and the army had set a bad precedent by forcibly removing an elected president. Only a credible election could grant Mnangagwa his desperately needed legitimacy. A

---

with Bloomberg TV on the 21st of September, 2018, when he was in New York for the United Nations General Assembly.

credible election with an undisputed outcome was also of paramount importance as it would help Zimbabwe open the doors to desperately needed foreign direct investment (FDI) for its prostrate economy. Foreign investors and governments had opted to wait for the outcome of the election before making any firm decisions.

The spoiler came the third phase of the electoral cycle. As observed in several other chapters in this book, on 1 August 2018 protests broke out in the Harare city centre as opposition supporters demanded that ZEC release the results of the presidential election. Their demand was partly precipitated by the lessons of 2008, and partly because the ZEC parliamentary election results had already been released, showing a landslide majority for ZANU-PF. (ZEC claimed it was still verifying the results.) However, a deep distrust in ZEC had prompted the opposition MDC-A to announce its own tally, which the party's agents had collected throughout the country, and these showed that Chamisa had a convincing win. MDC supporters felt that ZEC was deliberately prevaricating so that they could subvert the will of the people as they had done in 2008. The 1 August events 'resulted in the death of six (6) people, injury of thirty-five (35), and massive damage to properties'[35] after soldiers from the elite Presidential Guard were deployed to contain the demonstrations. Biti, who had announced Chamisa's apparent victory, was soon arrested for violating the law.[36] When it was finally officially announced that Mnangagwa had narrowly beaten Chamisa, the live TV broadcast was interrupted by MDC Vice-President Morgen Komichi who claimed that the results had not been verified by his party; Komichi was also later arrested and charged with interrupting the electoral process. Chamisa later contested the results at the Constitutional Court and lost on account of lack of 'primary evidence':

> The court finds that the applicant failed to place before the court, clear, direct, sufficient and credible evidence that the irregularities alleged to have marred the process, materially existed. There was no proof of the happenings of these irregularities as a matter of fact.[37]

---

35  Commission of Inquiry into the 1st of August 2018 Post-Election Violence in Zimbabwe, available at http://kubatana.net/wp-content/uploads/2018/12/Final-Report-of-the-Commission-of-Inquiry-18-DEC-18.pdf. Some reports claim seven people were killed and 17 injured.

36  By law, ZEC is the only statutory body that can announce election results and within it, only the ZEC Chairperson is mandated to announce presidential election results.

37  'Court upholds ED victory, Chamisa election case dismissed with costs', *The Chronicle*, 25 August 2018.

However, to this day, Chamisa and his MDC still refuse to acknowledge Mnangagwa's leadership as legitimate, thus escalating the tension and polarisation in the country.

## Foreign policy: a paradigm shift or a mirage?

Besides being 'open for business' in his economic trajectory, Mnangagwa's foreign policy is an area where there has been both continuity and distinct change. His pan-African focus was a clear progression from the Mugabe era. For instance, soon after his inauguration in November 2017, he paid courtesy calls on various Southern African Development Community (SADC) member states, principally South Africa, Botswana (whose president Seretse Khama had been an arch-critic of Mugabe), Namibia, Mozambique and Zambia. The visits were also meant to thank SADC for recognising the regime leadership change and not intervening on behalf of Mugabe. However, in a clear departure from his predecessor, Mnangagwa signalled his determination to change course in respect of relations with the western international community by making every effort to unfreeze the relationship. Zimbabwe's foreign policy had taken a belligerent and intransigent turn after the Land Reform Programme of the early 2000s with Mugabe defiantly quitting the Commonwealth in 2003 while the United States and the European Union imposed a variety of 'targeted' sanctions on the leadership, the ruling party and selected state and military institution. This move had caused Mugabe to craft his Look East Policy which sought to rekindle and strengthen relations with old 'all-weather friends' such as China and Russia that had helped nationalists' forces during the independence struggle.

While China has historically been an important ally both economically and politically, the vital importance of the West could not be undervalued, a reality that was not lost on the new president. As outlined in Chapter 13, from Mnangagwa's first speech on his return from his brief self-exile, he was emphatic about the need to take a new direction, a position he reiterated in his inauguration speeches (November 2017 and August 2018), his State of the Nation Addresses (SONA), at the WEF, SADC and AU summits. Zimbabwe also quickly applied to rejoin the Commonwealth. With this foreign policy U-turn, Mnangagwa thought he would be rewarded through FDI inflows, lifting of ZIDERA sanctions and doors being swung ajar for bailouts and lines of credit from the international financial institutions. Alas, the post-election violence in August 2018 and January 2019 eroded all the hopes and gains that been achieved in the run-up to the elections. The West hardened its stance while Mnangagwa and his political lieutenants, in frustration, reciprocated the gesture.

Thus, after the 2018 elections, Mnangagwa's foreign policy with regard to the West has shifted back to resemble that of his predecessor and mentor. The relationship with the UK that had initially looked the most promising is frosty again[38] while the US government has actually extended its sanctions on the country.[39] As relations soured, Mnangagwa again looked East, embarking on an eastern European tour in January 2019 to Azerbaijan, Belarus, Kazakhstan and Russia where he met with President Vladimir Putin.[40] During his interim presidency, he had gone to China where he had met his Chinese counterpart Xi Jinping in April, 2018, his first visit out of Africa since taking over from Mugabe. As Chapter 13 shows, Mnangagwa's re-engagement efforts now seem dead in the water.

## The economic quagmire continues

Many domestic and international business executives as well as political analysts and practitioners – including members of the opposition – considered Mnangagwa to be pragmatic and financially astute, and the right man to take Zimbabwe out of its economic morass. For instance, David Coltart, senior MDC leader and former Education Minister during the GNU, clearly belonged to this group. He wrote that he preferred Mnangagwa as Mugabe's successor purely from an economic point of view:

> Mnangagwa is business savvy and understands what needs to be done to save the ailing Zimbabwean economy suffering from a blistering liquidity crisis. For all his historical problems, he understands the running of the economy better than Mugabe, better than most ZANU-PF politicians (Coltart 2016).

Prior to his rise to the apex of power, Mnangagwa had admitted that Zimbabwe had fallen behind and needed to re-establish relations with both the West and the rest of the world if it was to escape from its

---

38  Zimbabwe was one of a few African countries not invited to the UK-Africa Investment Summit in January 2020, to the chagrin of the Zimbabwe government. 'UK snubs ED Govt', *NewsDay*, 15 January 2020.

39  Tanya Mugabe, *MyZimbabwe*, 6 March 2019.

40  The President aborted his tour to return home to attend to the January 2019 protests and riots that represented a potent threat to the very survival of his regime.

economic quagmire. In an unusually candid admission in an interview with the Chinese national television broadcaster in 2015, he lamented: 'You cannot say there are areas of our economy which we are happy with, infrastructure we are behind by 15-16 years, agricultural development the same, manufacturing, in fact capacity utilisation in some areas of our industry it is down to 20% ...'[41]

Mnangagwa pointed to the dire need for 'a massive reform process ...' including social and legislative frameworks, 'to bring Zimbabwe back to the table of nations'. He also expressed his admiration for the Chinese development model. Thus, a full two-years before he was catapulted into power, he had articulated a development model that Rwanda – following China – has been implementing and for which Mnangagwa has expressed his admiration. However, in practice, and perhaps due to the influence of his Minister of Finance, Mthuli Ncube, the government's economic policy has been more aligned to the market-driven, neo-liberal paradigm as expressed in the Transitional Stabilisation Programme (October 2018-December 2020) – the government's economic blueprint – and the 2019 Austerity for Prosperity[42] national budget.

Mugabe had rather half-heartedly implemented such an austerity programme during the ESAP era in the 1990s which he later abandoned with contempt after it proved too costly politically. While subsidies and price controls remained in place during the Mugabe regime,[43] Mnangagwa has steadfastly rejected calls to systematically control prices, opting instead for market-determined prices with a few exceptions such as the country's staple, mealie meal.[44] In other words, Mnangagwa has shifted from his predecessor's more state-driven economic policy to a more neo-liberal paradigm. In this respect, he has been unfavourably compared to Mugabe and many hard-pressed consumers have publicly expressed their nostalgia for the latter's more commandist approach to pricing policy even when it led to empty shelves.

Another area where Mnangagwa had sought to depart from his mentor

---

41 'Zim has lost 20 yrs – Mnangagwa', *NewsDay,* 15 July 2015.

42 This budget and its intent have been severely criticised and derided as 'austerity for poverty' or 'austerity for the poor and prosperity for the rich'. See, for instance: 'Austerity does not bring prosperity – ED, stop destroying our lives, please', *Bulawayo24,* 9 January 2019; 'Austerity for the poor, prosperity for the elites', *Zimbabwe Independent,* 7 December 2018.

43 'Zimbabwe Price Controls Cause Chaos', *The New York Times,* 3 July 2007.

44 The 2020 budget removed most subsidies with effect from January 2020 with the exception of roller meal.

was FDI and associated re-engagement with the West. Mugabe used every available opportunity, particularly international fora, to tell the West 'to go to hell'. For instance, in a speech at the Durban World Sustainable Development Summit in 2002, the former President reprimanded British premier Tony Blair in front of other leaders with his infamous quip: 'So, Blair, keep your England and let me keep my Zimbabwe'[45] receiving public applause for his jibe. Nonetheless, recently, Mnangagwa's administration has adopted some of Mugabe's bellicose language as his 'open for business' mantra has foundered and international financial institutions are maintaining their distance until Zimbabwe implements the promised economic and political reforms, including aligning the statutory laws to the national Constitution.

## Continued militarisation of politics and politicisation of the military

In a Sky News interview in August 2019, Mnanagagwa described himself as someone 'as soft as wool'[46] belying his moniker, the 'crocodile', i.e. cunning, patient, fearsome and ruthless. What is undeniable is that Mnangagwa was Mugabe's fixer during his long imperial presidency and was close to Mugabe both before and after independence. Moreover, Mnangagwa has had close military and security ties throughout his political career; he was Minister of State Security, Minister of Justice, Speaker of Parliament and Minister of Defence before achieving the post of Vice-President. He has been implicated in some of the darkest moments in Zimbabwe's history and is considered to be one of the primary architects of Zimbabwe's security state (Southall, 2017: 84).

In the 1980s, when he was Minister of State Security, Mnangagwa oversaw the Gukurahundi campaign against the Ndebele and in 2008, as Mugabe's Chief Election Agent, he orchestrated ZANU-PF's militarised campaign against the opposition after Mugabe had lost the first round to Tsvangirai. He did so in his capacity as chairman of the Joint Operations Command (JOC) which comprised of senior heads of the Zimbabwe

---

45  See, for instance, 'Hands off Zimbabwe, Mugabe tells Blair', *The Guardian*, 2 September 2002.

46  See video at: https://news.sky.com/video/mnangagwa-britain-is-better-with-female-pm-11463019. Mnangagwa had earlier described himself in the same words in an interview with the BBC in July 2018: 'I am as soft as wool. I am a very soft person in life, my brother. I'm a family person. I am a Christian.' See: https://www.bbc.com/news/world-africa-44619102

Defence Forces, the Central Intelligence Organisation (CIO), Zimbabwe Republic Police (ZRP), and Zimbabwe Prisons Service and its explicit mandate was to ensure that Mugabe won the run-off election (Human Rights Watch, 2008). His close relationship with the security sector, especially the military, ultimately helped him to win the ZANU-PF succession war and he reciprocated by appointing military men in strategic positions in the party and government.

The military has since continued to be a vital cog in the party-military regime as evidenced in key decision-making around the 1 August 2018 shootings and January 2019 protests, (see Chapter 8). Though the army denied culpability, blaming the demonstrations and the deaths on the protesters themselves, allegedly instigated by main opposition MDC-A, the Kgalema Motlanthe Commission of Inquiry revealed that the army used disproportionate force. Six months later, on 14 January 2019, the government deployed heavily armed soldiers across the country to quell the protests that had erupted after Mnangagwa had announced a 150% increase in fuel prices, which at the time made fuel in Zimbabwe the most expensive in the world.

> Soldiers fired live ammunition at the protestors and 12 lives were lost while about 78 people were left nursing gunshot injuries. The soldiers went on a rampage abducting and torturing civilians in various suburbs around the country. The gruesome activities by the military also resulted in the rape of women especially in Harare. Cases of masked and armed soldiers having unprotected sex with the victims have been recorded (Crisis in Zimbabwe Coalition 2019).

Section 213 of the Constitution states that 'only the President, as Commander-in-Chief', has power to authorise the deployment of the Defence Forces, and that, with his authority, they may be used within Zimbabwe 'in support of the Police Service in the maintenance of public order'. Though it was not clear who had deployed the armed forces in August 2018, it was evident who had done so in January 2019. The two episodes raise serious questions concerning not only who was in charge of the security forces, whether the former Commander of the Defence Forces (CDF) – now Vice-President – or the current CDF General Sibanda, or the President and Commander-in-Chief of the Defence Forces. The President further added to the confusion in the line of command by failing to reign in the offenders despite his assurances that 'heads would roll' over the abuses.[47]

The intrusive role of the military in civilian governance after the 2018 election contributed in no small way to impairing re-engagement. Nicole Beardsworth commented that 'it appears that all prospects for international re-engagement have stalled'.[48] She could not avoid drawing parallels with the Mugabe regime:

> While early in his presidency, many were willing to give the new president the benefit of the doubt, *it is increasingly clear that the new administration in Zimbabwe is both more authoritarian than its predecessor,* and *less strategic.* Having denounced the January 2019 protests as a Western-backed attempt at regime change, the ruling party has dusted off its old anti-imperial mantra as a cloak for their repressive actions (ibid. Our emphasis).

From independence to his ouster in 2017, Mugabe had relied heavily on the security sector, prompting some observers to describe Zimbabwe as a securocratic state. Within this sector, however, he depended more on the intelligence agencies – CIO and military intelligence (but more the former) – and the police, both regular and the Paramilitary Support Unit to enforce his will and maintain power. Due to the faction-ridden dynamics of the November 2017 Operation Restore Legacy and the attendant intra-security sector tensions and open hostilities, the military became the dominant player while the police and CIO (but not the military intelligence) played second fiddle in the 'new dispensation'. Therefore, to quell protests or nip them in the bud, Mnangagwa and his militarised administration resorted more to the military than the other organs of the security sector. The deployment of the Presidential Guard rather than the police in large part accounted for the deaths in August 2018 and those in January 2019. The strategic aim was to smother the protests in the cradle.

The lesson from 1 August 2018 and January 2019 is that the Mnangagwa regime, just like its predecessor, was quick to unleash security forces whenever there was perceived existential threat to power. The difference

---

47  In fact, the one who was in command of the Presidential Guard unit that deployed in the August 2018 event was later promoted from Brigadier General Anselem Sanyatwa to Major General and subsequently appointed Ambassador to Tanzania where he is now addressed as 'His Excellency'.

48  '"As soft as wool?" Reform and Repression in Zimbabwe', *Democracy in Africa*, 1 March 2019.

was the organ chosen to complete this mission; for Mugabe, it was the police and civilian intelligence; and for Mnangagwa, the military and military intelligence.

## Political intolerance and closing democratic/civic space

Under Mugabe's ruthless authoritarianism, publicly expressing dissent was a punishable offence backed by a barrage of laws some of which were worse than the colonial statutes. The most onerous were the insult laws under Criminal Law (Codification and Reform) Act and the notorious (now repealed) Public Order and Security Act under which scores of people were arrested, prosecuted, but only a few found guilty because of the flimsiness of the charges. Mnangagwa has retained these manifestly undemocratic laws and has also used them to stifle dissent.

Arrests and abductions of opposition and civic leaders and activists – like civil society leader Jestina Mukoko in December 2008 and journalist and activist Itai Dzamara who has been missing for five years – were commonplace[49] under Mugabe while Mnangagwa appears to have made abductions his stock in trade. In 2019, the abductions became so endemic[50] that the European Union, United Nations, France, Germany, Greece, the Netherlands, Romania, Sweden, the UK, Australia, Canada and the USA all condemned the spate of abductions and urged the government to act. In September 2019, the United States issued a statement registering their condemnation: 'Since January more than 50 civil society, labour, and opposition leaders have been abducted in Zimbabwe. No arrests have been made. We urge the government to take action and hold perpetrators of these human rights violations accountable.'[51] In all these acts of abductions, the regional body, SADC, has remained studiously but unsurprisingly silent.

Leading opposition members were not spared but were mostly subjected to state-sponsored intimidation and spurious charges. Several MDC Members of Parliament were arrested and charged for treasonable offences in 2019 alone.[52] They allegedly organised and participated in

---

49 Other abductees include Rashiwe Guzha, Dzamara Marceline Dzumbira and Paul Chizuze. In addition, some were abducted and later found dead including: Edwin Nleya, Cain Nkala, Tonderai Ndira, Abigail Chiroto and Patrick Nabanyama. See 'UN probes Zim amid abductions', *Zimbabwe Independent*, 20 September 2019.

50 Civil society groups reported that about 50 people had been abducted and arrests had been made. See for instance: 'Zimbabwe abductions: Dozens of protest leaders missing', *AJ Impact*, 22 September 2019.

51 See: https://twitter.com/usembassyharare/status/1173550395316232192?lang=en

52 See, for instance, 'MDC petitions Parly over arrests', *Daily News*, 23 January 2029.

the January 2019 fuel protests and were charged under the Criminal Law (Codification and Reform) Act.

Both hard and soft power were deployed to crush the protests. To this extent, and for almost a week starting on 15 January 2019 – and ending on 21 January 2019 – the party-military regime through the Minister of State Security imposed a total internet shutdown to suppress any publicity around the excesses committed by the security forces but also to disrupt communication and mobilisation of the protests by the organisers. Two civil society organisations – the Zimbabwe Lawyers for Human Rights (ZLHR) and Media Institute of Southern Africa Zimbabwe Chapter (Misa Zimbabwe) – successfully challenged the shutdown in the High Court which ruled that it was illegal and ordered the internet service providers and mobile network operators to immediately resume services. To Reuters, the fragile state's behaviour was growing evidence 'that the country is slipping back into authoritarian rule'.[53] In short, Mugabe's repressive policies were quickly assumed by Mnangagwa and there seems little to distinguish the two regimes.

## Emasculation of state institutions

Following in the footsteps of his political master, the new president also sought to emasculate key state institutions so as to consolidate his fragile rule. He started with the low-hanging fruits, dismissing all undesirable elements at the senior levels of security sector structures. Hence, both the ZRP and the CIO were 'restructured' e.g. in December 2017, a month after the military intervention, the head of the ZRP, Commissioner-General Augustine Chihuri was 'retired' and replaced by his deputy Godwin Matanga. Chihuri was reportedly against the military intervention[54] and was also suspected to be part of the G40 faction.[55] The ZRP changes were disguised as 'transformation' and rebranding ostensibly so as to win back public confidence which admittedly was at its lowest ebb since independence. In January 2018, barely three months after Mnangagwa's

---

53 'Zimbabwe court says internet shutdown illegal as more civilians detained', Reuters, 21 January 2019. Also see: 'Zimbabwe imposes internet shutdown amid crackdown on protests', *AJ Impact*, 18 January 2019.

54 He was conspicuous by his absence at the KG6 press conference on 13 November 2017.

55 Chihuri, who was also reportedly profoundly corrupt, subsequently faced charges of abuse of public office and faced arrest but had skipped the country to Malawi. See 'Ex-police boss Chihuri faces arrest', *The Chronicle*, 30 May 2019.

takeover, 'Government retired over 30 senior police officers from the rank of senior assistant commissioner and above, as it moves to transform the ZRP'.[56] However, at the operational level, the force continued as before. Soon after the January 2019 protests, the Zimbabwe Human Rights Commission – a constitutional body – bluntly reported that:

> ... the police were letting loose their dogs to attack those whom they suspected to have caused mayhem. Some residents reported losing their valuables such as cellphones to the soldiers and the police during their searches of peoples' homes and their property such as doors and windows were destroyed. Some members of the public highlighted that they were scared of reporting the cases to the police as the nearby police stations were barricaded by the army and they also feared that the police would victimize them. Others managed to make reports but were turned away (ZHRC 2019).

In early December 2017, just weeks after Mnangagwa was sworn in, the chairman of ZEC, Justice Rita Makarau resigned without giving any reasons[57] but reports alleged that she was pushed out. Like Chihuri, Makarau was also said to have been part of the G40 faction that was pushing for Grace Mugabe to succeed her husband. As a Mugabe loyalist, Makarau presided over the 2013 General Election in which Mugabe and ZANU-PF handed Tsvangirai and his MDC party their heaviest defeat; Mugabe's big 2013 victory was thought to have been orchestrated by ZEC. Two months after resigning, Makarau also 'suddenly' resigned from the Judicial Service Commission, again for unstated reasons. She had been the G40 preferred candidate to replace the retired Chief Justice Godfrey Chidyausiku while Lacoste had preferred Judge President George Chiweshe.[58] To replace Makarau as ZEC chair, Mnangagwa appointed Justice Priscilla Chigumba in early February 2018 to steer the country towards the 2018 elections. Her appointment was not without controversy as she had previously been questioned by the former Chief Justice Chidyausiku and the current Chief Justice Luke Malaba[59] on allegations of corruption. She was also accused

---

56 'Govt retires 30 top cops', *The Herald*, 19 January 2018. A day later, it was announced that the government had rescinded its decision on 19 of them: '19 dropped from top cops chop list', *The Chronicle*, 20 January 2018.

57 'ZEC chair resigns', *The Herald*, 9 December 2017.

58 'Rita Makarau quits JSC', *Zimbabwe Independent*, 9 February 2018.

59 'Mnangagwa Has failed By Appointing Chigumba As ZEC Chairperson', *Pindula News*, 1 February 2018.

of 'wearing Zanu-PF regalia' after pictures of her circulated wearing a 'Mnangagwa scarf'.[60] Throughout the pre-election period, Chigumba was heavily criticised for her handling of election management issues[61] and ZEC's independence formed a substantive issue in most election observer reports which argued that the body was not sufficiently autonomous and professional, and had a clear bias in favour of the ruling party.

Mnangagwa also continued where his mentor had left off with respect to other state institutions. His determination to consolidate power did not spare the judicial system. The independence and impartiality as well as the professionalism of the judiciary was severely tested after the January 2019 protests and riots. At least 1,055 people were arrested and appeared in court for looting, public violence, arson, malicious damage to property, assault and murder, among other crimes. The judicial processes involved raised the ire of the Law Society of Zimbabwe (LSZ) which issued a statement condemning the injustices that they claimed were being perpetrated by the judicial system. In part, their statement read:

> We have received reports from some members and in other instances we have observed practises that do not show that justice is being done. It would appear that no one is paying attention to the adage "Justice must not only be done but must be seen to be done." Irregular and illegal pre-trial processes and court processes appear to be collusively used to deny accused persons access to justice.
>
> The following instances of apparent injustice being done to accused persons have been brought to our attention:
>
> 1. Mass trials
> 2. Fast tracked trials
> 3. Routine denial of bail
> 4. Routine dismissal of preliminary applications
> 5. Refusal of access to medical treatment and
> 6. Trial and detention of juveniles
>
> We have also received reports of abduction of personas and or

---

60 'What's the story behind Mnangagwa's scarf', *News24*, 26 July 2018.

61 She was criticised by the opposition parties – especially the MDC Alliance – and civil society groups for her alleged bias in favour of Mnangagwa and his ZANU-PF party. She was however also subjected to personal sexist attacks which were condemned by ZEC and other gender activists. See for instance: 'ZEC Commissioneer blasts Chigumba "sexiest" abuse', *New Zimbabwe*, 17 July 2018.

their close relatives, assault, torture and denial of access to lawyers.[62] (LSZ statement, 23 January 2019).

Lawyers followed this up with a protest march to the Constitutional Court where they presented a petition. Some of the lawyers marching through Harare carried placards emblazoned with the words: 'Systemic beatings, detentions silence the rule of law' while other signs read '#No to judicial capture, #justice not politics; #no to militarization of magistracy'.[63] For his part, the Chief Justice responded by taking the unprecedented step of issuing a statement rebutting the lawyers' allegations:

> The allegations that the Judiciary is acting under capture of an external force remain unfounded, baseless and unsubstantiated. In the meeting held on 22 January 2019, the Chief Justice gave the Law Society of Zimbabwe (LSZ) his assurance that no directive or instruction was given by himself or the JSC to magistrates to dispose of cases before them in a particular manner. He maintains this position.[64]

Mnangagwa ensnared himself in controversy regarding the role he played in the release on bail of Tendai Biti, a senior leader in the opposition MDC-A. Biti, a lawyer, was arrested for announcing the 2018 presidential elections results on 30 July and for inciting violence. As stated above, ZEC has the sole prerogative to announce results and Biti's action was therefore illegal under the electoral law. He was released on bail. Mnangagwa posted a statement on Twitter telling the world that he had influenced the courts to release Biti. If his intention was to woo the opposition, or to limit the damage to done to Zimbabwe's reputation, his tweet had the opposite effect, generating fears that the judiciary could easily be captured by the executive. This fear was compounded because it was the same judiciary that would be handling Chamisa's election challenge in the Constitutional Court. Indeed, subsequently, the MDC accused the courts of bias after the High Court ruled that party leader Nelson Chamisa was illegitimate. Party spokesperson, Jacob Mafume told a press briefing in Harare that the court ruling was President Emmerson Mnangagwa's attempt to divert the

---

62 'The rule of law situation', Law Society of Zimbabwe Statement, 23 January 2019.
63 'Zimbabwe lawyers march to demand justice for jailed protesters', *Reuters*, 29 January 2019.
64 'Chief Justice slaps down capture claims', *The Herald*, 1 Febuary 2019.

MDC from focusing on real issues and to sanitise his own illegitimacy.[65] The same thrust applies to the state media. Section 61 of the Constitution requires the latter be impartial, independent and provide fair coverage to all political parties during elections. The national media –television, radio and print media – have always been ZANU-PF mouthpieces, a trend that has continued with Mnangagwa's presidency. So biased was the national broadcaster that almost all election observer groups, even when they differed in other respects, unanimously agreed on the partisan manner in which ZTV and other state-controlled media such as *The Herald*, *The Chronicle* and the *Sunday Mail* carried out their duties.[66] In addition, there was outrage at the excessive coverage on ZTV – the only station in the land – gives to Mnangagwa and his wife, who appear on the news almost daily, just as Mugabe and his wife once did. The opposition is rarely ever featured in the state media and, when they are featured, they are shown in a negative light.

The most egregious assaults on national institutions have been the amendments to the newly-minted supreme law, barely seven years after the Constitution was agreed and enacted in 2013. The first assault was in September 2017 by Mugabe but spearheaded and fiercely defended by Mnangagwa in his capacity as Vice-President and Minister of Justice. This resulted in Constitutional Amendment No. 1 in 2017 whose main effect was to change the procedure for the appointment of the top three judiciary officers – the Chief Justice, the Deputy Chief Justice and the Judge President of the High Court. The appointments will now be made by the President after consultation with the Judicial Service Commission and without the need for a public interview process as was provided for in the 2013 Constitution. At the time of writing in February 2020, this arbitrary change to the law will have momentous consequences. Power will be further concentrated in the hands of the president undermining his accountability to the public and to Parliament as well as eroding the checks and balances that the four-year constitution-making process had laboured to build. (See Chapter 10 for more detail.) Moreover, the Amendment bill includes 27 amendments, an omnibus constitutional bill, and a deceptive tactic used by the regime to hide the far-reaching

---

65 'MDC: Mnangagwa behind Mushore's judgment, congress will proceed', *NewZimbabwe*, 8 May 2019.

66 Significantly, the Generals' historic press conference on 13 November 2017 had been completely blacked out on all state media platforms, both electronic and print.

eviscerations on the national charter.[67]

The hold that Mnangagwa now has over strategic state institutions is a device used by Mugabe. Thus, there is very little that is new and positive in the 'new dispensation'.

## Conclusion

A recurrent theme in this and other chapters is that of great hope and expectation that are soon deflated when pledges are broken resulting in a pervasive frustration and despair. So, back to the question: did November 2017 mark a change from the iron-fisted rule of former president Mugabe or did Mnangagwa simply pick up where his predecessor had left off. Professor Lovemore Madhuku, once a bitter critic of the Mugabe regime, but now accused by some of being sympathetic to the Mnangagwa administration, passed an uncomplimentary verdict on the 'new dispensation'. Asked in an October 2019 interview if there a new dispensation in Zimbabwe, Madhuku replied:

> There is no new dispensation. Currently, there is a dispensation that has been going backwards. They have gone behind what we had in the 1980s. Our current leaders are trying to learn the bad portion of their old days. The bad portion of the old days were characterised by the mysterious disappearance of people, the heavy deployment of police and army at the smallest excuse; the old days where you found people in government who had no clue on how to turn around the economy, which is what we have at the moment. We don't have a new dispensation[68]

Notwithstanding his 'sell-out' tag, Madhuku was speaking for many when he dismissed claims of a new dawn in Zimbabwe. Indeed, the

---

67  For a comprehensive outline and critical analysis of the Bill, see Veritas, a legal and parliamentary watchdog; its website is: www.veritaszim.net

68  'I am not a sell-out, Madhuku', *NewsDay*, 14 October 2019. Madhuku, a professor of law at the University of Zimbabwe, was a founding member of the National Constitutional Assembly (NCA) in 1997 where he, together with many civic formations and activists, vigorously campaigned for a new constitution and for the rejection of the 2000 government-driven draft. He later broke ranks with his erstwhile colleagues and campaigned against the constitution making process which gave birth to the 2013 supreme law. He subsequently and controversially converted the NCA into a political party and stood as a presidential candidate in July 2018 where he received paltry support (2692 votes or 0.06% of total valid presidential votes) before joining the Political Actors Dialogue (POLAD) – a forum established by Mnangagwa but which Chamisa firmly refused to join. Madhuku is a fiercely independent-minded public intellectual who does not baulk at sailing against the wind, even alone.

'distress, trepidation and despondency within the nation' that former CDF Chiwenga described on 13 November 2017 remains and grows worse, a legacy that Mnangagwa has been unable or unwilling to change. Evidence provided in this chapter attests to the fact what happened under Operation Restore Legacy was a leadership change not a regime change. The Mugabe regime was a party-military regime with is roots deep in the memory of the civil war, and anyone who challenges this is an 'enemy'. The Mnangagwa regime is no different. It has picked up the Mugabe baggage of profound corruption, a deep sense of entitlement to rule and monopolise the perquisites of power by virtue of having participated in the liberation war and a resort to coercion and electoral manipulation to maintain control. In sum, change was not delivered in November 2017. As foretold by Fergal Keane just a week after the November putsch: '… this was not a revolution to bring liberal democratic principles into government. It was about power'.[69] Bratton would have agreed, and many Zimbabweans today would confirm that their analysis could not have been more prescient. November 2017 was a potential game changer but there have been no substantive changes in the governance of the country or regard for welfare of its citizens. The coup in November 17 gave people hope for a future, something for which the hard-pressed citizens of Zimbabwe longed, and which briefly blinded their judgement. Now they are all too aware, that it offered nothing more than a change in leadership.

## References

Rosenfield, B. (2018) 'The Politics of Rupture', *Left Voice*, 20 April.

Catholic Commission for Justice and Peace (CCJP) and Legal Resources Foundation (LRF) (1997) *Breaking the Silence, Building True Peace: Report on the Disturbances in Matabeleland and the Midlands, 1980-1989*. Harare: CCJP and LRF.

Coltart, D. (2016) *The Struggle Continues: 50 years of Tyranny in Zimbabwe*. Johannesburg: Jacana Media.

Crisis in Zimbabwe Coalition (2019) 'Darkness at Noon: Inside Mnangagwa's 'New' Dispensation'. Harare: Crisis in Zimbabwe Coalition.

Human Rights Watch (2008) '"Bullets for Each of You": State-Sponsored Violence since Zimbabwe's March 29 Elections', *Human Rights Watch*, 9 June.

---

69 'Mugabe has gone, but will Zimbabwe change?', *BBC News*, 22 November 2017.

Masunungure, E.V. (2008) 'A Militarised Election: The 27 June Presidential Run-off', in E.V. Masunungure (ed.) *Defying the Winds of Change.* Harare: Weaver Press.

Southall, R. (2017) 'Bob's out, the Croc Is In: Continuity or Change in Zimbabwe?' *Africa Spectrum*, 52/3.

Zimbabwe Human Rights Commission (ZHRC) (2019) 'Monitoring Report in the Aftermath of the 14 January to 16 January 2019 "Stay Away" and Subsequent Disturbances'. Harare: ZHRC.

3

# The July 2018 Elections in Zimbabwe: Watershed that Never Was?

Richman Kokera, Simangele Moyo-Nyede
and Jonathan Kugarakuripi

*'Madame President, Mr. Speaker Sir, allow me to reiterate that my Government is committed to entrenching a democratic society driven by respect for the Constitution, rule of law, mutual tolerance, peace, and unity. To this end, Government will do all in its power to ensure that the 2018 Harmonised General Elections are credible, free and fair.'*
(President E.D. Mnangagwa, State of the Nation address 20 December 2017.)[1]

## Introduction

Since its founding electoral contest in 1980, Zimbabwe's elections have been distinguished by the troubling conjoined twins of violence and intimidation anchored in a regulatory framework that has deliberately created an asymmetrical playing field. Prior to 2018, Zimbabwe had held eight legislative and six parliamentary elections. In terms of electoral integrity, all failed the test of being free, fair and credible, with an indisputable outcome. And, with the exception of the legislative race in 2008, ZANU-PF, led by President Robert Mugabe, emerged victorious at the polls.

---

1   <http://www.veritaszim.net/node/2293> emphasis added.

All elections were marked by *procedural uncertainty* meant to produce *certainty of outcome* i.e. the triumph of the incumbent ZANU-PF party and its leader. Further, all the country's pre-2018 elections were presided over by the towering political figure – or institution – of Robert Gabriel Mugabe, Zimbabwe's now late founding leader. He meticulously crafted an electoral system and electoral processes geared to produce a predetermined result. Violence and intimidation were institutionalised and solidified as part of the iron law of Zimbabwe's elections.

However, between the 2013 and 2018 elections, a major, historically unprecedented event occurred in the overt intrusion into the political domain by the military, the Zimbabwe Defence Forces. They, in November 2017, launched Operation Restore Legacy, an operation that culminated in the dislodgement of Robert Mugabe as the country's president and leader of the ruling party. He was immediately replaced by Emmerson Dambudzo Mnangagwa (popularly known as 'ED'), Mugabe's long-time confidante whom he had recently fired[2] for alleged serious misdemeanours including 'consistently and persistently' exhibiting 'traits of disloyalty, disrespect, deceitfulness and unreliability'.[3] As soon as Mnangagwa returned from his brief self-exile, he sought to draw a red line between his and Mugabe's regime, promising, in a well-orchestrated charm offensive, a 'new unfolding democracy', 'free, fair, credible, transparent and violence-free' elections.[4]

The November 2017 events – dubbed 'military assisted transition' in the state media – were received with rapturous celebrations and soaring expectations. The newly imposed leader reinforced this intoxicating feeling of hope in all his initial speeches, including his State of the Nation address in December 2017. This message of change was repeated ad inifinitum throughout the pre-election phase of the electoral cycle and at various fora, both domestic and international. To many in and outside the country, a new dawn was beckoning, including a clean break with the long and odious past of falsified elections. Mnangagwa assumed office just nine months before elections were constitutionally due. In the light of the newly declared 'New Dispensation', many

---

2  Mnangagwa had then fled to neighbouring South Africa, fearing for his life. He only returned two days after Mugabe had 'voluntarily' resigned.

3  'Breaking: ED Mnangagwa fired', *The Herald*, 6 November 2017.

4  One of the popular placards to welcome him back was 'Dawn of a New Era'.

legitimately expected the forthcoming harmonised electoral contest to be a watershed. Was it? This question offers the focus of this chapter.

## Why elections?

Elections have become something of a universal expectation with which political actors must conform in the process of government formation (Bratton 2014). In a democracy, elections are essential because everything is done with the approval of the citizen. As such, the right to rule is entrusted to an individual or party through a majority vote. The argument is that a government is not legitimate without the consent of the governed. Elections, therefore, demonstrate that a government is of the people, for the people and by the people; the process itself settles the legitimacy question. Even in autocratic states, leaders hold 'show' elections to justify their claim to power (ibid.). Furthermore, the absence of consent from the governed can create legislative deadlocks, which can only be broken through elections. They are the foundation of governmental power providing a right to govern and some recognition by the governed of that right. As long as such recognition stands, a government is assured of compliance.

In addition to what has been mentioned above, Wojtasik (2013) states that there are seven basic functions of elections: (i) delegation of political representation, (ii) selection of a political elite, (iii) legitimisation of those in power, (iv) control over authorities, (v) political accountability, (vi) creation of political programmes, and (vii) creation of a public image.

Zimbabwe, which in name is a democracy, has enshrined the right to vote in the highest law of the land. Section 67 (3) of the Constitution provides that 'every Zimbabwean citizen who is of or over 18 years of age has the right to vote in all elections and referendums'. Section 155(2) (b) says 'The State must take all appropriate measures, including legislative measures' to ensure that every eligible citizen has an opportunity to vote. Thus, the Zimbabwean government is mandated under the dictates of the 2013 Constitution to conduct elections after every five years.

Zimbabwe has, thus, always held elections when due, and Zimbabweans appear to agree that elections are the best way to choose their leader. See Figure 3.1 below, survey data from the past three rounds conducted by Afrobarometer suggest as much.

**Figure 3.1: Zimbabwean's most preferred method of choosing a leader**

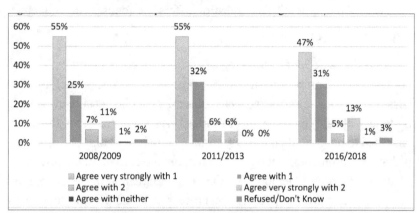

*Respondents were asked:* Which of the following statements is closest to your view? Choose Statement 1 or Statement 2. Do you agree or agree very strongly? 1. We should choose our leaders in this country through regular, open and honest elections. 2. Since elections sometimes produce bad results, we should adopt other methods for choosing this country's leaders.

## Brief history of elections in Zimbabwe

The history of elections in Zimbabwe demonstrates significant issues about the nature of politics in the country since independence. First, Zimbabwean elections have always had Mugabe and ZANU-PF at their core; second, most have been characterised by violence. Moreover, ZANU-PF has dominated Zimbabwean politics through abuse of state resources for the benefit and purposes of the party (see Figure 3.2). State machinery – such as the army, courts, police, and the media – has been used to feed and drive its purposes i.e. winning elections and staying in power. Even though democratic institutions and opposition political parties have been permitted, the absence of a level playing field has meant an absence of accountability.

By employing repressive measures, ZANU-PF has ensured that opposition parties are frustrated; access to media is kept to a minimum and acts of violence by state security agents are used to undermine and intimidate opposition members. For instance in 2002, the government instituted restrictive ordinances in the form of Public Order Security Act (POSA), which made it virtually impossible for other political parties to campaign, especially in the rural areas. Other measures restricted civil society organisation (CSOs) that advocated political reforms as they deemed their activities to be 'political' gatherings. Thus, civic electoral education was severely inhibited. Under POSA, any gathering of five or more people to discuss politics was interpreted as a political activity which would require authorisation by the police, and this was rarely granted, especially in ZANU-PF strongholds. The heavy presence of security agents and fear of this law made it difficult to discuss politics in public – even on public transport.

**Figure 3.2: Zimbabwe presidential election results, 1990-2018[5]**

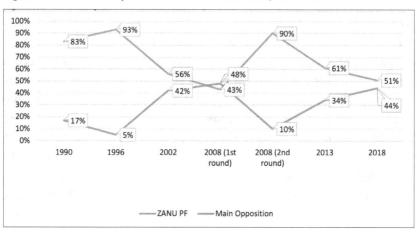

All this, it seemed, was about to change with the ouster of Mugabe and the installation of his long-time comrade, Mnangagwa, who appeared as if he wanted to revolutionise the way in which ZANU-PF played their political game. However, a test of his commitment to change came with the 2018 election which, based on his public addresses, promised to be an election like no other, a watershed; an election that would mark a break from the past.

## The pre-election environment

The 2018 election, unlike most previous elections in Zimbabwe, was characterised by a relatively peaceful pre-election environment. Rare were reports of active violence such as setting homes on fire and the amputation of body parts, which predominated the 2013 presidential run-off. However, instances of subtle voter intimidation and threat were present, such as the possible denial of food aid, or rumours that ZANU-PF could trace the way people voted through the Biometric Voter Registration (BVR) technology,

5    ZANU-PF has always dominated elections in Zimbabwe.

and reminders of retributive violence by ZANU-PF should MDC garner the majority of votes. Though since 1980 such threats have reflected the usual ZANU-PF approach to elections, the 2018 pre-election period saw the government taking strides to bring the Electoral Act in conformity with the Constitution. Zimbabwe, for the first time, would have a new voters' roll and, after more than a decade of isolation, foreign observers were invited. It did appear as if the promise of a new dispensation was on the horizon.

## Legal framework

The pre-election environment saw the introduction of a number of positive changes and appeared to be a major departure from past elections, more especially post-2000. One major positive attribute of the pre-election environment was the Electoral Amendment Act, which was signed into law on 28 May 2018 in order to align it to the 2013 Constitution. Although the Act failed to address all stakeholder concerns, the amendment saw the establishment of the Electoral Court and the Electoral Code of Conduct. Thus, provisions to accelerate the processing of cases of politically motivated violence and intimidation were put in place (Election Watch 2018). However, even with these achievements, critics still argue that more could have been done to level the playing field. For example, the Electoral Amendment Act is severely criticised for failing to speak to issues of transparency, particularly regarding the procurement and printing of ballot papers and the diaspora vote. The position of ZANU-PF on the latter remained unchanged, despite the new dispensation: diasporans would have to return home to register and/or vote. Thus, the ZANU-PF government disenfranchised millions[6] of Zimbabwean citizens living outside the country by not making provisions for postal voting. In addition, Mnangagwa's government failed to repeal repressive laws such as POSA and AIPPA,[7] which curtailed the ability of Zimbabweans to fully realise their constitutional rights. These outstanding issues contributed to the deterioration of the fragile relationship between the opposition and the electoral management body, ZEC, in the weeks prior to the election,

---

6   'Rough estimates: Millions of Zimbabweans abroad', *Mail & Guardian*, 19 April 2013. The Harare Office of the International Organisation for Migration (IOM) estimates that 500,000 to four million Zimbabweans are living abroad. However, the exact number is not known as the IOM claims that there are no reliable statistics of the exact number of Zimbabweans living in the diaspora.

7   Access to Information and Protection of Privacy Act (2002).

and compromised the image of the new era that Mnangagwa was trying to portray to the world (European Union Election Observation Mission (EU EOM 2018).

## Electoral challenges

One might ask if the amendments to the Electoral Act made it constitutional because in reality it remained seriously defective. First, according to the Act, election results may be deemed unfit as a result of malpractice i.e. corruption, violence and intimidation, but only if the perpetrator of such acts became the successful candidate. This provision directly contravenes section 155 of the Constitution which states that an election must be free from electoral misconduct regardless of the person responsible for them (Veritas 2018). Second, Part 23 of the Electoral Act stipulates the procedures to be followed during election challenges. These procedures are very difficult to follow and as a result all election petitions filed after the 2013 general election were not decided on their merits, thus creating an impediment to the principle of free, fair, peaceful and transparent elections (ibid.). Self-evidently, once an election violates these principles, it also violates the Constitution. More so, the Act states that only unsuccessful candidates can challenge elections. However, section 67 of the Constitution provides that every voter has the right to challenge an election.

Other downsides to the Act are: it is not easily accessible to the public and it is long, repetitive and sometimes obscure (ibid). Election Watch further asserts that there are many legal and technical errors. The Act remains unaligned to the Constitution, which is the supreme law in the land. One example of a technical error is that the procedures after polling in a presidential election are dealt with in both sections 37C and 110, which, however, are inconsistent with each other.

Thus, the shortcomings within the Electoral Act dealt an early blow to the government's promise of free, fair and credible elections and while the government's efforts to amend the Act to align it with constitutional provisions were commendable, they were simply inadequate.

## Training and education

The pre-election environment was also marked by an exciting departure from past elections in terms of Civic and Voter Education (CVE) initiatives. ZEC trained and commissioned 37 CSOs to assist in voter education. As a result, the democratic space opened up and the pre-election environment witnessed a commendable improvement in CVE initiatives by both CSOs and the Zimbabwe Election Support Network. In addition, a legal amendment removed the requirement for CSOs to disclose their sources of funding and no longer forced CVE funding through ZEC (ZESN 2018a).

## Voter registration

For the first time in the history of the electoral process in Zimbabwe, a new voter's roll was used in the harmonised elections i.e. presidential, parliamentary and local government elections that are held simultaneously, a practice that started with the 2008 elections. The BVR system involved taking photographs and fingerprints of registrants and proved a welcome development as it eliminated the possibility of ghost voters, a phenomenon that had previously been a bone of contention.

There were other conscious efforts made by ZEC to ensure that those who needed to register were able to do so, regardless of the often challenging requirements of proof of residence as provided for in the Constitution Paragraph 1 (2) of the Fourth Schedule. To lessen the burden of proof, citizens without the normal proof of residence could complete an affidavit and have it certified by the Commissioners before proceeding to register. This was especially beneficial to registrants in urban areas[8] and helped to ensure that citizens who wanted to vote were not excluded from doing so. Even election watchdogs like ZESN agreed that the 2018 voters roll was a significant improvement on the one used in 2013.

However, the roll was not without its problems. Firstly, the metropolitan cities were reportedly under-captured and possibly under-registered compared to rural counterparts thereby prejudicing voters in urban voters (EU EOM 2018). Secondly, an audit conducted by ZESN revealed that 9% of registrants were not found at their given addresses and were not known in the neighbourhood (ZESN 2018a). In addition, duplication of national registration numbers (IDs) was reported. Thus, critics of the voters' roll contended that too many duplicate IDs, plus evidence of the systematic alteration of ID prefixes, rendered the voters' roll unfit for use in the harmonised elections (EU EOM 2018).

By and large, and despite the problems identified above, the efforts by ZEC to produce a new voters' role signalled a significant break with the past and allowed ZEC to address major issues that had become endemic

---

8  Urban residents benefited mainly because people living in rented accommodation will quite often change their place of abode depending on rentals, thus this new proof of residence provision meant it was easier for them to register to vote.

within the previous voters' role administered over decades by the Registrar General, Tobaiwa Mudede.

## The independence and transparency of ZEC

The Zimbabwe Electoral Commission according to Section 235 of the Constitution is supposed to be independent and not subject to the direction or control of anyone. There are many instances where the transparency and independence of ZEC has been thrown into jeopardy and the Commission in many instances has acted in ways that are clearly not independent. Section 194 (1) (h) of the Constitution requires all tiers of government, including the electoral body, to foster transparency by providing the public with timely, accessible and accurate information, this is not reflected in the amended Electoral Act. ZEC has been criticised by many for not being transparent: such issues entail but are not limited to its failure to publish its procedural manuals, refusal to put the contract for printing ballot papers out to public tender and not disclosing how many of its staff have a security force background.

## Invitation and accreditation of observers

In a clear departure from the policies of his predecessor, President Mnangagwa opened the door to western poll observers. Teams from the United States of America, the European Union, (the Commonwealth and other international organisations had been shut out during a diplomatic stand-off with former Mugabe administration over charges of human rights abuses and electoral fraud. Thus, the return of these observer missions for the first time in nearly two decades was hailed by many.

## Domestic observers

While the invitation to international observers stole the limelight, there were also major improvements in the way in which domestic observers were allowed to operate. Numerous CSOs, NGOs and community groups monitored the harmonised elections with more freedom than in past elections. This was a positive step toward increasing the democratic space and a healthy indicator of progress toward competitive multi-party elections whereby CSOs could objectively and impartially operate and monitor the electoral process. The Election Resource Centre, ZESN, Heal Zimbabwe Trust, Habbakuk Trust, Veritas, Media Monitoring Project Zimbabwe (also known as Media Monitors Zimbabwe), the Media Institute of Southern Africa, Zimbabwe Council of Churches and the Evangelical Fellowship of Zimbabwe were among the CSOs that observed the elections. These organisations freely conducted various monitoring activities during the period preceding the 30 July elections and deployed teams of Zimbabwean citizen observers on election day.

## A skewed media

This chapter does not dwell deeply on the media dimensions of the elections as this is dealt with in considerable detail in Chapter 7. Thus, this section mainly highlights the media coverage of the elections and comments by observer groups as evidence of the skewed media landscape. Zimbabwe has a long history of suppression of press freedoms. This was the restrictive environment that characterised Robert Mugabe's rule. However, with the 'new dispensation', the political space somewhat widened. Journalists could cover contentious issues without being unduly harassed or unfairly detained. On this, the EU Observer report states that 'During the electoral period, media and journalists operated in a generally free environment, which only deteriorated in the wake of the incidents of 1 August in Harare' (EU EOM 2018). It should therefore be acknowledged that although media freedom fell short of constitutional prescription, it was a significant improvement on what Zimbabwean journalists had experienced during Mugabe era.

However, in terms of the state-owned media, ZANU-PF, as always, continued to dominate with Zimbabwe Newspapers Ltd (Zimpapers) and Zimbabwe television (ZTV) continuously singing the government's praises. This happened regardless of the fact that ZEC under section 160 (k) of the Electoral Act is mandated to allow media access to all political contenders, without which a fair election cannot be realised. A report by the independent media monitors noted that ZANU-PF received 53% of the media coverage (Media Monitors 2018). The media landscape in the pre-election phase of the electoral cycle is adequately summarised by the EU Observer Report which states:

> The state-owned media provided heavily biased coverage of the electoral process in favour of the ruling party. During the analysed period ZANU-PF received a total of 84.9%, 81.8% and 76.5% of election-related coverage 70% of air time on ZTV, Radio Zimbabwe and Classic 263, respectively. (EU EOM 2018).

## Party financing

Access to state funds for election campaigning demonstrated a continuation of ZANU-PF dominance. There was a clear disparity in terms of party financing. The former could as usual distribute free t-shirts and regalia and could mount very large billboards on approximately 610 sites.[9] The MDC-A, on the other hand had a hard time financing their campaigns, the party even admitted that they lacked the necessary funds to deploy observers at most polling stations (Mashava 2018). It is important to note that parties receive funds under the Political Parties (Finance) Act in proportion to the votes cast in the general election immediately prior. Under the provisions of the act, ZANU-PF and MDC had received $6,126,633 and $1,873,663 respectively (EU EOM 2018).[10] This disproportionate amount of party financing is further compounded by the fact that there is no legislation that places a cap on party expenditure. In addition, ZANU-PF enjoys the advantage of being the ruling party and can divert taxpayer's money for its own gain as has been the case in previous elections. In the face of such evidence, what changed in the 2018 election was the rhetoric, but in terms of conduct, ZANU-PF made few concessions.

## Electoral violence and voter intimidation

The 2018 election was not characterised by active voter intimidation and intense violence as in previous elections. However, instances of implicit violence were reported in the form of direct threats, pressure to attend rallies, partisan actions by traditional leaders, collection of voter registration slips (and other measures undermining confidence in the secrecy of the vote), manipulation of food aid and agricultural inputs, i.e., fertilisers, maize seed and other misuses of state resources.

Over four decades and primarily in the rural areas, ZANU-PF had collected citizens' private information on party allegiance, which was then used to determine who could access food aid. This information is usually provided by traditional leaders (though not all of them do so) and

---

9   'Zanu PF plots razzmatazz campaign', *Zimbabwe Independent*, 6 April 2018.

10  The allocation formula is based on the total number of votes cast for all the candidates of a party if they exceed the minimum threshold of 5% of valid votes cast in the preceding election. In 2013, ZANU-PF candidates won by large margins, and where they lost, it was often by small margins. So, the total number of ZANU-PF votes far exceeded those of MDC-T . The formula itself was correctly applied; it is the voting system that needs scrutiny. It does not matter if the vote is rigged by including coerced 'assisted voters', or the ballot boxes stuffed; the party with the largest nnumber of votes receives the largest allocation.

ZANU-PF village cell leaders who interact with the populace on a day-to-day basis. Secondly, local chiefs, who are supposedly non-partisan, only need to remind their community of the retaliation that took place when the opposition won in 2008. Colloquially referred to as 'shaking the matchstick box' [*Kuzunguza chikoko chemachisa*] (Cheeseman 2018), this phrase was sufficient to remind people of the threat that their homes would be burnt down as had been done in 2008, should they choose not to vote for ZANU-PF. In addition, absence of information about the BVR system was used to intimidate people who were told that party officials could track whom they had voted for, a tactic that ZANU-PF has used in the past elections (Cheeseman 2018).

Although such issues cannot be ignored, there was, nonetheless, tangible improvement on the ground as is supported by empirical findings from Afrobarometer (AB). Data collected under their auspices regarding the 2018 election demonstrated that while 76% of citizens still felt that they had to be careful when they spoke about politics, 25% of the registered voters who took part in the survey had been asked to show their voter registration slips, and 43% Zimbabweans said they personally feared becoming a victim of electoral intimidation or violence, these results show a real improvement on the 2013 election when 68% reported that they feared becoming the victims of political violence (Zimbabwe 2018 AB pre-election survey). However, certain issues demonstrated a change on the part of ZANU-PF – not a change for the better, but rather a possible change in tactics.

## The elections

President Mnangagwa had promised to deliver free, fair and credible elections under a new dispensation. Even though a single day of voting does not tell the whole story, it is a necessary part of the whole process. So, was there any reason to remain cynical about the president's promises as the day progressed?

For a moment, it looked as if Zimbabwe had finally turned a corner. However, it should be remembered that election days in Zimbabwe have historically been peaceful – 30 July 2018 was no exception. There was general agreement among observers that the voting process was well organised and took place in a peaceful environment both in rural and urban areas (African Union Elections Observer Mission 2018; European Union Election Observation Mission 2018; Election Support Network –

Southern Africa 2018; Commonwealth Observer Group, (COG) 2018; The Zimbabwe Human Rights Commission (ZHRC) 2018; ZESN 2018). Possibly encouraged by the peaceful pre-election environment and hoping for a real and credible election with unmanipulated results, voters turned out in large numbers. While there were long queues in the urban areas, this did not seem to be major concern for stakeholders. Moreover, isolated reports of some voters lacking awareness of their polling locations did not seem to negatively affect the voting process (EU EOM 2018). A further look at different aspects of the election day below would help us to put things into proper perspective. We start with postal voting.

## Postal voting

We have already referred to the pending issue of the diaspora vote above. Here, we take a quick look at postal voting as it relates to uniformed forces. It is well documented that the latter are denied the right to a free and secret vote as they are forced to vote in front of their superiors or challenged to show that they have voted for a ZANU-PF presidential candidate (Maringira 2016). Section 72 of the Electoral Act makes provision for postal ballots for the police to be distributed through a commanding office and for each individual officer to complete their ballot in secret and then return it directly to the ZEC through the postal system. Having police commanders administer postal voting is against the provisions of the Electoral Act and therefore an infringement of the officers' rights to a secret vote as enshrined in the Electoral Act (EU EOM 2018). Thus, the management of the postal system by the electoral management body still leaves a lot to be desired and is reminiscent of the conduct of postal voting during Mugabe's era, especially in 2008 (Maringira 2016).

## Assisted voters

As in past elections, the 2018 elections suffered from a notoriously high number of assisted voters. Key election stakeholders (ESN-SA 2018; EU EOM, 2018; ZHRC, 2018) raised a red flag about the high number of assisted voters witnessed on 30 July 2018. Forcibly assigning members of the community to a person who would assist them to vote is not new. In the past voters were told to claim illiteracy so that a ZANU-PF sympathiser could help them cast their votes (Asylum Research Centre 2015). Forced assisted voting is a form of intimidation and goes against section 133B (c) (i) of the Electoral Act. According to the ZHRC, seven areas, mainly in the ZANU-PF heartlands, which recorded the most assisted votes are Murehwa South, Gokwe North, Buhera South, Chivi North, Bindura North, Shamva North and Hurungwe West (ZHRC 2018). Findings from Heal Zimbabwe July 2018 report suggests that Hurungwe and Buhera were among some of the areas that recorded the highest number of human rights violations in the month of July, which was the month preceding the election and levels of intimidation were also high in these areas. The report also notes that some of the people were forced to volunteer for assisted voting. These decisions were made during community meetings and through the traditional leaders (Heal Zimbabwe 2018). Reasons for the high number of assisted voters could be intimidation, human rights violations and politicisation of food aid, because of these, voters were cowed to 'volunteer' for assisted voting for 'their own good'.

## Role of traditional leaders on election day

One of the major expectations in the turnaround was that traditional leaders would, in accordance with the law, desist from openly associating with any political party; acting in a partisan manner; furthering the interests of any political party; and respecting the fundamental rights and freedoms of their citizenry. However, the role played by traditional leaders in coercing villagers to vote for ZANU-PF is well known. President Mugabe ensured that they were well rewarded if they pledged support for his party and openly forced their subjects to support and vote for the incumbency. Nothing changed in the 2018 elections. The chiefs were neither neutral nor non-partisan. The Zimbabwe Human Rights NGO Forum (2018: 31) reports that traditional leaders were shepherding, with impunity, villagers to the polling booths with the instruction to vote for ZANU-PF in what is popularly known as 'sabhuku nevanhu vake' (a village head and his subjects). Thus, the influence or coercion of traditional leaders in elections remains a major hurdle to free, fair and credible elections (COG 2018).

## Disenfranchisement of potential voters

Zimbabweans went to the polls with enthusiasm and in large numbers to elect their president in a supposedly new dispensation. The expectations were high that the BVR exercise brought about a much-improved voters' roll where everybody who had registered to vote would find their name on the voters' roll on election day. Unfortunately, some potential voters could not vote either because their names did not appear on the voter's roll or appeared in a far-flung constituency e.g. a home area, which they had no hope of reaching in time (ESN-SA 2018; EU EOM 2018). In 22% of polling stations visited, EU EOM (2018) observed people being turned away. As in past elections, disenfranchisement of potential voters continues to compromise the credibility and fairness of elections (ZESN 2013).

## Counting at the polling stations and the collation process

Though the counting of votes was reportedly transparent, well-organised and meticulous in polling stations throughout the country, problems with ballot reconciliation, completion of the numerous originals of return forms, and packing election materials (EU EOM 2018) continue to paint a bleak picture. In addition, some polling stations failed to post election results at the polling station as required by law. Thus, the July 2018 elections did not live up to expectations.

While the collation process was considered good overall, instances where party agents did not receive copies of the completed results, and where results were not displayed outside the collation centres, reveal that there is still room for improvement. The figures presented to observers by ZEC were littered with errors casting doubt as to the accuracy and reliability of the figures (EU EOM 2018). The EU EOM noted that provinces with the highest margin of votes in favour of the ruling party, also had highest number of reports of subtle intimidation, vote buying and coercion of voters by traditional leaders.

## The election results

Once again, ZEC was found wanting in the way it handled the announcement of the presidential elections results. While, indeed, all the results were eventually announced as per the dictates of Section 67 and Section 110 of the Electoral Act (Chapter 2:13) within the prescribed five days, releasing the parliamentary results first, where ZANU-PF was clearly leading, and deliberately withholding the presidential results, fueled speculation and triggered anger among opposition party supporters who then protested (ESN-SA 2018; ZHRC 2018). The reader, and indeed the voter, is reminded of the five week delay in the announcement of the 29 March 2008 presidential election. This delay followed a carefully stage-managed announcement of both the senatorial and parliamentary results, so that both the MDC-T and ZANU-PF appeared on par in terms of the number of seats won. So, when in 2018 there appeared to be a break in the announcement of the presidential results, it seemed logical for opposition supporters to assume that ZEC was again tampering with the ballot. The delays reminded opposition party supporters of the deceptions of March 2008.

The errors made by ZEC in counting and collating the presidential results – even though observers seem to agree that these could not have changed Mnangagwa's lead – did not help the situation. Instead, they raised serious questions about ZEC's competency in the post-Mugabe era. Amendment (No. 20) Act 2013 Section 239 (a) (iv) of the Constitution of Zimbabwe requires ZEC to be efficient and transparent in counting the ballot. Initially, ZEC announced that Mnangagwa had won the presidential vote with 50.8% to Chamisa's 44.3%, only to revise the figures to 50.67% and 44.39% respectively, a week after the MDC-A has challenged the result in the Constitutional Court (ZHRC 2018; CCJPZ 2018). One must ask why the electoral management body had to wait for the court challenge to revise down Mnangagwa's win. So it was that ZEC's conduct continued to raise suspicion and mistrust, especially among the opposition. Critics wonder whether ZEC would have revised the results if there had been no court challenge (CCJPZ 2018).

## Post-election period

The post-election period was marked by three major events: the protest by MDC-A supporters, the killing of six protesters by the military, and the subsequent commission of inquiry led by Kgalema Motlanthe, former South African president. In the sections that follow, we consider how each of these impacted the outcomes of the harmonised elections.

## Protests and the crackdown

Although all went relatively well during the pre-election and voting period, events subsequently took a bad turn. The most disturbing post-election incident was the violence that erupted in central Harare on 1 August 2018. According to analysts, this was due to the unexplained delay in releasing presidential results, the continued accusations by MDC-A leaders that the elections had been rigged, and the growing impatience among MDC-A supporters,[11] who took to the streets in

---

11 Online articles and newspapers suggest that the opposition MDC-A supporters who took to the streets were many, but no accurate numbers have been provided.

and around Harare's central business district. It is argued that the demonstrations turned ugly resulting in property being destroyed, and six civilians (protestors and non-protesters) being killed in broad daylight with many being injured after military – not police – intervened to quell the demonstrations with live ammunition, a first in the history of Zimbabwean elections. It was reported by the ZHRC that the military moving around in military trucks, harassed and beat civilians in some suburbs in Harare – especially in the much-populated high-density areas. Journalists were ordered to switch-off cameras in an attempt to keep events out of the public eye and the world at large, and hide what were gross human rights violations. The deployment of the military, by the Defence minister in consultation with the Home Affairs minister and the Police Commissioner-General,[12] was a sharp reminder of past elections, which were marred with violence against opposition supporters. Many viewed the violence as evidence that Zimbabwe had not yet moved forward. The intervention of the military was condemned locally and internationally. Colm Ó Cuanacháin, Amnesty International's Acting Secretary General, said of the shootings; 'By using live ammunition against unarmed protesters, the army has broken the very same rule of law that they should protect'.

Mnangagwa's reaction to the clampdown that resulted in the death of unarmed civilians did not help the situation. Blaming it on the opposition and remaining silent about any wrongdoing on the part of security forces responsible for the killings was ill-advised (International Crisis Group Report, 2018). Instead, it merely emphasised the fact that the so-called 'new dispensation' meant little. The blame game reeked of the tactics of the old regime. Even as President Mnangagwa came to his senses and called for peace and calm, the Zimbabwean army, together with the police, continued to hunt down opposition supporters in their homes in the high-density suburbs of Harare (e.g., Mabvuku, Tafara, Glen View) (ZESN Report, September 2018). In addition, the crackdown and militarisation of post-election environment demonstrated a muzzling of freedom of expression, association and assembly.

---

12  There is evidence of a paper trail between the Defence Minister, the Home Affairs Minister and Police Commissioner General about the deployment of the military, and the defence Minister gave the go-ahead. This is provided for by the draconian POSA, which is not consistent with the 2013 Constitution. However, later during one of his rallies, President Mnangagwa took responsibility for the deployment of the soldiers.

## Citizens' trust in electoral processes eroded

The conduct of security forces using excessive might against citizens exercising their right to protest violated Zimbabwe's democratic values enshrined in the Constitution, and diminished trust in the elections which had, until then, been conducted in a much improved environment (COG 2018). Further incidents continued to erode citizens' trust and confidence in the electoral process, especially in relation to the participation rights of all stakeholders (EU Observers Report, 2018). These included a raid on the MDC-A's offices by the police on 1 August 2019 on the orders of Tandabantu Matanga, Police Commissioner-General, and the heavy-handedness of the security forces in disrupting a press conference by the leader of the MDC-A at the Bronte Hotel on 3 August 2018, even before it had commenced. These issues undermined citizens' and observers' trust and confidence in the electoral process.

## State of human rights in the new dispensation

It is well recorded that former President Mugabe employed repressive tactics to cling to power. So has anything really changed under Mnangagwa's government post the elections? ZESN's long-term observers reported incidents of human rights violations in their constituencies, though in most cases, they could not identify the perpetrators. When this could be established, ZANU-PF supporters and the military were identified as the main culprits. There were also reports of the military indiscriminately beating people (ZESN Report, September 2018). Zimbabwe Association of Doctors for Human Rights (ZADHR) reported that they treated patients that were injured during the crackdown; eleven with gunshot wounds.[13] Furthermore, ZADHR alleged that state agents tried to cover up post-election violence forcing pathologists at public hospitals to describe gunshot-wound injuries as stab wounds.[14]

## The Inquiry: the Motlanthe Commission

On 29 August 2018, President Mnangagwa appointed a seven-member Commission of Inquiry chaired by former South African President, Kgalema Motlanthe to look into the post-election violence. This was

---

13 'Doctors nail army in killings', *NewsDay*, 16 November 2018.
14 'Zimbabwe "state agents" tried to cover up post-election violence, say doctors', *The Guardian*, 19 November 2018.

viewed as a positive step by both the populace and the international community. There was, however, criticism that the president violated Section 110 (6) by establishing the Commission without seeking the advice of the Cabinet[15] and without publishing a proclamation as required by the Commissions of Inquiry Act (No. 4 of 1991) (Chapter 10), Revised 1996 Revision. It was argued that the president could not appoint a Commission to enquire into his own conduct, based on the allegations that under section 213 of the Constitution, the president is responsible for deploying the military and thus he must have ordered their deployment on 1 August 2018.

The Motlanthe Commission was established in terms of the Commissions of Inquiry Act (Chapter 10:07), published in Statutory Instrument 181 of 2018, and to give it a veneer of respectability, four of the seven Commissioners were from outside Zimbabwe. It was given a three-month period to establish its findings, recommendations and produce the final report. The terms of reference were designed to 'steer the Commission towards investigating post-election violence'. They contain a presumption that the appropriateness of the force used must be measured against the 'ensuing threat to public safety, law and order' (Mungwari 2019). Missing from the terms of reference was the necessity to investigate and establish the military chain of command in order to identify who authorised the deployment of soldiers and the order to shoot to kill (Mungwari 2019).

According to Mungwari, (ibid), the Commission's composition and terms of reference raised serious concerns. Some of the Commissioners[16] were viewed as sympathetic to President Mnangagwa and ZANU-PF.[17] Alex Magaisa, as quoted by Mungwari, argued that clearly partisan Commissioners will not be able to make a 'full, faithful and impartial inquiry' into any matter in which they have been already pre-judged and demonstrated partisanship (Mungwari 2019).

---

15 'Kgalema Motlanthe Commission in Zim "illegally formed" says think tank', *News24*, 5 September 2018.

16 The Commission comprised: His Excellency Kgalema Motlanthe (former President of the Republic of South Africa), who chaired the Commission; Chief Emeka Anyaoku (former Commonwealth Secretary General, Federal Republic of Nigeria); Rodney Dixon QC (United Kingdom); General Davis Mwamunyange former Chief of Tanzania People's Defence Forces); Professor Charity Manyeruke (Political Science, University of Zimbabwe); Professor Lovemore Madhuku (Faculty of Law, University of Zimbabwe); and Mrs. Vimbai Nyemba (former President of the Law Society of Zimbabwe).

17 'Autonomy critical for Motlanthe commission', *Daily News*, 25 November 2018.

## Key findings of the Motlanthe Commission of Inquiry

According to Derek Matyszak (2019), the Commission's report was tailor-made to Mnangagwa's requirements, primarily because it commences by contrasting his calls for peace before the elections with what is called 'overwhelming video evidence'[18] of MDC-A leader, Nelson Chamisa, inciting violence. The Commission considered evidence from various witnesses across the political divide and the generality of the populace. However, their findings were made when police investigations into some of the cases cited during the hearings had not been finalised. Nevertheless, the Commission was satisfied that the substantial evidence it received was sufficient. The highlights of their findings are as follows:

(a) The riotous demonstration had been incited, pre-planned and well-organised by the MDC-A and caused extensive damage;

(b) The particular circumstances prevailing on the day justified the deployment of the military to assist the police in containing the riots; and

(c) Six people died and 35 were injured as a result of actions by the military and the police.

From these findings, the Commission clearly blamed the MDC-A for the violent protests. It concluded by saying that evidence showed that the government deployed the military in accordance with the Constitution. That the deployment of the military was lawful, but the operational framework in terms of Section 37 (2) of Public Order and Security Act [Chapter 1 1:0 7] was not fully complied with in that the deployed troops were not placed under the command of the Harare Regulating Authority (The Zimbabwe Republic Police, Harare Central District Headquarters).

## Criticisms of the Commission's findings and lack of implementation

Analyst, Matyszak (2019), considers the recommendations of the Commission are disingenuous. The Commissioners called for perpetrators

---

18  Nelson Chamisa is said to have incited violence and demonstrations by alleging, a few days prior to the elections, that if MDC-A does not win the Presidential elections, the election would have been rigged and Tendai Biti announced that the MDC-A had won the Presidential election before a formal announcement of the results by ZEC was given.

of crimes on 1 August to be prosecuted by which they meant the demonstrators who destroyed property, while being very lenient on the soldiers who killed people. Writing that they are to be regarded as in 'breach of discipline', to be identified by 'internal military processes' and 'sanctioned'. Interestingly, one of the generals involved in the shooting, (then) Brigadier General Sanyatwe, was promoted a few months later to Major General, by President Mnangagwa. Mungwari (2019) argues that the Motlanthe Commission of Inquiry had a 'template' into which they only had to fit pre-enacted details. At the time of writring, the Commission's recommendations to those in power have not been implemented: there has been no compensation paid to victims or their families, nor has there been any report of retribution with regard to the soldiers that took part in the shooting. It must, however, be noted that in terms of the publication of findings, compared with the Mugabe era, it could be argued that there was an improvement – considering that the Dumbutshena Commission's findings in 1981, and the Chihambakwe Commission's report in 1985 were never made public.[19]

## The MDC-Alliance's legal challenge

On several occasions during the run up to the July 2018 elections, the MDC-A leaders had publicly warned that they would defend the vote. Indeed, on 1 August 2018, Tendai Biti claimed that Nelson Chamisa had won the presidential election; and after Emmerson Mnangagwa was declared the winner by ZEC, the MDC-A said they would file a court challenge, and did so by lodging an appeal to the Constitutional Court on 10 August 2018. This weighty petition and contestation forced a month-long postponement of Mnangagwa's inauguration, planned for 12 August 2018. The MDC-A accused ZEC of improper conduct, bias and fraud claiming that it had in fact won the presidency by over 650,000 votes. This court challenge was viewed as one that would bring about change to the court system in the hope that the legal challenge would be addressed by the court in a non-partisan and fair manner.

## Constitutional Court processes

After the submissions of written arguments by the relevant parties on an expedited schedule, the Constitutional Court held an unprecedented all-day hearing on 22 August. Nine judges led by Chief Justice Luke Malaba

---

19 'Gukurahundi inquiry reports lost', *NewsDay*, 22 April 2019.

were designated to hear the case. The principal argument was whether the MDC-A had called into question enough votes to reduce Mnangagwa's total to below the 50% plus one threshold. The MDC-A cited a catalogue of discrepancies including incorrect counting, 'ghost' polling stations and at some polling stations, more ballots being counted than there were registered voters. Chamisa's lawyers alleged that there was 'massive' doctoring of the vote to keep Mnangagwa in office. However, lawyers for the prsident insisted that there was insufficient evidence. During the proceedings, ZEC admitted certain mistakes and reduced the margin to 50.67% from 50.8%. In their responses, both Mnangagwa and ZEC argued that petitioners violated legal processes. In customary ZANU-PF style, before the court had given its final verdict, several senior party figures, including the leader of the Zimbabwe Liberation War Veterans Association, Victor Matemadanda, sent a congratulatory message to Mnangagwa. These were aired on the sole state broadcaster, ZTV. To some this was a form of intimidation. Would or could the Constitutional Court give a ruling contrary to the congratulatory messages?

## The Constitutional Court judgement

On 24 August 2018, the Constitutional Court of Zimbabwe dismissed MDC-A leader Chamisa's challenge to ZANU-PF leader Mnangagwa and declared the latter the election winner in an unanimous ruling by nine judges.[20] The court ruled that the MDC-A had failed to prove allegations of fraud during the elections and that there was a lack of evidence to support specific examples of allegations put before the court.[21] The Chief Justice noted that Chamisa refused both a recount and access to the ballot boxes. In handing down the judgement, Malaba said:

'It is an internationally accepted principle of election disputes that an election is not set aside easily merely on the basis that irregularities occurred. There is a presumption of the validity of the election. It is not for the court to decide an election; it is for the people. In the result, the following order is made: the application is dismissed with costs. Emmerson Mnangagwa is duly declared the winner of the presidential elections.'

In a first for the country, the proceedings were broadcast live on

20 'UPDATED: court-upholds ED victory... Chamisa election case dismissed with costs', *The Chronicle*, 25 August 2018.

21 ConCourt (2018).

state television for all to see. This would never have happened during Mugabe's era. Derek Matyszak, a legal expert, had predicted that the opposition faced an uphill struggle[22] given the courts' historic leaning towards ZANU-PF, saying that the outcome was predictable.[23]

## Other election challenges

### a) Electoral Courts

Other electoral complaints were filed at the four Electoral Courts (Harare, Masvingo, Mutare, and Bulawayo) and other election-related cases at the general division of the High Courts. These 2018 electoral challenges show that the democratic space had opened up in the post-Mugabe era. However, according to ZIEOM 2018, the total number of challenges was less than anticipated given the broad range of public complaints that the opposition made regarding the results of the National Assembly elections. Harare Electoral Court received a total of 41 electoral cases: sixteen challenged the results for National Assembly seats, eight challenged the result for Local Council seats, and one challenged the result for the Provincial Assembly of Chiefs' seat. The Bulawayo Electoral Court received a total of five electoral cases: two citing a number of mathematical errors that affected the validity of the results, including a difference of more than 40,000 votes which were cast for the president, more than the votes that were cast for the National Assembly election;[24] differences between V11 and V23 forms in favour of the incumbent; more than 100% voter turn-out in some polling stations in favour of the incumbent by 31,204 votes; lack of results being posted at 21% of polling stations and double tabulation of results at some stations. The court did not impugn ZEC, claiming it provided sufficient evidence to refute all allegations; and ultimately dismissed the petition with costs to the applicant, challenging the results for National Assembly seats. The Mutare Electoral Court received a total of three cases, with one filed to challenge the results for a National Assembly seat. The Masvingo Electoral Court received only one electoral case. The ZIEOM noted that for a number of pre-election cases, allegations of electoral malpractice were not investigated in a timely manner nor were judgments rendered

---

22 'MDC "faces an uphill struggle" in its bid to overturn Mnangagwa's election victory', *News24*, 22 August 2018.

23 Ibid.

24 The argument in this case was why the presidential results showed 40,000 more votes for the president than the National Assembly votes that were cast in Bulawayo in the same election.

before election day, undermining international conventions for citizens' right to effective dispute resolution and remedy (ZIEOM 2018).

### b) General Division of the High Court

A total of twenty petitions were filed challenging the outcome of parliamentary elections: nine by the MDC-A, four by ZANU-PF, three by independent candidates, two by MDC-T, one by National Patriotic Front (NPF), and one by the People's Rainbow Coalition. All these petitions could signify that there was a growing trust in the judiciary, although the outcomes reveal that little has changed within it since the 'second republic'. One interesting petition was that of Chegutu West, where ZEC initially announced the ZANU-PF candidate, Dexter Nduna, as the winner. However, it later admitted it had made an error and had inadvertently recorded the votes for the winning MDC-A candidate, Gift Konjana, as those for the losing ZANU-PF candidate and vice versa. While ZANU-PF acknowledged that a transcription error had been made and that its candidate did not receive the largest number of votes, the party challenged ZEC's decision to reverse itself, arguing that only the courts could change the outcome. As a result, the ZANU-PF candidate was declared the winner despite ZEC and the two political parties all agreeing that it was the MDC-A candidate who received the most votes. The MDC-A filed a petition challenging this result, but it was thrown out by the courts on technical grounds and the petition was not heard.

## Conclusion

For the umpteenth time, the 30 July 2018 harmonised elections produced a disputed presidential election. Many aspects of these elections failed to meet international standards. The events that followed confirmed that Mnangagwa had failed to convince the world that he was ushering in a new more democratic era. Although he sought to present the election as marking a new chapter in Zimbabwe after years of repression and economic decline, Mark Stevens the deputy head of the EU Missions, was nearer the truth when he concluded that though the election campaign and voting day were largely peaceful, multiple factors affected the fairness of the result. He added that 'The misuse of state resources, instances of coercion and intimidation, partisan behaviour by traditional leaders and overt bias in state media, all in favour of the ruling party, meant that a truly level playing field was not achieved.' The elections perpetuated the unfair dominance of ZANU-PF in Zimbabwean politics (Bratton and

Masunungure 2018). Apart from cosmetic changes to the electoral process such as the introduction of the BVR, limited changes to the Electoral Act, and peaceful pre-elections campaigns, the July 2018 elections were largely biased in favour of the incumbent, ZANU-PF. In addition, traditional leaders and food distribution continue to be used to further their political agenda. Arguably, the elections can be viewed as having taken the country a step backwards, judging by how the nation was left divided along political party lines.

The events of 1 August 2018 served as a sharp reminder of ZANU-PF's ability to quickly switch back to brutal tactics to silence dissent whenever the need arises. Indeed, the July 2018 elections were far from the watershed that they were expected to be. Indeed, a leopard never changes its spots.

## References

African Union Commission (2018) 'Report of African Union Election Observation Mission to the 31 July 2013 Harmonised Elections in the Republic of Zimbabwe'. https://eisa.org.za/pdf/zim2013au2.pdf

Afrobarometer (2018) 'Findings from a pre-election survey in Zimbabwe: June/July 2018'. https://afrobarometer.org/media-briefings/findings-pre-election-survey-zimbabwe-junejuly-2018

———— (2017) 'Afrobarometer Round 7, Survey in Zimbabwe, 2017'. https://afrobarometer.org/sites/default/files/publications/Summary%20of%20results/zim_r7_sor_en.pdf

Asylum Research Centre (ARC) (2015) 'Zimbabwe: Country Report'. https://www.refworld.org/pdfid/54b691994.pdf

Bratton, M. and E.V. Masunungure (2018) 'Heal the beloved country: Zimbabwe's polarized electorate'. Afrobarometer Policy Paper No. 49. https://afrobarometer.org/sites/default/files/publications/Policy%20papers/ab_r7_policypaperno49_heal_the_beloved_country_zimbabwes_polarized_electorate.pdf

Bratton, M. (2014) *Power Politics in Zimbabwe*. Boulder, CO: Lynne Rienner Publishers.

Commonwealth Observer Group (COG) (2018) 'Zimbabwe Harmonised Elections on 30 July 2018'. https://thecommonwealth.org/sites/default/files/inline/FINAL%20-%20Zimbabwe%20Preliminary%20Statement%20-%202%20August%202018_1.pdf

Constitutional Court of Zimbabwe (ConCourt) (2018) 'Constitutional Court

Judgement – Nelson Chamisa's Presidential Election Legal Challenge'. http://kubatana.net/2018/08/24/constitutional-court-judgement-nelson-chamisas-presidential-election-legal-challenge/

Election Support Network – Southern Africa (ESN-SA) (2018) 'Eminent Persons Observer Mission Report to the Zimbabwe Harmonised Elections 2018'. http://www.veritaszim.net/sites/veritas_d/files/ Eminent%20Persons%20Observer%20Mission%20Report%20to%20 the%20Zimbabwe%20Harmonised%20Elections%202018_0.pdf

European Union Election Observation Mission (EU EOM) (2018) 'Final Report Republic of Zimbabwe Harmonised Elections 2018'. http://www. veritaszim.net/sites/veritas_d/files/EU%20Election%20Observers%20 Final%20Report%20Zimbabwe%202018-.pdf

Heal Zimbabwe (2018) Human Rights Report (1-23 July 2018).

International Republican Institute and National Democratic Institute (2018) 'IRI/NDI Zimbabwe International Election Observation Mission Final Report'.

Maringira, G. (2016) 'Politicization and Resistance in the Zimbabwean National Army'. *African Affairs*, 116/462.

Matyszak, D. (2018) 'The Motlanthe Commission's anniversary of shame'. https://issafrica.org/iss-today/the-motlanthe-commissions-anniversary-of-shame

Mungwari, T. (2019) 'Zimbabwe Post Election Violence: Motlanthe Commission of Inquiry 2018'. *International Journal of Contemporary Research and Review*, 10/02.

Pigou, Piers (2017) 'After Elections, Zimbabwe Government's Legitimacy in Limbo'. https://www.crisisgroup.org/africa/southern-africa/zimbabwe/ after-elections-zimbabwe-governments-legitimacy-limbo

The Catholic Observer (2018) 'Catholic Commission for Justice and Peace in Zimbabwe Election Observation Report for 2018 Zimbabwe Harmonised Elections'. http://www.zcbc.co.zw/assets/ccjpz_election.pdf

Veritas (2018) 'Presidential Ballot Paper – Election Watch 34 / 2018'.

Wojtasik, Waldemar. (2013) 'Functions of Elections in Democratic Systems'. *Political Preferences*. 4. 25-38.

Zimbabwe Election Support Network (ZESN) (2018) 'Report on the 30 July 2018 Harmonised Election'.

———— (2018a) 'ZESN report on pre-election political environment and observation of key electoral processes'.https://www.zesn.org.zw/ wp-content/uploads/2018/07/ZESN-REPORT-ON-PRE-ELECTION-POLITICAL-ENVIRONMENT-AND-OBSERVATION-OF-KEY-ELECTORAL-PROCESSES.pdf

———— (2013) 'Report on the 31 July 2013 Harmonised Elections'. http://archive.kubatana.net/docs/elec/zesn_2013_harmzned_elec_ report_130913.pdf

Zimbabwe Human Rights Commission (ZHRC) (2018) 'ZHRC 2018 Harmonised Election Report'.

Zimbabwe Human Rights NGO Forum (2017) 'Predisposing the Scourge of Political Violence'. http://www.hrforumzim.org/wp-content/ uploads/2017/08/An-Analysis-On-Political-Violence-Reports.pdf

# 4

# Zimbabwe's Predatory Ruling Elite Coalition: Continuities Beyond Mugabe

## Eldred V. Masunungure

## Introduction

It is commonplace to refer to Zimbabwe's post-independence regime as a 'ZANU-PF regime' or a 'party-state' – the latter referring to ZANU-PF's conflation with the State. These terms are only partially correct, the missing parts being the military – especially post-2000 – as well as the business cartels which appear to be a more recent and still covert development with one having to dig deeper to unearth them. It is therefore more accurate to refer to the ruling regime as a tripartite elite coalition comprising the party, the military and business cartels that are unified by common interests of 'eating' and instrumentalising the state for that purpose. Though the members of this ruling elite coalition sometimes (and often) fight and factionalise over who gets what share, when and how – and some of the fights burst into the open for the media to salivate over – the coalition partners generally keep their peace in order not to rock the boat with all of them capsizing in it. Like any sailing ship, it needs a captain and in November 2017, the coalition decided to 'retire' their aging and chronically ill leader and replace him with his long-standing understudy.

On 15 November 2017, nine days after the incumbent president ignominiously dismissed his vice-president, an overt military intervention, followed by orchestrated public pressure and a parliamentary impeachment motion, culminated in the 'voluntary' resignation of long-time strongman,

President Robert Mugabe, and a power transfer to his former deputy, Emmerson Dambudzo Mnangagwa. Mugabe's departure was greeted with unguarded optimism and hope for a new trajectory following decades of pervasive economic failure, poverty, violence and suffering at the hands of the ZANU-PF leader and his long ruling party. Indeed, the new president promised to deliver a new 'open democracy', economic recovery and to end Zimbabwe's nearly two decades of international isolation. There were some early low-hanging fruits and policy reforms, including dealing with the ubiquitous extortionist police roadblocks as well as instituting indigenisation reform. These signalled a positive path by the Mnangagwa administration which dubbed itself the 'new dispensation' to draw a demarcation line between his regime and that of his predecessor.

Externally, President Mnangagwa also began reimaging himself as a friend of capital, an open economy and the West. A vigorous re-engagement and rapprochement strategy was aggressively pursued. However, faced with an unexpectedly robust and growing opposition threat in the July 2018 elections, the ruling party retreated to its old practices, doling out extensive patronage to gain political support and unleashing intimidation to threaten the opposition. By the end of the first year after the elections, the reform mantra had fizzled out. At the time of writing, the economy is teetering at the brink: spiralling inflation, shortages of fuel and some basic commodities, deteriorating incomes, high unemployment, rising poverty levels and hunger.

This chapter argues that, contrary to a reform trajectory, the Zimbabwe state exhibits continuities with the past. It examines the nature of the state, power dynamics and the modes of accumulation of the power elite. A triangle of power is in charge of the country, comprising the ruling ZANU-PF, the military, and the increasingly powerful business cartel. This is not an 'iron triangle' as such but is permeable from outside forces. The emerging discourse is in fact that the state has been 'captured' by business cartels in a manner analogous to the South Africa saga where the Gupta family allegedly captured the state under former president Zuma, a subject of a long-running Commission of Inquiry.

Looking through this prism, it was not surprising to see the deepening militarisation expressed through the appointment to strategic positions of top military officers who were instrumental to Mnangagwa's ascendancy to the presidential throne. To this extent, the military intervention was a manifestation of the unique party-military relations rooted in Zimbabwe's liberation war and consolidated in the post-independence period. With hindsight, the optimism of the post-Mugabe transition was understandable but soon proved premature or even unwarranted. There are far too many constraining legacies and structural issues to navigate and re-orient the state, business and societal relations towards a developmental trajectory. And, it is doubtful if the ruling party-military coalition has the will to undertake the required system overhall.

Not much serious academic work has been done to make sense of the almost novel characteristics of Zimbabwe's party-military regime and its intimate and shadowy relations with private parasitic cartels. This chapter hazards such an anatomy. In doing so, the notion of a predatory state or predatory governance has some heuristic value. As already suggested, the concept of a party-state should be extended to that of party-military-business state, that is, the ruling party, the military and business cartels all anchored in and feeding on the state. Jabusile Shumba (2018) makes some inroads into this largely unexplored terrain, and his work has been formative.

The dynamics shaped by the articulation of the formations outlined above have produced a new political economy in crisis, whereby, for instance, the once large if not mighty manufacturing sector has now virtually collapsed and been replaced by predatory and murky business cartels in the context of a rentier rather than a productive state. Thus, Zimbabwe now has a surfeit of 'innovative' mega projects like the Command Agriculture, dismissed by exiled former Cabinet minister Jonathan Moyo as 'Command Ugly-culture' that has allegedly fleeced the state of billions of United States dollars that find their way into the deep and bottomless pockets of the country's power elite.

It is under such circumstances that we find it misleading if not naïve to refer to the post-Mugabe trajectory as analogous to a developmental state of south east Asian countries from the 1960s to the 1980s. If anything, evidence points to an anti-developmental state in Zimbabwe. In any case, seldom is a predatory state also a developmental one. In the case of the Asian Tigers, the developmental nature of the political economy largely stemmed from the fact that the state was not only in command; it was also, and importantly, a disciplined one; a professional, bureaucratic state. A developmental political economy cannot thrive in a state where bureaucracy is riven by pathologies associated with what Goran Hyden (1983) called an 'economy of affection'. At best, the notion of a developmental state fits the first decade after which predation crept in and intensified over the last two decades in crisis-ridden Zimbabwe.

## The militarisation of the state and politics

The party-military-state complex denotes the umbilical cord between the party and the military in the context of the state such that the boundaries between the two become indistinguishable with the party-military-complex as the predator and the state as the prey. Under ZANU-PF's government, the institutional boundaries between the state and the executive are elusive, stifling the professional independence of other state institutions such as the bureaucracy, judiciary and the military. This indistinct boundary between the state and party is rooted in the liberation war and civil military relations, consolidated by the Africanisation of the civil service from independence in 1980, and accelerated in the 1990s up to the turn of the century.

The endurance of the party-military-state complex has been reinforced under President Mnangagwa's government with deepening militarisation. Faced with strong political opposition, the ruling elite invests in the development and consolidation of the repressive apparatus, which becomes the dominant political force and beneficiary of supposedly collective goods. As Bratton (2014: 7) notes, 'because autocrats rely on repression, they inadvertently strengthen the hand of the armed forces, who, in turn, are able to claim a share of both economic bounty and political decisions.'

The militarisation of the state and politics is not a new phenomenon. During the 1970s, as the struggle for independence intensified against a determined white colonial regime, a dual process of militarisation and politicisation occurred. This was the militarisation of white politics and of the Rhodesian state and the parallel process of politicisation of the Rhodesian security forces. Thus, the leaders of the Rhodesian security forces, led by General Peter Walls played a central and decisive role in the political direction of the country. General Walls, who attended the Lancaster House Conference in 1979, is credited with playing a cardinal role in the negotiations especially by convincing recalcitrant Ian Smith of the Rhodesian Front to co-operate. Walls attended as part of the Rhodesian delegation.

The parallel militarisation was in the nationalist movements, both in ZANU and in ZAPU. The moment the two nationalist parties decided to shift from a peaceful and constitutional mode of struggle for independence to armed struggle, they became militarised and created their armed wings – ZANLA for ZANU and ZIPRA for ZAPU. The ZANU/ZANLA and ZAPU/ZIPRA militarised movements had distinctive civil-military relations though none controlled the state unlike the case of the Rhodesian Security Forces. When ZANU/ZANLA won the independence elections in 1980, the party and its military wing inherited the state under the leadership of Robert Mugabe. They brought into the state the civil military relations they had during the armed struggle. In short, the Zimbabwe state and politics were militarised from birth and the umbilical cord tying ZANU – the party – to ZANLA – the military, were never severed. The war-time civil-military relations were reconfigured to fit the new dispensation especially given that the party and its military now controlled the state, and a powerful one at that. Not long afterwards, the post-colonial state was instrumentalised for predatory purposes and, in the process, business entered the equation to produce the party-military-business complex alluded above. This is the power matrix today.

Once power was won at independence, the next strategic thrust for ZANU-PF was to consolidate it: first by ensuring that it controlled the state apparatuses and, secondly, by embarking on a strategy of annihilating the opposition prior to establishing the long-cherished one-party state similar to that achieved by most countries in sub-Saharan Africa such as Zambia, Malawi and Tanzania. The first goal was easier to achieve than the second mainly because the independence constitution provided for the de-racialisation of the civil service to make it representative of the make-up of the population. This provision was used to craft the Africanisation Directive which enabled the new government to embark on a process of cadre deployment at all levels of the government, especially at central government level. Though competence was one of the factors for appointment into the civil service, loyalty trumped expertise. The cadre deployment benefited mostly those who were aligned with ZANU-PF and further, Mugabe favoured his own ethnic group such that strategic positions such as permanent secretaries and heads of parastatals and state-owned enterprises were predominantly from his Zezuru tribe. In the army, air force and intelligence services, former ZANLA military leaders were appointed to the top command positions notably the late General Solomon Mujuru (then Rex Nhongo) who was appointed commander of the Zimbabwe National Army. The ethnic factor also loomed large in such appointments, something Mugabe did with an eye on ensuring loyalty through ethnic affinity.

The second strategic goal, achieving a one-party state, proved to be a complicated and costly one which failed but not before thousands were killed in Matabeleland in what came to be called Gukurahundi, a genocidal crusade that reportedly claimed an estimated 20,000 lives, a vast majority innocent civilians[1] (see Chapter 1). The idea was to liquidate the opposition ZAPU led by Mugabe's long-time rival, Joshua Nkomo and to do so in its stronghold in the three Matabeleland provinces and parts of the Midlands. Nkomo and his party had been invited into Mugabe's government alongside a few white Cabinet ministers. The ferocity of the five-year scorched-earth Gukurahundi campaign between 1982 and 1987 ultimately forced Nkomo to accept a humiliating deal in which his party was swallowed by ZANU-PF, which made very few concessions in the 1987 Unity Accord. Nkomo was forced, against his convictions, to accept in the Accord a clause that provided for the establishment of one-party state. The one-party state project ultimately failed on account of both domestic and international developments. Domestically, the project was vigorously opposed by elements within the united ZANU-PF leading to the expulsion of Edgar Tekere (former Secretary General) who went on to form the opposition Zimbabwe Unity Movement (ZUM). ZUM posed a major challenge to ZANU-PF in the 1990 general elections. Internationally, the one-party goal collapsed on account of the sudden collapse of empirical socialism in the Soviet Union and its satellites that were all organised around the one-party system and from which Mugabe derived his inspiration. It is, however, vital to stress that though Mugabe reluctantly abandoned his dream, spiritually, he remained a prophet of the one-party state and this guided his governance style. Zimbabwe thus became a *de facto* one-party state after failing to achieve a *de jure* one-party status.

It is this spiritual attachment to the one-party philosophy that explains Mugabe's (and his party's) antipathy towards opposition parties and their intolerance of dissent that finds expression in violence and intimidation meted against any opposition party as well as civil society organisations that are perceived to pose an existential threat to the ruling party. In this schemata, the security sector, with the military in the lead, not only

---

1   CCJP and LRF (1997) noted in its introduction that the figure of '20,000 dead' originated with Joshua Nkomo's autobiography with 'other sources putting the figure as low as 700', and suggested that '[t]here is a need to resolve these disparities by methodological investigation.'

shares this perspective but is also an enforcer. The infamous 'strait jacket' speech by the security sector chiefs should be read and understood in this light.[2] This statement marked a real turning point in defining the civil-military relations in Zimbabwe, demonstrating beyond reasonable doubt what Samuel Huntington (1957) called 'subjective civilian control' of the military in contrast to the 'objective civilian control'.

In Huntington's objective model of civil-military relations, civilian control of the military is instituted through the maximisation of military professionalism, thus 'rendering them politically sterile and neutral. ... A highly professional officer corps *stands ready to carry out the wishes of any civilian group which secures legitimate authority within the state'* (Huntington 1957). This formula, however, needs to rest on something more substantial. For if soldiers are to become attitudinally disposed to their own subordination, they need to internalise the 'civilian ethic'. Concomitantly, the politicians must exhibit due regard for the internal autonomy of the fighting forces.

Under the subjective model, however, the 'military allegiance to government depends much more on informal linkages, merging of class interests, and so on' than on 'self-restraining military professionalism'. The problem in Zimbabwe, as in many other liberation war states, is that the military sees itself as subordinate, not so much to *any* civilian authority or government that wins power, but to a particular government formed by a particular party, in Zimbabwe's case, ZANU-PF. Achieving

---

2　In 2002, General Vitalis Zvinavashe, then the Commander of the Defence Forces (CDF) proclaimed: 'We wish to make it very clear to all Zimbabwean citizens that the security organizations will only stand in support of those political leaders that will pursue Zimbabwean values, traditions and beliefs for which thousands of lives were lost, in pursuit of Zimbabwe's hard won independence, sovereignty, territorial integrity and national interests. To this end, let it be known that the highest office on the land is a 'straight jacket' whose occupant is expected to observe the objectives of the liberation struggle. We will therefore not accept, let alone support or salute anyone with a different agenda that threatens the very existence of our sovereignty, our country and our people' (Statement by the Zimbabwe Defence Forces Commander Vitalis Zvinavashe, Harare, 9 January 2002).

　　And, in 2011, Brigadier General Douglas Nyikayaramba stated: 'Tsvangirai doesn't pose a political threat in any way in Zimbabwe, but is a major security threat. He takes instructions from foreigners who seek to effect illegal regime change in Zimbabwe. This is what has invited the security forces to be involved because we want to ensure we protect our national security interests... Daydreamers who want to reverse the gains of our liberation struggle will continue daydreaming. They can go to hell... they will never rule this country. We cannot keep quiet. We will continue speaking and as the security forces, we will not sit back and watch things going wrong (*Zimbabwe Daily*, 23 June, 2011).

objective civilian control of the military is going to be a herculean and long-term goal as long as the liberation war generation is alive and in strategic positions in the state and the security sector. That is part of Zimbabwe's thorny problem, one that is rooted in its protracted liberation war where the soldiers (the guerrillas) and their political leadership had a symbiotic and emotional attachment to each other. In the post-liberation period, the two stand together and fall together. Security sector reform under such circumstances is a hazardous enterprise for whoever initiates it. When change is felt, by the liberation movement, to be an imperative for survival, the change will be engineered from within and not from without. In the context of a party-military regime, as Zimbabwe is, change comes from within its circles. This is what happened at the end of 2017.

In November 2017, faced with blistering infighting over Mugabe's succession,[3] the military decisively intervened as arbiter, precipitating President Mugabe's resignation under a military lockdown. Thus, the 15 November 2017 event was a military solution to a political problem emanating from within the party wing of the party-military equation. It is instructive but unsurprising that senior military commanders (the command element) continue to view themselves at 'stock holders' of the Zimbabwean state. During the peak of the ruling party succession fights, then Commander of the Zimbabwe Defence Forces (CDF), General Constantino Chiwenga, issued a statement that articulated their position vis-à-vis the country; 'we are stockholders. Some are stakeholders. Stakeholders come and go and stockholders have nowhere to go, so we are stockholders, we come with it [Zimbabwe]'.[4]

Upon his ascension, President Mnangagwa has attempted to frame a discourse of reform[5] and himself as a born-again reformer. He also promised a 'new open democracy' and to turn around the economic fortunes of the country after two decades in which it has been mired in a syndrome of crises. However, faced with a reinvigorated opposition that

---

3  The succession infighting pitted the G-40 (fronted by party heavyweights including political commissar Saviour Kasukuwere, Johnathan Moyo (the Minister of Higher and Tertiary Education, Manicaland Minister of State, Madiitawepi Chimene and Mugabe's wife Grace Mugabe) against president Mnangagwa's Lacoste faction backed by senior military commanders and war veterans.

4  *Bulawayo 24*, 22 April 2016.

5  Fungai Kwaramba, '5,000 soldiers deployed to rural areas', in *Daily News*, 21 March 2018. See also *News24* at: https://www.news24.com/Africa/Zimbabwe/at-least-5-000-soldiers-deployed-to-zim-rural-areas-ahead-of-vote-mugabe-ally-claims-report-20180321.

was gaining momentum under the leadership of the youthful, charismatic firebrand, Nelson Chamisa, the military became actively involved in partisan politics and campaigning for ZANU-PF during the run-up to the 2018 elections. Ahead of the elections, civil society organisations monitoring the campaign corroborated reports of 'soldiers on leave' deployed in the rural areas to campaign for the party. Former Brigadier General Ambrose Mutinhiri, leader of the National People's Front (NPF) raised a similar claim when he met with the SADC team in March 2018. He stated that between 3,000 and 5,000 soldiers had been deployed in rural areas to campaign for ZANU-PF. Mutinhiri pointed as evidence that:

> The army confirms that by November 15, 2017, it had put over 2 000 of its officers and embedded them in every community in Zimbabwe, not just for the coup but for the forthcoming election. The number is now over 5 000. Zimbabwe cannot hold free, fair and credible election with over 5 000 army officers embedded in every village and street communities across the country.[6]

The claims were repeated by the MDC-T/Alliance[7] and former minister of Higher Education, Jonathan Moyo.

In response to assertions of military deployment, in July 2018, the army spokesperson issued a statement repudiating reports of military interference in the country's electoral process.[8] However, he confirmed military deployment under the Command Agriculture programme. And barely a month before the elections, former CDF Commander (now Vice-President Constantino Chiwenga) told supporters at a ZANU-PF rally in Mabvuku that the November 2017 military intervention code-named 'Operation Restore Legacy', which had forced the resignation of former president Mugabe, ends when President Emmerson Mnangagwa and his team in parliament and councils is voted into power.

> You came out in your numbers on November 18 demonstrating in peace and today we are saying in the same spirit, let's rally behind President Mnangagwa and all Zanu-PF candidates vying for local authorities, Upper and Lower House of Assembly seats come July

---

6    Ibid.

7    Ibid.

8    'Military: We won't interfere in election, will uphold Constitution', *newZWire*, 4 July 2018.

30 so that we conclude Operation Restore Legacy.[9]

The statement raised fears that ZANU-PF would not accept defeat and cede power if defeated in the polls. And when the opposition protested later what they perceived to be deliberate delays and manipulation of electoral results, the military opened fire leading to the death of six civilians. This incident delivered a near fatal blow to Mnangagwa's reform agenda. The culture of state-sponsored violence with impunity[10] reinforces the fear which undermines political participation and democratisation.

Following the November 2017 palace coup, ZANU-PF's conflation with the state deepened, with the military being increasingly embedded in party structures as well as in prominent positions in the state. Retired Lieutenant General Engelbert Rugeje was appointed Political Commissar of the ruling party (a strategic position that handles party internal elections and is responsible for growing party membership). Notably, there was a high number of top serving and retired military officers that participated in ZANU-PF primary elections including: Retired Brigadier Callisto Gwanetsa (Chiredzi South); Retired Major Mathias Tongofa (Chivi North); Retired Major Benjamin Mazarire (Masvingo Urban); Retired Colonel Ngoni Masenda (Hurungwe East) and Retired Brigadier Elasto Madzingira, Major Clifford Mumbengegwi and Colonel Patrick Maponga (Masvingo). In government, there is significant military presence in high-ranking positions including: Retired General Chiwenga (Vice-President), Retired Lieutenant General Sibusiso Moyo (Minister of Foreign Affairs and International Trade) and Retired Air Marshal Perence Shiri (Minister of Agriculture). The President also promoted Brigadier Generals Thomas Moyo and Anselem Sanyatwe from Brigadier level to Major General. The promotions were viewed as reward to Sanyatwe (Presidential Guard) and Moyo (Military Intelligence Department) who controlled critical units during the military intervention.

Not unlike the Mugabe regime, President Mnangagwa's power consolidation strategy betrays a tribal motivation – the Zezuru command element of the security sector was replaced by Mnangagwa's Karanga tribe: Valerio Sibanda (CDF), Elson Moyo (Air Marshall), Isaac Moyo (Central Intelligence Organisation, Director General) and so are

---

9  Vote ED to conclude Op Restore Legacy', *The Herald*, 18 June 2020.

10 Since independence, perpetrators of violence on behalf of the ruling party have either been allowed to walk scot-free or pardoned when convicted. Under President Mnangagwa, despite establishing a Commission of Inquiry into the July 2018 post-election violence, no perpetrator has been brought to book.

strategic appointments in government including the Chairperson of the Public Service Commission which oversees government staffing. The increased military presence defines the parameters of democratic politics in Zimbabwe. Having been assisted to oust Mugabe by the military, Mnangagwa's freedom to reform the military are severely limited, even if he wished to do so, which is very doubtful. Thus, retiring senior military officials associated with the 'smart coup', including Major General Douglas Nyikayaramba and Head of Presidential Guard, Brigadier Sanyatwe largely reflects factional political battles[11] rather than reform. Genuine political reform can also undermine the ruling party's political reproduction which in turn undermines the strategic interests of the ruling elite. In other words, party-military-state conflation is likely to be an enduring problem with all the perverse consequences for sustainable democratic reform and economic transformation. Further, the military, and the security sector as a whole, has been playing an expansive role since the new millennium when the Zimbabwe crisis escalated.

## Emasculation of key state institutions and policy making

The starkest demonstration that the securocracy[12] had expanded and outgrown its role beyond defence of nation and state was in its active involvement in core public policy matters. This military-role expansion was institutionalised in the revival and activation of the Joint Operations Command (JOC), first established by the leadership of the Rhodesian Security Forces, to co-ordinate operations against the intensifying war of liberation in the 1970s. The post-independence JOC comprised the heads of all security-related branches and agencies: the CDF, Commanders of the Army and Airforce, the Director-Generals of the CIO and Zimbabwe Prisons Service, and the Commissioner-General of Police. This time around though, the JOC's task (legally opaque) went beyond the co-ordination of a war effort (there was no war) to core policy making in virtually all policy areas, especially on issues that were identified or perceived as strategic. The military's first visible involvement was in the planning and execution (and attendant militarisation) of the land seizures from 2000 as part of the chaotic and often violent Fast Track Land Reform Programme (FTLRP). The military role expansion was accompanied by

---

11   There are credible and persistent reports of teething factional infighting pitting the Chiwenga camp against President Mnangagwa.

12   This is a term used in Zimbabwe, most by academics and elite civil society activists, to refer to the security sector as a whole.

an expanded definition of national security to include virtually all policy fields to the extent that the policy issue was felt to have implications – real or perceived – on the survival of ZANU-PF. However, key areas of special interest were those the president regarded as 'presidential preserves' and these included elections, agriculture, mining, telecommunications and energy – especially the fuel sub-sector.

As a matter of fact, the JOC has been credited with planning and executing some of the government's most controversial policy decisions and operations: the FTLRP in the 2000s, successive violent election campaigns, Operation Murambatsvina (Restore Order) (2005), which was ostensibly to clean up the cities, but left more than 700,000 homeless and without a source of income. This was followed by Operation Garikai/ Hlalani Kuhle (Live Well) (2005) which was purportedly designed to build houses for the victims of Operation Murambatsvina.[13] Chikorokoza Chapera (informal gold panning has ended)[14] (2007) was intended to weed out informal diamond miners in Chiadzwa in Manicaland; and Dzikisai Mitengo (Reduce Prices) (2007) was an operation which compelled businesses and manufacturers to slash the prices of goods by more than 50% in response to hyperinflation. Such policies were haphazard, inconsistent and served short-term political objectives but with disastrous developmental consequences.

Further, constitutionally independent state institutions such as the Zimbabwe Electoral Commission (ZEC) and law enforcement agencies, including the police, are often accused of being partisan and subordinated to the party-military-state. The ZEC's subordination to the regime is through military deployments in strategic positions. Some of the military officers (some servicing) appointed to ZEC over time include: Colonel Sobuza Gula-Ndebele (Head of the Election Supervisory Commission in 2002); Brigadier Douglas Nyikayaramba (Chief Elections Officer, 2002); George Chiweshe (Head, Zimbabwe Electoral Commission, 2005); and

---

13  Alexander and Tendi (2008), amongst others, argued that the 'operation' was a purge against the people who were suspected of supporting opposition parties, particularly the MDC while Operation Garikai benefited mainly ZANU-PF supporters.

14  Between 2006 and 2007, over 26,000 miners were arrested during this state clampdown operation. Chiadzwa was a theatre of several operations including Operation Hakudzokwi (Don't Return, meaning don't return to Chiadzwa), a successor to Operation Chikorokoza Chapera. According to human rights groups, 'over 200 people were killed in the diamond fields while thousands were maimed, tortured and brutalised in Marange'. There were also Operation Tasangana (We Have Met) and Operation Ngatizivane (Introduce Yourself).

Retired Major Utoile Silaigwana, a former military officer (now current ZEC's Chief Elections Officer). ZEC, mainly the logistics committee which oversees election logistics, is largely staffed by military personnel. The ZEC head admitted as much. Speaking to the parliamentary committee and civic groups in January 2018, the Chairperson of the ZEC, Priscilla Chigumba, revealed that about 15% of the Elections Management Body (EMB) was staffed with people with a military background.[15] Deployment of military officials in ZEC compromises its autonomy, and undermines the credibility of the institution in the public eye. ZEC's lack of transparency is also an issue perennially raised in election observer reports.

The judicial system also has been and continues to be a highly contested arena of state building in Zimbabwe. Poor justice delivery is commonly cited as one of the drivers of patronage politics and the demands from democracy reformers for the reform of the political system. Over the years, the ZANU-PF government systematically undermined the rule of law by intimidating judges and appointing pliant public prosecutors and judges to the judiciary. Judges perceived to be independent have been targets of intimidation and in response, they have either resigned or been forced into retirement. Bratton traces the mutilation of the judiciary to issues surrounding the Fast Track Land Reform Progamme (FTLRP) at the turn of the century, noting that the higher echelons of the judiciary system was 'restructured' in the image of the regime and this was after the Chief Justice and other 'politically incorrect' judges were condemned by senior ministers, including the Justice Minister. He writes:

> Emboldened by signals from party leaders, war veterans took it upon themselves to invade the Supreme Court. Ultimately, in 2001, the Chief Justice and two High Court judges, who happened to be white, were forced into early retirement under threats of physical harm. In place of Chief Justice Anthony Gubbay, for example, Robert Mugabe appointed Judge Godfrey Chidyausiku a former ZANU-PF minister and reliable ally. When others on the Supreme Court refused to resign, the government increased its size by promoting sympathetic jurists from the High Court (Bratton 2014: 78).

In August 2017, the ZANU-PF government enacted Constitutional Amendment (No 1) which grants the president sweeping powers in the manner in which the Chief Justice, Deputy Chief Justice and Judge of

---

15 'Former military staff part of Zec: Chigumba', *Zimbabwe Situation*, 28 February 2018.

the High Court are appointed. The amendment – declared null and void in a March 2020 Supreme Court ruling – allows the president to appoint judges who share ZANU-PFs 'philosophy' or show an inclination towards the ruling party.

In the civil service, the party-state ensured control over key institutions by appointing loyalists from the nationalist struggle to top positions in cabinet, government ministries, departments and parastatals. Bratton and Masunungure (2011: 5) observed that:

> when many competent senior officials, including experienced permanent secretaries, opted for generous early retirement schemes offered under the Economic Structural Adjustment Programme (ESAP) in the 1990s, ZANU-PF chose to fill these and other vacant civil service posts with individuals whose qualifications leaned more toward party loyalty than technical skills. The ZANU-PF regime's patronage based appointments to reward and control strategic institutions compromised bureaucratic quality and autonomy. By rewarding party cadres, serving and retired military personnel with access to parastatal jobs and state resources, the state created patronage opportunities leading to the failure of several State Owned Enterprises.[16]

The ruling party 'deployees' were able to manipulate control of key state institutions for narrow personal and political interests. The state also pursued *dirigiste* policies and redistribution (such as in indigenisation and empowerment) which served the ruling elite and patronage based primitive accumulation.

The enduring party-state-military complex and its overbearing role in policy making extends into the post-November 2017 dispensation, often undermining formal policy making structures. Under President Mnangagwa, ZANU-PF is ostensibly introducing reforms to emulate the Chinese Communist Party (CPC) model in which the party is supreme to the government. Mnangagwa has re-assigned the old guard (including Obert Mpofu and Patrick Chinamasa) to the party's headquarters ostensibly in a bid to reform the party, but in reality to consolidate his power. To make up for their loss of government positions, the party retained minister-level

---

16 Zimbabwe's 97 parastatals which used to contribute 40% of the country's Gross Domestic Product (GDP) in the 1980s and 1990s have been reduced to patronage troughs relying on perennial government support. See: https://www.theindependent. co.zw/2015/02/27/parastatals-increasingly-bleed-economy/

perks for the retired old guard. However, the ruling party reforms to emulate the CPC are creating two centres of power, one anchored in the party (the Politburo, the Soviet era body that makes and decides policy for the party in-between congresses) and the other in government, precipitating policy contradictions and clashes between the two. Thus, technocrats in the new government,[17] while initially thought to provide a glimmer of hope for reform, lack the necessary political capital. For instance, Professor Mthuli Ncube, the Finance Minister, has been publicly criticised over some economic policy decisions by the party's politburo members, including Obert Mpofu.[18] Senior ZANU-PF leaders often remind the government that the party is supreme. For instance, when former ministers were appointed full-time party workers at its headquarters, the party national spokesman (himself one of those left in the cold) said that it was in order to assert the party's 'supremacy over Government' and that they were following the Chinese and South African models. This was affirmed by many other senior party members, including Vice-President Chiwenga.[19]

Institutions of government, parastatals and public officials are caught in a web of corruption and mode of patronage governance that negatively impacts on delivery of public services. The high number of top-level corruption and abuse of state resources, open clash of government officials on key policy issues, and lack of distinction between the party and government, paralyses the delivery of public goods and services. State enterprises largely serve as feeding troughs for the well-connected political and military elites, impacting on service delivery. Various Auditor General's reports (2011–2017) have cited misappropriation and abuse of state resources and a number of government departments and agencies have received qualified audit opinions in successive years. This suggests that ministers and permanent secretaries (who are the accounting officers of ministries) were reluctant to act on recommendations of the

---

17  The most notable appointment is economist and former banker, Mthuli Ncube, as Minister Finance and Economic Development.

18  'ZANU PF Isolates Mthuli Ncube, "He Never Consulted Us" Says Obert Mpofu', *Zimeye*, 11 October 2018.

19  See for instance: https://www.facebook.com/288500807952079/videos/zanu-pf-is-superior-to-government-vp-constantino-chiwenga/2573265492905748/; https://dailynews.co.zw/articles/2013/12/08/zanu-pf-superior-to-govt-gumbo; https://news.pindula.co.zw/2018/09/11/zanu-pf-is-supreme-than-govt-khaya-moyo-hints-new-zanu-pf-departments-headed-by-former-ministers-will-direct-govt-policy/; https://news.pindula.co.zw/2018/09/16/zanu-pf-politburo-members-will-run-govt-through-the-ministers-party-is-supreme-mpofu-explains-rebirth/

Auditor-General and, importantly, they do so with impunity, knowing that they are protected at the top. Culprits include: the Grain Marketing Board (2011-2014),[20] the Zimbabwe Mining Development Company (2012-14), SEDCO (2012-2014), Allied Timbers (2012, 2013), and CSC (2011, 2012). According to one report, 'Audits showed that 38 SOEs surveyed made losses totalling $270 million in 2016. There were 93 SOEs in 2016 and the audits carried out showed that 70% of them were technically insolvent or illiquid'.[21]

The AG reports show a general picture of recurring findings and recommendations; the major systemic drivers of leakages include: lack of transparency in the award of state tenders (creating a privileged class of 'tenderpreneurs'), bad corporate governance practices, poor maintenance of accounting records, weak internal controls, unsupported expenditure and poorly constituted Boards of Directors and Audit Committees.

At the local government level, traditional leaders who are pivotal in local governance matters and national politics, remain very influential in rural Zimbabwe (estimated 67% live in rural areas) and continue to play a partisan role through their support of the ruling ZANU-PF party. This is despite the constitution clearly stating that traditional leaders should be non-partisan.[22] ZANU-PF has continued to manipulate traditional leaders to mobilise and campaign for the ruling party in elections and distribute food on partisan grounds.[23] In January 2018, Chief Charumbira who is the President of the Chief's Council, told delegates at the ruling party convention centre in Gweru that chiefs support the new ZANU-PF presidential candidate, President Emmerson Mnangagwa. Despite a High Court ruling on 16 May 2018, that traditional leaders must not interfere in partisan politics and ordering Chief Charumbira to publicly withdraw his statement that they support the ruling party, Charumbira did not comply.

---

20  Under President Mnangagwa government, GMB officials were also involved in arbitrage activities. The buying price of maize is higher than the selling price; GMB officials were buying maize from one depot and reselling the same stock to another GMB depot at higher buying price. This also distorted national grain reserve statistics due to multiple recording of the same stock sold across many depots.

21  'Govt Selling Off Stakes In State Owned Enterprises, Air Zim, ZESA And More. Right Move?' *Teczim*, 4 January 2018. Available at: https://www.techzim.co.zw/2018/01/government-selling-off-stakes-state-owned-enterprises-right-move/

22  Section 281 (2) of the Constitution requires traditional leaders not to be members of any political party or further the interests of any political party or cause.

23  The Zimbabwe Peace Project monthly human rights monitoring reports singled out traditional leaders amongst perpetrators of human rights violations, mainly partisan food distribution, especially during elections.

Instead, he petitioned the High Court, seeking rescission of the judgment. In January 2018, and to reward the chiefs toward the 2018 elections, Mnangagwa's administration bought 226 all-terrain vehicles for each one of them.

## Crony capitalism and state capture

The party-military-business elite is omnipresent, with its tentacles spread across the spectrum of key economic sectors from agriculture, banking and finance to mining, transport and energy sectors, especially electricity generation and fuel supply. The liberalisation – under the Economic Structural Adjustment Programme (ESAP) – of the banking sector in 1990s and associated indigenisation into the 2000s opened patronage and looting avenues that were exploited by the strategically located indigenous elites with perverse consequences for the national economy. The state was used as the milch-cow until today the udders are dry from over-milking. For instance, the state took over odious private debt through the US$1.7 billion[24] Reserve Bank of Zimbabwe (RBZ) Debt Assumption Act in 2013 while the Zimbabwe Asset Management Corporation (Private) Limited (ZAMCO) absorbed in excess of US$1 billion[25] Non-Performing Loans (NPL) ostensibly to turnaround struggling banks. Meanwhile, agricultural policies which have been maintained under the 'new dispensation' such as the Command Agriculture rarely extend beyond the logic of short-term political support to reward key constituencies (military chefs, courtiers and the party social base) in the process undermining fiscal stability and economic reform.

Despite the 'new dispensation', murky operations and rule of law violations continue unabated. To cite one instance, Vongai Mupereri, a ZANU-PF senior official in the Midlands Province, invaded Gaika Mine and despite a High Court ruling ordering his arrest, he has faced no

---

24  The full details and particulars of the entities and individuals involved in the Reserve Bank of Zimbabwe (RBZ) US$1.7 billion debt obligations have not been disclosed. However, the lines of credit were mostly included through the various RBZ quasi-fiscal programmes during Gono's tenure and largely benefitted ZANU-PF chefs and the military elite.

25  In order to secure their interests, indigenous investors banked security of their business interests with granting preferential loans to the ruling elite. For instance, Intermarket Banking Corporation including its founder Mr. N.M. Vingirayi (retired) funded General Mujuru's TRS Mujuru acquisition of shares in Willdale Holdings Limited (Willdale), which were on offer from Anglo America Corporation of Zimbabwe. Strangely, the deal was secured by untitled land belonging the General Mujuru in the Goromonzi area (Confidential memo).

consequences.[26] President Mnangagwa, has also allegedly been associated with a shadowy South African domiciled company, Moti Group. *The Sunday Times* of South Africa reported that its chairman, Zunaid Moti was arrested in Germany in August 2018 over an Interpol red notice[27] on alleged fraudulent activities in Russia.[28]

In the fuel sector, a huge and powerful cartel involving Trafigura (an international energy company), said to be fronted by one Kudakwashe Tagwirei,[29] was – until recently – allegedly involved in shoddy fuel dealings and brokering predatory international loans to the Mnangagwa administration. In October 2018, former ZANU-PF youth league member William 'Acie Lumumba' Mutumanje, a former ZANU-PF member, himself with a colourful but controversial past who had been appointed by the Finance Minister to head the Ministry of Finance Communications Taskforce – the appointment lasted only three days – claimed that the country had been captured by a cartel of business which control key economic sectors and participates in the black market. Mutumanje claimed the country's economy was in the hands of a businessman, 'Queen Bee', who controls the fuel industry and some Reserve Bank of Zimbabwe (RBZ) officials. The private and social media was immediately abuzz with speculation that Queen Bee referred to by Mutumanje was Tagwirei, who has been handed several lucrative government contracts. Tagwirei is the owner of Sakunda Holdings, which was until recently in a 50:50 partnership with Trafigura, an international company with vast interests in fuel. The company controls almost 70% of the fuel market in the country through its Puma Energy service stations. It is alleged that his company buys US dollars in the black market and still claim dollars from the RBZ fuel allocation. The cycle would be repeated with Trafigura accessing US dollars at concessionary rates from the RBZ. Tagwirei's Sakunda also provides funding for Command Agriculture in a seemingly opaque scheme that has largely benefitted chefs in government; such transactions are now

---

26 'ZANU PF stalwart Mupereri ignores court order, plots re-invasion', *Zim24News*, 15 April 2019.

27 Interpol issues a red notice when countries are unable to arrest suspects who have fled their policing jurisdiction.

28 'Controversial SA business tycoon arrected and detained in Germany', *The Sunday Times*, 26 August 2018.

29 Tagwirei has repeatedly been linked to the ZANU-PF and state Presidium, especially to the President and one of his vice-presidents.

the subject of intense but contested investigations by the Parliamentary Committee of Public Accounts. Here is Mutumanje in his own words:[30]

> ... the cartel is heavily connected to senior politicians, the army, intelligence, the judiciary, permanent secretaries and directors in government, commercial parastatals including RBZ, Minerals Marketing Corporation of Zimbabwe (MMCZ), National Oil Company of Zimbabwe (NOCZIM), Zimbabwe Revenue Authority (ZIMRA) and the Zimbabwe Electricity Supply Authority ZESA (ZESA). The syndicate also controls imports of key commodities such as Wheat and Maize and the subsequent value chain process and distribution in Zimbabwe. It also controls Gold and Diamond marketing.

The most powerful figures in the cartel include Vice-President Retired General Constantino Chiwenga, Minister of Foreign Affairs Retired Lieutenant General S.B. Moyo, Minister of Agriculture Retired Air Marshal Perence Shiri, Air Marshal Elson Moyo, Presidential Guard Commander Anselem Sanyatwe, former Central Intelligence Organisation (CIO) boss Happyton Bonyongwe, Minister of Transport Joram Gumbo, former ministers Obert Mpofu and Supa Mandiwanzira and controversial businessmen John Bredenkamp, Billy Reutenbach, Simon Rudland, Nicholas van Hoogstraten, and Ozias Bvute. [The origins of this powerful syndicate are linked to Zimbabwe Defence Industries (ZDI)'s business dealings in diamonds and timber logging during Zimbabwe's military intervention in the DRC war.

Under Mnangagwa, the ruling party remains deeply embedded with 'predatory capital' for personal and political interest. In the July 2018 elections, the ruling party launched a well-funded campaign with a fleet of new cars and buses, including generous regalia blitz with all the male supporters receiving T-shirts and caps and the women receiving *zambias* (wrapping cloths). The source of the funds has been questioned by expelled senior party officials including former Minister of Higher and Tertiary Education, Jonathan Moyo, suggesting that the ruling party was illicitly diverting money from diamonds revenue to fund its elections. Other reports claimed that the ruling party ran a multi-million campaign election with some funding sourced from China[31] and some local investors

---

30  Mutumanje's claims were posted in various social media outlets, including Twitter and Facebook.

31  In May 2018, *Zimbabwe Independent* reported that: 'Zanu-PF insiders said the party

in exchange for business deals. The Moti brothers' African Chrome Fields (ACF) is allegedly a top funder in exchange for lucrative platinum and chrome mining claims.

Predictably, unlike in developmental states, the emerging regime of accumulation does not engage in developmental investment and manufacturing, reflecting both the predatory logic of accumulation and the extractive nature of global capital. Rather, it is based on easy resource rents. Indeed, the political elite, most of whom were somehow involved in the liberation struggle, feel entitled to the country's wealth as if it were their own. The ZANU-PF ethos remains rooted in the idea that those who fought for liberation deserve to reap its benefits and they use this narrative to justify their predatory excesses. Economic players like companies – whether indigenous or foreign-owned – occasionally pay tributes to the party in return for security e.g. funding party programmes and meetings such as annual conferences and the congresses. These demands have often been exploited by enterprising party leaders and activists at various levels and in various parts of the country to extort the vulnerable companies and individuals in the name of securing their protection. Meanwhile, individuals and private businesses seen to be on the wrong side invite severe sanctions of one kind or another, while those who comply are often treated favourably e.g. getting lucrative state procurement contracts and deals and the favoured include Chinese and Russian capital.

The anti-developmental implications will be far reaching. Indeed, Zimbabwe was ranked the twelfth most corrupt country in the world and eleventh in Africa by Transparency International.[32] In 2019, it was number 158 out of 180 countries and remains one of the most corrupt countries in the world despite the 'new dispensation'. High-levels of corruption undermine Zimbabwe's economy, investment and growth. Combatting corruption will be central to Zimbabwe's political and economic governance reform if ever the country is to succeed. It is the elephant in the room and will not be easy to tame.

Genuine and sustainable reform will come at a heavy political cost to ZANU-PF as it undermines the repressive capacity and patronage systems that maintain loyalty of the party's key constituencies. Far-reaching reforms are thus unlikely; anti-corruption efforts rarely serve

has received huge funding from the Chinese who have also helped fund its previous campaigns. 'Zanu-PF launches 200 million campaign', *Zimbabwe Independent*, 4 May 2018.

32 'Zim poorly ranked in corruption index', *Daily News*, 27 January 2017.

beyond a smokescreen to fight political opponents. Upon Mnangagwa's ascension, several G-40 linked ministers were arrested on corruption allegations including former ministers Ignatius Chombo (Finance) and Saviour Kasukuwere (Local Government) but prosecution has been very half-hearted. Those responsible for corruption are seldom brought to account for the looting of state resources. This is consistent with the culture of impunity that Mugabe started and institutionalised as part of his mode of governance. Instead, corruption scandals are often reduced to rhetoric and corruption constitutes part of the reward system to various ZANU-PF party, military and government officials. The controversial appointment of Justice Loice Matanda-Moyo, wife of Foreign Affairs and International Trade Minister as head of the Zimbabwe Anti-Corruption Commission (ZAAC) has raised questions over president Mnangagwa's anti-corruption commitment on account that she may be compromised by her proximity to the citadel of power.

## Socio-economic and developmental costs

The Zimbabwe economy has undergone significant structural regression in the past four decades. It now has a highly informalised economy, high unemployment (by some accounts estimated at over 90%),[33] endemic poverty and hunger. By January 2018, the International Monetary Fund reported that informalisation[34] in Zimbabwe accounted for 60.6 % or close to two thirds of all economic activities in Zimbabwe, making it the second most informal economy in the world after Bolivia (Medina and Schneider, 2018). It is estimated that the informal sector is contributing between 40 and 50% of national output (Medina, Jonelis and Cangul, 2017).

The inexorable expansion of the disarticulated informal sector has been associated with the disintegration of the formal industry due to constraining economic and governance challenges. The poor investment climate has resulted in limited investment, closure or scaling down of companies, or migration of businesses to other countries. According to *Africa Check,* the country's bourgeoning informal sector (also known as shadow economy[35]) is now estimated to employ about 5.7 million people

---

33 'Destruction in his wake', *Africa Confidential*, 1 December 2017.

34 The informal sector is taken here to mean legal self-employment or unregistered small-scale legal economic activities (vending, operating tuck-shops, cross boarder traders and various micro enterprises).

35 This shadow economy does not (and cannot) pay taxes. The 2% transaction tax on electronic money transfers (introduced in October 2018) was largely meant to

(2.8 million small-scale business owners and 2.9 million employees). Out of the 2.9 million employees, only 22% – about 638,000 – are estimated to be full-time, paid employees, while 26% are temporary or seasonal or contract workers and 22% constitute unpaid workers.[36] Women and youth are the dominant participants in the shadow economy. Notably, only 14% of women are formally employed[37] and of the 6.3 million people employed in the informal economy, women make up 53%, thus, dominating a sector full of vulnerabilities and social insecurities, reinforcing the gendered nature and feminisation of poverty. For the youth, chronically high unemployment has created a 'lost generation' which is marginalised and alienated. Wageless life is no longer a temporary condition, but it is fast becoming the main mode of existence which is destined to stay for the foreseeable future (Raftopoulos 2013).

Importantly too, the reconfiguration of the economy has produced a disarticulated citizenry due to insecurity associated with the state's partisan patronage politics and electioneering. Following the land reform, more than 300,000 households were resettled on the land but without security of tenure remain vulnerable to the regime's political demands, especially uniquivocal loyalty. Similarly, in the mining sector, artisanal and small-scale miners who often fail to comply with onerous compliance requirements are either dispossessed or enter into mining syndicates with party-military and state elites and security agents for protection. In the informal sector, without security of tenure, vendors – most of whom are women – have suffered forced eviction, confiscation of their wares by the police and payment of bribes to unscrupulous police officials and ruling party militia for protection. Consequently, citizens lack autonomy of action. Stark inequalities in power and status thus create vertical chains of dependency secured by patronage and coercion. The state has an interest in the growth and persistence of the informal economy precisely because it serves the political objective of sustaining the social base for which the formal sector can no longer provide adequate security. The labour unions will obviously also suffer from depleted membership as a result of the shrinking formal sector.

The consequences of collapse of the formal economic production

---

address this by capturing this huge unharnessed tax base.

36 'Are 5.7 million people employed in Zimbabwe's informal economy? No', *Africa Check*, 12 May 2014.

37 GoZ, 2014.

systems and informalisation[38] have led to a weak export base and widening trade balances and perennial budget deficits. Further, the informal economy is trapped in low productivity and unable to stimulate economic transformation. Since dollarisation in 2009, Zimbabwe has exported more US dollars than it has brought in through declining exports and low Foreign Direct Investment (averaging only three percent of GDP since 2010). The situation has led to severe forex shortages. And in response, money creation through domestic money market instruments has generated a mismatch between electronic money balances and forex, leading to arbitrage, a rampaging of black market currency trading and inflation. Meanwhile, a weak tax base and patronage policies have generated a chronic fiscal imbalance characterised by growing disparity between revenues and expenditure resulting in high-levels of fiscal deficits. Public spending has reached unsustainable levels with central government expenditure accounting for 27% of GDP and with a deficit as high as 11% of GDP in 2017. Public sector employment costs currently consume up to 90% of the budget leaving no leg room for developmental projects. Without this, funding for social protection, basic healthcare and education has significantly declined over the years culminating in poor and inadequate social service delivery.

Despite the 'open for business mantra', the situation in the country has at best, remained stuck. The economy continues to sputter along, characterised by deep structural constraints including: sustained trade deficit, debt overhang, forex shortages, patronage and corruption. The degeneration of the socio-economic situation is punctuated by spiralling inflation, falling value of incomes, shortages (of basic goods, medical drugs, fuel), deteriorating social service delivery, failing basic healthcare and intermittent civil-service-wide industrial action (especially by doctors and nurses). Public health workers have been on persistent industrial action since the 'new dispensation'. Four months after Mnangagwa's inauguration, a month-long doctors' strike in December 2018 and earlier industrial action by nurses in April 2018 paralysed healthcare delivery, causing unnecessary loss of lives. Then, in 2019 was a four-month old strike by doctors which only ended with the philanthropic intervention of a private sector company who offered an attractive package of remuneration

---

38 According to the CZI's 2019 CZI Manufacturing Sector Survey, industry's capacity utilisation fell by 11.8 percentage points to 36.4% in 2019 from 48.2% recorded in 2018. 'CZI: Capacity ulitlisation to fall to 27%', *The Standard*, 16 February 16, 2020.

and improved conditions to enable the doctors to effectively perform their work.[39] It is a grave indictment on the predatory state that a private sector player had to intervene while the state itself and its predatory private sector allies are sapping state coffers dry.

The state of public hospitals is appalling, with antiquated equipment and shortages of drugs and personal protective equipment. The degraded capacities of the state are evident across all service delivery institutions. Cyclone Idai in early 2019, which claimed more than 350 lives, destroyed infrastructure, housing and livelihoods also exposed shocking and embarrassing disaster unpreparedness on the part of the Zimbabwe government which had to rely on generous donations from international organisations and local well-wishers. With better preparedness, some lives would have been saved and damage minimised.

Meanwhile, citizens' patience has literally run out and the initial guarded optimism associated with the 'new dispensation' first waned and then disappeared, replaced by frustrations as well as deep and fast-growing despair. Threats of civic unrest over the deteriorating socio-economic conditions are an ever-present danger. In January 2019, the labour movement (Zimbabwe Congress of Trade Unions) organised a well-observed three-day stayaway (which later degenerated into riots ) in response to a three-fold fuel price increase and deteriorating economic conditions. The state responded with its trademark lethal force, killing at least sixteen civilians as well as inflicting 87 gunshot injuries and over a thousand arrests, providing chilling signs of political regression. Without genuine political commitment to reform, the future looks very bleak. The chronic and deteriorating economic crisis will undoubtedly pose a serious risk to civil and political stability.

## Conclusion

Over the years, the country's developmental capacities have been undercut by a narrow party-military coalition which relies on violence and patronage to retain power and accumulate wealth. In response to declining economic performance and growing political threats, the Zimbabwe state has increasingly assumed unrestrained predatory characteristics. The combined dominance in the state of the party-

---

39 'Zimbabwe doctors end strike after billionaire's offer', https://www.bbc.com/news/world-africa-51205619. It should be noted though that the health practitioners were not only striking for a living wage (in a country where the elite earn millions) but for adequate medicines, and basic personal protective equipment such as rubber gloves.

military coalition, in alliance with business, facilitates pervasive anti-developmental accumulation which undermines any development potential, leading to widespread popular discontent. When faced with serious threats to power from an organised political opposition, the state turns to violence, patronage-driven short-term programmes and endemic corruption that undermine sustainable economic transformation. The increasing political threats to ZANU-PF power have in turn paved the way to the growing power and overt influence of the military which controls the repressive state apparatuses.

The November 2017 military intervention, rather than rupture, was a power elite reproduction project. The securocracy, especially the military, is the prominent beneficiary of promotions in civilian state positions and business opportunities. Fundamental political and economic reforms will be needed to re-orient the party-military-state, and its relations with business and society, towards a developmental trajectory. However, reform will of necessity come at a political cost to ZANU-PF as such reforms undermine the repressive capacity and patronage systems that maintain loyalty of the party's key constituencies. Meaningful reforms will require a fundamental shift in political culture, within and beyond ZANU-PF, towards a more inclusive vision and political practise that focuses on the benefit of all citizens. Going by the past four decades, especially the last two, such an outcome is highly unlikely, and even unthinkable.

## References

Alexander, J. and B. Tendi (2008) 'A tale of two elections: Zimbabwe at the polls in 2008', *Association of Concerned African Scholars*, Bulletin 80: Special Issue on Zimbabwe (II).

Bratton, M. (2014) *Power Politics in Zimbabwe*. Boulder, CO: Lynne Rienner.

Bratton, M. and E. Masunungure (2011) 'The Anatomy of Political Predation: Leaders, Elites and Coalitions in Zimbabwe, 1980-2010'. Development Leadership Program, University of Birmingham.

Catholic Commission for Justice and Peace (CCJP) and Legal Resources Foundation (LRF) (1997) *Breaking the Silence, Building True Peace: A Report on the Disturbancse in Matabeleland and the Midlands, 1980-*

*1988*. Harare: CCJP and LRF.

Government of Zimbabwe (GoZ) (2014) 2014 *Labour Force Survey*. Harare: Zimbabwe National Statistics Agency.

Human Rights Watch (2009) 'Diamonds in the Rough: Human Rights Abuses in the Marange Diamond Fields of Zimbabwe'. New York: Human Rights Watch.

Huntington, S.P. (1957) *The Soldier and the State: The Theory and Politics of Civil-Military Relations*. Cambridge, MA: Harvard University Press

Hyden, Goran (1983) *No Shortcuts to Progress: African Development Management in Perspective*. Berkeley and London: University of California Press..

Medina, L. and F. Schneider (2018) 'Shadow Economies Around the World: What did we learn Over the Last 20 years'. IMF Working Paper No. 18/17.

Medina, L., A.W. Jonelis and M. Cangul (2017) 'The Informal Economy in Sub-Saharan Africa: Size and Determinants'. IMF Working Paper No. 17/156.

Shumba, J.M. (2018) *Zimbabwe's Predatory State: Party, Military and Business*. Durban: University of Kwazulu-Natal Press.

# 5

# Political Parties in Zimbabwe's Constrained Democratic Space

Eldred V. Masunungure and Stephen Ndoma

*Political parties created democracy and ... modern democracy is unthinkable save in terms of the parties .... The most import-ant distinction between modern political philosophy, the dis-tinction between democracy and dictatorship, can be made best in terms of party politics. The parties are not therefore merely appendages of modern government; they are in the centre of it and play a determinable and creative role in it.*
(Schattschneider 1942: 1)

## Introduction

Robust political parties lie at the heart of a functional democratic society. But parties cannot perform their heralded, normative functions in a political space that is unduly constrained. Post-independence Zimbabwe is an exceptionally difficult operational terrain for opposition political parties as well as for most non-state actors, such as civic society, which are often shackled by a myriad of constraints that range from legal to extra-judicial.

Significantly, political parties in the country are almost as old as its founding as a modern, territorially unified state in 1890 under British colonial suzerainty. Paradoxically, in light of the legendary limitations of political space in the country, Zimbabwe has the deceptive distinction of being one of the few countries in Africa that escaped the universal continental trend toward a one-party state after attaining their independence. And yet, the country has never operated as a functional or full-blown multi-party state. At best, Zimbabwe has had a defective multi-party system with a 'malign', dominant ruling party around which other parties orbit, mostly struggling to make their presence felt. The polity has occupied the grey zone between one-party and multi-party systems. In sum, political parties have remained a constant in Zimbabwe's political history; it is the latitude of political space that has changed over time. By and large, it has been constrained, always more inclined towards shrinking than expanding. It is this dynamic that this chapter seeks to analyse.

## Defining political parties, types and functions

Political parties are a necessity in most modern political systems irrespective of their status as democracies or dictatorships or occupying a grey zone in-between. The previous statement is explicit in making an indissoluble link between political parties and democracy. But, how are political parties defined in the contemporary political world? Various definitions abound. One such is 'an organised group of people with at least roughly similar political aims and opinions that seeks to influence public policy by getting its candidates elected to public office'. A political party is a conduit through which people can speak to the government and influence governance processes within a specific polity. Three key components are necessary for a political party to be operational and these are: leaders, active members and followers. A political party is:

> a political organisation that typically seeks to attain and maintain political power within government, usually by participating in electoral campaigns, educational outreach or protest actions. Parties often espouse an expressed ideology or vision bolstered by a written platform with specific goals, forming a coalition among disparate interests[1]

Giovanni Sartori, the twentieth century Italian political scientist and renowned student of political parties and democracy, defined a party as: 'any political group identified by an official label that presents at elections, and is capable of placing through election, candidates for public office' (Hofmeister and Grabow 2011). In other words, power – its acquisition

---

1  Wikipedia, The Free Encyclopaedia, https://en.wikipedia.org/wiki/Politics.

and retention – is a unifying motive of all political parties. To this extent, parties fall into two straightforward categories: they are either in power or want to be.

A fundamental principle upon which political parties are conceived, created and nurtured is that of participation. One major primary function of political parties is not only to participate in the formation of political opinion but also that of representing people in Parliament. This representational role can only be performed after participation in elections; hence, at a minimum, political parties need to take part in elections for them to perform that function. In a way, a party's political contribution and its political weight or impact is closely tied to elections. The will of the voters is of significant importance. One key attribute of any political party is their 'fighting spirit' – their readiness for political action and political confrontation – and their aspiration to take over and retain governing power. It therefore follows that competition among political parties is the instrument by which to gain political power and the whole organisation of a political party is ultimately subject to this aim. The more organised political parties are, the better their chances of meaningfully competing in elections and of acquiring posts of political representation. On the other hand, opposition political parties also perform an important function in a democracy as they help to keep the ruling party in check through their 'watchdog' role. In addition, vibrant opposition political parties normally serve as a political alternative in the future.

## Functions of Political Parties

What then are some of the functions of political parties? Hofmeister and Grabow (2011) define some of the functions that political parties perform in a political system as:

(a) Political opinion-making – this relates to the articulation and aggregation of social interests.

(b) Selection – for any political system to be viable and compete with other political parties, there is need for that formation to recruit personnel to run the affairs of that party; to mobilise people for its various structures; and to mobilise those who will vote for it during elections.

(c) Integration – for a political party to be taken seriously, whether as a ruling party or otherwise, a key function of that formation is the development of a political programme through which its various integrated activities can be rolled out.

(d) Socialisation and participation – these lie at the heart of core functions performed by political parties as they seek to sell their ideology.

(e) Exercise of political power – any political party worthy of its salt sets its sights on controlling the levers of government and retention of power.

(f) Legitimating function – political parties in a way contribute to the legitimacy of the political system by establishing the connection between citizens, social groupings and the political system, the parties contribute in anchoring the political order in the consciousness of the citizens and in social forces.

## Types of party systems

Literature reviewed shows that a number of party systems exist around the globe and these differ depending on context. Below we discuss one of the typologies of the political party systems that exist in different political systems:

**Single party systems** – a key feature of this system is that there is no competition. Single party systems (*de jure* or *de facto*) are characterised by the oppression of political competition and democratic freedoms. The Communist Party in China and Cuba are good examples of such a system; while Zimbabwe has largely been a *de facto* one-party system in the pre-2000 era and the post 2013 period.

**Predominant party systems** – in this system, one of several political parties[2] holds the majority in government for a sustained period, for example the Congress Party of India, 1947-1975, and Swedish Social Democrats 1945-1998.

**Two-party system** – here, two major political parties dominate in nearly all elections and at every level of government; the majority of elected offices are members of one of the two major parties. Under this system, one party typically holds a majority in the legislature and is usually referred to as the *majority party* while the other is the *minority party*. The United States is an example of a two-party system in which

---

2 For example, India has approximately eight national parties, 53 state parties and 2,485 unrecognised parties and Sweden has eight national political parties.

the majority of elected officials are either Democrats or Republicans.

**Moderate multi-party system** – under the moderate multi-party system there are four to five parties, with all of them holding less than 50% of votes/seats. Coalition governments are inevitable in such a scenario, and this has been the experience in countries such as Denmark and Germany.

**Fragmented multi-party system** – a critical feature of a fragmented multi-party system is the existence of multiple parties (6+) in the legislature, for example in Israel, Netherlands and Belgium.

## Defining democracy and democratic space

The word 'democracy' has its roots in the Greek words 'demos' meaning people and 'kratos' meaning authority or power.' It was coined by the ancient Greeks who established a direct form of government in Athens in 507 BC. All 'adult males would gather to discuss issues and they would vote by a show of hands'. In the words of former US President Abraham Lincoln, democracy is a government 'of the people, by the people and for the people' (Becker and Raveloson 2008). The underlining message in Lincoln's definition is that a democracy is a political system by which a government is chosen by the people and its key deliverable is that of serving the people. There are two basic forms of democracy – direct and representative democracy. In a direct democracy, 'all citizens, without the intermediary of elected or appointed officials, can participate in making public decisions.' This system can only work well in situations where there are relatively small numbers of people who can discuss issues and arrive at decisions by consensus or majority vote (as in Switzerland). However, it is difficult to achieve in the modern world because of the size and complexity of populations and hence the most common form of democracy in the contemporary world is representative where citizens elect officials to make political decisions, formulate laws and administer programmes for the public good on their behalf.

Democracy is a system of government that bases its legitimacy on the participation of the people. While democratic governments come in many varieties, they are uniformly characterised by three key components: competitive elections, the principle of political and legal equality, and a high degree of individual freedom or civil liberties. In a lecture entitled

'What is Democracy?', Larry Diamond (2004) described democracy as a system of government with four key elements: (i) a system for choosing and replacing the government through free and fair elections; (ii) active participation of the people, as citizens, in politics and civic life; (iii) protection of the human rights of all citizens; and (iv) a rule of law in which the laws and procedures apply equally to all citizens. Dahl (1971: 3) identified eight criteria in defining democracy: the right to vote; the right to be elected; the right of political leaders to compete for support and votes; elections that are free and fair; freedom of association; freedom of expression; alternative sources of information; and institutions that depend on votes and other expressions of preference. Thus various key principles form the substructure of democracy and these comprise – a government based upon the consent of the governed, majority rule, minority rights, guarantee of basic human rights, free and fair elections, equality before the law, due process of law, constitutional limits on government, social, economic, and political pluralism, values of tolerance, pragmatism, co-operation and compromise.

Having zeroed in on the definition of democracy, we will shift our focus to a definition of 'democratic space'. According to Horner and Pudderphatt (2011), this refers 'to the arena that exists between the state and the individual in which people interact to hold the state accountable, shape public debate, participate in politics and express their needs and opinions.' The two authors further contend that such a space can only be deemed democratic when 'it is underpinned by the values of liberal democracy such as individual autonomy, political freedom, representative leadership, accountable governance and respect for human rights'(ibid.). For Shah Alam Khan, 'democratic space is an unwritten permission to think. A fundamental consideration and respect granted by a state to its subjects to raise a voice of dissent and disagree. It is this democratic space which forms the basis of a vibrant democracy.'[3]

## Brief History of political parties in Zimbabwe

Political parties in Zimbabwe are a product of a country's socio-economic and political history. The Rhodesian Front (RF), formed in March 1962, left an indelible footprint with its white supremacist policies. The party which during its existence changed its name to the Republican Front Party and the Conservative Alliance Zimbabwe (CAZ) won all twenty Assembly

---

3    Shah Alam Khan, 'Democratic Space – What Is That?' *Countercurrents*, 3 June 2009.

seats reserved for whites in both the 1979 and 1980 elections, and fifteen of the twenty seats allotted to whites in the 1985 elections. Principal black parties which faced bans from the repressive colonial regime emerged to fight for liberation. Among these key political formations were the Southern Rhodesia African Congress (1957), the National Democratic Party (1960), the Zimbabwe African People's Union (ZAPU) (1961), the Zimbabwe African National Union (ZANU) (1963). After a protracted war, the Lancaster House agreement was brokered in 1979 under the auspices of the British government which saw elections organised in February 1980. These were contested by nine political parties, including ZANU-PF, led by Robert Mugabe, and ZAPU (which registered under the name Popular Front). Of the 80 Assembly seats elected from the common rolls, ZANU-PF took 57, the Popular Front (or ZAPU) twenty, and the UANC, three. In the July 1985 elections, ZANU-PF won 63 seats, PF-ZAPU, fifteen. Following the deadly Gukurahundi experience (1982-1987), ZAPU and ZANU finally agreed to merge in late 1987 under the ZANU-PF banner. The merger of the two political parties was seen by some as a positive step in promoting unity in Zimbabwe, although others saw it as a threat to multi-party democracy and the fulfilment of Mugabe's cherished dream for a one-party state. This desire was actually an integral part of the Unity Agreement which expressly stated that: 'Zanu (PF) shall seek to establish a one-party state in Zimbabwe' (Chiwewe 1989: 283).

According to law professor Welshman Ncube, the Unity Accord ushered in a new political climate and 'various sectors of the population of Zimbabwe felt released from the constraints of party-political rivalry which had inhibited virtually all democratic expressions about national problems'. Ncube argues that people were able to direct their attention to real issues and could air their views without being mistaken as supporters of ZAPU or dissidents'.[4] One of the manifestations of this newly found sense of freedom saw one of the party's stalwarts, Edgar Tekere forming the Zimbabwe Unity Movement (ZUM) in 1989 after being expelled from the ruling party for speaking out against corruption and the one-party state.

The Movement for Democratic Change (MDC) was launched a decade later in September 1999 and was initially supported by the Zimbabwe Congress of Trade Unions, under the leadership of Morgan Tsvangirai. Following disagreements over a decision to participate in the 2005 Senate elections, the party later split in two and split further resulting in splinter

---

4    Ibid

parties, for example, the MDC-99 under Job Sikhala and the People's Democratic Party under Tendai Biti. With the inconclusive elections of 2008, the main political parties in Zimbabwe bowed to SADC-led mediation and worked together under a Government of National Unity (GNU) which was consummated in February 2009. Under this structure, Robert Mugabe of ZANU-PF retained the presidency, while Morgan Tsvangirai became the Prime Minister and Arthur Mutambara of the smaller MDC formation, the Deputy Prime Minister. The squabble-ridden GNU's life span was terminated by the general elections in 2013 which saw ZANU-PF retaining its ruling party status with a majority in Parliament.

Intra-party factionalism has been a common and defining feature of both major parties. For the opposition, this is a self-inflicted wound that weakens their capacity to fight robustly against the ruling party; a source of severe vulnerability independent of the toxic legal and political environment. On the other hand, ZANU-PF has capitalised on these weaknesses to consolidate its hold on power. After the death of Tsvangirai in 2018, the MDC-T split again into two factions, one led by Nelson Chamisa and the other by Thokozani Khupe. The MDC formation led by Chamisa later merged with several other political parties and splinter groups[5] to contest the 2018 harmonised elections as the MDC Alliance (MDC-A) while MDC-T, the faction led by Khupe decided to go it alone.

ZANU-PF was also faction-ridden ahead of the 2018 elections, with the Lacoste faction allegedly fronted by Emmerson Mnangagwa annihilating the G-40 faction through a military-led intervention in November 2017. Even the National Patriotic Front and the National People's Party (led by Joice Mujuru) which contested in the 2018 harmonised elections were offshoots of the faction-torn party. Lastly, side by side with the more established political parties are some fly-by-night, ideologically bankrupt political entities which emerge before elections only to disappear thereafter. Nonetheless, as election outcomes have confirmed since 2000, ZANU-PF and the MDC Alliance continue to dominate the polls and this trend is likely to continue given the present configuration of political forces. In fact, the post-2000 elections have consolidated the two-party system.

---

5  'Zimbabwe Opposition Launches MDC Alliance Ahead of 2018 General Elections, *VOA Zimbabwe*, 6 August 2017.

## Constrained democratic space during the First Republic

Zimbabwe's law regarding the registration of political parties is relatively easy. There are no laws compelling them to register in order to exist (Masunungure 2006). The only time registration is obligatory is during elections when a party wants to contest by fielding a candidate. That is, a candidate is required by law to be proposed and endorsed by a certain number of registered voters in their constituency and has to pay a candidacy deposit which is returned if they get a certain stipulated threshold of valid votes cast. The Political Parties Finance Act (PPFA) of 2001, (first enacted in 1992 and amended in 1997 before being repealed in 2001 only to be replaced by a 'new' by the same title) explicitly defines a political party as 'an association of persons the primary object of which is to secure the election of one or more of its members to a local authority or Parliament' (ibid.). A cursory look at the framework of the PPFA of 2001 indicates that political parties are free to regulate their affairs as they deem fit. The state does not interfere in the running of their 'domestic' affairs (ibid.).

State-led political party financing is spelt out in the PPFA which stipulates the requirements for accessing public funds not only to run elections, but to finance political party activities even outside the electoral arena. By law, any political party that garners at least 5% of the vote in the previous election is eligible to receive public fees, but to date only two political parties – the ruling ZANU-PF and the main opposition MDC – have enjoyed this privilege. Most political parties in Zimbabwe depend on the financial (and other) resources of generous individuals, businesses and private organisations. Political parties are not required by law to disclose their source of donations from within the country, nor is there a set ceiling on such contributions, nor do they need to account for public funds that have been availed to them. Contributions from 'well-wishers' are also a key source of funding for major political parties while some revenue is generated from sale of membership cards, party regalia and literature. Business interests also contribute significantly to the funding of the major political parties such as ZANU-PF and the MDC.

Given the undisputed need for financial resources to run a political party, funding for these formations is a key issue in the electoral process. Logically, this means that currently the two main political parties (ZANU-PF and the MDC-A), which qualify to receive public funding under the PPFA contest elections in a sound financial state at local authority, parliamentary and presidential elections level. This was evident in the 2018 harmonised elections as ZANU-PF fielded candidates in all the 210 constituencies while the other contestants struggled to do the same. State-party conflation places ZANU-PF in a very advantageous position when compared with other contestants.

According to ZESN (2018), a look at the material used for campaigning by political parties, reveals that ZANU-PF was financially advantaged receiving its share of US$6,126,633.17 while the MDC-T only received US$1,873,663.83 as provided for under subsection 3(1) of the PPFA. However, at the time of writing, a court case is still to be concluded on which party is entitled to get the US$1.8 million following the split of the MDC-T.[6] Political parties are not even required by law to account for the public funds availed to them.

When Zimbabwe achieved its independence, the then Prime Minister Robert Mugabe was acclaimed because of his message of reconciliation on 18 April 1980, Independence Day: 'If you were my enemy, you are now my friend. If you hated me, you cannot avoid the love that binds me to you and you to me'.[7] The move toward reconciliation was however short-lived as evidenced when Mugabe sent the North Korean trained contingent of the Zimbabwe National Army to Matabeleland to quell disturbances. The years 1983-87 saw the army committing atrocities with reports indicating that up to 20,000 people were killed in an operation named 'Gukurahundi' (CCJP and LRF 1997). Most atrocities were committed against people sympathetic to the late nationalist Joshua Nkomo and people generally opposed to the centralisation of power in Harare. Nkomo eventually agreed to a National Unity Accord which saw him serving as vice-president following a merger of his party under the banner ZANU-PF, thus eliminating the only major opposition party.

Some analysts note that the Gukurahundi massacres 'set the tone for Mugabe's response to future attempts at political opposition' (Jafari 2003). Even though small political parties such as ZUM had no realistic chances of unseating Mugabe, the late founding president did not hesitate 'to resort to violence and intimidation to ensure that no opposition party gained a foothold in Zimbabwean politics (ibid.). For example, a ZANU-PF television advert broadcast during the 1990 presidential race threatened

6  VOA Zimbabwe Service, (2018) 'Khupe MDC Attacks Chamisa Group Over $1.8 Million State Funds', 1 June. Available at: https://www.voazimbabwe.com/a/nelson-chamisa-thokozani-khupe-state-funds-political-parties/4419478.html

7  'Robert Mugabe: From liberator to tyrant', *BBC News*, 6 September 2019.

constituents who did not wish to support ZANU-PF. The advert, which featured a car crash, had the announcer state: 'this is one way to die. Another way is to vote for ZUM. Don't commit suicide. Vote ZANU-PF and live.' (Ibid.)

Use of dirty tricks to outmanoeuvre the opposition became further entrenched after the emergence of the MDC in 1999 as ZANU-PF determined to emaciate the opposition. This hostility became even more apparent after the MDC and civic organisations, which included the National Constitutional Assembly (NCA), defeated Mugabe in the February 2000 Constitutional Referendum and the MDC won 57 out of the 120 contested seats in the 2000 parliamentary elections. Alex Magaisa contends that the defeat of Mugabe's constitutional proposal was historic in two ways – it showed the world 'that Mugabe could be defeated, and it was the first time that he had lost a plebiscite.'[8] Unfortunately, it also proved to be a double-edged sword, as it awakened Mugabe and ZANU-PF to the danger that they could lose to the opposition.

Thereafter, ZANU-PF adopted the twin strategy of attacking whatever institution it deemed to support the opposition MDC while maintaining its core support through the confiscation and redistribution of privately-owned assets, especially the white-owned farms. This was achieved by ZANU-PF's relentless violent attacks on the opposition party which were aimed at breaking the opposition's back and its ability to organise and mobilise the huge swing vote of the brutalised and traumatised commercial agricultural workers many of whom were forcibly displaced from the farms where they had worked and settled. The invasion of farms from 2000, fronted by the war veterans and often co-ordinated by the security forces, was one method used to harass farm workers while violence against the opposition served to instil group fear. David Coltart (2006) notes that the 'first two murders of white farmers, chillingly well and gruesomely executed, struck fear into the hearts and minds of the farming community.'

To reinforce this view, Joseph Winter contends that the invasion of the white-owned farms served a number of purposes for Mugabe and his party. Among their aims were to remove a source of opposition funding; to provide a means by which war veterans could intimidate black farm workers who were largely seen as opposition supporters; and a way of

---

8   'Morgan Tsvangirai: From a nickel miner to an icon, How Morgan Tsvangirai rose to become one of the greatest figures in Zimbabwe's recent history', *Al Jazeera*, 15 February 2018.

ensuring that the opposition could not campaign in the rural areas.[9] He also argues that besides the aforementioned objectives, the invasion of the white-owned commercial farms served to re-energise ZANU-PF supporters who had lost faith in the party, while attracting new supporters through land handouts.[10] Efforts to obliterate the opposition were quite evident in the run up to the 2002 presidential election as ZANU-PF upped its game against the opposition, for example in November 2001, police detained several MDC leaders and activists in connection with war veteran Cain Nkala's murder, including Fletcher Dulini Ncube (MP), the MDC's Treasurer and Shadow Industry and Commerce Minister.[11]

Efforts to deny the opposition political breathing space were also demonstrated by the government's enactment of three pieces of legislation before the March 2002 presidential election: the Public Order and Security Act (POSA), the General Laws Amendment Act and the Access to Information and Protection of Privacy Act (AIPPA). POSA, which was passed in January 2002, replaced the Law and Order Maintenance Act of 1960 (LOMA), one of the few pieces of legislation retained from the Rhodesian era. POSA created an uneven electoral field as it has hindered the opposition's ability to organise meetings; while AIPPA has culminated in the intimidation of the independent print media, a key outlet for the opposition, which is denied equal access to the government-controlled media. The MDC has accused the police of using POSA to ban its meetings and arrest its supporters in order to cripple the opposition's effectiveness. For example, before the 2000 presidential elections, with POSA in place just two months before the poll, the late Robert Mugabe is said to have addressed roughly 50 rallies unhindered while the late Morgan Tsvangirai who was the MDC's candidate only managed to hold eight rallies. Reports also indicated that the police used POSA to disrupt or prevent 83 MDC rallies between January and March 2002. In July 2011, the then Minister of Industry and Commerce under the Government of National Unity (Welshman Ncube) and at least twenty other senior members of the smallest of the three parties within the ruling coalition – the Movement for Democratic Change-Ncube

---

9   'Robert Mugabe: From liberator to tyrant', *BBC News*, 6 September 2019.
10  Ibid.
11  Zimbabwe, Country Assessment, October 2002, Country Information and Policy Unit Immigration and Nationality Directorate Home Office, United Kingdom, https://www.ecoi.net/en/file/local/1339067/1329_1200479267_zimbabwe-october-2002.pdf

(MDC-N) were arrested for violating provisions of POSA.[12]

In a further display of paranoia, opposition leaders were attacked left, right and centre and sometimes on trumped up charges. Treason trials[13] involving the late opposition leader, Tsvangirai, and then MDC secretary general, Ncube, culminated in their acquittal in October 2004, but provide clear evidence that the ruling party was prepared to undermine the opposition in all possible ways including distracting the party leadership from core organisational issues.[14] A statement made by Mugabe at a rally in the year 2003, was evidence that his administration was not prepared to yield or even share power, 'let the MDC and its leadership be warned that those who play with fire will not only be burnt, but consumed by that fire'.[15] Coltart (2006) showed that 90% of the MDC members of parliament (MPs) elected in June 2000 had suffered some human rights violation; 24% survived murder attempts and 42% had been tortured while state agents are reported to have murdered three MDC MPs.

One of the most vicious attacks against the opposition was on 11 March 2007, when the late MDC leader Morgan Tsvangirai was mercilessly beaten by state security agents while preparing to attend a prayer meeting in the suburb of Highfields. This was during the Save Zimbabwe Campaign – a broad coalition of civil society organisations and members of the political opposition-attempted to hold a prayer meeting at Zimbabwe Grounds in Highfield, Harare. Instead of being apologetic, the late former President Mugabe boasted of 'bashing' the opposition leader at a ZANU-PF rally on 29 March 2007. He remarked, 'of course he [opposition leader Morgan Tsvangirai] was bashed. He deserved it. I told the police to beat him a lot. He and his MDC must stop their terrorist activities...'.[16] These remarks demonstrate Mugabe's brazen violation of human rights with a clear message intended to decimate the opposition. Addressing a rally in Kadoma District in Mashonaland West province ahead of the June 2008 presidential election runoff, Mugabe threatened to arrest the opposition

---

12 'Zimbabwe police arrest, then release, top leaders', *Christian Science Monitor*, 10 July 2011.

13 'Opposition leader cleared of treason by Zimbabwe court', *Zimbabwe Independent*, 16 October 2004.

14 It should perhaps be noted that aside from the stress caused, it diverted the leaders' focus, as they have to concentrate on consulting with lawyers, raising legal fees, preparing their defence, etc.

15 'Robert Mugabe: From liberator to tyrant', *BBC News*, 6 September 2019.

16 Human Rights Watch, 'Bashing Dissent, Escalating Violence and State Repression in Zimbabwe', 2 May, 2017

leaders over election campaign violence for which his opponents blamed the ruling party supporters. In the address Mugabe warned, 'we are warning them that we will not hesitate to arrest them, and we will do that in broad daylight. They think they are protected by the British and the Americans. The law of the country has to be observed.'[17] In another clear case of an opposition that is under siege, the late Tsvangirai had to seek refuge at the Dutch embassy in Harare after pulling out of the 27 June 2008 presidential election runoff saying his supporters would risk their lives if they voted.[18]

As part of efforts to choke the opposition, state-sponsored violence and intimidation were twin weapons used by ZANU-PF to obstruct opposition political parties. For instance, in the run up to the June 2008 presidential election runoff, Tsvangirai disclosed that more than 50 people had been killed and 25,000 people displaced in political violence. The outspoken MDC political leader noted that '... I have been saddened that Zimbabweans are willing to shed the blood of other Zimbabweans over political differences'.[19] The Human Rights NGO Forum noted in its December 2008 reports that the cumulative totals for January – December 2008 were six politically motivated rape cases, 107 murders, 137 abductions/kidnappings, nineteen cases of disappearances, 629 of displacements and 2,532 violations on the freedoms of association and expression.[20] The International Coalition for the Responsibility to Protect noted that prior to the presidential election runoff in June 2008, the security services and the ZANU-PF militia coalesced to unleash a campaign of intimidation, torture and murder against opposition activists, journalists, polling agents, public servants, civic leaders and ordinary citizens suspected of voting for the opposition party, MDC. The organisation noted that human rights violations including torture, beatings, mutilations and rape were perpetrated against leaders and supporters of the opposition.[21] All this was done under an operation code named 'Operation Makavhoterapapi?' (Operation Where Did You Put Your Vote?).[22]

---

17  'Mugabe threatens opposition leaders over violence', *Reuters*, 16 June 2008.
18  'Zimbabwe's Tsvangirai takes refuge in embassy', *Reuters*, 23 June 2008.
19  'Zimbabwe's Tsvangirai says 50 dead in poll violence', *Reuters*, 27 May 2008.
20  Zimbabwe Human Rights NGO Forum, 'Political Violence Report, December 2008', 13 February 2009.
21  The International Coalition for the Responsibility to Protect (ICRtoP), 'Crisis in Zimbabwe'. http://www.responsibilitytoprotect.org/index.php/crises/crisis-in-zimbabwe.
22  Human Rights Watch, 'Bullets for Each of You, State-Sponsored Violence since

The state-ruling party-military conflation is another factor that has resulted in democratic space shrinking for opposition political parties. Zimbabwe's army generals vowed never to salute the opposition candidate, Tsvangirai, if he were to become president. For example, shortly before the 2002 presidential election which Mugabe won amidst claims of rigging by the opposition MDC, senior army officers held a press conference where they affirmed their loyalty to ZANU-PF and vowed never to serve under the opposition presidential candidate Morgan Tsvangirai. A few weeks before the 2002 presidential elections, the government arrested Tsvangirai on treason charges. The military has thus provided a critical bedrock of support to ZANU-PF. For example, Major General Martin Chedondo was quoted at Cleveland Shooting Range telling the army to vote for Robert Mugabe in the 2008 presidential election runoff or resign from the military. He is reported to have said, 'soldiers are not apolitical… only mercenaries are apolitical. We have signed up and agreed to fight and protect the ruling party's principles of defending the revolution. If you have other thoughts, then you should remove that uniform'.[23] The perception that opposition political parties are often silenced by the government finds traction among Zimbabweans with Afrobarometer (AB) data (July 2012) showing that a majority (62%) of the adult population in Zimbabwe was of the opinion that the opposition is often/always silenced by the government. Three out of ten (31%) said this was 'never/rarely' the case while 7% of the survey respondents professed ignorance on the subject matter.

## Political parties and party systems in Zimbabwe: from dominant one-party state to a two-party system

A closer look at political parties and party systems in Zimbabwe shows that party systems post-independence have oscillated from dominant one-party (1980-1999) through two-party system (2000-2013) and, legislatively speaking, back to dominant party system (post-2013). In fact, post-2013, there were two tendencies whereby, in the legislature, we have had a dominant one party (courtesy of ZANU-PF's two-thirds majority) but a two-party system outside Parliament. We discuss these oscillations below:

### Zimbabwe as a dominant one-party system (1980-1999)

On 18 April 1980 Zimbabwe hoisted its flag in place of the British Union

---

Zimbabwe's March 29 Elections', 9 June 2008.
23 'General Says Back Mugabe or Quit Army', *The New York Times*, 1 June 2008.

Jack, a symbol of colonial conquest. The new flag signified the dawn of a new era for a country that had experienced a bitter, protracted struggle in its quest for independence and democracy. Thus, Zimbabwe joined the comity of nations as an accommodative multi-racial society anchored on the late Prime Minister Robert Mugabe's reconciliation policy. Having borne the brunt of colonial domination and Smith's oppressive regime, expectant Zimbabweans looked forward to a new socio-economic and political order and trajectory that would satisfy their desires. On the social front, the post-independence government espoused egalitarian principles as the new leaders were strong believers in socialism.

On the political front, the young nation had five main political parties: the Zimbabwe African National Union (ZANU), Zimbabwe African People's Union (ZAPU), ZANU-Ndonga, United African National Congress (UANC), and the RF, which was later renamed the Conservative Alliance of Zimbabwe. In October 1987 and in accordance with the Lancaster House Accords, the Constitution of Zimbabwe was amended to end the separate roll for white voters and to replace the whites whose reserved seats had been abolished; among the new members were fifteen whites in the Senate and House of Assembly. Marred by Gukurahundi disturbances in the Midlands and Matabeleland provinces in the better part of the 1980s, ZANU-PF and PF-ZAPU agreed to unite in December 1987, in a union that was solemnised through the historic Unity Accord on 22 December 1987. Elections in March 1990 saw the then President Mugabe and his party, ZANU-PF, romping to victory, winning 117 of the 120 election seats.

ZANU-PF was the dominant political force during the first decade of independent Zimbabwe with election results in 1980, 1985 and 1990 confirming this. In the 1985 elections, ZANU-PF increased its majority, holding 67 of the 100 seats. This gave then Prime Minister Mugabe the opportunity to make changes (including those related to land restoration) to the 1979 Lancaster House Constitution, which saw an end to the civil war. The 1987 Unity Accord also saw the party spreading its tentacles and grip on the country's political landscape. In the same vein, the Mugabe-led ZANU-PF had as one of its key agendas, the establishment of a one-party state, an idea which was rebuffed and resisted by even stakeholders from within the ruling party ZANU-PF.

Mugabe's plans to establish the one-party state also suffered a stillbirth as the powerful wave of democratisation swept across the African continent. The formation of ZUM, following the expulsion of a ZANU-PF son, Edgar Tekere, was a clear signal that not all party stalwarts were willing to accept the idea of the one-party state. Tekere's ZUM contested the 1990 elections with some success. The UANC, still led by Abel Muzorewa, merged with ZUM in January 1994. Lupi Mushayakarara, launched the United Democratic Front (UDF) party with other key players: former Rhodesian leader Ian Smith, Muzorewa, and Ndabaningi Sithole. The Forum Party of Zimbabwe (FPZ) was formed in March 1993 under the leadership of the late former Chief Justice Enock Dumbutshena while Margaret Dongo, a well-known former member of ZANU-PF also launched a party in 1998, the Zimbabwe Union of Democrats (ZUD). The formation of these political parties was a clear indication that progressive forces on the political scene abhorred the one-party project, which ZANU-PF was attempting to impose on the people of Zimbabwe.

Nonetheless, in the 1995 parliamentary elections, ZANU-PF won an overwhelming majority of parliamentary seats with 118 of the 120 seats, while ZANU-Ndonga won two seats. To illustrate ZANU-PF's dominance, 55 (almost half) of ZANU-PF's parliamentary candidates stood unopposed. As for the 1996, presidential elections held in March 1996, ZANU-PF presidential candidate Robert Mugabe won, claiming over 90% of the vote in an election when he stood against Abel Muzorewa and the ZANU Ndonga leader Ndabaningi Sithole. Due to threats of violence, Sithole and Muzorewa withdrew their candidacies shortly before the election (though their names remained on the ballot). Sithole (who was under virtual house arrest due to charges of attempting to assassinate Mugabe) withdrew after claiming that Mugabe's ZANU–PF was undermining his campaign, whilst Muzorewa pulled out after the Supreme Court turned down his bid to postpone the elections on the basis that the electoral rules were unfair (as state funds were only available to parties with fifteen or more seats in parliament).[24] In December 1997 Sithole was convicted of conspiring to assassinate Mugabe; he appealed but died while out on bail.

## Zimbabwe – the transition from dominant one-party to two-party system, 2000-2013

The adoption of the Bretton Woods prescribed Economic Structural Adjustment Programme (ESAP) in 1991 – which the government half-

---

24 'Zimbabwe President's Last Rival Withdraws from Election', *New York Times*, 16 March 1996.

heartedly implemented – and its adverse social impacts eroded some of the gains of the 1980s decade. The deterioration of economic conditions provided a perfect climate for the birth of a stronger opposition movement that was later to challenge ZANU-PF's desire to rule Zimbabwe into perpetuity. The deterioration in macro- and micro-economic circumstances fuelled the growth of discontent. During the 1990s, student, trade unionists and workers often demonstrated to express their displeasure with government policies. For the greater part of the 1990s, through its control of the media and security forces, the ZANU-PF government seemed to have mastered the art of keeping organised political opposition to a minimum. To compound matters, the government further undermined the economy by making unbudgeted pay-outs of Z$50,000 to war veterans, which led to a crash of the Zimbabwe currency on 'Black Friday', 14 November 1997. Then, in 1998, Mugabe unilaterally sent several thousand troops to the DRC, a move which had a huge impact on the national fiscus given 'the cost of maintaining an estimated 6,000 troops, aircraft and armoured vehicles was at least US$1 million in a day'.[25]

Thus it was that the year 1999 marked a turning point in the country's political history as a new party emerged, to pose a real threat to ZANU-PF's grip on power. On 26 February 1999, more than 300 people from a cross-section of society met together and adopted various resolutions, primarily the formation of the working people's convention that in turn gave rise to the Movement for Democratic Change (MDC) on 11 September 1999 at Rufaro Stadium in Harare. In January 2000, the party had its inaugural congress at the Chitungwiza Aquatic Complex where the late Morgan Tsvangirai was elected president, deputised by the late Gibson Sibanda, both former trade union leaders. Given the general dissatisfaction in the country on many fronts, the MDC had national appeal and gave citizens hope for a multi-party democratic dispensation and political pluralism.

Sceptics felt that the alliance would collapse under the weight of the conflicting interests of its broad constituency. ZANU-PF simply labelled the party a stooge of the West. However, the MDC's first opportunity to flex its political muscle against Mugabe's government came in February 2000 when a referendum on a draft national Constitution was proposed. The MDC, with the aid of civil society organisations (CSOs) led the opposition to the draft, and the government lost the referendum. Although parliamentary elections held in June 2000 were marred by localised

---

25 'DRC intervention "affordable"', *The New Humanitarian*, 16 December 1998.

violence, after less than a year in opposition, the MDC captured 57 (almost half) of the contested 120 seats in the Parliament of Zimbabwe. This was to be the trend in future polls, the MDC won in most urban centres and provinces of Matabeleland; ZANU-PF remained a hegemonic force in the rural areas of Mashonaland, Manicaland and the Midlands, where its power of coercion was more effective.

The MDC also posed serious challenges in the 2002 presidential election and the 2005 parliamentary elections. In the inconclusive elections of 2008, the main MDC formation, then under the late Tsvangirai, posed the most serious threat to ZANU-PF, forcing the former liberation movement to the negotiating table and the establishment of a Government of National Unity (GNU) where ZANU-PF and the two MDC formations shared power. In the 2005 parliamentary elections, ZANU-PF won 65% of the parliamentary seats while the MDC won 34% of the legislative assembly seats. In the 2008 harmonised elections, ZANU-PF won 48% of the parliamentary seats while the main opposition party, the MDC- T secured 47% of the House of Assembly seats.

However, the growth of the MDC has been very uneven with 'splits and counter splits'[26] dogging the movement as the struggle against ZANU-PF's dominance intensified. The movement has along the way splintered into the MDC-T under Tsvangirai, the MDC-M under Welshman Ncube, the MDC 99 under Job Sikhala and the MDC Renewal led by Tendai Biti. The GNU marked the only phase in the country's history when ZANU-PF was forced to share power with other political parties as Zimbabwe continues to practice multi-party politics within a single dominant party system. Indeed, the squabble-prone GNU was terminated through the 2013 harmonised elections which saw ZANU-PF reclaiming its super majority status in Parliament.

## A hybrid of a dominant and two-party party system after 2013 harmonised elections?

The 2018 harmonised elections took place against a backdrop of critical developments on the country's political landscape. The first was that

---

26  Many reasons have been offered the way in which the MDC has essentially undermined itself: (a) persistent, and often brutal, attacks both physical and psychological by ZANU-PF taking a toll on both individuals and the party; (b) persecution leading to a sense of entitlement, in a manner not dissimilar to the way in which ZANU-PF still demands rewards for a war fought over four decades ago; (c) power being an inducement after now more than two decades of resistance.

elections were taking place after the departure of Mugabe from the political scene following his resignation as president on 21 November 2017 after a military intervention code named 'Operation Restore Legacy'. He was replaced by his long-time confidante Emmerson Mnangagwa, who went on to represent ZANU-PF as their presidential candidate in the harmonised elections held on 30 July 2018. The MDC-T, however, had suffered a heavy blow ahead of these elections with the death of its founding president, Morgan Tsvangirai, on 14 February 2018. Nelson Chamisa, one of the three vice-presidents of the party, was elected as interim president of the MDC-T at an emergency meeting of the party's National Executive Council and contested Mnangagwa in a two-horse race.

Chamisa was contesting the election under the banner of MDC Alliance (MDC-A) – an electoral bloc formed between seven opposition political parties[27] on 6 August 2017 (three of whom had splintered from the original MDC). The two main contenders (ZANU-PF and the MDC Alliance) both had to contend with factionalism before confronting each other in the national elections. A record 23 presidential candidates took part in the elections while 127 political parties were said to have registered with the Zimbabwe Electoral Commission (ZEC) in May 2018. According to Zimfact, there were 35 registered political parties in Zimbabwe in June 2017, but the number rose to 75 in October 2017, a month before Mugabe's resignation and to 112 by March 15, 2018.[28] Despite the proliferation of opposition parties, most of which have been described as 'briefcase' or 'fly by night' and fragmented; attempts at coalition building have generally failed primarily because of ego but also because some candidates were allegedly encouraged to stand by the ruling party in order to divide the opposition.

As with previous elections, ZANU-PF won a parliamentary majority while the outcome of the closely contested presidential race between Mnangagwa and Chamisa required a stamp of approval from the Constitutional Court before it could be conferred on the former (see

---

27 The MDC Alliance was an electoral pact formed on 6 August 2017. The Alliance consisted of: Movement for Democratic Change-Tsvangirai (MDC-T) led by Nelson Chamisa; Movement for Democratic Change-Ncube, led by Welshman Ncube; People's Democratic Party, led by Tendai Biti; Transform Zimbabwe, led by Jacob Ngarivhume; Zimbabwe People First, led by Agrippa Mutambara; Zimbabwe African National Union-Ndonga under the leadership of Denford Musiyarira; and Multi-Racial Christian Democrats led by Mathias Guchutu.

28 'Zimbabwe now has 127 registered political parties, more could be on the way', *The Zimbabwe Mail*, 2 May 2018.

Chapter 3). In conclusion, the emergence of the MDC in 1999 has seen the erosion of ZANU-PF's dominance on the political scene; and despite fierce resistance a two-party system is gradually gaining ground. However, despite the zero-sum nature game of politics in the country vis-à-vis the heavily fragmented opposition, it is very probable that the two-party system will subsist for many more years to come. It should however be noted that the ruling party, ZANU-PF, has always put winning an election over the good of the country. The period of the GNU was a case in point. At the time of writing, four years before the next election, the war veterans have already stated that they are preparing for it[29] and the Herbert Chitepo Ideological College will ensure that they lend their weight to the narrative.

## Political parties in the 'New Dispensation'/ 'Second Republic'

As has been the trend, a number of new political parties emerged on the political scene ahead of the harmonised elections. Related to this development was the move towards strategic coalition building among the opposition. The first coalition, the Movement for Democratic Change Alliance (hereafter referred to as MDC-A), was formed on 6 August 2017. This was an alliance of seven political parties with three of the member parties being splinter parties from the original MDC.

As described above, 21 November 2017 will be recorded in history as one that people understood as a watershed moment. The military coup saw power shifting from Mugabe's 37-year rule to that of his long-term ally Mnangagwa, who was alleged to be fronting the Lacoste faction of ZANU-PF. Mnangagwa rewarded his allies from within the civilian and military rankings with key positions within the ruling party and government as the ZANU-PF strategically positioned itself ahead of the envisaged watershed elections that were scheduled for 30 July 2018. As in previous elections, the party maintained a firm grip on the rural areas, while the MDC-A's hold on the urban areas appeared intact. Nonetheless, divisions within both main parties seemed both strong and counter-productive – power struggles that culminate in the people's voice being ignored and trampled upon. After the elections, one of the coalition's partners, Transform Zimbabwe, pulled out of the MDC-A pact, choosing to stand alone rather than dissolve and become part of the grand MDC. On the other hand, the People's Democratic Party formerly led by Tendai Biti and the MDC

---

29 'War vets to anchor ZANU-PF's 2023 campaign', *NewsDay*, 15 January 2020.

formation led by Welshman Ncube, have since dissolved and integrated into the Nelson Chamisa-led mainstream MDC and this was endorsed at the MDC-A's congress in May 2019.

Besides the MDC-A, two coalitions were also formed to contest the 2018 harmonised elections. One of them, the Coalition of Democrats (CODE) was formed on 9 August 2017. The group endorsed Elton Mangoma as their presidential candidate in the 2018 general election. The second was the People's Rainbow Coalition (PRC) under the leadership of Joice Mujuru, the country's former vice-president and leader of National People's Party. A strong sign of a fragmented coalition, the launch of the PRC was a direct counter to the MDC-A led by the late MDC-T leader Morgan Tsvangirai which Mujuru and her partners refused to join over a litany of issues, chief among them the party's name.

As has been the trend, a number of new political parties emerged on the political scene ahead of the harmonised elections. Related to this development was the move toward coalition building ahead of these elections as the opposition parties took aim at unseating ZANU-PF after the ouster of Robert Mugabe. The MDC-A was a union of seven political parties with three of the member parties being splinter parties from the original MDC. The opposition parties in the MDC Alliance include Morgan Tsvangirai's MDC, Professor Welshman Ncube's MDC formation, Tendai Biti's People's Democratic Party, Agrippa Mutambara (Zimbabwe People First), Jacob Ngarivhume (Transform Zimbabwe), Multiracial Christian Democrats and ZANU-Ndonga. The MDC Alliance was led by Nelson Chamisa.

A pre-election public opinion poll conducted by the Mass Public Opinion Institute on behalf of the AB Network in Zimbabwe in April/ May 2018 revealed that among the political party alliances/coalitions, MDC-A emerged as the best known and most popular ahead of the 2018 harmonised elections. On the other hand, the survey data also showed that the ruling party ZANU-PF was the 'most liked' political party, although by less than half of the adult population (46%). Support for political party alliances/coalitions was also a majority view ahead of the elections with 56% of the adult Zimbabwean population endorsing the coalitions as they felt that the opposition parties can do better in the 2018 elections if they form a coalition rather than compete as separate entities.

**Figure 5.1: Awareness of political-party alliances | Zimbabwe | 2018**

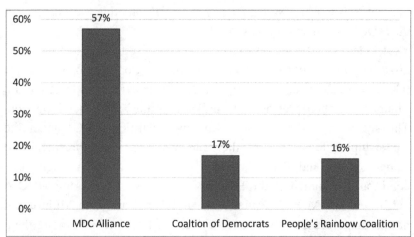

*Respondents were asked:* Have you ever heard of the following political alliances: (a) The MDC Alliance? (b) The Coalition of Democrats? (c) The People's Rainbow Coalition? (% who say 'yes)

**Figure 5.2: Trust in political parties | Zimbabwe | 2018**

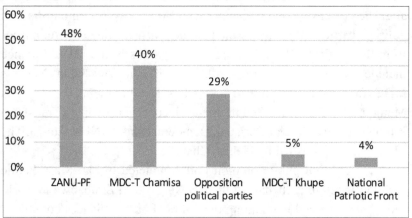

*Respondents were asked:* How much would you say you trust the following or haven't you heard enough to say? (% who say they trust).

The pre-election survey also revealed that less than half of adult Zimbabweans had faith in the ruling party ZANU-PF or the opposition. The poll showed that just 29% trusted the opposition political parties 'somewhat / a lot'. However, when analysis is conducted for distinctive opposition political parties, survey data shows that two-fifths (40%) of adult Zimbabweans had 'somewhat /a lot' of trust in the MDC-A led by Nelson Chamisa while only 4% said the same about the People's Democratic Party, the National People's Party and the National Patriotic Front. However, close to half of the adult population (48%) reported that they trust the ruling party ZANU-PF 'somewhat / a lot'.

## Media Coverage

The pivotal role of media freedom upon which civil and political rights and liberties are enshrined in the 2013 Constitution cannot be over-emphasised. The law in Zimbabwe, through Section 160J of the Electoral Act, requires all media outlets, both print and electronic, to ensure that 'all political parties and candidates are treated equitably in the news media, in regard to the extent, timing and prominence of the coverage accorded to them...'[30] However, the so-called new dispensation did not result in any significant changes to the media's coverage of political parties ahead of the harmonised polls. Chapter 7 in this volume deals with the media terrain in more detail while Chapter 3 also alludes to the skewed and biased media coverage, especially the public or state-controlled media.

In 2018, the Media Monitoring Project of Zimbabwe (MMPZ) conducted a study from 11-24 February 2018 ahead of the harmonised elections. It concluded that the media in Zimbabwe falls short of all standards of fair and balanced coverage of the country's political actors. ZANU-PF and MDC-T dominated the coverage with 94% of the space and time, whilst the remaining fifteen parties accounted for 6% of coverage. This is a reflection of the lack of diversity in the representation of political actors. The study assessed both the state and privately-owned media pointing out that while all state-owned media outlets are constitutionally obliged to be fair and impartial, their coverage of MDC-T was either neutral or negative, while ZANU-PF consistently received more favourable attention.[31]

Figure 5.3, based on the ZESN report on the 2018 harmonised elections, reveals the biased media coverage which distinctly favoured the incumbent, while being unfair to the opposition and smaller political parties.[32] The Network noted that a total of 49 political parties were covered by the media in the period from proclamation to election day.

---

30 Zimbabwe Election Support Network, 'Report on the 30 July 2018 Harmonised Elections'.

31 'Baseline Study on Election Reporting in Zimbabwe's Mainstream Media – 1st Quarter 2018', *MMPZ*, 13 June 2018.

32 Ibid.

The coverage of presidential candidates was heavily biased towards the incumbent, Mnangagwa, with 57% in all media, followed by Chamisa of the MDC-A with 15%. Nkosana Moyo of the Alliance for the People's Agenda (APA) had the third highest coverage with 5%. The remaining 20 candidates shared the remaining 23%.[33]

**Figure 5.3: Media coverage of presidential candidates | Zimbabwe | 2018**

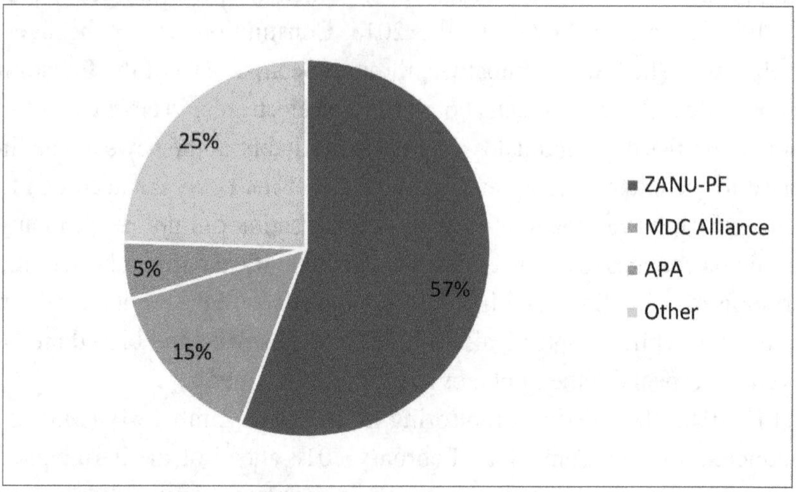

Source: ZESN Report on the 30 July 2018 Harmonised Elections

## Performance of political parties in the July 2018 harmonised elections

As noted above, Zimbabwe's legal framework does not require political parties to register, hence there is normally a proliferation of entries ahead of elections, parties whose intention is to contest or confuse the electorate. Prior to the Nomination Court sitting on 14 June 2018, there were reports that 133 political parties wanted to contest the 2018 harmonised election. This number dropped to 55 after the Court had sat as some parties did not submit candidates for consideration.[34] Possibly due to resource constraints, ZANU-PF was the only party to hold primary elections throughout the country. The MDC-A relied on a hybrid process where meetings were convened for the Alliance's members to reach consensus on whom would represent them in the various parliamentary constituencies and local council wards. For the most part, primary elections were held whenever

33  Ibid
34  Zimbabwe Election Support Network, 'Report on the 30 July 2018 Harmonised Elections'.

interested candidates failed to agree and, in some instances, aggrieved party members chose to stand as independents. As for the smaller parties, the candidate selection processes were unclear, with reports that the leadership made arbitrary decisions as to whom would represent them.

A record 23 candidates, (up from five in 2013 and four in 2008) contested the 2018 presidential election. Only four of these candidates were female, a small improvement on the 2008 and 2013 elections when all the candidates were male. Once again, ZANU-PF flexed its political muscle as it was the only party that managed to field candidates for all 210 National Assembly seats. The MDC-A failed to field candidates in three constituencies: Hurungwe East, Chiredzi West and Insiza North.[35] The PRC sought to contest in 74% of the constituencies while Khupe's MDC-T contested 52% of the 210 seats. In some cases, the contesting political parties had more than one candidate seeking election on the party ticket (twin-candidature) in the same constituency.[36] The MDC-A had the highest number of double candidates, with two candidates in constituencies such as Mazowe North, Mazowe South, Mazowe West, Muzarabani North, Goromonzi West, Bikita East, Gutu Central, Gutu North, Gutu West, Masvingo South, and Zaka West. The major impact of fielding double candidates was that of splitting the votes and giving ZANU-PF an upper hand in those constituencies. Table 5.1 below shows the number of candidates fielded by each of the major parties.

**Table 5.1: Candidates fielded by the main political parties| Zimbabwe harmonised elections | 2018**

| Political party | Number of candidates fielded in 210 constituencies | Total number of candidates | Number of constituencies with more than one candidate | Number of constituencies where parties did not field candidates |
|---|---|---|---|---|
| ZANU-PF | 210 | 211 | 1 | 0 |
| MDC Alliance | 206 | 220 | 14 | 4 |
| PRC | 156 | 157 | 1 | 54 |
| MDC-T | 109 | 110 | 1 | 101 |
| NPF | 94 | 95 | 1 | 116 |

35  Ibid.
36  Ibid.

| Political party | Number of candidates fielded in 210 constituencies | Total number of candidates | Number of constituencies with more than one candidate | Number of constituencies where parties did not field candidates |
|---|---|---|---|---|
| CODE | 43 | 44 | 1 | 167 |
| ZAPU | 36 | 37 | 1 | 174 |

Source: ZESN Report on the 30 July 2018 Harmonised Elections

Of the 1,958 local authority wards in Zimbabwe, 90 were unopposed, 84 of which had only ZANU-PF candidates while the MDC-A fielded six candidates for the remainder of the unopposed wards.[37] Although the political field was broad with 55 political parties, ZANU-PF and the MDC-A and, to an extent, the PRC and MDC-T stood out in terms of the visibility of their campaigns. The two main contending parties, ZANU-PF and the MDC-A, held bumper rallies in different parts of the country. ZANU-PF had many more, bigger and more expensive billboards for its presidential candidate compared with the MDC-A.

The Zimbabwe Electoral Commission announced presidential election results which showed that ZANU-PF's candidate Emmerson Mnangagwa won the poll with 2,460,463 (50.8%) votes to Nelson Chamisa's 2,147,436 (44.3%). At the parliamentary level, ZANU-PF won 144 of the 210 constituencies, representing 68.57% of total seats; the MDC-A garnered 64 seats, representing 30.47% while the National Patriotic Front represented by Masango Matambanadzo and independent candidate Temba Mliswa won a single seat each. Compared to the 2013 election, ZANU-PF lost sixteen seats while the MDC-A gained fifteen. The outcome of the 2018 harmonised elections confirmed that ZANU-PF is still the dominant political party while the MDC-A remains a force to reckon with. Table 5.2 shows the results for the National Assembly elections as announced by ZEC.

---

37 Ibid.

**Table 5.2: National Assembly Results | Zimbabwe harmonised elections| 2018**

| Party | Number of seats won in 2018 | % of seats (2018) | Number of seats won in 2013 | Comparison with 2013 (change in seats) |
|---|---|---|---|---|
| ZANU-PF | 144 | 68.57% | 160 | -16 |
| MDC Alliance | 64 | 30.47% | 49 | +15 |
| Independent | 1 | 0.48% | 1 | - |
| NPF | 1 | 0.48% | N/A | - |
| **Total** | 210 | 100% | 210 | - |

Source: ZESN Report on the 30 July 2018 Harmonised Elections

## Zimbabwe's political parties after the July 2018 Harmonised Elections

In a high-stakes game, Chamisa of the MDC-A challenged the 2018 election outcome in the Constitutional Court. However, the case was dismissed on the basis that they failed to produce enough evidence to prove electoral fraud. Despite this, the MDC-A has continued to question the legitimacy of President Mnangagwa. Thus, the post-election phase has been marred by persistent introverted bickering between ZANU-PF and MDC-A while the country's socio-economic and political crisis escalates by the day. ZANU-PF continues to demonstrate an insatiable desire to maintain its political grip by attempting to pummel the opposition, particularly the MDC-A into submission. The sense of freedom granted to the opposition parties before 30 July 2018 continues to fast evaporate with many questioning the sincerity of the commitment to reforms by the so-called 'new dispensation'. The 1 August 2018 cold-blooded killing of at least six protesters by the army after an MDC Alliance organised demonstration against the delayed announcement of the presidential election results (see Chapters 1 and 3), alleged abductions of opposition members and the government's heavy-handed response to January 2019 national shutdown have led some Zimbabweans to conclude that there is no difference between the 'new' and the 'old' dispensation.

Nonetheless, in theory, once an electorate has granted a mandate to a political party to run the affairs of state, it bequeaths it with responsibilities and obligations towards its citizens. The electorate has a right to expect the chosen party to deliver on its pre-election promises. ZANU-PF is indeed confronted with the intractable task of dealing with a multi-dimensional crisis. As the chronic socio-economic crisis rages, some stakeholders, including the president himself, have called for a national dialogue. However, the two main players have both laid conditions for this to take place. Nonetheless, smaller political parties have come to the negotiating table under the Political Actors Dialogue (POLAD) platform established by President Mnangagwa. POLAD is chaired by Retired Justice Selo Nare (National Peace and Reconciliation Commission) and Margaret Mukahanana-Sangarwe (Zimbabwe Gender Commission). Most Zimbabweans and outside observers see the prospects for success as negligible in the absence of the MDC-A which has adamantly boycotted the process.

## Democratic space under the Second Republic: a case of old wine in new bottles?

As stated above and more fully in Chapter 3, the immediate post-coup phase and the run-up to the elections seemed to suggest that President Mnangagwa meant what he said and that he and his party had adopted a more liberal and accommodative agenda. However, if the populace had invested in hope for a better future, it was short-lived as suggested by developments following the July 2018 elections.

Despite some positive reports about the elections (see Chapter 3), Mnangagwa's administration unleashed excessive force when at least six civilians were killed during a protest against delayed release of election results on 1 August 2018. As significantly, the immediate post-July 2018 phase saw the government launching a massive crackdown on the opposition.[38] Further, a number of activists, human rights defenders, civil society leaders and opposition leaders have been arrested and charged with 'subverting constitutional government'[39] as provided for under section 22 of the Criminal Law (Codification and Reform) Act [Chapter 9:23] (hereinafter referred to as the Criminal Code) after the protests that occurred in most major cities and towns in Zimbabwe in January

---

38  'CiZC condemns Closure of Democratic Space', *The Zimbabwean*, 16 March 2019.
39  International Commission of Jurists, 'Zimbabwe: Subverting a Constitutional Government. A Legal Briefing Note'.

2019.[40] The protests were sparked by a 150% in the price of fuel that was announced by Mnangagwa before he left the country for a four-nation tour in Asia. Since then the political space has continued to shrink with the opposition persistently denied its freedom to demonstrate or to hold rallies. Indeed, MDC-A spokesperson Nkululeko Sibanda remarked:

> You can't ask a dog to do a cat's job. The removal of Mugabe did not change anything for them [ZANU-PF]. They just continued in a much more ruthless and aggressive manner. Democratic space has been further restricted; soldiers now shoot and kill unarmed protesters on the streets. Demonstrations and rallies don't happen, they are blocked...' [41]

The NCA leader Lovemore Madhuku echoed similar sentiments, remarking that the Mnangagwa government is incompetent, and more brutal than that of Mugabe.

> There is no new dispensation. I think currently, if you have anything, there is a dispensation that has been going backwards. They (current leaders in government) have gone beyond what we had in the 1980s. Clearly, they are actually trying to learn the bad portion of their old days. That's what they are doing; the bad portion of the days where the mysterious disappearance of people, the heavy deployment of the police and the army at the smallest excuse; the old days of this where you find people in government who have no clue on how to deal with the situation, how to turn around the economy. That's what we have at the moment, so we have no new dispensation at all.[42]

Besides the suppression of citizens' right to protest, the 'new dispensation' has demonstrated a glaring democratic deficit through the 'unbundling and cosmetic repackaging' of laws such as the Public Order and Security Act (POSA) and the Access to Information and Protection of Privacy Act (AIPPA).[43] According to Veritas the provisions of the successor piece of legislation to POSA 'have been slavishly copied in the Bill so that all POSA's undemocratic features have been retained' and hence 'the draft Bill is not new wine in an old bottle: it is the same old wine in the same bottle but with a new label.'[44] There is now indisputable evidence that the little democratic space that existed during Mugabe's tyrannical rule is fast disappearing. All the elements that typify repression

---

44 Ibid.

– abductions, kidnappings, torture, disregard of the Constitution and questionable judicial rulings – seems to be firmly in place.[45]

## In search of a functional multi-party system in Zimbabwe's shrinking democratic arena

Zimbabwe's history and context does not provide a fertile ground for political parties to run for national elections and have the capacity to gain control of government offices, separately or in coalition. This is compounded primarily by the party-military-state conflation (see Chapter 8) which hinders the growth and free operation of competing parties. Even if opposition political parties were to flourish and win elections in a free and fair manner, would Zimbabwe's security sector be willing to accept the transfer of power? Zimbabwe's history is replete with examples when the military have made their position clear either overtly or covertly in a bid to instil intimidation and fear in the populace. During the 2002 presidential elections, the late Vitalis Zvinavashe, then Commander of the Zimbabwe Defence Forces declared that the security forces would not salute anyone without liberation war credentials; and the extent to which party-military-state fusion is embedded in the body politic is obvious when one considers the tainted and bloody presidential election run-off in June 2008, when 153 MDC supporters were killed (Howard-Hassman 2010), hundreds tortured or maimed, and the 1 August 2018 killing of at least six civilians. Indeed, 'Operation Restore Legacy' offers just another a clear demonstration that ZANU-PF and the military are inseparable twins. It is thus irrefutable that ZANU-PF has a profoundly unfair advantage over other political parties whether home-grown or, as they say, 'foreign-backed'. In addition, the incumbency factor places them in an advantageous position strategically and financially on many fronts.

If, however, opposition parties have always been constrained politically, financially and through coercion, they have also been their own worst enemies as they have failed to unite for a purpose, preferring instead to go it alone on a path of fragmentation even when it is evident that they have better chances as a coalition. The self-serving egos and parochial interests have been counter-productive to the opposition ranks while making them more vulnerable to ZANU-PF ploys to splinter them further. Intra-party factionalism has also undermined their credibility and done a disservice to their electorate, as instead of challenging the ruling party on policy,

---

45 'Democratic space has shrunk', *NewsDay*, 21 August 2019.

they undermine each other. In sum, the odds are heavily staked against the opposition, whether new or established while providing fertile grounds for ZANU-PF to continue with its dominance.

## Conclusion

The emergence and development of political parties in Zimbabwe in the last thirteen decades has been shaped by the largely restrictive socio-economic and fraught political context. From the decades through pre- to post-independence, political parties have been active. In the pre-independence era, nationalist political parties found themselves operating within a very constrained environment as they fought hard to dismantle the repressive colonial regime. In fact, most such parties were legally eliminated especially when they posed – in reality or perception – a mortal threat to the hegemonic regime. This approach to the black opposition parties was inherited hook, line and sinker by the liberation movement now in power.

With the attainment of independence in 1980, ZANU-PF's bid to establish a one-party state was a clear example of concerted efforts to create political monopoly, a hegemonic ambition challenged by the constellation of opposition parties who also inhabited the country's political universe. Since the turn of the twenty-first century, Zimbabwe's political space has been shrinking and its democratic development largely blocked. The incumbent's compelling imperative to retain power, and at any cost, points to an extended period of increasingly constrained democracy and a shrinking political space for parties that stand in opposition in Zimbabwe. The road to a fully functional multi-party democracy is going to be long, hard and anything but linear.

## References

Baviskar, S. and F.T.M. Malone (2004) 'What Democracy Means to Citizens – and Why It Matters', *European Review of Latin American and Caribbean Studies*, 76.

Becker, P. and J-A Raveloson (2008) *'What is Democracy?'* Antananarivo: Frederick-Ebert-Stiftung.

Catholic Commission for Justice and Peace (CCJP) and Legal Resources Foundation (LRF) (1997) *Breaking the Silence, Building True Peace: Report on the Disturbances in Matabeleland and the Midlands, 1980-1989*. Harare: CCJP and LRF.

Chiwewe, W. (2009) 'Unity Negotiations' (pp. 242-287). in C. S. Banana (ed.), *Turmoil and Tenacity: Zimbabwe 1890-1990*. Harare: College Press.

Coltart, D. (2006), 'MDC Legal Affairs Department Report, 2000 to 2005'. Harare: MDC. 20 February.

Dahl, A. (1971) *Polyarchy: Participation and Opposition*, New Haven, CT: Yale University Press.

Diamond, L. (2004) 'What is Democracy?' Lecture at Hilla University for Humanistic Studies, Iraq, 21 January

Howard-Hassmann, R.E. (2010) 'Mugabe's Zimbabwe, 2000–2009: Massive Human Rights Violations and the Failure to Protect'. *Human Rights Quarterly*. 32/4.

Hofmeister, W. and K. Grabow (2011) 'Political Parties, Functions and Organisation in Democratic Societies'. Singapore: Konrad Adeneur Stiftung.

Horner, L. and A. Puddephatt (2011), 'Democratic Space in Asia-Pacific: Challenges for Democratic Governance Sssistance and Deepening Civic Engagement'. GSDRC Publications.

Jafari, J. (2003) 'Attacks from Within: Zimbabwe's Assault on Basic Freedoms through Legislation', *Human Rights Brief*, 10/3.

Masunungure, E. (2006) 'Regulation of Political Parties Zimbabwe: Registration, Finance and Other Support'. Harare: ZESN.

Zimbabwe Election Support Network (ZESN) (2018) 'Report on the 30 July 2018 Harmonised Elections'. Harare: ZESN

# 6

# Public Opinion Before and After the July 2018 Harmonised Elections

### Anyway Chingwete and Stephen Ndoma

*...even in the least democratic regime, opinion may influence the direction or tempo of substantive policy. Although a government may be erected on tyranny, to endure it needs the ungrudging support of substantial numbers of its people.*

(Key 1961: 3)

*'To hell with public opinion.... We should lead, not follow'*
(US State Department Official, 1973)

Nearly a century ago in 1921, British jurist and historian James Bryce asked, rather rhetorically: 'Is there ... no other way in which the people can express their mind and exert their power? Can any means be found of supplying that which elections fail to give?' (Bryce 1921:153). He then supplied the answer: 'Polling is the only explicit and palpable mode yet devised of expressing the people's will'. Everywhere, elections are held infrequently and yet every day citizens hold views about how they are governed and what they would like those in government to deliver in terms of both tangible and intangible public goods. In short, how do people speak truth to power in between elections held, in most cases, every four or five years?

Public opinion surveys, such as Afrobarometer – an Africa-wide survey research network – puts it, are about 'giving voice to Africans'. This chapter is about the aggregate of the views citizens hold regarding matters that affect or interest them, ranging from the quality of elections, popular expectations about the quality of governance, public assessments of the direction of the country to the salience of policy issues (e.g. employment, food security, service delivery, currency reform, corruption indigenisation). In 2018, these are the issues that animated Zimbabwean voters before, during and after the elections. Because what public opinion is (or is not) is seldom well understood, the chapter begins by discussing what this phenomenon is.

## What is public opinion?

Even after decades of intense scholarship, the meaning of 'public opinion' remains complex and problematic, with little consensus on what it indicates. Nine decades ago, Robert Binkley (1928: 389) lamented the 'uncertainty in the meaning of the term "public opinion"':

> The problem of public opinion is deep rooted; it is found in all fields of social thought. It perplexes sociologists, political theorists and historians, and he would be rash indeed who should presume to present any solution to the entire problem .

Earlier, according to Binkley, a Round Table had been convened in 1924 which laid bare the difficulties of defining public opinion:

> Some members of the Round Table believed that there is no such thing as public opinion; others believed in its existence but doubted their ability to define it with sufficient precision for scientific purposes. Others again, more sanguine or perhaps more credulous, believed that the term could be defined, but were of different minds concerning the kind of definition that should be adopted (ibid.).

In exasperation, the Round Table concluded that it would be wise to 'avoid the use of the term public opinion, if possible' (ibid.). Since the Round Table's 'surrender', the term has been in vogue and public opinion polling in most open regimes is one of the major games in town, especially during the election cycle. Indeed, prominent political scientist Austin Ranney (1990: 127) has asserted that 'public opinion is the cutting edge of a nation's political culture' and thus, that all governments and most political actors 'treat public opinion as a mighty force'.

Notwithstanding the nuances around what public opinion is and about who constitutes the 'public' and whose opinions should count most – individuals, groups or elites – a common thread can be discerned. It is that 'public opinion' is the 'aggregate of views amongst members of a society'. Following Davison (2017), public opinion is an aggregate of the individual views, attitudes and beliefs on a particular subject, expressed by a significant proportion of a community at a particular time. In other ways, Davison views public opinion as not restricted to politics and elections, but embraces citizens' views on different topics. Importantly, public opinion is not sought for its own sake but, primarily, in order to influence policy makers and the decision-making processes. Thus, for Key (1961: 14), 'Public opinion consists of those opinions held by private persons which governments find it prudent to heed'.

## The importance of public opinion

For citizens, including its leaders who understand the importance of a public voice, public opinion has been used as a valued resource in programming and planning. It has also found its space in advocacy work, monitoring and evaluation and in advancing research work. Failing to provide 'an ear' to a citizen's voice signifies failure to embrace democracy and failure to embrace the citizenry's ideas in providing policy direction.

For nations striving to democratise or maintain their democratic tenets, citizens' views play a critical role in shaping the politics, economy and social well-being of a country. Most scholars, who contributed to the body of knowledge about democracy, have in their definitions outlined the relevance of a public voice. Pennock (1979: 7) defines democracy as 'Government by the people, where liberty, equality and fraternity are secured to the greatest possible degree and in which human capacities are developed to the utmost, by means including free and full discussion of common problems and interest.'

Pennock views democracy as incomplete without the participation of the ordinary citizens. In drawing up the equation for democracy, citizens' views cannot be ignored. Weale (1999: 14) explicitly see the interplay of laws, policies and public opinion in defining democracy, 'in a democracy, important public decisions on questions of law and policy depend, directly or indirectly, upon public opinion formally expressed by citizens of the community, the vast bulk of whom have equal political rights.'

We often see then that democracy thrives well when citizens' views are not suppressed. Public opinion has been legitimised as a pillar of African democracy, leading to the growing expectation that public voices must be heard in policy debates. Most western countries have out-performed their African peers in embracing public opinion. Democracy is all about people and it is the voice of the people that matters in shaping the course of action governments take in defining the country's policy direction. One of the co-founders of the Afrobarometer Project, Professor Gyimah-Boadi, echoed that, 'we believe that African societies thrive well when African voices count in public policy and development, and so over the past twenty years, Afrobarometer (AB) has demonstrated that the views of ordinary citizens can indeed be heard and made to count.'[1] It is against such a background that Zimbabwe has tried to open space for public opinion, although the country is still far from effectively harnessing the public voice into policy processes and policy development.

## The evolution of public opinion in Zimbabwe

Prior to independence, Zimbabwe, like most of its African peers, registered a dearth in public opinion. During colonial times and the period just after independence, public opinion was an area to which governments paid little attention. According to Bratton et al. (2005), 'Political leaders and technocrats thought that they knew best what the people wanted'. With the transition from colonial rule to independence, political leaders saw the importance of public opinion, but could only rely on periodic national censuses and household production or consumption surveys, conducted essentially for planning purposes. During this era, little systematic evidence was collected about living conditions, let alone mass preferences.

Early post-independence, Zimbabwe conducted its first census in 1982, followed by the August 1992 census, with some Inter-Censul Demographic Surveys (ICDS) in 1987 and 1997. In between the censuses and the ICDS, not many citizens' views about their experiences and political behaviour was collected, although that period probably mattered most in terms of understanding peoples' hopes and aspirations for a new Zimbabwe. The little research that was conducted at the time suffered from methodological deficiencies.

It was only in the late 1990s, that a new wave of 'Public Opinionists' emerged. The idea was to tap into citizens' perceptions on topical issues around the economy, politics and social issues, thereby connecting the

---

1 'Afrobarometer lays foundation for "next generation" of giving voice to African citizens', Afrobarometer Press Release, Accra, 6 June 2019.

citizenry with the policy makers. We see here the birth of institutions such as the Target Research, a marketing and social research agency, established in 1993, the Mass Public Opinion Institute (MPOI) (1999),[2] the Zimbabwe Economic Policy Analysis and Research Unit (ZEPARU) (2003), Research and Advocacy Unit (RAU), in 2006 and Research Projects such as the Afrobarometer (AB).[3]

Realising the missing link in policy formulation as public opinion, MPOI felt that tapping citizens' perceptions would likely fill this gap. The Institute believes that public policy should be informed by public opinion and that good governance prospers where policy makers are informed by public opinion. The AB Network, a continental non-partisan research agency in Africa, was also initiated around this time. Its main thrust is to provide a voice in policymaking processes. The AB Project is primarily driven by its catchy slogan 'Let the people speak' or 'let the people have a say'.

Afrobarometer findings have become a key source giving voice to Africans, and helping to break the monopoly of elites, experts and opinion leaders in political and policy debates. As outlined in its survey manual, the AB Project enables ordinary Africans to become more informed about what other people in their countries and across the region think, and amplify popular voices that might not otherwise be heard. The survey findings may verify, challenge, or complement the formal statistics collected by the state.

## The significance of public opinion in Zimbabwe

In Zimbabwe, whilst some segments of society harbour a hostile attitude to research outcomes, others have embraced public opinion. Commenting on the first wave of the 2018 pre-election survey,[4] (hereafter referred to as

---

2  MPOI is a non-profit, non-governmental research organisation established and registered in January 1999 as a Trust in accordance with the laws of the Republic of Zimbabwe to undertake, publish, and discuss public opinion research. The Institute's main objective is to gauge public opinion on topical governance issues and matters of public concern and make this known to policy makers and implementers, as well as to the public itself.

3  AB is a comparative series of public attitude surveys that assess citizen attitudes to democracy and governance, markets, and civil society, among other topics. The surveys have been undertaken at periodic intervals since 1999. Having begun with twelve countries in the first cycle in 1999, AB coverage has progressively increased and currently covers at least 34 African countries.

4  The 2018 Wave 1, Pre-election survey was conducted by MPOI in conjunction with the Institute for Justice and Reconciliation (IJR), with technical support from

the May 2018 survey), a local senior political analyst had this to say to the opposition political parties:

> I think any argument that dismisses the latest findings from Afrobarometer/MPOI survey on the basis that it will give ZANU-PF (Zimbabwe African National Union Patriotic Front) an upper hand is a lousy argument. You have been given the pulse of the nation 15 months ahead of an election. Take the findings, interpret them and identify your weaknesses and get busy to convince people by addressing key areas![5]

Commenting on the same survey findings and arguing along the same lines, a senior Movement for Democratic Change–Tsvangirai party (MDC-T) member had this to say; 'we must not dismiss the Afrobarometer survey results but work harder to surprise our sceptics. Thanks to the survey. I think my colleagues will agree with me that we are now even more motivated to win the elections. We are not deterred as the survey has given us more impetus to confront the regime with better policy alternatives and strategies to win.'

The MDC Alliance (MDC-A) acknowledged the value of the survey findings, even though they may have found them unfavourable. The party was quick to offer its official position and acknowledged the importance of social science surveys.

> The MDC-T *takes very seriously* scientific studies which help to inform us of the political environment in which we operate. As such, the MDC-T will always take its time to thoroughly study the recent report that was published by MPOI and working in conjunction with Afrobarometer,' the party said in a statement. Naturally, the MDC-T will use the report to inform its strategies going forward. These types of surveys assist us in providing data on the electoral environment (emphasis added).

We see here how political parties embraced the pre-election research findings for their programming and planning i.e. reflecting the importance of the citizen's voice. Naturally, people would be suspicious of such findings if they repeatedly contradicted events on the ground or if there

---

the AB project. The survey interviewed a nationally representative sample of 2,400 Zimbabweans between 28 April and 12 May 2018, i.e. some three months before the election.

5    'Afrobarometer report timely warning', *The Financial Gazette*, 19 May 2017.

was a persistent mismatch between the findings and the in-country political and economic status. With a solid methodology, reasonable sample size, and thoroughly trained interviewers, consumers of survey research can be assured of sound public opinion data. Over two decades, MPOI and its affiliates have been successful in supplying unadulterated data on public opinion from both its surveys and its qualitative Focus Group Discussions[6] (FGDs).

## Challenges with public opinion in Zimbabwe

Researchers use different methods to measure public opinion, although the most common are polls that are quantitative in nature, conducted to gauge people's opinions about a particular policy or thematic area. With a single poll, researchers are able to generalise findings and provide information on what proportion of the sample hold a particular view. For example, the May 2018 survey, findings on the economy revealed that, '65% of Zimbabweans reported their economic status as "fairly bad" or "very bad"'.

Such quantitative findings provide the heartbeat of the citizenry, but fall short of explaining why. However, generally the FGDs will offer some explanation as to why people hold the opinions they do.

In Zimbabwe, reaction to research findings has always been antithetical. Some consumers (government, political parties and the media) are quick to accept the survey data if/when they are favourable to their aspirations. On such occasions, they will embrace the research methodology without questioning the selection of research participants, coverage, and questions, etc. The reverse is true when the findings do not concur with their perspective. For example, findings that are critical of the president and his allies are often viewed as advocating or spearheading 'a regime change agenda'. Needless to say, democracy is based on fact and a reasoned exchange of opinion; it is necessarily undermined when advocates assume an intransigent opinion and see all alternatives as betrayal.

---

6   A focus group is a small-group discussion (ten to twelve participants) guided by a trained facilitator. It is used to learn about opinions on a designated topic, and to guide future action. FGDs are often used as a means of triangulation with other data collection methods. Participants are chosen to participate in FGDs on the basis of defined criteria by the researcher, for example, province, ethnicity, gender, age and education. Homogeneity is a key consideration when conducting the FGDs with participants of similar characteristics participating on their own. The main weakness of FGDs is that data generated from them is not statistically representative of the entire population due to the smaller number of participants involved.

Susan Booysen reveals the effectiveness of public opinion in programming. In response to the 2018 pre-election survey findings, which showed stronger support for ZANU-PF than for the opposition MDC-T and its Alliance (see Appendix 2), Booysen warned the latter to act on the findings rather than ignore them as they did the 2012 Freedom House pre-election findings:

> The main opposition party should have learnt the hard way after ignoring similar findings from a survey by Freedom House in 2012 – just a year before the 2013 harmonised elections – which gave President Mugabe and his party a favourable view, which it (MDC-T) pooh-poohed. The dire consequences of casually dismissing the findings were the comprehensive defeat of the opposition in the 2013 harmonised election.'[7]

Reflecting on the same survey, a senior member of MDC-T argued that the survey findings did not address some of the salient issues affecting Zimbabweans, saying: 'I think the results are disappointing because they do not capture the mood in the country'.[8]

Responding to the seventh wave of the AB survey (held between January and February 2017), the MDC-T, excoriated MPOI for reporting its findings on 'trust', where the late – then 93-year-old – President Mugabe garnered modest trust (trusted 'somewhat' or 'a lot') by 64% of Zimbabweans, against 56% for his party (ZANU-PF) and only a third (32%) for the opposition political parties. Reported by *News24* (13 May 2017), the MDC-T dismissed the survey as 'irrelevant'. The leader of one of the breakaway factions from the MDC, the People's Democratic Party (PDP) also questioned the methodology that was used to collect data in this survey.

In this chapter, we ask salient questions about the reception of public opinion research findings: When does public opinion data become valuable? Is it only when it aligns to the consumers' expectations or should we not take the findings at face value? When should citizens speak their minds? Is it only when it suits certain segments of the society or when it is necessary to do so? In the context of Zimbabwe, does fear affect the way citizens respond to survey research? With regard to the former, we argue that citizens' views matter. And with regard to fear, Chikwanha et

---

7 'Afrobarometer report timely warning', *The Financial Gazette*, 19 May 2017.
8 Ibid.

al. (2004) argued that the history of violence and the power of propaganda might have an effect on how citizens respond to survey questions. They posit that 'People who trust the ideological pronouncement of the official government media are very much more likely to give the President a positive rating', but go on to say that Zimbabweans might feel so intimidated by ZANU-PF surveillance and control that they may be unwilling to express political opinions honestly, but will rather say what they think the government wants to hear.

However, we do have built-in checks into the survey design to try and counteract the effect of fear undermining a citizen's ability to be honest. Testing the results, Chikwanha et al. found that citizens who were fearful (need to be careful when discussing politics), were twice as likely to give a negative rating to the President. Chikwanha et al. argue:

> In other words, despite their fear, people are willing to take the risk of speaking truth to power. The courage of ordinary people is confirmed by the lack of relationship between feelings of political fear and the frequency with which people actually engage in political discussion. In these respects, ZANU PF has not enjoyed complete success in compelling citizens to keep quiet or to toe the official party line.

Further, for every interview, we ask interviewers to document their experience with their respondents. In a May 2018 pre-election survey, large majorities of respondents were reported to be friendly or in-between (97%), co-operative or in between (98%) and honest (94%). In all cases, only 6% or less were reported in the negative. We do conclude that whilst we cannot rule out the effect of 'fear', citizens are willing to allow themselves to be interviewed, and to volunteer a significant amount of their time. Many people welcome being asked for their opinions on issues which they have often felt no one cared about.

Apart from the scrutiny and backlash that can follow the release of public opinion surveys, collecting the data can be easily managed in a propitious and non-hostile political space. Chingwete and Muchena (2008) argue that political instability in Zimbabwe negatively affects the conduct of research, especially in areas where the ruling ZANU-PF party commands a majority. Whilst institutions such as MPOI have found ways of dealing with precarious situations, we acknowledge how risky such environments can be to field researchers. However, the early months of Mnangagwa's rule saw the opening up of political space, allowing a more conducive environment for researchers, and survey participants who felt freer to express their own opinions about the political, economic and social standing of their lives and their country.

Whilst other factors such as poor road networks, a bad infrastructure and a collapsed economy explain why conducting research in Zimbabwe is extremely expensive and time-consuming, these might be lesser challenges than those associated with conducting survey research in a polarised and hostile environment.

The following section scrutinises public opinion as it relates to the 2018 pre-election and post-election period. What were citizens' political values ahead of the harmonised elections? Did the electorate have any worries or apprehensions over the 2018 elections? If, yes, what were they? Why did they intend to vote? We detail citizens' views regarding their economy and the political standing of the country. On matters relating to the former, we try to answer such salient questions as: what did people want? How did citizens evaluate their own economic conditions (micro-level) and that of their own country (macro-level)? Do they foresee a real transformation at both micro- and macro-level in the post-Mugabe era? Considering the unfolding events in the economy, do they feel the country is going in the right or wrong direction? Finally, we also present citizens' view on what they consider as solutions to the current economic challenges. Do citizens believe things will improve in the near future; and, if so, who do they think is capable of bringing salvation to a troubled nation?

## Citizens' voice on the economy ahead of the 2018 Harmonised Elections

From the May 2018 pre-election survey, almost two-thirds of adult Zimbabweans (65%) evaluated their 'present' economic conditions and that of their country (74%) as bad. Zimbabweans also expressed their disillusionment about the direction the country was taking. This level of pessimism was apparent in other economic evaluations. A clear majority (62%) felt that the country was going in the wrong direction, with only a third (32%) being optimistic. Bratton and Masunungure (2018) reported that 'Perhaps surprisingly, the public mood on this issue hardly changed as a result of the November 2017 presidential transition from Mugabe to Mnangagwa; in February 2017, a similar proportion (60%) already considered that the country was going in the wrong direction'. Indeed, the level of pessimism has only continued to rise since 2012 when it was 41%, to 63% in 2015, where it has more or less remained ever since.

Bratton and Masunungure (2018) show some correlation between citizens' evaluation of economic performance and the direction of the country. They note that 'more than eight in ten persons (81%) who regard the present condition of the Zimbabwean economy as "very bad" also see the country going in the wrong direction (see Figure 6.1 below). Bleak assessments of the country's future prospects are similar among those who see present personal living standards as 'very bad' and macro-economic conditions as getting 'much worse'.

**Figure 6.1: Country directions by economic conditions | Zimbabwe | May 2018**

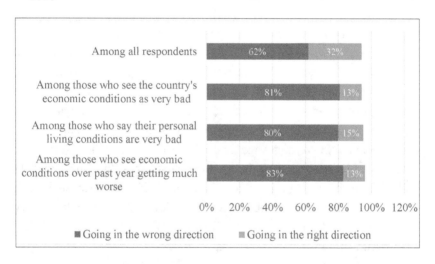

*Respondents were asked:* Some people might think the country is going in the wrong direction. Others may feel it is going in the right direction. So, let me ask YOU about the overall direction of the country: 1. Would you say that the country is going in the wrong direction or the right direction? 2. In general, how would you describe:

  a. the present economic condition of this country?

  b. Your own present living conditions?

Looking back, how do you rate economic conditions in this country compared to twelve months ago?

## Citizens' priority areas for development

To win the hearts of the electorate, political leaders and the government at large are expected to address the many challenges citizens encounter on a daily basis. Most African citizens decry the level of government commitment in addressing their needs. The same applies with regard to their political leaders, who are mostly seen to be active during the election campaign period, but disappear after their election into office. Do political leaders take time to listen and understand the issues affecting their constituencies? When formulating policies, does the view of the citizen count? Findings from a Global Parliamentary survey (2012), show a disconnect between what parliamentarians view as their role against what they perceive citizens expect of them. Members of parliament view law-making as their most important role, even though they know that their electorate consider this to be solving the constituencies' problems.

Just two months before the July 2018 election, the pre-election survey asked citizens to single out the most important problems the election campaign should address. Respondents were asked to mention a maximum of three issues. Figure 6.2 below provides an aggregate of all three responses. The top three issues are employment (64%), management of the economy (39%) and wages and salaries (25%). For the first time the latter found its space among the top three challenges, though previously ranked at fifth place in 2015 and ninth in 2013. The persistent cash shortages in Zimbabwe and the increasingly devaluation of the temporary 'local currency' (Bond Note and the Real Time Gross Settlement - RTGS), have significantly weakened the local currency.

**Figure 6.2: Most important problems campaign should address: | Zimbabwe | May 2018**

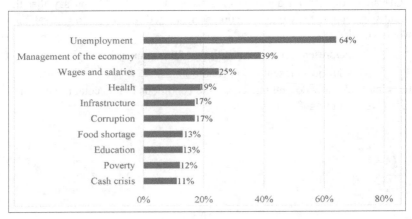

*Respondents were asked:* In your opinion, what are the three most important problems facing this country which the forthcoming election campaign should address? (Figures will not add to 100% because each percentage aggregates up to three responses per interviewee.)

Singing from the same hymn book, participants in post-election FGDs,[9] organised by MPOI and IJR, believe that resolving unemployment in Zimbabwe could offer a step forward in addressing a myriad of challenges facing the nation: including unwanted pregnancies and corruption, as well as the many profound problems in the education and health sectors. In order of importance participants consider the government should attend to the following: currency/salaries/cash/money issues, jobs/reopening of industries/creating a favourable environment for investment, inflation, corruption, rule of law, fuel shortages and pricing, resolving the challenges in the health and education sectors as well as addressing the land issues. With regards to currency stability, participants expect their government to abandon the Bond note, and introduce a new currency, which should be monitored to ensure its stability in value and availability. Others believe the adoption of the South African Rand or the United States dollars would probably bring sanity to a cash-strapped economy. In their own words' participants had this to say:

That's why I am saying that the government should create employment. Right now, ladies are being impregnated at the age of 18 years, but they don't even have the napkins or anything, and would end up loitering in town. And then we blame them for loitering in town, without considering that they don't have means for living. As a result, I think creation of employment by the government might help. (Bulawayo Urban, Female, 25-49 years)

What I think as important for the government to address is the currency problems. They must change the currency for us because all that we are talking about stems from the currency. If they can change to US dollars or any other currency that we can use across countries because our challenges are stemming from the currency. (Harare Urban, Female, 18-24 years)

---

9   The FGDs took place in April 2019, eight months after the July 2018 harmonised elections. A total of ten FGDs were held across six provinces: Harare, Bulawayo, Matabeleland South, Mashonaland West, Masvingo and Manicaland provinces. Fieldwork was conducted from 11-13 April 2019.

## Political values ahead of the 2018 Harmonised Elections

### Public support for regular, open, and honest elections

The AB pre-election survey held in May 2018 showed that adult Zimbabweans embrace the need for regular, open and honest elections: more than eight out of ten adult Zimbabweans (84%) said that they supported the need to choose leaders in this way. Afrobarometer surveys conducted between 2009 and 2018 confirm this with more than 75% of adult citizens holding this opinion over the review period. This view was however most widespread in 2012 with 87% of the surveyed adult population in support (Figure 6.3).

**Figure 6.3: Support for regular, open, and honest elections | Zimbabwe | 2009-2018**

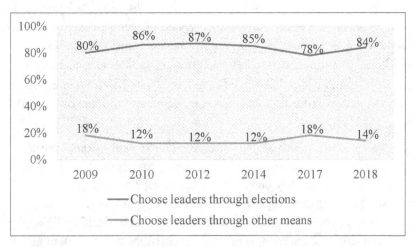

*Respondents were asked:* Which of the following statements is closest to your view? 1.We should choose our leaders in this country through regular, open, and honest elections. 2: Since elections sometimes produce bad results, we should adopt other methods for choosing this country's leaders – (% who 'agree' or 'agree very strongly' with each statement).

### Public Attitudes to Voting

MPOI's 2018 Wave 2, pre-election survey (hereafter referred to the June/July 2018 survey)[10] showed that adult Zimbabweans generally regard voting as a civic duty. Three out of five adult Zimbabweans (60%) said they felt this way while 39% indicated that they regard voting as a matter

10  The 2018 Wave 2, pre-election survey was conducted by MPOI in conjunction with the IJR, with technical support from the AB Project. The survey interviewed a nationally representative sample of 2,400 Zimbabweans between 25 June and 6 July 2018.

of choice. More rural-based Zimbabweans (62%) than urbanites (54%) and more men (61%) than women (59%) are likely to state that voting in elections is a civic duty (Figure 6.4).

**Figure 6. 4: Public attitudes to voting | Zimbabwe | 2018**

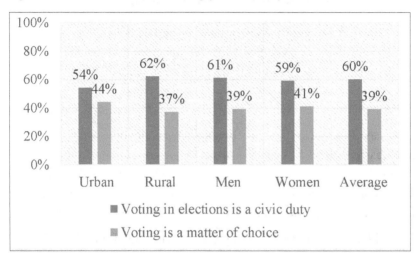

*Respondents were asked:* Which of the following statements is closest to your view? Choose Statement 1 or Statement 2. [Interviewer: Probe for strength of opinion] Do you agree or agree very strongly? 1. Voting in elections is a civic duty 2. Whether or not I vote in elections is my choice to make.

NDI pre-election FGDs[11] held in March 2018 also confirmed that Zimbabweans believe that voting is important. Most participants who had taken part in the FGDs held across the country's ten administrative provinces said that they were eager to vote in the July 2018 harmonised elections due to their belief that voting is equal to voice and choice. They also held the view that the electorate has power to influence the country's future trajectory by means of the ballot. However, a few were of the opinion that voting was not important due to rigging.

I think voting is important in the sense that whoever is governing is given that mandate by the people and therefore that person can

---

11  Seventeen FGDs conducted from 3-10 March 2018 in the country's ten administrative provinces: Harare, Bulawayo, Mashonaland Central, Mashonaland East, Mashonaland West, Manicaland, Matabeleland North, Matabeleland South, Masvingo and Midlands provinces. Participants for each FGD averaged ten, with each group divided across the main demographics: province, gender, age and location (rural/urban). Separating participants by these demographics provides them with a freer space to openly discuss issues.

be able to bring change in the country. (Masvingo Urban, Female, 18-24 years)

Voting is a good thing because it is my right to choose the leader I want. (Chitungwiza Urban, Male, 25-49 years)

I think it gives me the opportunity to be heard on the things that I want. It is my voice that gives the opportunity to decide on the direction I want my future to take. Voting gives me the opportunity to contribute to the affairs of the state. (Masvingo Rural, Male, 25-49 years)

Asked if they thought the 2018 harmonised elections were important, most participants who answered in the affirmative emphasised that these elections were different in that there were new contestants; a new promise of free and fair elections; and a competition which gave them hope for a better Zimbabwe. Below are quotations buttressing this view:

I think voting this time is important because the leadership of the country has changed and the president said that we needed free and fair elections, which is now different from Mugabe's era. (Masvingo Rural, Male, 25-49 years)

Voting this year will be very important because it will be the first presidential election when Mugabe is not a candidate. People think if they vote this time, they will elect someone that they like. (Manicaland Rural, Male, 18-24 years)

I think it's more important this time around because in previous elections we would just vote but we already knew who was going to win. (Matabeleland South Rural, Male, 18-24 years)

FGD participants also had hope that the elections were going to be free because of the presence of international observers, and new technology. However, participants wondered if the military would allow free and fair elections, some seemed fatigued, believing that the election outcome is always the same due to rigging while others were resigned to the idea, that nothing changes with voting.

Reinforcing the belief held by FGD participants in the March 2018 NDI qualitative study, the May pre-election survey showed that adult Zimbabweans believe that they have power as voters to choose leaders who can help them improve their lives in the future. This view found takers among almost eight out of ten adult Zimbabweans (77%) while 18% held a different view. No significant differences existed by urban-rural location and even by gender (78% in urban areas vs. 77% in rural areas and 78% men vs. 77% women) (Figure 6.5).

**Figure 6.5: Perceptions of power to influence circumstances | Zimbabwe | 2018**

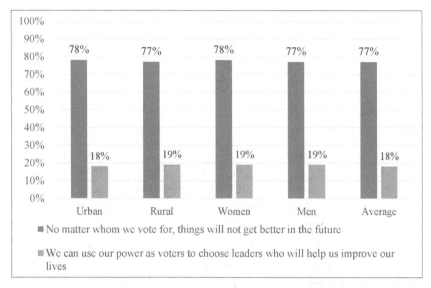

*Respondents were asked:* Which of the following statements is closest to your view? Choose Statement 1 or Statement 2. [Interviewer: Probe for strength of opinion] Do you agree or agree very strongly? 1. No matter whom we vote for, things will not get better in the future. 2. We can use our power as voters to choose leaders who will help us improve our lives

## Public support for multi-party politics and rejection of military rule

It is also instructive to note that the 2018 Wave 2 pre-election survey, revealed that Zimbabweans are generally desirous of a political space which allows multi-party politics to flourish. This was manifest as almost eight out of ten citizens (77%) disapproved (with 54% strongly disapproving the existence of a one-party state. On the other hand, a fifth (20%) approved of a situation where only one political party is allowed to stand for election and hold office. More urbanites (82%) than rural residents (70%) and more men (80%) than women (73%) were inclined to hold this view (Figure 6.6).

**Figure 6.6: Support for multi-party politics | Zimbabwe | 2018**

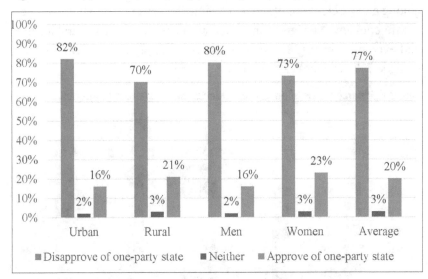

*Respondents were asked:* There are many ways to govern a country. Would you disapprove or approve of the following alternatives? Only one political party is allowed to stand for election and hold office.

Closely interwoven with support for multiparty politics is overwhelming evidence that Zimbabweans reject military rule with eight out of ten adult citizens being of this inclination. More urban-based residents (83%) than rural residents (76%) said they reject military rule.

**Figure 6. 7: Rejection of military rule | Zimbabwe | 2018**

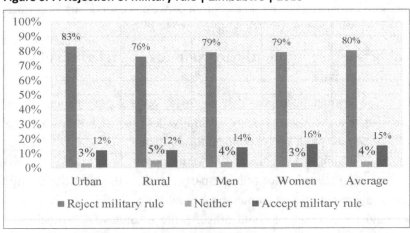

*Respondents were asked:* There are many ways to govern a country. Would you disapprove or approve of the following alternatives? (a) Only one political party is allowed to stand for election and hold office. (b) The army comes in to govern the country. (c) Elections and Parliament are abolished so that the president can decide everything.

## Perceptions of freedom of expression

Section 61 (i) of the Constitution of Zimbabwe states that every person has the right to freedom of expression, which includes – (a) freedom to seek, receive and communicate ideas and other information; (b) freedom of artistic expression and scientific research and creativity; and (c) academic freedom. Despite this constitutional guarantee, did Zimbabweans feel that their freedom to express themselves was guaranteed ahead of the 2018 general elections? As Figure 6.8 shows, adult Zimbabweans' perceptions of freedom of self-expression have fluctuated since 2009. In January/ February 2017, almost half of adult citizens reported that they were 'not very free' or 'not at all' free to speak their minds. This is not surprising given that a trend analysis commencing with the year 2009 showed that 48% of the adult population considered that they were 'not very' or 'not at all' free to express themselves openly. This opinion was at its highest in 2010 (67%), but dropped to 53% in 2012 during the period of the Government of National Unity, and dropped again to 43% in 2014 before showing a slight upward trend to 47% in 2017.

**Figure 6.8: Trend in freedom of expression | Zimbabwe | 2009-2017**

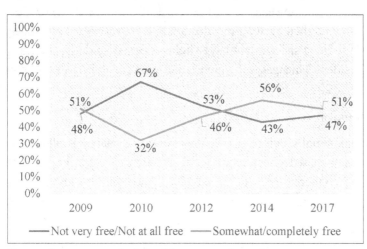

*Respondents were asked:* In this country, how free are you to say what you think?

**Figure 6.9: Trends in perceptions of self-censorship | Zimbabwe 2009-2018**

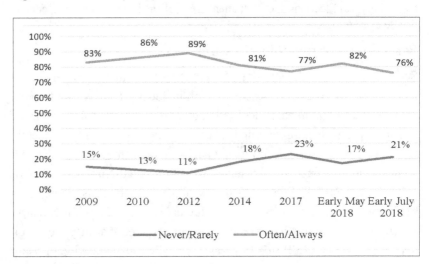

*Respondents were asked:* In your opinion, how often in this country do people have to be careful of what they say about politics?

Self-censorship is high.[12] AB survey statistics conducted between 2009 and June/July 2018 show that at least 75% of adult citizens indicate that they are 'often' or 'always' careful about what they say. This self-censorship was expressed by the largest proportion of adult Zimbabweans in 2012 (89%) though it went down to 76% in 2018 (Figure 6.9). We therefore postulate that Zimbabweans are forced to self-censor and hence their freedoms are curtailed even during election time. However, as previously suggested, political space might have slightly opened up during the early rule of President Mnangagwa, which is not the case during the time of writing (early 2020).

## Apprehension over 2018 elections

Public opinion polls before the 2018 harmonised elections show that Zimbabweans shared concerns about them. Hence as the build-up to the elections gathered momentum, anxieties among adult Zimbabweans increased with regard to certain processes. According to Afrobarometer pre-2018 election surveys, citizens were worried about aspects of a newly

---

12  It is the nature of public opinion that it will reveal contradictions, so while Chikwanha et al. (2004) stated that people who are fearful will often overcome their fear to express their opinions, our data also reveals (see Figure 6.9), that self-censorship, particularly with respect to politics, has always been high (more than 75% of the adult population over the review period). On the other hand, with regards to general freedom to say whatever they think, the outlook is better, as depicted in Figure 6.8.

introduced biometric voter registration (BVR) system. In early July, 25% reported that an unauthorised person had demanded to see the serial number on their BVR slips. Although these concerns dropped slightly from higher levels in early May, more than a quarter of adult citizens continued to feel anxiety about the secrecy of the ballot; 28% thought that 'powerful people' could somehow 'find out how you voted', 26% were concerned that their vote would not be counted while 45% thought that incorrect results would be announced (Figure 6.10).

**Figure 6.10: Perceptions of likelihood of election irregularities | Zimbabwe | May-July 2018**

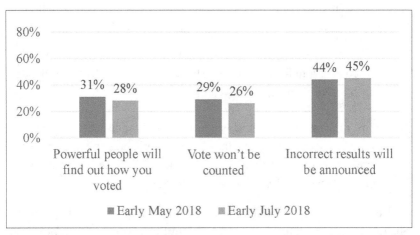

*Respondents were asked*: In your opinion, how likely will the following things happen in the 2018 elections: 1. Even though there is supposed to be a secret ballot in this country, powerful people will find out how you have voted? 2. Even though you will cast a ballot, your vote will not actually be counted? 3. Even after all ballots are counted, an incorrect result will be announced? (% who say 'somewhat likely' or 'very likely')

The pre-election FGDs confirmed the existence of some deep-rooted fears. The qualitative study showed that citizens had unanswered questions about the issue of photographs and fingerprints under the BVR system. The FGD participants were also troubled about the secrecy of the vote. There was fear that technology or the use of computers can be manipulated to reveal how someone had voted.

What are they going to do with my photo? Are they assuming that I will not vote? Or do they want to come where I stay and then do what to me? (Bulawayo urban female vendor, 18-35 years)

...it has never happened all these years that photographs of me are taken for registration purposes and after that they are demanding serial numbers which we write on the cards, where are those cards going? (Midlands Rural, Female, 18-24 years)

The Zimbabwe Electoral Commission (ZEC) also received criticism as some participants felt that the electoral management body had not done enough to teach people how the BVR system works during the voter registration process. Nevertheless, there were others who felt that vote secrecy was guaranteed as they understood the process. Nonetheless, this category of participants had worries about elderly and rural residents whom they imagined would not understand the secrecy of the ballot and hence felt that these people were vulnerable and would be manipulated.

...but for the elderly it will change how they vote, most of them will just go and vote for the ruling party because of that. (Matabeleland North Rural, Female, 25-49 years)

...in rural areas you find soldiers that do not wear uniforms intimidating the elderly that they have their pictures and fingerprints from when they registered to vote so they will trace for rebellious voters. (Masvingo Rural, Male, 25-49 years)

Zimbabweans also expressed concerns about the final stages of the election and especially the role of the military within the process. As Figure 6.11 shows, in both the May and July surveys significant minorities of citizens reported that they expected that:

- incorrect election results would be announced: 44% in May, 45% in July
- the armed forces would not respect the election result: 41% in May, 44% in July
- post-election violence would occur: 40% in May, 44% in July

**Figure 6.11: Popular concerns about election's final stages | Zimbabwe | May-July 2018**

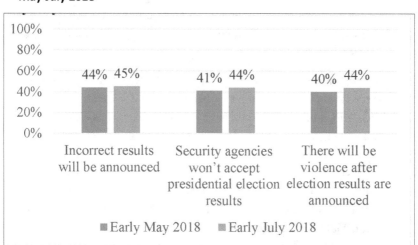

*Respondents were asked:* In your view, how likely is it that: 1. Even after all ballots are counted, an incorrect result will be announced? 2.Security agencies will not accept the result of the presidential election? 3. There will be violence after the announcement of election results?

Whereas participants in the NDI pre-election FGDs of March 2018 were passionate about the need to see free and fair elections in 2018, they felt that this was very unlikely because of Zimbabwe's unenviable record of intimidation. They were also concerned about violence. A few participants made references to the 2008 elections when people had their limbs hacked off:[13]

> I do not think that elections will be free and fair elections because already people in the rural areas were told that if they do not vote for Mnangagwa, they would be beaten. (Masvingo Rural, Male, 25-49 years)

> There will never be a free and fair election because the new president uses force for things to be done in his way, he uses the army. So, he is going to use the army so that the outcome of the election will be in his favour. (Bulawayo Female Vendor, 18-35 years)

Assisted voting was also a focus of uneasiness for some FGD participants who strongly disliked it on the basis that it renders secrecy

---

13 'Wife of Mugabe rival burned alive after having feet hacked off', *Mail Online*, 12 June 2008.

null. Participants felt that the process results in forced voting, hence they considered the process should be confined to the blind i.e. not the elderly in general. Participants opined that any voter who needed assistance should receive it from a person they know or from party agents, not the police or the soldiers.

> For me, the issue of assisted voting makes one vote for someone he or she doesn't like because that person will be scared that whoever is assisting him or her would have known how one has cast the vote. (Mashonaland East Rural, Female, 25-49 years)

> ... it does not guarantee the secrecy of one's vote because certain people will know how you have voted. This will likely cause conflicts after elections and may result in targeted violence. (Manicaland Rural, Male, 18-24 years)

> That is tricky in that the person being assisted will be assisted even in the voting, they will even be told who to vote for. (Bulawayo Urban Female Vendor, 18-35 years).

There was also a broad consensus by participants that chiefs or village heads are politicised because they tell people to vote for a certain party and it was also difficult for one to live in an area if they have different views from the chief or village head. According to these participants, this manifests in traditional authorities distributing food aid on partisan grounds and upon production of a voter registration slip. Furthermore, FGD participants reported that some of the traditional authorities had threatened some people with eviction if they failed to vote to order:

> The chiefs are the major problem as they urge people to support their party ZANU-PF. These chiefs are very influential and they accumulated a following for ZANU-PF. (Masvingo Rural, Male, 25-49 years)

> ...chiefs have their allegiance to a particular political party. Because they support a certain party, they force you to vote for that particular party so that you will receive agricultural inputs and food aid such as potatoes. (Manicaland Rural, Male, 18-24 years)

## Public Opinion on the Zimbabwe Electoral Commission

ZEC is mandated with running Zimbabwe's elections. Discharge of its mandate has always been under the spotlight with its neutrality being questioned because of the way the electoral management body has handled elections. AB surveys show that in 2010, more than 50% of survey respondents were sceptical of ZEC, and of the view that it sacrifices neutrality for partisan interests. In early May 2018 and early July 2018 (31%) and (34%) respectively shared this view (Figure 6.12).

While failing to attract full endorsement, popular trust in ZEC has been on an upward trend over the past decade. In 2010, ZEC recorded the least proportion of adult Zimbabweans who had faith in it with only 31% stating that they trust ZEC 'somewhat' or 'a lot'. This is unsurprising since the electoral management body had superintended the controversial run-off presidential elections in June 2008. In May 2018, 46% of adult citizens said they trusted ZEC 'somewhat' or 'a lot' and in June/July 2018, the proportion rose to 51% (Figure 6.13).

**Figure 6.12: Is ZEC neutral or biased? | Zimbabwe | 2010-2018**

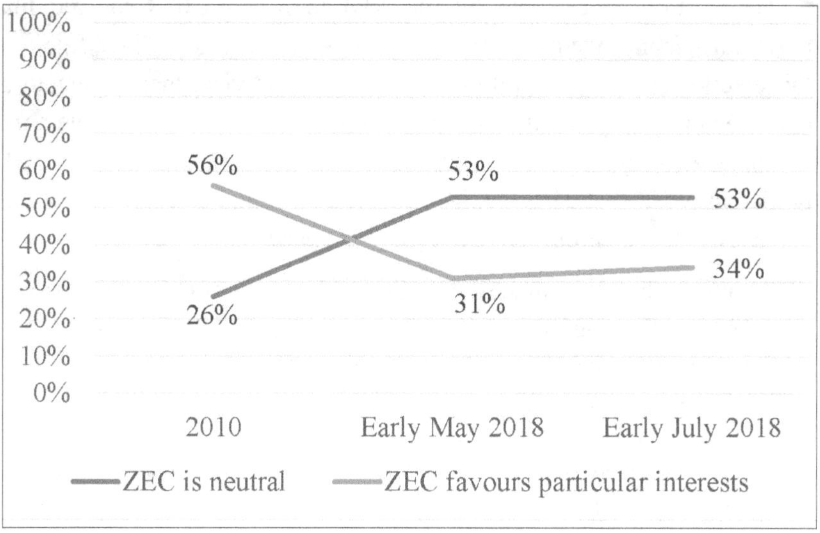

*Respondents were asked:* Which of the following statements is closest to your view? Choose Statement 1 or Statement 2. 1. The Zimbabwe Electoral Commission performs its duties as a neutral body guided only by law. 2. The Zimbabwe Electoral Commission makes decisions that favour particular people, parties or interests.

**Figure 6.13: Trust in Zimbabwe Electoral Commission | 2009-2018**

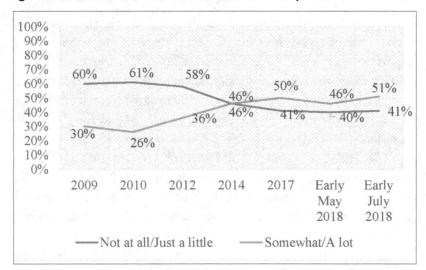

*Respondents were asked:* How much do you trust each of the following, or haven't you heard enough about them to say? (% who said 'not at all'/'just a little' or 'somewhat/a lot').

Pre-election FGDs held by the NDI in March 2018 showed that FGD participants were sceptical of ZEC's capacity to deliver free and fair elections with most participants being of the view that the electoral management body is devoid of independence, citing the electoral commission's history and refusal to announce results. Other FGD participants felt that ZEC is aligned with the ruling party ZANU-PF and is represented by employees from only one party.

> I am not happy with ZEC because in the past, ZEC worked with ZANU-PF to rig elections. I do not know about the current ZEC though; whether it is different or it is still the same old ZEC. (Manicaland Rural, Male, 18-24 years)

> ZEC is referred to as 'ZANU Electoral Commission'. Therefore, the only election that ZEC can administer as free and fair is a ZANU-PF election and not a national election. (Masvingo Rural, Male, 25-49 years)

> There is nothing ZEC can do for us to have a free and fair election, they are not just trustworthy, if they are told what to do, they will just follow orders. (Bulawayo Urban Female Vendor, 18-35 years)

There was also a feeling that the ZEC leadership is compromised given that it is chosen by the president and thus serves at his command. A recurrent message that came from seven of the seventeen FGDs was that the security apparatus is allied with ZEC.

> I do not think so because they work in accordance to the commands of the president, so if the president says let us do this, they will not question it. (Manicaland Rural, Male, 18-24 years)

> It is not independent because it works with people from the Central Intelligence Office. (Masvingo Rural Male, 25-49 years)

> It is not independent for many reasons: First, people say that it is made up of ZANU-PF employees and second, it is made up of war vets, of which they are all ZANU-PF members. (Manicaland Urban, Female, 25-49 years)

For some participants, the electoral management body is not transparent as was made apparent by its failure to explain the issue of photographs or fingerprints during the BVR exercise. Some FGD participants were curious about the resignation of former ZEC Chairperson Rita Makarau:[14]

> ...if it was independent, Rita Makarau would not have resigned. She resigned because she had seen that the people had seen all her rigging tricks and so she decided to quit. (Matabeleland North Rural, Female, 25-49 years)

> With regard to ZEC, I don't have confidence in that organisation because Rita Makarau was appointed to lead that BVR exercise but she resigned midstream and no one has reasons for her resignation. (Midlands Urban, Male, 25-49 years).

However, some participants felt that ZEC is fair and independent and were waiting to see how it would handle the 30 July 2018 elections. They expressed the view that President Mnangagwa wants ZEC to work without fear. Some also applauded the commission for running a good/ credible/ fair BVR process and were optimistic that ZEC could deliver a free and fair election if closely watched:

---

14 ZEC Chairperson Rita Makarau resigned from her post on 9 December 2017 without giving reasons for doing so. Speculation was that she was forced to step down because of her alleged loyalty to deposed president Mugabe and the G40 faction.

ZEC will conduct a great job because I see Mnangagwa as someone who wants to cut all ties with the bad past. ZEC will do a good job without fear because Mnangagwa is on record saying this year people are free to vote for whom they want. (Manicaland Rural, Male, 18-24).

## Fear of political intimidation or violence during election campaigns

Levels of election-related fear in Zimbabwe, while consistently high, have varied dramatically, dropping from a high of 83% in 2009 – a year after the violent June 2008 presidential runoff elections – to 42% in 2014 before climbing back up by ten percentage points in 2017. These figures dropped before the watershed harmonised elections of July 2018, possibly because of the relatively quieter environment (Figure 6.14). However, the proportion of adult Zimbabweans fearful of becoming victims of political violence or intimidation remains alarming.

**Figure 6.14: Trend in fear of political intimidation or violence during election campaigns | Zimbabwe | 2009-2017**

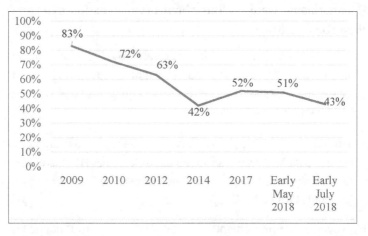

*Respondents were asked:* During election campaigns in this country, how much do you personally fear becoming a victim of political intimidation or violence? (% who say 'somewhat' or 'a lot')

Apprehension over violence was also evident among citizens who took part in the NDI pre-election FGDs of March 2018. These FGDs showed that citizens were concerned about an eruption of violence in the run up to, during and after the July 2018 harmonised elections. Some participants in eleven out of seventeen FGDs expected violence to occur before the elections. Some participants felt that violence was inevitable as party clashes were likely to occur during the campaign:

> I think there will be violence before elections, because Mugabe has started his own party and now there is enmity between the police and the soldiers. And with Mnangagwa and Chamisa contesting a 50/50 election, I think there is potential for violence before the elections happen. (Bulawayo Urban, Male, 18-24 years)

> I think this violence will take place towards the voting period and especially in rural areas. (Chitungwiza Urban, Male, 25-49 years)

In four of the seventeen groups, participants thought that violence would occur on election day. Female FGD participants were more likely to say that violence would discourage them from voting. In fourteen of the seventeen FGDs, it was thought that violence would occur after the elections, especially if the opposition were to win – there was a sense that the army would not yield power. It was also felt that if ZANU-PF were to win, people would inevitably conclude that the election process was rigged.

> I think violence will likely occur after election if Mnangagwa should lose the election. Currently, President Mnangagwa is confident that he will win the election and therefore he will be shocked if he loses. (Masvingo Rural, Male, 25-49 years)

> Violence will come after the elections. It is not possible now to start any violence because they are promising free and fair elections. Perhaps violence will happen after the elections, when they have either won or lost. (Harare Urban Male Vendor, 18-35 years )

## Discussion of political matters

Public opinion surveys show that the Zimbabwe polity consists of three groups, namely those who say (i) they 'never' discuss political matters, (ii) they discuss political matters on an 'occasional' basis and (iii) that they discuss political matters on a 'frequent' basis. In 2009, 23% said they 'never' discuss political matters when they get together with their friends or families, and there was a three percentage points rise to 26% in 2012 and another rise by three percentage points in 2014. The year 2017 witnessed the highest proportion of adult Zimbabweans (41%) who said they never discuss political matters when they come together with their friends or family. However, there was a noticeable decline by seventeen percentage points to a quarter (25%) in May 2018 when the Mnangagwa administration came to power (Figure 6.15). If fear prohibits people from talking about contentious issues, how can citizens participate in the country's political processes?

Afrobarometer surveys conducted in Zimbabwe in January/February 2017 and pre-election surveys of May 2018 revealed that 64% in 2017 and 76% in 2018 claimed that they had to be careful about how they vote 'often' or 'always' (Figure 6.16). This would appear to indicate that citizens are apprehensive of voting and have to do so with caution to avoid unfortunate consequences. The question we cannot avoid is whether citizens freely vote for a candidate of their choice or whether coercion takes over freedom to choose?

## Perceptions of free and fair elections in Zimbabwe

Given ZEC's centrality in the management of elections, citizens'perceptions of how free or fair an election has been is likely to align with their assessments of ZEC. According to the AB surveys, no more than 56% of the population have ever judged a national election as generally free and fair (either 'completely free and fair' or 'free and fair, but with minor problems'). A third (33%) rated the 2013 election as generally free and fair in the May 2018 pre-election poll, down from 48% who rated the same election that way in the 2017 survey.

**Figure 6.15: Discussion of political matters | Zimbabwe | 2009-2018**

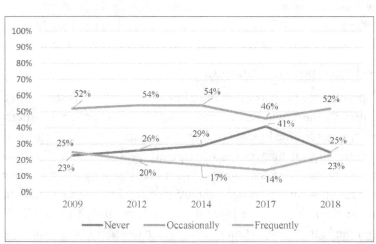

*Respondents were asked*: When you get together with your friends or family, would you say you discuss political matters frequently, occasionally, or never?

**Figure 6.16: Trend in carefulness during voting in elections | Zimbabwe | 2017-2018**

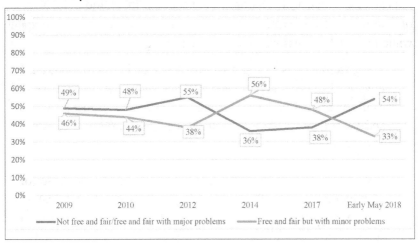

*Respondents were asked:* In your opinion, how often, in this country do people have to be careful about how they vote in an election? Figure 6.17

.**Figure 6.17: Trend in perceptions of freeness and fairness of elections | Zimbabwe | 2009-2018**

*Respondents were asked:* On the whole, how do you rate the freeness and fairness of the last national election?

Asked about the likelihood of free and fair elections in July 2018, most participants who took part in the NDI FGDs of March 2018 expressed scepticism noting that the people running the process are partisan and belong to one political party. In addition to election manipulation, they cited intimidation by chiefs and traditional authorities, and fear of the military which they expected to be violent if ZANU-PF does not win, media bias and partisan food aid.

> I do not think there will be free and fair elections because the leader of ZEC was placed there by the president. (Mashonaland Central Urban Male, 18-24 years)

> ...the first thing is that the opposition political parties are yet to be given space on TV to say whatever they want. (Midlands Urban Male, 25-49 years)

> I have a huge concern; these people are put there to intimidate people in rural areas because they are threatened with the issue of being taken back to war. They are threatened that they will not get agricultural inputs. (Mashonaland Central Urban, Male, 18-24 years)

A few participants were however positive about possibility of free and fair elections pinning their hopes on promises of change as well as the fact that new people were now responsible. There was also a feeling that the eyes of the world were on Zimbabwe and the hope that this would improve the conduct of elections in the country. In addition, the presence of international observers gave hope to some of the FGD participants while the BVR process would eliminate rigging.

> The government is saying it will have free and fair elections, but I think it's just because of the fact that many countries are looking at Zimbabwe and they are just saying that to please the other countries and yet things will be different on the ground. (Masvingo Rural Male, 25-49 years)

> If we take a look at the government, they are making promises of inviting the SADC, Africa Union, EU and anyone else that can to monitor the elections so maybe if this happens there might be a slight change of making things fair. (Harare Urban Male Vendor, 18-35 years)

> This time it can be different because we have different people now. There is Mnangagwa who emphasized that he wanted free and fair elections but, well, since they are the same people, we would not know. (Harare Urban Male Vendor, 18-35 years)

However, for some the hope evaporated. This depressed mood was captured through NDI post-election FGDs conducted in September 2018.[15] Doubt was palpable among participants who raised questions about the way the results had been announced, the delays, accuracy of the results, and concerns about the number of votes vis-à-vis the number of voters:

> The elections were free but not fair because counting took time than ever before; yet in the past election votes used to be counted in a very short space of time, so I think the delays in the counting contributed to the lack of fairness of the elections. (Masvingo Urban, Female, 18-24 years)

> I think, it totally wasn't fair, because the numbers that were being announced, contrasting them with population of where I stay, the announced figures, were way too big, they didn't tally. It wasn't fair, it was just lies. (Bulawayo Urban, Male, 25-49 years)

Some considered that the vote was tilted in ZANU-PF's favour because of threats from headmen as well as distribution of agricultural inputs and food aid on partisan grounds. Others were not happy about threats of war or a repeat of 2008, a media dominated by ZANU-PF and even ZANU-PF's celebrations before the final results had been declared.

## Voting Intentions ahead of July 2018 elections

The two pre-election surveys showed that ZANU-PF candidate Emmerson Mnangagwa had an edge over his main rival Nelson Chamisa. In the May pre-election survey, data showed that Mnangagwa would garner 44% of the vote while his nearest rival, Chamisa of the MDC, would realise 28% of the vote. In the July 2018 pre-election poll, survey data showed that if presidential elections were held tomorrow, ZANU-PF would attract 42% of the vote compared to 31% for the MDC-T (combined Chamisa party and Alliance). Voting intentions of 26% of voters were unknown, thus limiting inferences that could be drawn about the actual state of the presidential race.

Using the NDI pre-election FGDs conducted in March 2018, groups were split about the likely winner of the elections with an overall inclination towards ZANU-PF. Participants who felt that the latter would win the 2018 harmonised elections cited both positive and negative reasons for

---

15 Seventeen FGDs across Zimbabwe. The post-election FGDs were conducted from 12-15 September 2018 in the country's ten administrative provinces

their conclusion. Among some of the reasons cited was that ZANU-PF has a tradition of winning i.e. people were used to voting for the party hence it was obvious that the party would romp to victory. Some of the participants felt that Mnangagwa has made good promises/performed well/will be given a chance to deliver while others cited the rural support/support base as the reason ZANU-PF had an edge over the MDC:

> Yeah, my view is that, they will win through free and fair elections, because there are divisions within other parties. So, ZANU-PF is still one and other opposition parties are becoming many and also there are many independents. So those people's votes will be separated and ZANU-PF will win. (Matabeleland North Rural, Female, 25-49 years)

Other reasons given were that ZANU-PF always rigs elections and had already secured victory because of the issue of serial numbers/BVR questions. That the ruling party would resort to the use of the army in its quest to assert power, and that ZANU-PF would take advantage of the infighting within the MDC camp following the death of Morgan Tsvangirai. Some citizens who saw MDC as a likely winner gave positive reasons for doing so, namely: it is the people's/majority choice, people want change or tired of ZANU-PF, Chamisa and/or the MDC were gaining in popularity. Yet others gave negative reasons including: ZANU-PF infighting/National Patriotic Front splitting vote and ZANU-PF weakening, while a few thought the chances were 50-50; the main question being what the army would do in the event of the MDC romping to victory.

> Based on history they never won freely and with the backup they have, they never win fairly. If MDC wins aaah obvious it will be fair because they don't have inside men who can manipulate the vote for them. (Bulawayo Urban, Male, 18-24 years)

Participants in the NDI pre-election FGDs in March 2018 offered pointers as to what Zimbabweans thought about the two leading presidential candidates ahead of the watershed elections. The FGDs showed that the victorious presidential candidate (Emmerson Mnangagwa) was largely viewed by citizens as an ideal candidate because he was viewed as a good, capable, patient and strategic politician; an individual who had handled his dismissal from government in November 2017 well. Others felt that Mnangagwa deserved the presidency because of the role he had played in removing former President Mugabe from power. Still others thought that he deserved a chance because of efforts to woo international investors under his 'Zimbabwe is Open for Business' banner. There was also a feeling that Mnangagwa is open to communication as shown by his Facebook page.

> His strength is that he is making promises so many people are endearing with him after hearing of the promises, his weakness is that he doesn't fulfill many of his promises. (Midlands Rural, Female, 18-24 years)

> I see him as someone who attracts foreign investors, that's the only thing I can say I know. (Masvingo Urban, Female, 18-24 years)

> I see him as a good person, he looks like someone who is humble because when he was fired from the government and the party and it's not like he is someone who could not take action, but he had to study the situation first, so he is a good person, any person who exercises restraint during very difficult situations is someone who is good. And any good person studies the situation first before taking any action. (Mashonaland East Rural, Female, 25-49 years)

> ...he is a hardworking man and he tries his best to run around. (Midlands Urban, Male, 25-49 years)

His critics cited a failure to fulfil his promises, a lack of tangible achievements (at the time of the research), an ineffective 100 days in office, an absence of new investors, being in government for too long in the company of Robert Mugabe, and a politician with a bad history.

> He has one weakness; I think he is being overshadowed by his past mistakes, so given that he was part of that, people no longer see him as someone who is able to do anything good. (Harare Urban, Female, 18-24 years)

> Mnangagwa's strength is experience in his political career. (Chitungwiza Urban, Male, 25-49 years)

There was also a group of participants who said they didn't know enough about him.

On the other hand, Mnangagwa's main rival, Chamisa[16] was in the

---

16 Nelson Chamisa was appointed to serve as Minister of Information, Communication

eyes of participants 'a good speaker/communicator', 'energetic', 'a man of the people', capable and intelligent. Some participants made reference to his 'good performance in Parliament and as minister' and as someone who appears knowledgeable and can deliver. His 'leadership' qualities were also cited as attractive to some voters while others described him as educated, brave and loyal – beaten, he still stuck with MDC. His young age was also regarded as a major positive factor:

> He has good communicating skills and is loved by the people and he has a charismatic character. (Masvingo Urban Female, 18-24 years)

> His strength is that he is book and streetwise smart. He knows the game; he is courageous because he was elected as a student that time when he was in his first year at college. (Bulawayo Urban Male, 18-24 years)

> His strength is in his ability to talk. He states facts and with courage, he is not afraid of saying what he wants even if he is in front of Mnangagwa or anyone, he says what he wants. (Manicaland Urban, Female, 25-49 years)

FGD participants also felt that the youthful opposition leader is handicapped by a number of weaknesses with most of them inclined to say that he is too young – some described him as politically immature, 'too speedy' and 'thinks too fast':

> ... he is power hungry. He did not wait for himself and other party members to mourn, rather he quickly saw himself as the new leader. (Mashonaland Central Urban, Male, 18-24 years)

> His weakness is that he is too young to rule. (Midlands Rural, Female, 18-24 years)

## After the Harmonised Elections: public evaluation

Through pre-election public opinion polling, adult Zimbabweans spoke about their expectations, apprehensions, and their voting intentions. The 30 July 2018 harmonised elections took place as scheduled and ZANU-PF leader Emmerson Mnangagwa was declared the winner, although he needed the Constitutional Court to uphold his victory. How did citizens

---

and Technology as part of the Government of National Unity (GNU) in Zimbabwe between 2009 and 2013.

evaluate the run-up period to the elections? Generally FGD participants who took part in post-election FGDs organised by the NDI in September 2018 felt that the pre-election period was good or better because they were peaceful/no violence, 'free and exciting', people were free to talk about anything, to support anyone, they were not coerced to go to rallies, there was no intimidation, unlike previous elections when people were afraid to admit to being opposition supporters. There was a perception that all political parties were free to campaign and that people were free to vote for candidates of their choice.

> The atmosphere was very good in the area where I stay because everyone was free to talk whatever he or she wanted. (Midlands Urban, Male, 18-24 years)

> In our area things were all right. There was no intimidation or any fear that we used to witness in the past where we could see that when there was a ZANU-PF rally, everyone would be forced to attend, but this time around people were free to choose what they wanted to do, whether attending or not, they were free to choose. (Harare Urban Female, 25-49 years)

Nonetheless, the election was not without its problems. FGD participants pointed out that in the run up to the elections, there were demands for BVR slip serial numbers by ZANU-PF officials or traditional leaders,[17] political distribution of food/inputs, intimidation to support ZANU-PF/threats to MDC supporters, intimidation after attendance at MDC rallies, limited ability to speak openly, difficulties for the MDC to campaign in some areas and threats from ZANU-PF supporters that an opposition win would not be accepted.

Asked in September 2018 what they thought about a post-election ZANU-PF, some FGD participants spoke glowingly about the ruling party with Mnangagwa being commended for appointing a good Cabinet (see Appendix 1) that had seen the removal of the old guard which was replaced with new technocrats. Some felt that the party was very organised and working hard to strengthen party structures. The Zimbabwe is Open for Business mantra also received support as it was seen as marking a new and positive route to that of the former president, Robert Mugabe. There was also a feeling that the party has many resources and would hang on to

---

17 'New rules and ghost voters threaten Zimbabwe's vote', Mail & Guardian, 19 July 2018.

power for some time. A key message that came out of the FGDs was that the party's future is bright if they can deliver on their promises, bring in investors, and groom younger leaders to take charge of the party.

There were however some participants who predicted that ZANU-PF has a difficult future because it's getting old, can't deliver on its promises and is rocked by party divisions. Worse still, some participants reported that they couldn't see any change as prices rose after the election, while cash shortages went on unabated and joblessness remained rife.

## Depressed public mood post-2018 elections

FGDs conducted by the MPOI in April 2019, showed that Zimbabweans are generally pessimistic about the country's trajectory under the leadership of President Mnangagwa. This arises from government's lacklustre responses to the many challenges engulfing the nation. These include: continuing tension between Mnangagwa and his political arch-rival Chamisa's lack of strategic leadership, shrinking political space, economic challenges, unfulfilled promises, selfishness, lack of shared vision among Zimbabweans, oppression and absence of peace:

> I don't see any right direction by Mr Mnangagwa, just because he used to promise people that fifty thousand jobs are available in the days of his campaigns, but now the unemployment rate is really high, there are no jobs, he only wanted to buy our votes. (Masvingo Rural, Male, 25-49 years)

> I can see that our country is moving towards destruction because Mnangagwa's party has not been able to change anything in this country; things are getting harder and thus causing many problems. (Masvingo Rural, Female, 18-24 years)

FGD participants were also generally downbeat about the country's economic situation indicating that the post-election period in Zimbabwe was far worse than that which obtained before the 2018 harmonised election. Participants bewailed the lack of fuel in the country with supply bottlenecks that have driven fuel prices to unaffordable prices and seriously increased the cost of transport, thus worsening the economic status of an ordinary Zimbabwean. The lack of disposable income, unaffordable basic commodities and a currency that was continuously losing value against the USD, all ranked high among the concerns of ordinary Zimbabweans following the 2018 elections.

Before elections, we had better jobs, money was available but right now because of inflation, our money is useless. (Manicaland Rural, Male, 25-49 years)

Even if I get a dollar that dollar won't be able to buy anything. (Mashonaland West Urban, Female, 18 – 24 years)

Today, even if you get the money, first, it will not buy you anything; it's like useless paper in your hands. (Masvingo Rural, Male, 25-49 years).

Others outlined the challenges in the health sectors: primarily focussing on the costs for accessing health facilities and medication, shortages of drugs in hospitals, and the ballooning costs of education. In summary, participants representing the voice of their peers are calling for government's action in resolving a profound economic crisis:

In terms of health, many people are dying because of lack of medicine as things are not stable because the government sometimes does not have foreign currency to buy medicines. And in hospitals they also experience shortages of medicines, so I see things are bad. (Manicaland, Urban, Female, 18-24 years)

We can no longer afford to pay school fees for our children and hospital bills, there is no treatment that we are getting at the hospital it's either there is no medicine or they will tell you to go and buy at pharmacies. (Mashonaland West Rural, Male, 25-49 years)

Indeed, more depressing still is the fact that participants in this research felt life was better prior to election than it was afterwards. The FGDs revealed a sense of desperation and despondency among participants with citizens feeling that their last hope of a better Zimbabwe was shattered by the outcome of the July 2018 elections: In a sense of desperation, participants had this to say:

I want to say that things have become more difficult for me since the elections. (Mashonaland West Urban, Female, 18-24 years)

It was bad, but it was better (meaning life before election). Things are now worse because time and again things are going up. (Matabeleland South Rural, Male, 25-49 years)

I am not happy with what happened after 2018 elections because before elections in this country, there were price controls during Robert Mugabe's reign. When they used to increase prices even when he was out of the country, by the time he arrives at the airport, all the prices could be reduced to normal rates. (Harare Urban, Female, 18 -24 years)

Asked to make a projection of both the economic and political condition, twelve months from the research period, most participants expressed despond: a few believed that without a change in government and its leadership, prospects of a better future are non-existent. A very few were optimistic, (one participant from Mashonaland West, urban, female group and one participant from Manicaland rural male group) said they were looking up to Yahweh for a resolution to the national crises, with some believing that the current president will work out a better plan for the country.

I see life being difficult for me because previously it was hard for me and up to now it is still hard for me, my family is suffering and there's nothing I can do so I'm seeing the next 12 months, life being hard for me. (Manicaland Rural, Male 25-49 years)

I think it's going to be worse as long as Pfee is there. ED Pfee [ED-in full is Emmerson Mnangagwa-the current President of Zimbabwe, pfee-is a Shona word translated in political terms to mean-being in power] as long as is there it's going to be worse. (Harare Urban Female 18-24 years)

I think the political situation will be worse because there is no unity in the country. MDC, ZANU-PF and other parties should come together to form one party by sharing ideas, with MDC coming in and ZANU-PF coming with their ideas and by so doing things will change for the better. (Harare Urban, Female, 18-24 years)

Things will be good, as with my beliefs all things are controlled by God and the Egyptians suffered for 40 years and we are almost getting there so things may change because it's God who can make it happen, so things may change. (Mashonaland West Urban, Female, 18-24 years)

Macro-economic projections were no different from predictions at micro level. Citizens believed that Zimbabwe's only hope is in reviving its own industries, creating a favourable environment for foreign investment and ensuring stability within its own currency. A few others only hoped for change when the two main protagonists (MDC-A and ZANU-PF) were able to unite and work together. In summary, most participants were doubtful of any meaningful change within the next twelve months. It might not be the right time to sing 'a dawn of a new era has landed'. Zimbabweans felt as if the nation was slowly regressing to life as it was experienced during the hyper-inflationary and violent period of 2008.

> Things are going to get worse than they already are. If no improvement is done in the industries we will remain where we are. (Masvingo Rural, Male, 25-49 years)

> There is going to be economic decline because our currency has only value in this country so it's difficult for trade to flourish given that our money only has value in this country. (Masvingo Rural, Female, 18-24 years)

> Chamisa (Leader of the MDC-Alliance) and Mnangagwa (current president of Zimbabwe) must help each other with ideas on how to run the country so that it is stable because it looks like things are heavier for Mnangagwa on his own. (Masvingo Rural, Female, 18-24 years)

## Public expectations post-2018 elections

Just as it was before the harmonised elections, the most common expectation for Zimbabweans from both the quantitative and qualitative research was job creation. In the September 2018 FGDs, the cry for jobs far outweighed any other call. Engagement with the world, encouraging foreign investors and making sure that cash is available were key demands from citizens:

> I think it will be good if they repair roads and create employment so that the skilled and semi-skilled are absorbed without any form of discrimination. (Masvingo Urban, Female, 18-24 years)

> I am expecting them to fix the economy so that we are able to get money for opening of business and not for them to just operate for 2 minutes and then chase them away. (Manicaland Rural, Female, 18-24 years)

I want president Mnangagwa to ensure that we have cash in the banks, because cash shortage is the major issue. More so, I want him to stabilize prices so that they won't keep rising. (Midlands Rural, Female, 25-49 years)

Nine months after the harmonised elections, (April 2019), the currency issue was the main problem that citizens wanted the government to solve. Other problems included: lack of jobs, absence of price controls, fuel shortages and inadequate supplies of medication in clinics and hospitals. Key to note also was that most of these problems were perceived as tied to the currency issue.

They should fix money issues, then everything will be fine. (Matabeleland South Rural, Male, 25-49 years)

I think that even if they can't change the currency, there is no problem, as long as they can control the prices; I think inflation will be better. (Harare Urban, Female, 18-24 years)

Unemployment and corruption, because it is difficult to secure a job without corruption, if you don't know anyone at a company, there is no job for you. (Manicaland Urban, Female, 18-24 years)

The health sector is more urgent than compensating white farmers. We do not have enough medicine and the public hospitals are in poor shape. (Harare Urban, Male, 25-49 years)

## Public opinion and perceived way forward post-2018 elections

Public opinion post-2018 elections shows that Zimbabweans are weary of the crisis that besets the nation and want both economic and political solutions to the problems bedeviling the nation. One of the most preferred solutions proposed by FGD participants in the September 2018 FGDs was that of dialogue and unity which is understood as a precondition for the country to move forward. Some participants also called for stakeholders to move away from the perpetual election mode, bury political differences and work together. In some FGD groups, mention was made of the need to form a government of national unity while others underlined the need for Mnangagwa and Chamisa to sit down and find a way forward. On the economic front, FGD participants emphasised the need for dealing with corruption, (re-)opening businesses and job creation.

> In my opinion, things can work out if people unite, dialogue regardless of one's political affiliation and if jobs are created we don't want a scenario where people are employed after consideration of political affiliation and need for seed to be distributed to everyone since we are all Zimbabweans and help each other, I see things going on well. (Manicaland Urban, Female, 18-24 years)

> I think that all of us are Zimbabweans, that's the first thing, we are all Zimbabweans, let's forget about politics. All of us should work for the country for it to move forward, and leave politics. (Mashonaland West Rural, Male, 25-49 years)

> I think the best-case scenario is for them to form a GNU because if we look back to 2008-2009 multi-currency came and things started moving forward. (Bulawayo Urban, Female, 25-49 years)

There was also a call for Zimbabwe to have its own currency, and ensure the availability of cash. Similar sentiments were also echoed in the April 2019 FGDs. Indeed, the public has spoken through public opinion on their desires, post-2018 elections.

## Conclusion

This chapter has attempted to define the concept of public opinion which has evolved over time and become an important aspect of democratic practice in the developed world while the same cannot be said of the developing world. It is important to stress that while literature suggests that public opinion plays an important role in the policy cycle and growth of democracy, Zimbabwe's political environment has not proved conducive to the acceptance of the merit of public opinion surveys. Research organisations face a restrictive environment as they go about their business and this does not augur well for critical players whose primary aim is to bridge the gap between ordinary citizens and policy formulators, implementors and evaluators.

In addition, in situations where research organisations are able to collect data and reach the critical phase of dissemination, they also face many profound challenges, more particularly underutilisation of the research data. This normally emanates from attitudinal problems associated with stakeholders. Experience has shown that policymakers in Zimbabwe are skeptical or dismissive of research when it doesn't suit their agenda or world view. To respond negatively or with a closed mind to information provided from the citizens whom a government must serve, is to ignore the potential for democratic growth that is implicit within research surveys.

The significance of public opinion polling cannot be over-emphasised. Pre-2018 and post-2018 election quantitative and qualitative researches conducted by MPOI and its partners brought to the fore key issues affecting Zimbabweans regarding the pre-election environment – their expectations, apprehensions, political values, perceptions of freedoms and voting intentions, etc. After the elections, Zimbabweans have also spoken about their experiences. What the research data tells us is that adult citizens are in anguish because of an unabating socio-economic and political crisis that shows no signs of easing. They have also spoken about what they want for the future of Zimbabwe. The ball is now firmly in the policy makers' courts to act or not on the socio-economic and political issues that affect the general populace as explored through public opinion polling.

## References

Binkley, R.C. (1928) 'The Concept of Public Opinion in the Social Sciences', *Social Forces*, 6/3.

Bratton, M. and E.V. Masunungure (2018) 'Public attitudes toward Zimbabwe's 2018 elections: Downbeat yet hopeful?' Afrobarometer Policy Paper No. 47.

Bratton, M., R. Mattes and E. Gyimah-Boadi (2005) *Public opinion, democracy, and market reform in Africa*. Cambridge: Cambridge University Press.

Bryce, J. (1921) *Modern Democracies*. New York: The Macmillan Company.

Chikwanha, A., T. Sithole and M. Bratton (2004) 'The Power of Propaganda: Public opinion in Zimbabwe'. AfroBarometer Working Paper No. 42.

Chingwete, A.N., and E. Muchena (2009) 'The Quest for Change: Public Opinion and the Harmonised March Elections', in E.V. Masunungure (ed.), *Defying the Winds of Change*. Harare: Weaver Press.

Davison. W. Philips (2017) 'Public Opinion', *Encyclopaedia Britannica*, Available at Key, V.O, Jr. (1961) Public Opinion and Democracy. New York: Knopf.

Pennock, J.R. (1979) 'Democracy Definitions'. - University of Notre Dame.

Ranney, A. (1990) *Governing: An Introduction to Political Science (5th ed.)*. Englewood Cliffs, NJ: Prentice Hall International.

Weale, Albert (1999) *Democracy*. London: Macmillan.

# 7

# Zimbabwe's Media Policy and Regulatory Landscape: A Reflection of the Country's Fluid Politics[1]

Nhlanhla Ngwenya and Tabani Moyo

## 1. Introduction

The normative role of the media in the democratisation of any society cannot be overstated. For there is no doubt that a vibrant media in any democracy informs the public about daily events, and through clarification of issues, helps the public to make informed choices; provokes debate that leads to public participation; scrutinises the role of public officials and investigates abuse of office, etc. But at the same time, the media can also be used to propagate hate and entrench stereotypes as well as demobilise citizens through uncritical assumptions and the support of failed ideologies.[2] If the media within a country is either supine or acts as a puppet, they fail in their role as the Fourth Estate within the political system.

The power of the media has not escaped Zimbabwe's ruling elite, who have been in power since independence from colonial rule in 1980. They have used the media as a conduit for propaganda and as an instrument with which to shape public opinion in their favour, thereby entrenching their hegemonic dominance within Zimbabwe. Their objective has been

---

1  This is an expanded version of our article under the title Zimbabwe's Media Policy: A mirror of politics of the day which appeared on https://medium.com/@the.accent/zimbabwes-media-policy-a-mirror-of-politics-of-the-day-5493e70661d

2  Nyamnjoh (2005).

to inculcate a system of values, attitudes, belief and morality that has the effect of supporting the *status quo* as the natural order of things.

It is against this background that this chapter seeks to underline the fact that while media is an important cog in the democratic well-being of any democracy, the opposite is true for the Zimbabwean ruling class. We will assess the ideological grounding of media-policy formulation in the country and show how that has impacted on the normative role of the media in Zimbabwe's struggle for democracy between 2000 and 2019.

## 2. Political and Socio-economic Environment

As with every sector in Zimbabwe, the media operates within the country and its product is a function of the political and socio-economic environment. It is no secret that since 2000, the country has been in a series of crises. Some have attributed this to a 'crisis of transition' typical of many developing societies[3] while others like Murithi and Mawadza[4] argue that Zimbabwe's problems stemmed from complex political and economic factors that intertwined with national, regional and international factors rooted in both historical and contemporary issues. Whatever the diagnosis, the ramifications of the crises have manifested themselves for all to see. The most evident being the unending political squabbles, themselves a function of the intense intra- and inter-party political contestations for power within the ruling party and the opposition; the erosion of civil, socio-economic and cultural liberties, and the general culture of fear and impunity, which are all a consequence of a dysfunctional state, as noted by Mlambo and Raftopolous (2010). The fluidity of socio-economic and political crisis reached a tipping point on 15 November 2017, when a military coup lead to a change of guard: founding president Robert Mugabe (now late) was replaced by one of the former deputy presidents, Emmerson Mnangagwa. This, according to Moyo (2019), represented an arrested transition, which entrenched *de facto* party-military rule in Zimbabwe rather than offering change in the form of democratic governance and the supremacy of constitutionalism. It is within this context that the media law and policy regulatory framework should be understood as an area of contest between the violent footprints of pre- and post-independent Zimbabwe. This is

---

3    Moore (2003).
4    Murithi and Mawadza (2011).

further articulated by Kagoro[5] who states that Zimbabwe barely achieves a decade without plunging from one crisis to another. Therefore policy formulation in Zimbabwe is located in the contested terrain of power politics, which by extension shapes socio-economic and legal realities upon which Zimbabwe sits.

It is against this background that Mlambo and Raftopoulos (2010) concluded that Zimbabwe was in the 'throes of a severe' pervasive catastrophe, which had turned a once vibrant country into an international pariah and a proverbial basket case. Every year, UNDP's Human Development Index reports on the dramatic deterioration of Zimbabwe's economic and socio-political life. Indeed, since the late nineties, the country has registered declining human development with the worst decline recorded between 2000 and 2019. Accordingly, the World Bank (2019) reports that extreme poverty rose from 29% in 2018 to 34% in 2019, with a total number of 5.7 million people living in abject poverty.

By 2005, the crisis was so severe that it had set the country backwards by about 50 years, to the levels of an individual average income of 1953 in then Southern Rhodesia.[6] Clemens and Moss observed that this alarming decline resulted in Zimbabwe being the only country with such a fast-shrinking economy outside a war situation. They further contend that income losses were even worse when compared to war-torn countries in the sub-Sahara such as Ivory Coast, DRC and Sierra Leone. Annual GDP declined from 7% in 1996 to minus 10% in 2007; the manufacturing sector shrunk by more than 47% between 1998 and 2006 and production in the agriculture and mining sectors also plummeted, among other indicators of economic decline.[7]

The ripple effects of the economic shrinkage resulted in the dramatic decline in the general standard of living, with unemployment levels rising from 50% in 1999 to above 80% in 2009.[8] A decline in service delivery, notably crippling power and water shortages, resulted in the spread of water-borne diseases: 4,288 people died of cholera (out of 98,592 cases) between August 2008 and August 2009 (WHO, 2009). The country also witnessed severe food commodity shortages coupled with hyperinflation which rose to 89.7 sextillion per cent by November 2008, racing past

---

5   'An analysis of Mbeki's trip to Zimbabwe', *Power 98.7*, 17 December 2019.
6   Clemens and Moss (2005).
7   Coltart (2008).
8   Adebajo and Paterson (2011).

Yugoslavia's record inflation rate and only failing to break the record held by Hungary in 1946.[9]

The health sector was not spared. While the Zimbabwean government had demonstrated commitment to improving healthcare in post-independent Zimbabwe with life expectancy rising from 54.9 years in 1980 to 63 years in 1988; increased levels of child immunisation to 81% by 1999, compared to 48% for Sub-Saharan Africa, and a reduced infant mortality rate by 80% to 49 deaths per 1000 by 1988, this record crumbled between 2000 and 2010, as people were faced with a collapsing health delivery system.[10] By 2002, Tren and Bate (2005) note as an example that the immunisation coverage for diphtheria, pertussis and tetanus (DPT) had dropped to 58% and in 2003, life expectancy had fallen by 23 years from its 1985 level to just 33 years. Moreover, although life expectancy had risen to about 47 years in 2010, it remained the fourth lowest in the world (UN, Human Development Index, 2010).

The education sector faced a similar contraction, undoing the successes of the first fifteen years after independence. In 2009, UNICEF research on the education sector graphically captured the collapse. According to their findings, 66 of the 70 schools that the agency visited across the country were abandoned, while in those schools that were operational, only a third of the pupils reported for class. The school attendance rate had dropped from over 80% to about 20%. Due to the introduction of the multi-currency system in 2009 and the payment of a teachers' incentive by parents, itself a response to the state's evident failure to deliver on its responsibilities, schools re-opened with those few pupils who could afford the teachers' subsidies, mainly paid in US currency.[11] To make matters worse, between 2000 and 2010, approximately 45,000 teachers had reportedly left Zimbabwe for better employment opportunities outside the country leaving staffing deficits of 30% across both primary and secondary schools.[12]

By the time 2015 drew to a close, it appeared there was no end in sight for the troubled Zimbabwean economy, with government failing to pay its civil servants and meet other social services needs. Isolated protests organised by groupings and representative bodies of affected civil servants

---

9   Hanke (2009).
10  Tren and Bate (2005).
11  Chisaka (2011).
12  Shizha and Kariwo (2011).

took place but were ruthlessly crushed.

Then on 15 November 2017, the unimaginable happened. President Mugabe was toppled in a military coup and replaced by his former vice president, Emmerson Mnangagwa. This was done with the glaring support of most Western countries, Britain taking a front seat through the visible hand of former Ambassador Catriona Laing. Notably, the military intervention took pace a few days after General Constantino had returned from China where he had gone ostensibly on an official trip. The public's honeymoon, however, was short-lived. On 1 August 2018 and 14 January 2019, the Zimbabwe Defence Forces (ZDF) killed a total of 23 unarmed civilians.[13] The mask of an administration that took power with the promise of reform and a mantra of being 'open for business' fell away, as the government reverted to its default settings of hard-line violence and a militarised state. The coup, despite its promise, gave birth to yet another fragile state, suffering heavily from the crisis of governance and legitimacy.[14]

## 3. The more things change, the more they remain the same

On 30 July 2018, Zimbabwe held its elections against a backdrop of previously contested outcomes following allegations of rigging and manipulation, when the results were consistently won by former president Robert Mugabe and ZANU-PF.

The 30 July elections were thus significant in that Mugabe was no longer a player. Equally significant was that his long-standing nemesis, former Prime Minister Morgan Tsvangirai, was not alive to contest the 2018 elections.[15]

The absence of the two protagonists undoubtedly changed the complexion of the country's politics as Mugabe's successor, Mnangagwa, who stood as ZANU-PF's presidential candidate, promised to break with Mugabe's intransigent politics, stating in his inauguration speech on 24 November 2017 that he would strengthen and ensure the pillars of democracy are respected in Zimbabwe. This raised hope that he would move with speed to implement outstanding socio-economic and political reforms ahead of the 2018 elections.

---

13  NGO Forum (2019).

14  'Back to the future for us: Mnangagwa's false start', *Zimbabwe Independent*, 19 November 2018.

15  Morgan Tsvangirai, the leader of the MDC-T since its formation in 1999, died of cancer on 14 February 2018.

However, it is common cause that the presidential elections took place without any of the envisaged reforms. Worse still, the outcome was yet again disputed with the MDC-Alliance led by Nelson Chamisa mounting a constitutional court challenge, which they lost in the Constitutional Court.[16]

The elections were fuelled by hope. They were supposed to cleanse Zimbabwe of its previously disputed election results, open the country's socio-economic and political democratic space and boost a surge of international goodwill; all of which are necessary to foreign direct investments, and critical if the country's socio-economic ills – characterised by 90% unemployment, corruption, and mismanagement of national resources – are to be overcome. Instead, the 2018 elections produced yet another disputed election at a time when the country began to show all the signs of reliving the 2007-08 hyperinflationary period: acute fuel, foreign currency, drug and food shortages, erosion of incomes, and increases in the prices of basic commodities.

### The media structure in Zimbabwe

There are 157 registered media organisations in Zimbabwe covering the national spectrum through broadcasting, print and online media services, according to the Zimbabwe Media Commission (ZMC, 2019)[17]. However, the news organisations are mainly distributed in the categories of television, radio and print media services. There are two national radio stations, AB Communications' ZiFM and the StarFM, which are owned and controlled by Zimpapers. Further, there are eight provincial commercial radio stations namely: Skyz Metro FM, Bulawayo; Nyami Nyami FM, in Kariba, and Diamond FM, in Mutare; 98.4 Midlands FM, Gweru; Capitalk, Harare; Breeze FM, Victoria Falls; Hevoi FM, Masvingo and YAFM, Zvishavane. Save for Skyz FM, Breeze FM and YAFM, the rest are subsidiaries of the two national commercial stations, while Skyz FM and Breeze FM are owned by the Zimbabwe Election Commissioner Qhubani Moyo, and YAFM is owned by a former ZBC CEO, and former employee in the President's Office, Munyaradzi Hwengwere.

In terms of television, the Zimbabwe Broadcasting Corporation (ZBC) has maintained a statutory monopoly, protected by the law. In addition to the television monopoly, the broadcaster controls four national radio

---

16 'ConCourt releases full 2018 election judgement', *Zimbabwe Independent,* 8 November 2019.

17 The Zimbabwe Media Commission Database of Registered Media Houses (2019).

stations namely: Radio Zimbabwe, Classic 263, National FM and Power FM.

The national print media is dominated by Zimpapers which controls national newspapers and community newspapers respectively. Nationally, the stable publishes two weeklies, the *Sunday Mail* and the *Sunday News*, while publishing *The Herald* and the *Chronicle* as its dailies. It also publishes two tabloids: *H-Metro* and *B-Metro* covering Harare and Bulawayo respectively. Further the table publishes *Kwayedza* and *uMthunywa* catering for two main vernacular languages namely Shona and Ndebele respectively.

The private media is very small, being dominated by a few big players. The Alpha Media Holdings (AMH) publishes two weeklies: *The Standard* and the *Zimbabwe Independent*. It also owns and controls the *NewsDay*, a daily newspaper. On the other hand, the Associated Newspapers of Zimbabwe (ANZ) owns and controls a single weekly, the *Daily News on Sunday* and a single daily, the *Daily News*. Modus publications owns the *Financial Gazette*, a weekly newspaper. AB Communications publishes a single weekly, the *Business Times*. For the purpose of this analysis, our focus will be on the national weeklies and dailies i.e. not the community media, to which the writers only have limited access. (The Zimbabwe Media Commission's database could not establish which ones were operational and which had closed down.)

However, the people of Zimbabwe also receive radio services through Shortwave Broadcasting, especially accessing the Voice of America's country focused broadcasts under the *Studio 7* channel.

## 4. Policy and regulatory framework

While the foregoing synopsis of the country's available media may give an impression of diversity and an enabled democracy, in fact, this is only a veneer for the underlying challenges that the media face in Zimbabwe and the ideology grounding their regulation. The ruling elite, while feigning to democratise the media space by allowing different media voices, has not provided the legislative instruments to protect and promote media freedom, which are essential for the democratic well-being of citizens. Instead, as the country enacted a new Constitution in 2013, which enshrines adequate safeguards for the media, and allows it to play a critical role in nurturing democracy, the state has maintained the laws[18] which erode the rights due

---

18 Access to Information and Protection of Privacy Act (AIPPA) (2002) and The

to the media, and by extension to all Zimbabweans.

Faced with the dramatic economic decline in the aughts, which triggered poor service delivery, itself a breeding ground for public dissent against ZANU-PF, the ruling party adopted a repressive trajectory in a bid to contain swelling opposition. This culminated in government tightening its control of the media in a bid to manufacture consent19 when it enacted or reviewed at least five laws that were all aimed at muzzling the free flow of information though the media while also restricting the spaces on which citizens could dialogue and debate their own issues.

The laws include Access to Information and Protection of Privacy Act (AIPPA) (2002), Broadcasting Services Act (2001), Interception of Communications Act (2007), Public Order And Security Act (2002) and several provisions of Criminal Law (Codification and Reform) Act (2004).

## 5. Rebranding AIPPA

The Zimbabwean government conceded for the first time since the enactment of AIPPA and the BSA that they should be replaced as they are not compatible with the new constitutional dispensation. Appearing before the Parliamentary Portfolio Committee on Media, Information and Broadcasting Services in Harare on 18 February 2016, the then Permanent Secretary for Information, Media and Broadcasting Services, George Charamba, said AIPPA and BSA fall far short of meeting new emerging issues. He outlined the compelling six key emerging issues as:

- need to comply with the new (2013) constitution
- developments in the broadcasting and print sectors
- the macro-technological changes
- changing societal tastes
- the need for conformity to the strategic goals of the nation and convergence of technological and global information factors.[20]

Indeed, Zimbabwe's draconian media laws have reduced the electorate to second-class citizens and the use of repressive laws to silence dissent has left government is isolated by the international community, giving it pariah status.

Following the 2017 election, President Mnangagwa appointed a

---

Broadcasting Services Act (BSA) (2001).
19  Herman and Chomsky (2002).
20  Parliamentary Portfolio Committee on Media Information and Broadcasting Services Report (2016).

new minister, deputy minister and permanent secretary in the Ministry of Information, Publicity and Broadcasting Services and charged them to attend to media laws reforms. However, government-led media law reforms had already commenced in the Mugabe regime when his administration reluctantly buckled to pressure over the alignment of existing laws to the 2013 Constitution, and was working on three Bills to replace AIPPA namely the Freedom of Information Bill (FoI), Zimbabwe Media Commission Bill (ZMC)[21] and the Information/Data Protection Bill.

The lead agent in this process is the Inter-Ministerial Taskforce on Media Law Reforms, which is chaired by the Ministry of Justice and Parliamentary Affairs, targeting two laws for alignment, namely AIPPA and the BSA. However, the current bills that have been gazetted to unbundle these infamous laws are the Freedom of Information Bill and the Zimbabwe Media Commission Bill and, in our view, they are worse than laws that they are supposed to replace, literally freezing the country in a time warp. The third Bill, the Data Protection/Privacy Bill is yet to be gazetted. (Once the Bills have been gazetted, they go to Parliament for public consultations and debate before being passed into law.)

With these infamous laws under the spotlight, there was at first hope for real change. Alas, the more things change the more they remain the same. The people of Zimbabwe are now focussing on the Parliament of Zimbabwe in the hope that it will take its rightful position in applying itself in defence of the Constitution and push back attempts at smuggling in retrogressive laws and clauses more applicable to a dictatorship than a democracy.

Specifically, therefore, Parliament's role is to ensure, through the separated powers, that the bills are surgically broken down detail by detail, so that all provisions in violation of the Constitution are excised.

### 5.1 Background to the media laws

As stated above, the turn of the twenty-first century witnessed the introduction of a number of repressive pieces of legislation in Zimbabwe which, to date, continue to severely curtail the enjoyment and exercise of fundamental civil liberties by its people. Amongst others, these include the Broadcasting Services Act (BSA) in 2001, the Access to Information and Protection of Privacy Act (AIPPA) in 2002, the Public Order and Security

---

21  Cabinet Implementation Matrix (2018).

Act (POSA) in 2002, the Criminal Law Codification and Reform Act in 2005 and the Interception of Communications Act (ICA) in 2007.

These laws, and their arbitrary and selective application and implementation by state authorities since promulgation, have elicited a sustained campaign by media freedom activists, human rights defenders, progressive political activists, and other varied sectors of society for substantial reform, the freeing of the media space, diversification of media products, and protection of information and expression liberties.

In addition to the pressure levelled by civic groups in Zimbabwe for such legislative reform, regional human rights bodies such as the African Commission on Humanand Peoples' Rights (the Commission) have adjudged these laws to be repressive, undemocratic and in violation of the African Charter on Human and Peoples' Rights (the Charter), to which Zimbabwe is a State Party. In its 2002 report, following a fact-finding mission to Zimbabwe, the Commission made strong recommendations on the need for reform of AIPPA and POSA. This was echoed in its 2009 decision in the case of the *Independent Journalists' Association of Zimbabwe vs. Government of Zimbabwe,* in which sections 79 and 80 of AIPPA, were declared contrary to the Charter.

Despite such sustained pressure, the media landscape has not meaningfully developed over the last decade. The print and electronic media continue to be used by political parties to further personal and party-political agendas, score political points and often as propaganda tools – especially the publicly-owned but state-controlled and highly politicised Zimpapers and ZBC.

A number of amendments have been made to these repressive statutes since their promulgation; such changes have nevertheless not been substantive, neither have they been implemented in good faith. The reforms are largely cosmetic and do not address the restrictive aspects of these laws that continue to hinder fundamental rights and freedoms. This lack of progress and liberalisation can largely be attributed to a weak legislature, which has been held hostage to an all-powerful executive reluctant to democratise a legislative environment which currently entrenches their power and keeps the public uninformed and largely directionless.

The aim of this analysis is to measure the impact that these amendments and the new laws that have been introduced have had on the exercise of fundamental media freedoms: freedom of expression and the right to access to information, both of which are protected in the Constitution of Zimbabwe, and all of which the Zimbabwe government is obliged to respect, protect, promote and fulfil in terms of its regional and international obligations.

## 6. Parliament has a duty to protect the Constitution

The foundational and existential role of Parliament is defined in the supreme law of the land through Section 119 (1-3), which reads:

(1) Parliament must protect this Constitution and promote democratic governance in Zimbabwe.

(2) Parliament has the power to ensure that the provisions of the Constitution are upheld and that the state and all institutions and agencies of government at every level act constitutionally and in the national interest.

(3) For the purposes of subsection (2), all institutions and agencies of the State and government at every level are accountable to Parliament.

Parliament, therefore, bears the most complex role in the republic as it is the only institution mandated with the duty to 'protect this Constitution'. The drafters of the Constitution were alive to the narrow interests of power retention by the executive, which would compromise the supreme law. Indeed, this possibility is exemplified in the two sponsored bills that will undermine the Constitution of the land.

Therefore, focus was on Parliament to rise above the narrow polity of the day and uphold the Constitution through the Parliamentary Legal Committee (PLC) and its committee on Media, Information and Broadcasting Services. Over the years, it has shown its ability to close ranks and act in defence of the supreme law of the land, the Constitution.

Furthermore, Parliament has a proactive role through Section 119 (2) that empowers the house to ensure that '... the State and all institutions and agencies of government at every level act constitutionally...' Parliament has the powers to summon anyone in Zimbabwe, except a sitting president, in performing this right

Having established the foregoing, it is critical to note that both Bills are beyond the reach of the constitutional litmus test. With regards to the FoI Bill, the following issues are of concern:

Though the Bill makes marginal improvements to the current access to information regime under AIPPA and other various sectoral laws, much work needs to be done before it reaches the standards set out in Section 62 of the Zimbabwe Constitution as well as in the African Union's Model Law.

The Bill has no specific provisions in terms of the minimum requirements for information officers. While this might be governed by each public or private entity in respect of the skills set, it would be prudent to have some generic minimums that such individuals should possess.

The fact that the Zimbabwe Media Commission has a duty to 'ensure that the people of Zimbabwe have fair and wide access to information,' does not justify making it the guardian of the right to access information in Zimbabwe. The Bill's Memorandum rightly states the Zimbabwe Human Rights Commission is the guardian of human rights in Zimbabwe, including the right to access information. Therefore, the ZHRC should be the Commission responsible for the monitoring and enforcement of this Bill.

Sections 243(1) (a) – (d) of the Constitution sets out the functions and duties of the ZHRC. These duties are already wide enough to cater for the protection and promotion of the right to access information as set out in this Bill. There will, therefore, be no need to amend the Zimbabwe Human Rights Commission Act or grant any extra duties to the ZHRC in order for it to monitor the promotion and enjoyment of the right to access information in terms of this law.

It will only be necessary to ensure that the ZHRC is well resourced in terms of funding and is equipped for this work through the appointment of commissioners that have knowledge about the access to information laws and processes.

Voluntary disclosure has over the years not worked with public bodies, let alone private bodies. There is need to reconsider this approach and put in place mechanisms that promote proactive disclosure of information from public bodies.

The discretionary powers of information officers must be prescribed and guided according to the constitutional principles on the right to access information. The period of deferment under Section 11 (2) (c) needs to be specified or at least to be consistent with the timelines for responses to information request. The information officer is currently given power to determine that period, which might create arbitrage.

It is therefore recommended that the Bill only repeal those parts of AIPPA that relate to access to information. As it stands, Section 41 of the

Bill seeks to repeal AIPPA in its entirety; this will mean that there will be gaps in terms of legislation that regulates the protection of personal information and privacy in Zimbabwe.

On the other hand, the following concerns about the ZMC Bill are paramount:

In its present state, the ZMC Bill, with its the significant flaws, could further undermine the media's operating environment. The current bill has two major omissions: the first on the relationship between the ZMC and any other self-regulatory mechanisms; the second is in relation to the ZMC's responsibilities to promote access to information as set out in Sections 18 and 35 of the current Freedom of Information Bill.

The first omission relates to the possibility of a hybrid regulation of the media landscape as clearly set out in Section 249 (3) of the Constitution. The promulgation of a new media law in the form of a Zimbabwe Media Commission Act provides Zimbabwe with an opportunity to migrate from the current State Regulation/ Dual Regulation model to a co-regulatory regime whereby the internationally respected self-regulatory mechanism would be enhanced with the co-operation of the State.

Sections 18 and 35 of the Freedom of Information Bill currently identify the Zimbabwe Media Commission as the Commission responsible for the monitoring and exercise of the right to access information in Zimbabwe. The current version of the Zimbabwe Media Commission Bill is silent on how the Zimbabwe Media Commission will handle these additional functions assigned to it by the Freedom of Information Bill.

In addition to the above, and in the spirit of ensuring that the Bill is more closely aligned to the letter and spirit of Section 61, 248, and 249 of the Constitution, we observe that there is need for a holistic approach towards assessing all the sections that are in violation of the charter.[22]

Expectations are high that Parliament will fulfil its role without fear or favour as it is (a) the last frontier in defending the Constitution, and (b) it should enable the populace a voice through a consultative process. Both are critical for an institution with an existential mandate to defend and strengthen the Constitution. It should be noted that the Ministry of Information Publicity and Broadcasting Services consulted the media stakeholders, but it 'forgot' to capture their views in the draft, resulting in the executive sponsoring unconstitutional Bills to Parliament.

---

22 See Appendix 1 – Sections of the ZMC Bill that are in violation of the constitution as of March 2020

Almost twenty years ago, the late Dr Edson Zvobgo, then chairperson of the PLC, which was vetting AIPPA on its compliance to the Constitution, stated that:

> ... This Bill, in its original form, is the most calculated and determined assault on our liberties guaranteed by the Constitution ... what is worse, the Bill is badly drafted in that several provisions were obscure, vague, overbroad in scope, ill-conceived and dangerous ...

Twenty years on, Zimbabwe is again calling on the Parliament of Zimbabwe to rise above party polity, as Zvobgo and his team once did. Parliament should be encouraged by the United Nations' official endorsement of 28 September, the International Day for Universal Access to Information, to push back unconstitutional bills and recommend the current administration to domesticate the international instruments to which it is signatory, thereby strengthening the country's institutions of democracy, reads:

> In its Proclamation dated 30 September 2019, the UN re-affirmed the 2030 Agenda for Sustainable Development and the commitments therein to promote peaceful, inclusive societies to spur development of which access to information is a key ingredient.
>
> This can be achieved by ensuring unfettered public access to information and the protection of fundamental freedoms in line with national legislation, international agreements and best practice.[23]

## Information/ Data Protection Bill

At the time of writing, the text of the Information/Data Protection Bill was yet to be shared with the stakeholders as the Ministry of Media Information and Broadcasting Services and the Ministry of Information Communication Technologies were wrestling with each other over who should control the same.

Policy is following the politics of the day. The ruling party is locked into its default settings: militancy, violence, disproportionate responses to challenges on the ground, and policy inconsistency, while affecting to free the media. So, the law-making process is grounded. What is likely to finally emerge from this process is the re-packaging of AIPPA under three

---

23 'Statement on UN Proclamation on International Day for Access to Information 2018'. MISA Zimbabwe, 18 October 2019.

new equally proscriptive legal entities.

## 6. Open for business, but not for broadcasting!

The Broadcasting Services Amendment Bill is a highly contentious Bill (as of June 2019), which is supposed to make changes to the existing Broadcasting Services Act, which regulates broadcasting services in Zimbabwe. Several controversial issues could very well cripple the broadcasting industry in Zimbabwe if not remedied.

The first is the amount of foreign funding and/or ownership a local radio or television station can receive. According to the current Bill, foreign ownership in a local broadcasting service provider cannot exceed 20%. This is problematic because broadcasting by its nature is a capital intensive industry. Insisting that local funding should make up at least 80% of the capital will mean that broadcasting services will be challenged to raise adequate operational capital.

Secondly, the Bill prohibits donations of either equipment or funding to broadcasting services. Yet, in the main, community radio stations cannot do without such support. For example, a church-based organisation cannot donate radio broadcasting equipment to a local community for the purpose of setting up a religious or faith-based community radio station. Such restrictions are an indirect way of curbing would-be radio and television entrepreneurs from establishing their own broadcasting services. We therefore contend that there is need to allow foreign entities to fund the establishment of broadcasting services in Zimbabwe. As the industry develops and becomes more self-sustaining, government can always reduce the amount of foreign ownership in local ventures, if it continues to see these as a threat.

The Bill also seeks to maintain the structure and stature of the BAZ which has through its behaviour shown that it operates at the mercy of the Ministry of Information, Media and Broadcasting Services rather than being an independent regulator. Yet again, another pointer that policy follows the politics of the day in Zimbabwe.

## 7. It's the politics stupid!

A closer analysis of the evolution of media regulation in Zimbabwe expose the main reasons behind the media's failure to attain their true stature as key catalysts to democracy in Zimbabwe. For example, in February 2000, the then Information Minister, Chen Chimutengwende, complained in *The*

*Herald*, a state-run newspaper,[24] that the media's operating environment was 'too relaxed' and that such state of affairs has allowed 'the penetration of media organisations with a political agenda to destroy the government and country'.[25] He added: 'We are not living in normal times... there is a fierce battle for the hearts and minds in Zimbabwe and we just have to win it'.[26] And true to the prediction, a frenzied law-making spree ensued resulting in arrests of dozens of under the above stated laws.

Even as Parliament cautioned the executive against adopting undemocratic laws that impinged on citizens' fundamental rights, it appeared the die was cast. For instance, despite the PLC's adverse submissions on AIPPA, during which the chair of the committee described the law as the 'most calculated and determined assault on our liberties' while questioning the rationale behind government's demand 'in a democratic and free society to require registration, licenses and ministerial certificates in order for people to speak', the law was still forced through Parliament and enacted in 2002.[27]

Less than two years after the enactment of the law government's most radical critic, the *Daily News*, which by September 2003 had become the most popular news outlet, was forcibly closed using the same Act. Three other private papers faced a similar fate, buttressing the view that the law was an instrument used to erode the media space by closing all platforms that provided a counter hegemonic narrative.

The fact that there were almost no convictions of journalists who had been arrested only betrayed the precise reasons for such legislation, which was the very antithesis of the country's claims to upholding democratic principles.

This hardline stance was predicated on three main pillars, all interrelated and anchored on the power retention matrix: control, siege mentality and self-preservation. The first included, the freezing of the airwaves; annihilation of channels of criticism and spaces for activism while setting the agenda and entrenching hegemony through controlling the public sphere. The second involved inculcating a siege mentality by relentlessly projecting though domineering state media outlets the idea

---

24 'Government proposes measures to clamp down on independent press; President lashes out at the private media', MISA, 10 February 1999.

25 Ibid.

26 PLC Report (2002).

27 Minutes of the ninth meeting of the Parliamentary Legal Committee held on Wednesday 23 January 2002 in room 305.

that the country's sovereignty was under threat by the West. The third entailed preservation of the ruling elite, who were sold to Zimbabweans as the best custodians of their democratic and developmental aspirations as enunciated in the ethos of the country's liberation struggle. Any alternative was thus presented as neo-colonial, treasonous and a threat to Zimbabwe's political and socio-economic fibre. These reasons – singularly and or collectively – became the mould for legislative framework at a time when ZANU-PF battled for survival.

## 8. Bombed into silence

Apart from the use of controversial laws to justify shutting down the media, extra-legal means also took root. This saw the wanton beating of journalists working in the private media by (mostly) ZANU-PF activists and government supporters aggrieved at the private newspapers' criticism of their favoured party; torture of journalists, and bombing of private media premises. The culprits, who were often known, enjoyed a culture of political impunity. The first indication of the extent to which suspected state functionaries would go in using extra-judicial means to silence the media was in 2000, when the *Daily News* offices were bombed in the central business district of Harare after several government officials and their supporters criticised the paper's coverage of political violence in the run-up to 2000 parliamentary elections. A second and more powerful blast wrecked the paper's printing press the following in January 2001.[28] This followed the then Information Minister Jonathan Moyo's remarks that it was only a matter of time before Zimbabweans put a stop to what he called the newspaper's 'madness'.[29] A third bomb targeted the paper's Bulawayo offices in February 2002.[30] In August 2002, another bomb exploded in the Harare studio of the Voice of the People radio station (Radio VoP), which broadcasts locally produced programmes via a Radio Netherlands transmitter in Madagascar.[31] No one has ever been charged. Neither has there been any update on the progress (or not) of the investigations. Between the bombs, several foreign correspondents and journalists were either deported or barred from entering Zimbabwe.[32] Pro-ruling ZANU-PF militias seized numerous copies of private newspapers; journalists and

---

28  'Bombs wreck Zimbabwe Newspaper printing press', *The Telegraph*, 29 January 2001.

29  'Zimbabwe newspaper bombed', *BBC News*, 28 January 2001.

30  Ibid.

31  'Zimbabwe: Radio Station bombed', *allAfrica*, 30 August 2002.

32  MISA Zimbabwe (2015).

readers of these papers were assaulted and detained, and the private press was effectively banned from circulating in ZANU-PF strongholds.

## 9. Hostile buy-outs

The concerted efforts to capture the media and thereby control the public sphere as political tensions rose assumed another sinister dimension after the controversial 2002 presidential elections, which ZANU-PF won amid widespread allegations of rigging, with reports of the country's secret service, the Central Intelligence Organisation (CIO), had acquired a controlling stake in the now defunct Zimbabwe Mirror Newspapers Group, publishers of *The Daily Mirror* and *Sunday Mirror*.[33] Newspaper reports linked two of the group's shareholders – Unique World Investments and Zistanbal, which together own 70% of the company – to the CIO. The then central bank governor, Dr Gideon Gono, had a stake in Unique World Investments. Gono was also reported to be the owner of the weekly *Financial Gazette* through the paper's main shareholder Octadew Investments.

This left the *Zimbabwe Standard* and *Zimbabwe Independent* as the only newspapers in the country in between 2003 and 2008 that were not controlled or linked to the state or members of the ruling party.

## 10. An illusion of reform

The formation of a coalition government in 2009 following the signing of the Global Political Agreement saw the easing of inter-party tensions over contestation for power. Among a host of issues the ruling parties agreed to address was the opening up of the media. They agreed the following:[34]

(a) the government shall ensure the immediate processing by the appropriate authorities of all applications for re-registration and registration in terms of both the Broadcasting Services Act as well as the Access to Information and Protection of Privacy Act;

(b) all Zimbabwean nationals including those currently working for or running external radio stations shall be encouraged to make applications for broadcasting licences in Zimbabwe, in terms of the law;

---

33 'Mediagate – the big plot', *Zimbabwe Independent*, 13 April 2006.
34 Article 19 of the Global Political Agreement signed in 2008 by the three parties, ZANU PF, MDC-T and MDC led by Arthur Mutambara.

(c) in recognition of the open media environment anticipated by this Agreement, the Parties hereby:

i) call upon the governments that are hosting and/or funding external radio stations broadcasting into Zimbabwe (Shortwave Radio Africa, Voice of the People and the Voice of America) to cease such hosting and funding; and

ii) encourage the Zimbabweans running or working for external radio stations broadcasting into Zimbabwe to return to the country;

(d) steps be taken to ensure that the public media provides balanced and fair coverage to all political parties for their legitimate political activities; and,

(e) the public and private media shall refrain from using abusive language that may incite hostility, political intolerance and ethnic hatred or that unfairly undermines political parties and other organisations. To this end, the inclusive government shall ensure that appropriate measures are taken to achieve this objective. Upon signing the GPA, a column written under the pseudonym Nathaniel Manheru, allegedly run by the president and government spokesperson George Charamba, temporarily ceased penning its polarising and hatred-laden opinions on 21 February 2009 in compliance with the provisions of the GPA. Unsurprisingly, it bounced back with vicious attacks on the opposition, civil society and private press within a month.[35]

The underlying political motives to the agreement are obvious. They are intended to give an impression of reform while entrenching the same regulatory framework that led to the decimation of the media in the first place. It was hardly surprising that save for the licensing of several newspapers very little progress was made in comprehensively democratising the media space in the four-year tenure of the coalition government. This is because most of the key objectives were used as political bargaining chips by the ZANU-PF component of government to extract more concessions from the two MDCs.[36] Even the most visible milestone of the coalition government, the licensing of newspapers, came as a result of political compromises by the parties and their behind-the-scene horse-trading on the Constitution of

---

35 'Zimbabwe: Fare Thee Well, Manheru', *allAfrica,* 2 March 2009. See also MMPZ (2009).
36 Mukundu and Ngwenya (2013).

the Zimbabwe Media Commission.[37] One of the negotiators from ZANU-PF, Patrick Chinamasa, laid bare the toxic politics that characterised the reform agenda, even as the ruling parties appeared to be driven by a democratic ethos. Expressing his party's displeasure with the exclusion of one of the individuals it had nominated to sit on the ZMC, he called on his political counterparts to 'negotiate on the basis of the political realities...' given that '...we are...political animals with political biases'.[38]

However, despite the politicisation of media reforms, the ZMC managed to grant licenses to scores of media houses somewhat changing the country's media landscape.[39] These include mainstream daily newspapers, entertainment and professional magazines and community newspapers, among other media production houses. However, most of the media houses have struggled to stay afloat due to harsh operating environment. And those that have survived have limited reach as they are largely found in commercial centres dotted along the highways adjoining the country's major towns. As a result, the majority of people in the rural areas are left outside the information ring.

## 10.1 Newspapers

More than 70 publishing licenses have been granted by the ZMC since its formation in 2009. However, though this cast the country as having a diverse print media industry, the print news market is dominated by three main publishing houses. These include the Zimbabwe Newspapers (1980) Ltd, which has four daily papers and at least three weeklies; Alpha Media House (AMH), which publishes one daily and two weeklies. The other big player is the Associated Newspapers of Zimbabwe (ANZ), the publishers of the *Daily News*, the *Weekend Post* and *Daily News on Sunday*. The Modus Group, publishes a single newspaper, *The Financial Gazette*. The rest of the print media comprise small publications that range from fashion and sport magazines to small private community newspapers circulating in small provincial towns. However, some of the provincial newspapers are published infrequently as they also battle with sustainability challenges.

## 10.2 Radio stations

There are currently fourteen licensed FM stations in the country. Four are run by the state-run broadcaster, Zimbabwe Broadcasting Corporation

---

37  Ibid.

38  'Zimbabwe Media Interviews – Parliamentary Committee Under Fire', *The Herald*, 5 August 2009.

39  ZMC Database (2019).

(ZBC), two are owned by private entities affiliated to the state, the remaining eight are provincial commercial stations, of which only two had started broadcasting by early 2016. There are no licensed community radio stations in the country. There are also three exiled stations broadcasting into Zimbabwe from their foreign bases: SW Radio Africa; Radio VoA and Studio 7, all of which were forced to broadcast from outside Zimbabwe by the severe restrictions on establishing a radio station in the country. These three stations have become a feature of the Zimbabwean media terrain. And due to their popularity especially in the rural areas, the police have in the past swooped on citizens who owned short-wave radio sets distributed by civil society organisations in a bid to curtail access to the stations' content.[40] However, this has not deterred the stations as they have sought to leverage the ICTs to expand their reach. The stations and other community radio initiatives that are awaiting licensing are broadcasting through a free-to-air satellite platform dubbed ChannelZim, taking advantage of the increased use of the free-to-air decoders by ordinary Zimbabweans.

### 10.3 TV stations

The country only has one TV station run by the state-controlled ZBC. There has also been a steady increase in the number of those accessing satellite TV. The increase has been attributed to the low quality, poor programming and propaganda oriented state-controlled radio and television company.[41]

### 10.4 Online media and bloggers

Blogging in Zimbabwe has been on the rise with a number of Zimbabweans creating their own blogs to tell their own stories in a country where the dominant voices in the news are those of public and government figures. Apart from blog sites, there are also several online publications that have become vital sources of alternative information for Zimbabweans, especially those who live in the diaspora. These mainly include *ZimLive. com, ZimMorningPost.com; New Zimbabwe.com; Zimeye.org; Nehanda Radio; MyZimbabwe; zimdiaspora.com; herZimbabwe.com; bulawayo24. com; thezimbabwemail.net* among a host of other online publications. All the mainstream media also have functional websites which are interlinked with the their social media pages.

### 10.5 Internet access

Zimbabwe's mobile and internet penetration rates continue to rise as millions get connected. According to the regulator, POTRAZ,[42] as at the third quarter of 2019, a total number of 12.9 million active mobile subscriptions increased compared to 12,394,383 subscriptions as of 2015. While the number of internet subscriptions at a record 8,577,936 compared to 5,815,518 subscribers in 2015. Likewise, the internet penetration rate is pegged at 58.9% compared to 44.5% recorded in the first half of 2015. This growth has largely been catalysed by the increase in the number of people with access to mobile phone technology; duty-free importation of ICT gadgets; increased investment in the communication infrastructure.

## 11. Lingering political controls

Despite some progress made in trying to open up the media space such as the licencing of new publications which include but are not limited to the *NewsDay, Southern Eye, Daily News on Sunday;* new commercial radio stations under AB Communications and Zimpapers stables respectively, political controls linger, reducing all that has been done into quantitative reforms. Government is still to fully comply with provisions of the 2013 Constitution, enjoining it to promote and safeguard media freedom, freedom of expression as well as ensure independence of the media it controls.[43] To make matters worse, rather than adhere to the constitutional provisions, government announced in 2015 that it is in the process of drafting a law that will regulate the use of the internet under the guise of preventing cybercrimes.[44] While such a law will not be unique to Zimbabwe but in line with international practice, it is the ostensible political motivation that discredits the intention. The announcement followed disquiet over the faceless blogger, Baba Jukwa, who appeared to be posting on Facebook, information that reflected badly on the ruling elite ahead of 2013 elections. So popular was the blogger that at its peak the page commanded more than 400,000 followers.

Following the eruption of ZANU-PF succession wars which saw the ouster of the then Vice-President Joice Mujuru and other veteran party leaders on 2 April 2015, government was quick to blame the media and warned that it would descend on the private news outlets, all in a bid to contain the ugly conflict. In an elaboration of the remarks made by his Minister, Chris Mushohwe, a few days previously, Information Secretary George Charamba was quoted in *The Sunday Mail*[45] openly threatening to tighten the media space:

---

43   MISA Zimbabwe (2016).
44   'POTRAZ seeks to curb cyber crimes', *The Herald,* 15 April 2015.
45   'Media and a channel of noise: An interview with Information Secretary George Charamba', *The Sunday Mail,* 11 October 2015.

I will recommend most effective ways of controlling errant behaviour in the newsroom. So you will have a piece of legislation that seeks to restrain rather than to enable media practices... Don't feel unfairly treated when the hammer descends on you because *wada mabrickbats* [you invite brickbats] yet you are staying in a glass house.

However, these threats should not be viewed in isolation. They merely reflected the ruling party's thinking with regards media regulation, which simply demonstrated its enduring paranoia about free flowing information especially when it felt threatened.

Ahead of its 2015 Annual Conference, the ZANU-PF Central Committee recommended a tougher approach in handling the private media and non-governmental organisations. It stated:

> The private media and pirate radio stations are used to spread falsehoods. The party should, therefore remain vigilant and implement appropriate strategies to protect Zimbabwe. Activities of non-governmental organisations should also be monitored as they continue to represent the interests of the West... The machinations of the West to undemocratically unseat Zanu PF will continue. The party security machine should be ready to deal decisively with those that are bent on subverting our hard won independence and sovereignty.[46]

## 12. Conclusion

The foregoing discussion demonstrates that legislation and regulation of the media in Zimbabwe have never been about adequately safeguarding the media space or engendering its key role in promoting democracy. Instead, its motives are to maintain the political status quo while ensuring that those whose voices are critical of the ruling elite remain muffled. While this chapter offered a brief summary of the period between 2000 and 2019, it will be a misrepresentation of the history of the media in Zimbabwe if it were read in isolation; it should rather be understood as a continuum of media evolution from independence in 1980. Ferreting through archival documents on the media soon thereafter will reveal the fixation of the ruling class with controlling the media space for self-preservation. Of course, each of the four decades of post-independent

---

46 'Zanu PF threatens to crush media', *Zimbabwe Independent*, 18 December 2015.

Zimbabwe has given rise to a few independent voices, but these have served more as symbolic gestures, a disguise to give the impression that that the government supports a democratic society and a free press. The reality is very different.

# References

Adebajo, A. and M. Paterson (eds) (2011) 'State Reconstruction in Zimbabwe'. Cape Town: UCT Centre for Conflict Resolution.

Chisaka, B.C. (ed.) (2011) 'State of the Zimbabwean Education Sector in the 21st Century'. Harare: Human Resources Research Centre.

Clemens, M. and T. Moss (2005) 'Costs and Causes of Zimbabwe's Crisis'. Washington, DC: Center for Global Development.

Coltart, D. (2008) 'A Decade of Suffering in Zimbabw: Economic Collapse and Political Repression under Robert Mugabe'. Washington, DC: Cato Institute Center For Global Liberty and Political Analysis.

Hanke, S.H. (2009) 'R.I.P Zimbabwe Dollar'. Washington, DC: Cato Institute.

Herman, E.S. and N. Chomsky (2002) *Manufacturing Consent: The Political Economy of the Mass Media*. New York: Pantheon Books.

MISA Zimbabwe (2014) 'Citizens or Subjects - An investigation into the impact of current Media Laws on Zimbabweans' freedom of expression and other related freedoms'. Harare: MISA Zimbabwe.

————— (2015) 'Reporting in the Line of Fire: Media under Siege'. Harare: MISA Zimbabwe.

————— (2016) 'State of the Media Report: 2015'. Harare: Misa Zimbabwe.

Mlambo, A. and B. Raftopoulos (2010) 'The Regional Dimension of Zimbabwe's multi-layered crisis: An Analysis'. Paper presented to the conference, 'Election processes, liberation movements and democratic change in Africa', Maputo.

MMPZ (2009) 'The Language of Hate: Inflammatory, Intimidating and Abusive Comments of Zimbabwe's 2008 Elections'. Harare: Media Monitoring Project Zimbabwe.

Moore, D. (2003) 'Zimbabwe's Triple Crisis: Primitive accumulation, nation-state formation and democratization in the age of neo-liberal globalisation', *African Studies Quarterly*, 7/2,3.

Moyo, J.N. (2019) *Excelgate: How Zimbabwe's 2018 Presidential Election was stolen*. Harare: SAPES Books.

Mukundu, R. and N. Ngwenya (2013) 'So near yet so far: The tragedy of media reforms since the GPA'. Johannesburg: OSISA.

Murithi, T. and A. Mawadza (eds) (2011) *Zimbabwe in Transition: A view from within*. Johannesburg: Institute for Justice and Reconciliation.

NGO Forum (2019) 'The New Deception: What has changed?' Harare: Zimbabwe Human Rights NGO Forum.

Nyamnjoh, F.B. (2005) *Africa's Media: Democracy and the Politics of Belonging*. London: Zed Books.

POTRAZ (2015) 'Abridged Postal and Telecommunications Sector Performance Report. Third Quarter 2015'. Harare: Postal and Telecommunications Regulatory Authority of Zimbabwe.

Shizha, E. and M.T. Kariwo (2011) *Education and Development in Zimbabwe: A Social, Political and Economic Analysis*. Rotterdam: Sense Publishers.

Tren, R. and R. Bate (2005) 'Despotism and Disease: A report into the health situation of Zimbabwe and its probable impact on the region's health'. Johannesburg: Africa Fighting Malaria.

World Bank (2019) 'An overview of the Zimbabwean Context'. Washington, DC: World Bank.

# 8

# The Security Sector:
# The Elephant in the Room?

## Pedzisai Ruhanya

## Background and context of Zimbabwe's long history of military politics

The war of liberation in the 1970s charted the political future of Zimbabwe. The two military groups which led the war – Zimbabwe People's Revolutionary Army (ZIPRA) affiliated with Zimbabwe African People's Union (ZAPU) and the Zimbabwe African National Liberation Army (ZANLA) affiliated with the Zimbabwe African National Union (ZANU) – formed the foundation of the Zimbabwean army. The two political movements, ZAPU and ZANU, dominated the political scene after independence in 1980 and eventually merged into one party called the Zimbabwe African National Union – Patriotic Front (ZANU-PF) in 1987.[1] The war of liberation was articulated as the main source of political legitimacy, as the majority of the political elite participated in the armed struggle. Robert Mugabe himself was the President of ZANU and overall leader of the armed guerrillas. His vice-president, Mnangagwa, now president of both party and state was also a member of the ZANLA forces, although his 'struggle credentials' were questioned during the political campaign against him led by Mugabe's wife, Grace, before the first family

---

1   Between 1982 and 1987, over 20,000 PF-ZAPU supporters were massacred by the security forces, mainly in Matebeleland and Midlands Provinces. This put pressure on the party leadership to agree a settlement to save their supporters form further elimination.

was toppled by a military coup in November 2017. It is clear, therefore, that since independence the military has played a major role in the political and electoral affairs of Zimbabwe.

Zimbabwe became a majoritarian democracy in 1980 at the end of a bitter war of independence triggered by the Unilateral Declaration of Independence by Ian Smith's Rhodesia Front in 1965. From 1980, in all of the independence elections, in 1985, 1990, 1995 and 1996, the ruling ZANU-PF enjoyed huge mandates from the electorate, arguably on the basis of its liberation credentials.[2] Such political legitimacy through elections also meant that the newly established Zimbabwean government had huge responsibilities and the expectations that it would democratise state institutions, including the news media, to reflect the new political dispensation, (Ruhanya 2014). However, at the beginning of the aughts, Zimbabwe was grappling with deep political and economic crises which were, amongst other things, a result of the failed structural adjustment programmes implemented in 1990, corruption, attempts to impose a one party-state, involvement in regional war in the Democratic Republic of Congo in 1998, democratic deficits and rising poverty among the working class, student and workers' strikes, and civil society organisations calling for constitutional reforms (Saunders 2000; Hammar and Raftopoulos 2003), Raftopoulos and Sachikonye (2001: 145) posit that there were workers strikes from the late 1980s as a response the state's attempts to weaken the organised and restive unions through deregulation, and to the deteriorating impoverishing effects of economic liberalisation programmes. Faced with such challenges, ZANU-PF and government responded with some undemocratic measures that targeted labour unions, opposition political parties and the opposition press in order to maintain his political grip on power. Through a raft of legal and extra-legal measures, the state sought to suppress dissent. These autocratic measures surprised many as they were inconsistent with the ethos and values of the former liberators, and they galvanised others to democratically challenge the independence heroes.

Mustapha and Whitefield (2009: 216) observed that in Zimbabwe the ruling (ZANU-PF) party initially had legitimacy as a liberation movement and the rightful ruler who represented the liberated black majority of the population. At independence in 1980, ZANU-PF arguably inherited an effective state apparatus and professional civil service and retained its legitimacy through the effective delivery of social services, such as a democratised and accessible education and health delivery systems.

However, Mustapha and Whitefield (2009: 216) submitted that by the late 1990s and then more rapidly after 2000:

... the logic of the Zimbabwean state was rapidly transformed. With a worsening economic crisis and the strictures of structural adjustment, the state became partisan as it strove to maintain control. Support for the party increasingly trumped merit as the basis of civil service recruitment.

Alexander (2009: 189) seems to agree with this explanation, suggesting that the ZANU-PF's strategies of the mid-1990s left it politically vulnerable. It is observed that:

Structural adjustment, a stalled land reform programme, declining state capacity and accountability, and elite corruption combined to undermine the political capital derived from the delivery of development and the nationalist mantle.

Alexander (ibid.) highlighted some of the factors that facilitated the decline of the state and the ruling party's political power under Mugabe's stewardship. Such scholarly insights are shared by Hammar and Raftopoulos (2003: 4), who posit that: 'Zimbabwe's deepening economic and political crisis was well under way long before the dramatic events triggered by the constitutional referendum in February 2000.'

Alexander (2009:185) submits that the combination of a new and vibrant political opposition, the violent farm invasions of the largely white-owned farms, and the holding of deeply flawed and disputed elections, changed the political situation in Zimbabwe in 2000. She argued that the upheavals were rooted in both complex legacies of the nationalist struggle and the socio-economic pressures of the 1990s, but suggests that two specific events reshaped the possibilities for Zimbabwe politics in 1997:

The first of these was the ZANU-PF government's decision to accede to the demands of material compensation made by the war veterans of the 1970s liberation war. The second was the designation of over 1 400 mostly white-owned commercial farms for compulsory acquisition by the state (ibid.).

precipitating what critical voices have termed the 'crisis' of 2000, and what the government has termed the 'third *chimurenga*' or uprising, of descendants of those previously disadvantaged by colonialism after 1890. The period 1997 to 1999 was, therefore, a crucial historic era in opposition politics and Zimbabwean democratisation struggles. Firstly, civic society groups, such as students, labour, academics and the church, came together in 1997 to form the National Constitutional Assembly (NCA). Raftopolous (2013: 972) points out that different voices of opposition politics in post-colonial Zimbabwe have also constituted their presence through the discourse of constitutionalism. He suggests that the emergence of the NCA in 1997 represented a convergence of a critique of the state led by ZANU-PF around the issues of political democratisation and economic change, and constructed through the organisational frameworks of the churches, the emerging human rights organisations, and the labour movement, persuasively pointing out that:

> As the constitutional movement gained momentum between the late 1990s and into the 2000s, the dominance of the human rights messaging took precedence over economic issues, a shift that contributed to the rupture between rights and redistributive issues that has continued to mark the political discourse in the country. This emphasis on the part of the constitutional movement was the result of the mobilisation of a coalition of classes and organisations, largely in the urban areas, around the lack of accountability of the post-colonial state, in the context of the post-1989 changes in global politics and the dominant paradigm of human rights, democratisation and economic neo-liberalism that framed Western interventions in the South from this period. This convergence of factors led to ZANU(PF)'s construction of the constitutional movement as a Western intervention, completely ignoring both the national conditions that gave rise to its existence and the longer history of activism around human rights and constitutional issues that marked anti-colonial struggles in the country (Raftopoulos 2013: 972-3).

The Zimbabwe Congress of Trade Unions (ZCTU), led by its Secretary General, Morgan Tsvangirai, was at the centre of mobilising and organising the formation of the NCA, using its national structures and resources. The NCA's role was to push for democratic constitutional reforms resulting in a draft constitution which was rejected by ZANU-PF in a referendum. In March, 1997, the ZCTU organised an effective mass stay-away from work by both public and private sector workers to protest against food and fuel price rises (Saunders, 2000). The ZANU-PF government was taken by surprise at such an audacious challenge to its power. President Mugabe's government immediately sought action to ensure that stay-aways would be avoided. To make the government's displeasure clear, mysterious assailants burst into Tsvangirai's office in December, 1997, and beat him up, in turn deepening the governance crisis.

In January, 1998, after two days of riots over a steep rise in food and fuel prices in the country, mainly in the capital Harare, Mugabe's government met in an emergency session and decided to establish a programme of limited price control. However, at this stage, the situation could not be contained, as the economy continued to free fall (Raftopoulos and Sachikonye, 2001). What it is significant is that the political and economic crises that engulfed the state in the late 1990s were not represented by any opposition political party because opposition politics were weak and in disarray.

As Alexander (2009: 188) notes; in the mid 1990s:

... workers and civil servants struck repeatedly. Others were also unhappy with the shifts of the late 1980s and 1990s; the independent press was blossoming and grew increasingly outspoken and critical, students protested over time and again not least over corruption, intellectuals vocally expressed their disenchantment, and civic groups were formed to demand political rights, state accountability and constitutional rights.

However, with a growing national outcry and wide consensus there was a push to politically confront the political hegemony and failed policies of the regime of President Robert Mugabe and ZANU-PF, who had been in power since independence from Britain in 1980. Some leaders of the NCA, mainly from labour, left the civic body and formed the Movement for Democratic Change (MDC) in September, 1999. Like the NCA, the MDC was formed under the stewardship of ZCTU. The new opposition party, the MDC, was made up of many disparate groups with contradictory interests e.g., workers, employers, white commercial farmers, peasants, students and non-governmental organisations under the umbrella of the NCA (Hammar and Raftopoulos, 2003).

What brought these contradictory forces together was the desire to remove ZANU-PF and Mugabe from power and, in the long run, to (re) democratise state politics. The newly formed opposition party attempted to offer an inclusive ideological framework with which to confront, and compete with, the existing socialist political edifice of ZANU-PF

(Ruhanya, 2014). The ruling party's political ideology was premised on the struggles for independence against successive racist white supremacist regimes in Rhodesia. ZANU-PF also championed populist redistributive policies, which MDC and other opposition parties found difficult to challenge.

However, through successive mass demonstrations and protests by public servants, industrial workers, students, civil society and opposition political parties between 1997 and 1999, Mugabe's government succumbed to pressure, mainly from NCA and ZCTU, calling for democratic reforms and concomitant cost of living adjustments that were accepted to meet demands for political reforms (Saunders, 2000). Mugabe conceded to the widespread outcry, expressed through demonstrations in Zimbabwe, together with other demands that the 1979 Lancaster House Constitution was too heavily influenced by the country's colonial past. On 21 May, 1999, President Mugabe announced the convening of a Constitutional Convention to draft a new Constitution to address the demands of the protestors while recognising the political trajectory of the country's independence struggles. Mugabe constituted the Constitutional Commission, which was made up of the country's Members of Parliament and selected civic society individuals, to draft the new national law. After a year of gathering people's views, in February, 2000, a Constitutional Referendum was held. The NCA, the MDC, ZCTU and white farmers whose land was being threatened with seizures by the government mounted an organised campaign against the Draft Constitution, denouncing it for not taking into account the views of the people and for entrenching executive powers that would allow future governments to be unaccountable to citizens. The Draft Constitution was rejected in a Referendum on 12 and 13 February, 2000. For Alexander, the constitutional referendum was a transformative moment in Zimbabwe's emerging democracy:

> The referendum marked a watershed. The campaign itself occasioned widespread popular mobilisation around an agenda that focussed not just on anger over economic hardships but on civil rights, state accountability and specifically the curtailment of the autonomy of an executive that had gathered power over the preceding decade, not least through legal and constitutional amendments (Alexander, 2009: 192).

Hammar and Raftopoulos believe that the referendum victory by the opposition challenged the hegemonic and increasingly authoritarian rule of President Mugabe and the ruling party. They observed:

Despite a prior trend of opposition, this marked a particular watershed in Zimbabwe's post-independence political history, precipitating dramatic shifts in the country's political, economic, social, cultural and spatial landscapes; shifts whose ongoing dynamics and extensive effects have generically – though not without fierce contestation – come to be termed 'the Zimbabwe crisis' (Hammar and Raftopoulos, 2003: 1).

However, Alexander (2009: 192) pointed out that many of groups that were mobilised against the state and Mugabe during the crisis were disparate groups with disparate interests, including white farmers, black smallholders, business people, professionals, workers and students, who came to form the MDC in September, 1999. These groups, therefore, lacked a coherent framework for their opposition politics, apart from their dislike of Mugabe's authoritarian practices and the need to protect their individual and corporate interests. For instance, the workers found themselves working hand in glove with their employers (capitalists), who were partly responsible for their economic miseries. However, Alexander insightfully argues that what was crucial about the unity of these disparate voices was that:

The work of civics, churches, unions, alongside the MDC meant that debates over Zimbabwe's political future took place all over the country – in the remotest rural areas, on white farms and in the corners of every township. The result was the defeat for the ZANU-PF government in February 2000. This was the first national defeat ZANU-PF had suffered, and it stunned the party's leaders (2009: 192).

Raftopoulos (2013: 972) and Hammar and Raftopoulos (2003: 1) share Alexander's view, saying that ZANU-PF's referendum defeat by a coalition of opposition and civic forces challenged its state power and galvanised the dissenting groups to demand further governance reforms in a period of political and economic instability. ZANU-PF was badly fractured so it turned to its military component to retain power. The military then became involved in partisan politics holding the decisive power block on any attempts to democratise Zimbabwe using elections as a signifier of a democratic transition.

Following the formation of the opposition MDC in 1999, the military was involved in torture, kidnappings and killings of opposition supporters in the 2000 parliamentary elections. Before the 2002 elections, all senior military officers pledged that they would not serve under a president other than Mugabe and the army joined the campaigns of intimidation of opposition supporters. The army also participated in the 2000 land reforms which saw the forceful expropriation of land from white farmers. In 2001, Mugabe pledged troops on white-owned farms to 'speed up' the process, which resulted in the death of more than a dozen white farmers.

Most notably, the army launched a violent campaign in the June 2008 presidential-election run-off after Mugabe lost the 29 March presidential election to MDC leader Morgan Tsvangirai. Mugabe won the run-off through military intervention but the outcome was dismissed by the international community. Apart from being regularly mobilised to solve Mugabe's political problems, the military has also acquired power over decision-making in various levels of the state. The military is deployed to the commissariat of ZANU-PF and the Zimbabwe Electoral Commission (ZEC) to campaign and administer elections respectively. Its personnel occupy various positions in government ministries such as agriculture, land, justice and economic development. They ran state programmes such the Fast Track Land Reform (FTLRP) and, of late, the Command Agriculture scheme. Retired members of the military with a liberation background are appointed as judges of the High Court such as the current Judge President, Retired Major General Justice George Chiweshe. Others head key government parastatals such the Grain Marketing Board and the National Railways of Zimbabwe. While in these positions, members of the military are involved in partisan distribution of food handouts in times of drought and before the elections. Those deployed in the justice system have been accused of subverting the rule of law through its selective application against opponents of the regime. The same applies to retired military personnel in the police force. They rarely arrest members of the ruling party for human rights abuses or other crimes.

## Militarisation of the executive post-Mugabe

The vice-like grip of the military on political and electoral affairs has continued without changes in the post-Mugabe era making it the bedrock of Mnangagwa presidency. After the military coup in November 2017, which toppled Mugabe, the military was twice involved in the shooting and killing of seven civilians in the post July 2018 elections and the murder of sixteen civilians during the January 2019 protests over the cost of living. The purpose of military involvement was to maintain ZANU-PF grip in the electoral and public affairs of Zimbabwe and to block any efforts of a democratic transition where ZANU-PF will be weakened.

In this regard, given their power, economic influence, and their monopoly of coercive force with which to shape or break the transition, the role of the security forces, mainly the army, is and has been crucial. In fact, the undeniable truth is that the ZANU-PF militarised patronage network, which has been running the country since 1980, has been intensified, emboldened and fortified by covertly, overtly and systematically placing the security apparatus at the centre of governance. Actually, President Mnangagwa has gone two steps further than former President Mugabe in conniving with securocrats to capture key civilian institutions responsible for giving citizens opportunities to freely participate in democratic processes. The ubiquitous presence of the army is civilian and public affairs does not point to a new era of democracy but rather one of democratic regression: civilian politics is not the arena of military competence. For instance, ZANU-PF has been a dominant political party in Zimbabwe responsible for providing policies that destroyed the economy and political freedoms in Zimbabwe, and our current president, has been at the helm of those failed policy makers for 39 years. Instead of bringing sanity and real freedom of choice to ZANU-PF supporters, Mnangagwa enrolled himself and the party for capture by securocrats. Today, key decisions are made by military personnel retired purposefully to assume political posts from civilians. For the first time in history, Zimbabwe has witnessed four generals who led the November 2017 *coup d'etat* being retired to occupy most important policy making positions in the country: the foreign affairs and agriculture portfolios, the ZANU-PF commissariat and the office of vice-president. If this level of militarisation was openly achieved before his election in 2018, what more commissions and agencies not usually in the public eye will follow? Militarisation of state and civilian institutions by soldiers with tattered human rights records cannot be described as a 'new era', but a further reversal of freedoms over an electorate compromised by fear.

## Competitive authoritarianism in Zimbabwe and military state capture

Employing Levitsky and Way's (2010) analytical spectacle of competitive authoritarianism, our contention is that the Zimbabwe state has been fully captured by the security sector and a securocratic state, which partially fits with what Levitsky and Way (2002) termed a 'competitive authoritarian regime'. The two scholars noted that four key institutions of the state are targeted and/or captured: the electoral system; the legislature; the judiciary; and the media (ibid.).

Competitive authoritarian regimes are civilian regimes in which formal democratic institutions exist and are widely viewed as the primary means of gaining power, but in which the incumbents' abuse of the state places them at a significant advantage vis-a-vis their opponents. Such regimes are competitive in that opposition parties use democratic institutions to seriously contest for power, but the elections in which they participate are not democratic because the playing field is heavily skewed in favour of incumbents who manipulate the state apparatus for power retention. Competition is thus real but unfair (Levitsky and Way, 2010: 5). It is generally the electoral aspect that has left many regimes endorsing authoritarian states as largely democratic. This view is supported by Howard and Roessler (2006: 365) who posit that, 'these regimes feature regular, competitive elections between a government and an opposition, but the incumbent leader or party typically resorts to coercion, intimidation, and fraud to attempt to ensure electoral victory.'

Schedler (2002) warns against obsession with elections as a measure of democracy. It is submitted that most who do this appear to forget that the modern history of representative elections is a tale of authoritarian manipulation as much as it is one of democratic triumph. Elections can occasionally result in a 'liberalising electoral outcome', which can lead to a new government considerably less authoritarian than its predecessor. This electoral system can leave the electorate with competitive authoritarianism, a hybrid of both democracy and authoritarianism, which can cause democratic institutions such as the judiciary, legislature, executive to become undemocratic. This is what Diamond (2002) describes as pseudo democracy – the system is neither entirely democratic nor entirely authoritarian; Schedler (2002) describes it as the foggy zone between an open liberal democracy and closed authoritarianism.

In Zimbabwe, this hybrid system was more visible during the events leading to the military coup that pressured Mugabe to resign. Four fundamental state institutions – media, legislature, judiciary and the electoral system – were demonstrably captured by a faction aligned to the current president, Emmerson Mnangagwa, and military interests. They were thus used as ZANU-PF zones of military politicking.[3] This capture is either direct – through the rapid recruitment of security sector personnel by those institutions or indirect – through patrimonial recruitments enforced upon these institutions. This military strategy has been both sophisticated and clandestine to the extent that an external analysis might fail to appreciate the depth of military recruitment and appointments in political affairs. The government has encouraged its troops to attend university studies in order to pass the meritocracy test.[4] Such foggy demarcation is even worse with members of the Central Intelligence Organisation (CIO) as they are harder to distinguish from civilians. Many appointments of what the public assume to be the latter are, in effect, patriotic members of the intelligence services recruited to spy on public officials and institutions.

## Media capture by military interests in Zimbabwe

A first priority is the capture of the state media and moves to stifle the independent media by military interests. As argued in Levitsky and Way (2002), the media is always a target of competitive authoritarian regimes because it is a double-edged sword: on the one hand, it can be used to remove the regime of power; on the other, it is a potentially powerful propaganda tool that can undermine the opposition's political appeal. In Zimbabwe, apart from reliance on repressive legislation such as the Access to Information and Protection of Privacy Act (AIPPA), the Broadcasting Services Act (BSA), the Interception of Communications Act (ICA) and the Public Order and Security Act (POSA) among others, the ZANU-PF government has maintained a military presence though senior leadership positions at the Zimbabwe Broadcasting Corporation (ZBC), the Broadcasting Authority of Zimbabwe (BAZ), the Zimbabwe newspapers' group (ZIMPAPERS) among others. In the lead up to the coup, such strategic influence helped the military to control the narrative in the state media and have a degree of influence on how the private media reported unfolding events. A cursory overview of the military architecture

---

3   This is both a specific and main theme identified across primary and secondary data.

4   Interviews, Bulawayo Province, 29 July 2017.

within the state media shows that in 2009, eight senior retired security sector members were appointed by the then Minister of Information and Publicity, Webster Shamu (CiZC, 2012): Brigadier General Epmarcus Kanhanga (Zimpapers), Retired Colonel Rueben Mqwayi, Brigadier General Elasto Madzingira (both BAZ), Brigadier General Benjamin Mabenge, Major General Gibson Mashingaidze (both ZBH), Brigadier General Livingstone Chineka (Transmedia) Brigadier General Collin Moyo (Kingstons) and Colonel Claudius Makova (New Ziana).[5]

Denis Magaya, the son of ZANLA High Command member Cde Arthur Magaya, was a short-lived ZBC Board Chair in 2014 alongside Professor Charity Manyeruke, UZ Dean of Social Studies who is linked to the security sector and a close ally to the former first lady, Grace Mugabe; and Cleopatra Shingirai Matanhire-Mutisi, the wife of Brigadier General Francis Mutisi among others.[6] The message is very clear, military interests need to be protected in all key areas of state power and the media is one of them. As a result, the state-controlled media has been very vibrant in diverting attention from the political and economic decay that is undermining the social well-being of Zimbabweans; laying the blame instead on targeted sanctions imposed by certain Western countries on key ZANU-PF leaders.[7]

While the securocrats have succeeded in muzzling private media through legal and extra-legal regimes, the same cannot be said of other alternative media such as diasporic online platforms and social media. With the proliferation of social media networks, the latter, the state media has faced serious challenges in executing its propaganda in Zimbabwe. Opposition political forces have resorted to social and private media for publicity and mobilisation. The social movements (Tajamuka and Pastor Evan Mawarire's This Flag) have effectively mobilised citizens for protest against deepening economic crises in the country that almost 'shut-down-Zimbabwe' in 2016.[8] One of the advantages presented by social media is its ability to provide anonymity or enabling individuals to adopt multiple personalities. This has been an existential headache for the state actors,

---

5   'Mahoso appointed to the Broadcasting Authority of Zimbabwe board', *The Zimbabwean*, 7 October 2009.

6   'New board for ZBC announced', *The Herald*, 17 February 2014.

7   Over 150 ZANU-PF officials were put on targeted sanctions by the government of the United States. The European Union has since removed all but the late president Mugabe and his wife Grace Mugabe.

8   '2016 political highlights', *Zimbabwe Independent*, 23 December 2016. '

more so when social media users have mastered online applications that can hide the IP addresses of the computers from which information is being sent.

However, the security sector has been working hard to subdue this media space as well. This can be seen through attempts to ensure social media is out of reach for many citizens by barring mobile telecommunications from providing promotions, the promulgation of the Cyber Crime Bill in 2016, which was followed by the appointment of the Cyber Security, Threat Detection and Mitigation in October 2017. Phillip Valerio Sibanda, the ZNA commander, revealed this strategy through state media in August 2016 when he claimed that social media use by 'insurgents' and 'regime change agents' (probably against vested security sector political interests) has emerged as a security threat.[9] He continued:

We are already dealing with these threats. As an army, at our institutions of training, we are training our officers to be able to deal with this new threat we call cyber warfare where weapons — not necessarily guns but basically information and communication technology — are being used to mobilise people to do the wrong things. We will be equal to the task when the time comes.[10]

This security sector policy statement must be understood in the context of the military-dominated political economy in Zimbabwe. First, social movements have used social media and proven capable of undermining ZANU-PF hegemony, if left uncontrolled. This threatens the interests of the securocrats as pursued through ZANU-PF and the conflation of the military with the party when the two have morphed into one. This can be seen through the events prior to and following the coup. Three of the leading actors that led to Mugabe's ouster have since occupied senior government positions with the former army commanders having been promoted.

Second, the security sector at a time of social protests in 2016 was convinced that protesting against Mugabe and his failure to better the lives of the poverty-stricken majorities in Zimbabwe was a threat to their permanent interests and a reversal of their liberation struggle gains.[11] To state it more clearly, the securocrats have seen their role as protecting and perpetuating ZANU-PF dominance to the extent of warning that the army

9    *Nehanda Radio*, 5 August 2016.
10   Ibid.
11   Interviews, Matabeleland South Province, 6 August 2017.

was not going to surrender the country's sovereignty to the opposition MDC nor salute its leader, Morgan Tsvangirai.[12] How is that the military saw the attack on Mugabe as an attack on themselves? Robert Mugabe was key to the military's political strategy of capturing ZANU-PF and the state. He was installed in his position by the military against stipulated party procedures after the Mgagao Declaration of October 1975. Thus, demonstrating against a conduit of military interests is tantamount to protesting against security sector dominance and this has led to the general's outburst.

As already alluded to the government, in the wake of social uprisings of 2016, sought to curb promotions that mobile operators administer. Curbing data promotion was intended to lower social media activity as the data prices were too high for many ordinary citizens. One of the strategies the government has used to crack down on social media protests was to stigmatise the perpetrators as 'cyber terrorists', and therefore a threat to national security and stability. It is not a coincidence that the shutdown of mobile communication by the Postal and Telecommunications Regulatory Authority of Zimbabwe (POTRAZ) was followed by General Sibanda's press statement i.e. they wanted to curb campaigning ahead of the 2018 election.[13] POTRAZ's decision to arm-twist telecommunication service providers to stop programmes offering cheap access to mobile telephony was clearly aimed at limiting the number of citizens who can access social media. This was arguably meant to muzzle of social movements which rely on social media. Failure to view these events in the same political schematic package will be a clear-cut miscarriage of political science and the subdued role of the military in the coup in Zimbabwe. So, the media is a fundamental military politicking zone that will always defy or define transition in Zimbabwe. In the context of the G-40 vis-à-vis Team Lacoste factions of ZANU-PF, it was apparent that the state media is captured and used by the latter against the former. This also corroborates the previous assertion that the securocrats are in the Team Lacoste and that the state media was captured by the securocrats, hence the state media, at the time, was used to further former vice-president Mnangagwa's political ambitions and campaigns. The state media's failure to report that it was

---

12 On eve of the 2002 presidential elections, Zimbabwe Defense Forces Commander, the late General Vitalis Zvinavashe, convened a media conference and warned the electorate that the armed forces would not salute anyone without liberation credentials if that person were to win the election.

13 'Mandiwanzira Bans Internet Data Bundles', *ZimEye*, 10 August /2016.

under siege from the military as a way of explaining the coup in Zimbabwe is significant in suggesting its complicity.

## The role of security apparatus seizure of the electoral process in Zimbabwe.

Occasionally, elections in competitive authoritarian regimes lead to the victory of the opposition. The 2008 elections in Zimbabwe is a case in point. However, the very real threat of losing power gave rise to the increased role of the military in the electoral management system. The capture of electoral system by securocrats has seen the outcome being manipulated during and after elections and skewed the electoral environment to benefit the ruling ZANU-PF party. Capturing the political arena has given the system the certainty of continuity despite electoral pressure from the opposition. The strategy is executed through deployment of the security sector within campaign teams and war veterans to instil fear. Pre-election military terror campaigns undermine or sabotage the opposition, while the exploitation of state media reminds the electorate that voting ZANU-PF is a better alternative that the punitive consequences which will result from a vote for the opposition. Finally, and in addition, state institutions responsible for administering elections are filled by securocrats capable of sacrificing professionalism out of loyalty to ZANU-PF and knowledge of the rewards that will follow.

Firstly, the military has directly and indirectly taken charge of the election processes and made it very hard that anyone not aligned to it would win the presidential office. It forms part of ZANU-PF philosophy. Meredith (2007: 1) observes President Mugabe clearly stating, 'our votes must go together with our guns. After all, any vote we shall have, shall have been the product of the gun. The gun which produces the vote should remain its security officer – its guarantor. The people's votes and the people's guns are inseparable twins.' Literature on electoral processes in Zimbabwe reveals that that after the security sector successfully installed Robert Mugabe at the helm of ZANU-PF, all elections have been militarised.[14] In 1980, the governor of Zimbabwe-Rhodesia indicated that elections might not be conducted in some ZANU-PF strongholds due to violence perpetrated by ZANLA forces during the election campaign, only

---

14 This was a general theme across the interviews held. It simply indicates that the military has been in use in all elections in which ZANU-PF has been involved. Interviews, July-August 2017.

to change his decision few days before the election.[15] ZIPRA forces were also not immune from doubling as campaign teams for Joshua Nkomo.[16] We now have a culture where we allow the securocrats to influence election results.

The security sector that installed Robert Mugabe after capturing ZANU went on to force PF-ZAPU into the 1987 Unity accord after it had been satisfied that the Central Intelligence Organisation (CIO), 5th Brigade and other militia had done their assigned campaign strategy across ZAPU strongholds.[17]

An estimated number of deaths amounted to around ten thousand and more following the ZANU-PF militarised campaigns in the Matabeleland region before the 1985 election; the style used in 2008 presidential run-off elections was not dissimilar.[18]

This legacy of violence remains in the hearts and minds of Zimbabweans as they approach elections and has often been invoked to instil fear and influence the choices made by the electorate. Retired members of the security sector and war veterans have helped to pursue and enhance military capture of the electoral process through the use of violence and threats of violence, forcing a 'sell-out'[19] tag on opposition members and supporters in their door-to-door ZANU-PF campaigns; they are scattered across the country's communities to indoctrinate, monitor and spy on citizens at household levels, they are used to ensure the electorate perceives them as ZANU-PF creators, kingmakers and fathers of the army; they capture and (mis)use public resources (schools, government projects, local government infrastructure) to further ZANU-PF political interests; they preside over the ZANU-PF capture of government food handouts and using them in 'food-for-a-vote' campaigns in hunger stricken villages and they undermine and frog-march traditional leaders at kraal head level

---

15 'Joshua Nkomo letter to Robert Mugabe from exile in the UK', *Nehanda Radio*, 24 December 2013.

16 Interviews revealed that ZIPRA forces were key campaign teams for PF-ZAPU and to date have been pivotal in Matabeleland as part of ZANU-PF war veteran campaign machinery.

17 Interviews, July-August 2017.

18 See *Breaking the Silence, Building True Peace: A Report on the Disturbances in Matabeleland & Midlands 1980-1989*, compiled by the Catholic Commission for Justice & Peace and the Legal Resources Foundation, September 2001.

19 An epithet used and abused widely during the war against adversaries.

to vote for ZANU-PF.[20] Under such circumstances, the election results are predictable before the elections are held. The electoral process is thus captured.

Reminiscences of pre-election ZANU-PF military exercises such as: Operation Gukurahundi (1983-87) land reform (2000), Operation Murambatsvina (2005) and Operation Makavhoterapapi (2008) are still fresh in the minds of victim communities. The current clampdown on vendors that coincides with voter registration in Harare is another example; it must be understood as more of a political strategy of sabotaging opposition strongholds than clearing the streets. These 'military operations' have been a systematic long-term strategy of rigging the electoral environment in that they have all been strategically timed and of implemented towards contested presidential elections; targeted within areas where ZANU-PF has performed dismally in a previous election; and merciless violence has been employed without judicial remedy. The 2008 June Presidential re-run elections were 'militarised elections' and it is because of the security sector's capture of the electoral process that Robert Mugabe emerged as the winner. These military operations have sent a clear message to the electorate that the military is ZANU-PF; it kills for a vote and 'voting it out' without protection is suicide.

Electorates and presidential candidates have been continuously reminded and assured – always towards presidential elections – of a repeat of similar operations and/or worse if in any event, ZANU-PF loses a presidential election. The most notable assurance came in the run-up to 2002 presidential elections when the then ZDF commander the late General Vitalis Zvinavashe released a press statement in the state media saying:

> We wish to make it very clear to all Zimbabwean citizens that the security organisations will only stand in support of those political leaders that will pursue Zimbabwean values, traditions and beliefs for which thousands of lives were lost, in pursuit of Zimbabwe's hard-won independence, sovereignty, territorial integrity and national interests. To this end, let it be known that the highest office in the land is a straitjacket whose occupant is expected to observe the objectives of the liberation struggle. We will, therefore, not accept, let alone support or salute, anyone with a different agenda

---

20 Interviews, July-August 2017. See also, 'This is no election. This is a brutal war', *The Guardian*, 22 June 2008.

that threatens the very existence of our sovereignty, our country and our people.[21]

This statement can arguably be described as the beginning of active military involvement in the country's politics. It demonstrates the conflation between the party and the state and the party and the military and it sets the stage for future military's overt interventions in the country's political life. General Nyikayaramba, Chedondo, ZPS General Paradzai Zimondi among others in the run-up to the 2008 June presidential elections made similar threats to the electorate and those with presidential ambitions. In addition, Robert Mugabe issued a solidarity statement clearly toeing the line drawn by the securocrats in the same period when he said:

> The war veterans came to me and said, 'President, we can never accept that our country which we won through the barrel of the gun can be taken merely by an 'X' made by a ballpoint pen. '*Zvino* ballpoint pen *icharwisana ne* AK? (Will the pen fight the AK rifle?) Is there going to be a struggle between the two? Do not argue with a gun.[22]

ZNA Major General – Douglas Nyikayaramba has recently emerged as a spokesperson for the ZANU-PF military electioneering team. During the GNU era, he was chosen to represent military presence in the constitution-making committee and he advocated for a constitutional clause that will ensure that Mugabe is 'president for life' and told the nation that:

> I am in ZANU-PF and ZANU-PF is in me and you can't change that… Truly speaking, I am ZANU-PF and ZANU-PF is in me and you can't change that … I am sure everyone, including yourself, has now woken up to realise that he [Tsvangirai] is not the right candidate… The bottom line is that I will not surrender; I will not salute someone like that personally… What he [Tsvangirai] is saying is nonsense. We are dealing with a national security threat…[23]

On September 2017, in the run-up to the July 2018 elections, Major General Douglas Nyikayaramba, in a ZANU-PF military politicking crusade, commandeered chiefs assembled at Four Brigade in Masvingo to ensure that President Robert Mugabe wins the 2018 elections. He unequivocally asked:

---

21 Zimbabwe: Press Freedom, 16 January 2002. Available at: https://www.africa.upenn. edu/Urgent_Action/apic-011602x.html
22 'President Mugabe's statement', *The Herald*, 23 June 2008.
23 *Financial Gazette*, 18 July 2011.

Did anyone ever say to a traditional chief that you are old, leave the chieftainship for me? That is unheard of. What will happen to the chief's aides? We need to remind each other. No chief was voted for. No son has ever ordered his father to step down from his role as leader of the family, so the same applies to our case with President Mugabe. That is what we should remind each other when we meet. Whites want divide-and-rule, and they saw that Mugabe is the nerve centre of the country. Let us not sell the country for the love of sugar. We are here to strengthen the relationship between chiefs, the President and the army.[24]

Militarising an election environment nullifies the results of an election as an indicator of the people's democratic choice, they rather signify an expression of the people's choice of life over death. No matter how independent the Zimbabwe Electoral Commission (ZEC) might try to be, if the context of the electoral process is not liberated from military capture, elections will continue to be neither free nor fair. An election-based transition that is contrary to military interests is impossible. ZEC is among the most politicised bodies in Zimbabwe with its administration infiltrated by un-uniformed agents of the security sector and its political compradors. In 2002, an ex-colonel in the ZNA Sobuza Gula-Ndebele was appointed to chair the Election Supervision Commission (ESC) whilst Brigadier General Douglas Nyikayaramba was ESC Executive Officer and this military-led team presided over the running of first contested presidential elections post-Unity Accord. The former was later promoted to Attorney General in 2008 – a move seen as a direct reward for the 2002 flawed election services. In 2013 Justice Rita Makarau, a Supreme Court judge, was appointed Chair of ZEC, a ZANU-PF Trojan horse. It is said that she is a tried and tested conduit and security sector interests are safe in her hands. It is she who has presided over the Bio-metric Voter registration wherein, Robert Mugabe has made contentious launching services that have shown ZEC's continued bondage to ZANU-PF.[25]

## Zimbabwe's militarised judiciary

The judiciary at all levels is expected to be very active in setting a clear demarcation between the political terrain and the military topography and

---

24  'Major General Nyikayaramba urges chiefs to ensure Mugabe wins 2018 election', *Pindula News*, 12 September 2017.
25  'Makarau State House visit riles MDC', *Daily News Live*, 15 September 2017.

reprimanding security personnel for crossing from the latter to the former. However, due to its capture by securocrats, the judiciary has failed to play its constitutional oversight role through judicial activism; it only acts when cases have been placed before it. Indeed, many politically charged cases have been put before it; but perceivably stage-managed by ZANU-PF, the courts have been unable to fulfil their role or scrupulously examine the interests of their clients.[26] The judicial system has been captured by military interests through recruitment of military personnel, ZANU-PF agents and loyalists, and the system has lost its credibility in the public domain.

Capture of the state judiciary intensified with the emergence of MDC as a serious threat to ZANU-PF's political hegemony. The ZANU-PF military operation, the FTLRP which targeted white commercial farmers whom the government believed to be financial and electoral aids of the newly formed MDC, led to the outright judicial capture by military interests. This, in turn, led to the resignation of Chief Justice Anthony Gubbay, and judges Nicholas McNally and David Bartlett, among others, after the security sector allowed war veterans to dance on top of Supreme Court tables.[27] Commenting on the same issue and displaying disregard of the courts, President Mugabe remarked:

> The courts can do whatever they want, but no judicial decision will stand in our way. They are not courts for our people and we shall not even be defending ourselves in these courts?[28]

He further disapproved and criticised the court declaration of the land reform as unlawful in 2000 labelling judges as 'guardians of 'white racist commercial farmers. Later, in 2005, when High Court Justice Tendai Uchena's ruling allowed Roy Bennett, an imprisoned opposition MP to contest elections from prison, Robert Mugabe dismissed the decision as

---

26 In Jealousy Mbizvo Mawarire v Robert Gabriel Mugabe N.O, Morgan Richard Tsvangirai N.O, Arthur Guseni Oliver Mutambara, N.O, Welshman Ncube and the Attorney General. [SC 146/13, CCZ 18/13], Mr Mawarire successfully filed an application seeking an order directing the President to proclaim the elections to be held (after amendment) by 25 July and the Constitutional Court ruled in his favour. It had always been a ZANU-PF desire to have early elections before electoral reforms whereas opposition parties in the GNU preferred them to be done after electoral reforms agreed in the GPA had been completed. Mawarire was either sent by ZANU-PF or his actions were encouraged by ZANU-PF to secure a winning strategy.

27 See <www.pindula.co.zw>

28 'The abusive relationship between the Executive and Judiciary', *NewsDay*, 20 September 2016.

'stupid' and the justice concerned reversed the judgment.[29] From year 2000 onward, Mugabe used his party's militarised patronage network to populate the judicial bench at a time when a critical land reform case was before the courts. It was through the work of these loyal judges with the help of the Constitutional Amendment Number 17 Act (2005) introducing section 16B in the Constitution that the illegal exercise in farm seizure and violation of property rights was legalised, although the SADC Tribunal ruling declaring these actions illegal (*Mike Campbell (Pvt) Ltd et al. v. Republic of Zimbabwe*). The late Chief Justice Godfrey Chidyausiku (former ZANU-PF MP and Deputy Minister); Justice Guvava (the former's niece), Justice Charles Hungwe (founder of the Zimbabwe National Liberation War Veterans Association); the current Chief Justice Luke Malaba (beneficiary of the land reform), former Judge President Rita Makarau, current Judge President George Chiweshe (a Retired Brigadier General, Chair of ZEC during disputed 2008 elections) were among other justices that have found their way to the judicial system through the patronage network resulting in the *de facto* capture of the system by security sector interests.[30]

The judiciary has demonstrated too much ineptitude when it comes to cases that involve the vested interests of ZANU-PF securocrats. It must be remembered that war veterans were key architects of the farm invasion in early 2000s and, putting war veterans on the judicial bench was a clear statement that ZANU-PF will do anything to protect the security sector, even if it violates the Constitution. In reference to a recent dismissal of the case challenging the adoption of bond notes, Alex Magaisa, a Kent University legal expert aptly sums up the decay in the judiciary as follows: 'Taking matters to Chiweshe's court is like goats taking a petition to a hyena!'[31] The judiciary cannot act independently. For example, during the 2016 national demonstrations by social movements and opposition parties calling for electoral reforms, the High Court declared as unconstitutional the violent clampdown of peaceful demonstrations by the police on August 26, 2016. President Mugabe (in solidarity with the police) at a ZANU-PF youth rally captured on

---

29  Zimbabwean general election, 2008 - IPFS, March 2007. Available at: https://ipfs.io/ipfs/QmXoypizjW3WknFiJnKLwHCnL72vedxjQkDDP1mXWo6uco/wiki/Zimbabwean_general_election%2C_2008.html

30  See <www.pindula.co.zw>

31  'George Chiweshe', *Pindula*. Available at: www.pindula.co.zw/index.php?title=George_Chiweshe&mobileaction=toggle.

national television criticised the court ruling as 'reckless disregard to peace'.

The National Prosecuting Authority (NPA) is another militarised judicial body with more than half its staff drawn from the security sector. Dismissed Prosecutor-General (PG), Roy Goba, attested to this fact during public interviews when he stated that its 'personnel – mostly seconded from the police, air force, army and prisons – are unqualified for their job, thereby compromising the justice delivery system while factionalism is also rampant in the crucial institution.'[32] Indeed, the NPA has been affected by factional loyalties within ZANU-PF with many recruits allegedly aligned to their war veteran ally, the then Minister of Justice, Emmerson Mnangagwa. Former Prosecutor General Johannes Tomana was dismissed over allegations of abuse of office. He connived in protecting suspected military intelligence personnel who were accused of a failed bombing attempt at the Gushungo dairy plant – a suspected Mnangagwa faction's ploy against Grace Mugabe and her faction attested to the veracity of militarisation of this body.[33] In 2014, the Zimbabwe Law Officers' Association (ZILOA) filed an application at the Constitutional Court challenging the constitutionality of the recruitment of military personnel to the NPA. The NPA has subsequently been discredited for being used to pursue Mnangagwa's presidential ambitions.[34] A former military man, he has been working tirelessly to ensure that the military regains its control over the judiciary and, fortunately for him, Parliament has rubber stamped his plans. Mnangagwa has argued that the Head of State must be above every institution to the point of even appointing the Speaker of Parliament.

## The Legislature – tied hand and mouth by military political machinations

The legislature through the constitution is the main watchdog with responsibility to ensure that the security sector does not usurp government from the people. However, the preceding accounts of state capture by military interests have occurred not only under parliamentary oversight, but Parliament has connived with military conduits and often acted as a conduit itself. Parliament was captured in 1980, when it was populated by ZANU-PF – a party viewed as a political extension of the dominant

---

32 'NPA staffed with unqualified soldiers', *Zimbabwe Independent,* 25 August 2017.

33 'Tomana tribunal concludes', *NewsDay*, 26 January 2017.

34 *Zimbabwe Independent*, 25 August 2017.

securocrats of that day. Although its dominance has been weakened since the 2000 elections, the securocratic system has successfully recaptured the legislature following the so-called miraculous ZANU-PF electoral victory in 2013.[35] Consequently, the legislature has been reduced to rubber stamping even the most ridiculous military ploys to reverse the democratic gains achieved during the era of the GNU. That the first amendment Bill giving the president uncontested powers to appoint top judges sailed smoothly through parliamentary safeguards reveals a great deal about the way in which critics, even in the opposition, have been silenced by military interests. Three important pointers can be singled out: Parliament failed to defend the Constitution in the face of a powerful executive; Parliament failed and continues to fail to reprimand the army generals who violate the Constitution, which prohibits them from supporting any political party, including ZANU-PF, in public; Parliament is populated with retired security sector personnel who have been planted to enhance military interests in the executive.

It is democratic practice to allow entry into legislative politics to any citizen regardless of background. But it is not what appears to happen in ZANU-PF. The security sector has increasingly disallowed general citizens from accessing legislative positions by capturing ZANU-PF and assuring their permanent first-preference is observed in all major nominations for parliamentary seats.[36] Indeed, most non-military parliamentarians are friends, family or relatives of influential securocrats. As a result, the military legacy is jealously protected and preserved. Transition efforts have to paddle through this complex military network cognitive that this same network will seek to perpetuate their vested interests. However, if a major division within the security sector emerges and/or if its compradors in ZANU-PF decide to shake-off the military shackles, it is this same network that will lead to regime breakdown.

## Conclusion: the military factor in Zimbabwe's political affairs

This chapter has demonstrated the ubiquitous nature of the security apparatus, particularly the military, in the public, political and electoral affairs of the state and captured key democratic contested zones in Zimbabwe such as the judiciary, the legislature, the electoral field and the

---

35  Interviews, June-July 2017.
36  Interviews, July-August 2017.

media. The capture of these key democratic zones is to maintain the grip of the ruling ZANU-PF party's power over the state. The role of the security apparatuses in the democratisation and transition politics in Zimbabwe has oftentimes been associated with violence against opponents of the ruling party, who have little recourse to justice, as recently exposed in the securocrats clampdown against civilian protests in August 2018 and January 2019 when unarmed citizens were shot and killed with impunity. The chapter also revealed that the role of the security apparatus in partisan politics has not changed since the fall of Mugabe in November 2017 but has been further entrenched through capture of both key party and state institutions such as the ZANU-PF commissariat department and the Zimbabwe Electoral Commission. While evidence has been adduced about the role of the security apparatus in blocking pathways to a possible democratic transition in Zimbabwe by playing a decisive role in both party and state politics, what requires further study is the role of security apparatus in the political economy of the country. Further investigation of how the security apparatus is woven into the patronal, parasitic and clientelistic networks of the ruling party will helps to explain the vice-like grip of the repressive state apparatuses. Such further studies will help to devise methods to disentangle the security apparatus from involvement in the public, political and electoral affairs in partisan ways.

## References

Alexander, J. and B.M. Tendi, (2008) 'A Tale of Two Elections: Zimbabwe at the Polls in 2008', *ACAS Bulletin*, 80.

Alexander, J. (2009) Zimbabwe since 1997, Land and the language of war" in A.R. Mustapha, and L. Whitefield, (eds), *Turning Points in African Democracy*. Woodbridge: James Currey.

Diamond, L. (2008) 'Democracy in Retreat'. Available at: https://www.realclearpolitics.com/articles/2008/03/democracy_in_retreat.html

Donno, D. (2013) 'Elections and democratisation in authoritarian regimes.' *American Journal of Political Science*, 57/3, 703-716.

Hammar, A., B. Raftopoulos and S. Jensen (2003) *Zimbabwe's Unfinished Business: Rethinking Land, State and Nation in the Context of Crisis*. Harare: Weaver Press.

Howard, M.M. and P.G. Roessler (2006) 'Liberalizing Electoral Outcomes in Competitive Authoritarian Regimes', *American Journal of Political Science* 50/2, 365-381.

Levitsky, S. and L.A. Way (2010) *Competitive Authoritarianism: Hybrid Regimes after the Cold War*. Cambridge: Cambridge University Press.

———— (2002) 'Elections Without Democracy: The Rise of Competitive Authoritarianism', *Journal of Democracy*, 13/2, 51-65.

Masunungure, E.V. (2008) 'A Militarised Election: The 27 June Presidential Run-off', in E.V. Masunungure (ede.), *Defying the Winds of Change*. Harare: Weaver Press.

Meredith, M. (2007) *Mugabe: Power, Plunder and the Struggle for Zimbabwe's Future*. New York: PublicAffairs.

O'Donnell, G. and P.C. Shmitter (1986) *Transitions from Authoritarian Rule: Tentative Conclusions About Uncertain Democracies*. Baltimore: Johns Hopkins University Press.

Raftopoulos, B. (2013) 'The 2103 Elections in Zimbabwe: The End of an Era', *Journal of Southern African Studies*, 39/4, 971-988.

Raftopoulos, B. and L. Sachikonye (2001) *Striking Back: The Labour Movement and the Post-Colonial State in Zimbabwe 1980-2000*. Harare: Weaver Press.

Ruhanya, P. (2014) 'Alternative Media and African Democracy: The Daily News and Opposition Politics in Zimbabwe – 1997-2010'. Unpublished PhD Thesis, University of Westminster, London.

Saunders, R. (2000) *Never the same again: Zimbabwe's growth towards democracy 1980-2000*. Harare: Edwina Spicer Productions.

Schedler, A. (2002) 'The Nested Game of Democratization by Elections', *International Political Science Review*, 23/1, 103-122.

# 9

# Untangling the Gordian Knot: Zimbabwe's National Dialogue

Stephen Ndoma

## Introduction

Zimbabwe held watershed elections on 30 July 2018. Indeed, they were a defining moment in that Robert Mugabe's name was missing from the ballot paper after his ouster by a military coup on 17 November 2017 after almost four decades at the helm of the country's affairs. Another key feature was the absence of the opposition icon, Morgan Tsvangirai, who died in February 2018. For ZANU-PF, Mugabe's name was replaced by that of his long-time confidante turned rival, Emmerson Mnangagwa. Nelson Chamisa, in turn, replaced the late Tsvangirai. The ruling ZANU-PF party won 69% of the 210 elective seats in Parliament, and the Zimbabwe Electoral Commission (ZEC) announced that Mnangagwa had beaten the other 22 presidential candidates to garner 50.8% of the vote. The main opposition, the MDC Alliance (MDC-A), challenged this election result which was later upheld by the Constitutional Court.

The pre-election period was relatively peaceful compared with previous polls. The opposition MDC-A was even allowed to take its campaign into ZANU-PF strongholds, a rare occurrence under Mugabe's rule. Even the European Union's observers were allowed in by the 'new' authorities after the 2002 ban on the bloc was lifted. However, while the elections were held in a relatively peaceful environment, the immediate post-election period presented a dramatic reverse. On 1 August 2018, the army killed at least six civilians in Harare, following a protest over ZEC's delay in announcing the results. This event reconfigured the socio-political landscape in Zimbabwe, serving to demonstrate that 'old' habits cannot simply be wished away. Indeed, subsequently, both domestic and international players expressed serious doubts about the 'new dispensation'. As a result, President Emmerson Mnangagwa set up a Commission of Inquiry chaired by former South African President Kgalema Motlanthe to probe the post-election violence.

Since the post-election killings of civilians, the socio-economic and political landscape has not shown a semblance of normalcy; on the contrary, the situation has deteriorated. The immediate post-election phase saw the opposition and civil society organisations claiming 'over 150 attacks upon their supporters and staff, including cases of abduction, sexual abuse, torture and assault'.[1] On 8 August 2018, the main opposition party, the MDC-A, through its spokesperson Nkululeko Sibanda, revealed that many of their senior officials had gone into hiding, fearing arrests or abductions after the election.[2] One of the most vivid signs that the environment was not conducive for the opposition was the endeavour by opposition leader Tendai Biti (whose People's Democratic Party had formed an election alliance with the MDC) to seek asylum in neighbouring Zambia; he was later handed over by the Zambians to Zimbabwean authorities.

Then came the January 2019 national shutdown called for by the Zimbabwe Congress of Trade Unions (ZCTU) and the subsequent internet shutdown by government, both post-election signs of a fragile post-2018 election scenario. To compound matters, the government reacted in a heavy-handed manner as it tried to control the protestors by deploying the army to arrest the situation, prompting stakeholders (especially the Church and the National Peace and Reconciliation Commission) to call for national dialogue (ND) amongst Zimbabweans in order to find a lasting solution to the crisis.

It is against this background that the author seeks to discuss the subject of NDs. In so doing, the concept is defined and the contexts in which dialogue can take place are discussed, as are the factors that affect NDs. There is also a brief discussion of the history of NDs in Zimbabwe. The chapter is premised on the compelling imperative for ND in the country.

---

1 'After disputed elections, Zimbabwe government's credibility is in jeopardy', *Mail and Guardian*, 21 August 2019.

2 'Opposition Leader Returned to Zimbabwe Despite Court Order', *VOA News*, 9 August 2018.

The findings of Focus Group Discussions (FGDs)[3] will also be used to explore what public opinion has to say about the value of ND: do they endorse it or not? How do they regard its chances of success? The chapter also considers key stakeholders in the process dubbed 'Political Actors Dialogue' (POLAD), and its agenda. There is also an exploration of the contestable issue of the 'right' mediation process. Lastly, the writer will hazard a discussion on prospects for the ND project.

## Zartman's ripeness theory as guiding theoretical framework

According to William Zartman (2008), the concept of a ripe moment for ND centres on the parties' perception of a mutually hurting stalemate (MHS) – a situation in which neither side can win, although a continuing conflict will be harmful to each (not necessarily in equal measure or for the same reasons). Also contributing to 'ripeness' is a recently avoided catastrophe. This further encourages the parties to seek an alternative policy or 'way out,' because suffering might only increase unless something is done to settle the conflict. The MHS is grounded in a cost-benefit analysis and is consistent with public-choice notions of rationality. These theories assume that a party will pick what is best for itself, and that a decision to change strategies is induced by increasing the pain associated with the present course of the conflict, thereby making change a rational choice from a cost-benefit point of view. Zartman (2013) suggested that 'ripeness' was the critical factor that finally triggered agreements during negotiations in the Sinai (1974), South West Africa (1988), El Salvador (1988), Mozambique (1992), and others while a lack of ripeness led to the failure of attempts to open negotiations between Eritrea and Ethiopia in the late 1980s and within Sudan for decades.

Using this theoretical framework, this chapter analyses the extent to which the conditions presently obtaining in Zimbabwe are or are not at a stage where the key players have reached a point where negotiations can take place. From a cursory look, it can be argued that the crisis or conflict situation is not as ripe as it was in 2008 when the Global Political Agreement (GPA) process was initiated, culminating in the formation of a Government of National Unity (GNU).

---

3  Twenty FDGs were held by MPOI across the country's ten administrative provinces from 1-4 April 2019.

## The concept of national dialogue and its Zimbabwean context

National dialogues are mechanisms used by societies to manage issues of national concern – often long-standing causes of conflict that have given rise to crisis situations. Blunck et al. (2017) define NDs as 'nationally owned political processes aimed at generating consensus among a broad range of national stakeholders in times of deep political crisis, in post-war situations or during far-reaching political transitions'. NDs seek 'to expand participation in political transitions beyond the political and military elites' and are aimed at addressing crises of national importance that have or can have repercussions for the whole of society. These can be severe political deadlocks or blocked political transitions. In these situations, NDs seek to ease tensions, to reach political agreement or even to establish a new institutional framework, fulfilling a crisis management function (ibid.). NDs normally involve wider societal consultations which may be premised on broad-based change processes or, alternatively, narrow objectives. They often include national elites, the government, opposition parties, the military, civil society, business, religious and traditional actors. History is replete with examples of NDs undertaken in a variety of political contexts and environments, such as Benin, Tunisia, Egypt, Libya, Morocco and Yemen. NDs usually consist of clear, well-defined structures which normally feature plenary and working groups, defined rules, and procedures for dialogue and decision making. NDs may take place over days or years, and their size and composition will vary depending on contexts. NDs may take the form of consultations, commissions, high-level problem-solving workshops, and/or referendums. Writers also contend that inclusion of large segments of society in NDs is critical as it enhances chances of generating buy-in for its outcomes.

The narrative of NDs is not a new phenomenon in Zimbabwe – the Tripartite Negotiating Forum (TNF) has been in existence since 1998 and has proved a critical forum for national discourse where socio-economic matters can be discussed and negotiated by social partners. Since 1978, Zimbabwe has had three significant NDs, leading to the Lancaster House Agreement, the National Unity Accord (1987) and the Government of National Unity (2009).[4] Some analysts argue that political dialogues in Zimbabwe largely borrow from the Shona traditional culture of '*dare*'

---

4 'National Dialogue not new to Zim', *The Patriot*, 16 May 2019.

where issues are resolved through 'arbitration, adjudication, mediation and negotiation'.[5]

NDs are typically convened at times 'when the fundamental nature or survival of a government in power is in question'.[6] Thus, they are usually intended as a means of redefining the 'relationship between the state, political actors, and society through the negotiation of a new social contract'.[7] In such historical moments, pro-change and anti-change forces emerge. The government – generally anti-change – often initiates NDs with the aim of regaining legitimacy by controlling the negotiating process and outcomes. Pro-change forces, on the other hand, envisage NDs as an opportunity for re-defining the future of the state and society. For these reasons, 'both pro-change and anti-change actors have often been able to agree on NDs as a negotiation format'.[8]

## What makes or breaks national dialogues?

Paffenholz et al. (2017) outline factors related to the political context and process that often play a part in the success or failure of NDs. The potential enablers or constraints include the resistance or support of national elites to the process, public support or frustration, the support or resistance from regional and international actors, local dialogue expertise, and experiences from prior negotiations. Related to this are architectural or process issues related to the ND – among other issues, the design of an ND shapes the level of representativeness and the distribution of power within the process, and thus the likelihood of reaching sustainable agreements.

One key design issue identified as critical to NDs include the representation of actors and selection process – sometimes elites have co-opted participants loyal to them which can hinder the broader participation and legitimacy of the process. A second revolves around the decision-making procedures which determine which actors hold decision-making and ultimately veto power. A third concerns the support structures for involved actors – such support structures can assist participants to build coalitions and enable groups to advocate for their respective interests. A fourth factor is that of coalition building among actors in the ND – coalition building is viewed as a powerful strategy for actors to make their

---

5   'POLAD: It will work, not only for economics, but conflict resolution', *The Sunday News*, 26 May 2019.

6   Ibid.

7   Ibid.

8   Ibid.

voices heard. The choice of facilitator is also viewed as critical. NDs are almost always facilitated by a party neutral to the negotiations. Finally, the literature reviewed shows that NDs have three key features:

- They serve to embrace the various and diverging interests of all stakeholders during processes of political transition;
- They can be understood as a kind of 'creative space' within which ideas of national unity, reconciliation and peace-building can prosper;
- They cannot replace the need for democratic elections and an effective constitution, but can provide a normative and practical framework conducive to building trust and enhancing confidence in a conflict-stricken state (ibid.).

## Multiple calls for national dialogue in Zimbabwe

Zimbabwe is at crossroads because of a deepening socio-economic and political crisis. One stark issue is the refusal by the main opposition leader, Nelson Chamisa, to recognise President Mnangagwa as the legitimate Head of State. The MDC Alliance insists that Emmerson Mnangagwa stole the elections and that a stolen election cannot produce a legitimate leader. The opposition insists that the Constitutional Court 'glossed over or ignored evidence that points either to grand theft of the election or the fact that Mnangagwa did not muster the required constitutional 50% plus one threshold'.[9]

On the other hand, the ruling ZANU-PF party dismisses claims by the MDC-A as 'mere political gamesmanship'. It argues that the MDC-A did have its day in court and lost after failing to produce 'primary evidence' to support its claim of electoral theft. ZANU-PF further argues that it had a resounding victory in the parliamentary elections (a more than two-thirds majority) which has not been challenged. Thus, 'the ruling party is not willing to consider any negotiation that does not start with an unequivocal acceptance of the legitimacy of the Mnangagwa presidency'.[10] This stalemate based on the question of legitimacy is one of many issues that have triggered calls for ND in Zimbabwe.

Analysts and members of the clergy have been at the forefront of calling for the ND. This call began in August 2018, and grew louder after the existing political and economic crisis was accelerated by fuel hikes

---

9 'What are the realistic chances for political dialogue in Zim?', *Zimbabwe Independent*, 7 December 2018.

10 Ibid.

in January 2019. The 150% fuel price increase announced by President Mnangagwa on state television led to protests between 14 and 16 January 2019, and the state responded in a heavy-handed manner. The Human Rights NGO Forum reported that it:

... recorded at least 844 human rights violations during the shutdown. Consolidated statistics so far reveal the following violations: killings (at least 12); injuries from gunshots (at least 78), assault, torture, inhumane and degrading treatment, including dog bites (at least 242), destruction of property, including vandalism and looting (at least 46), arbitrary arrests and detentions (466), displacements (under verification).[11]

The national shutdown was also hijacked by criminal elements who took advantage of the protests leaving many properties vandalised and businesses exposed to looters. Government also shut down the internet (illegally) leaving Zimbabweans cut off from the rest of the world.

In line with the incessant calls for ND, the August 2018 Commission of Inquiry recommended:

the establishment of multi-party reconciliation initiatives, including youth representatives, national and international mediators to address the root causes of the post-election violence and to identify the implementing strategies for reducing tensions, promoting common understanding of political campaigning, combating criminality and uplifting communities.[12]

The January 2019 national shutdown heightened calls for ND in Zimbabwe. Below are key state and non-state actors who are at the forefront of making such calls.

## The Zimbabwe Council of Churches (ZCC)

Founded in 1964 from the Rhodesia Missionary Conference and then the Rhodesia Christian Council, the Zimbabwe Council of Churches (ZCC) is made up of 26 Christian denominations and ten para-church organisations. In its 2019 New Year statement, the ZCC acknowledged that the country is sinking into the doldrums and offered to create a platform for the two main political rivals, i.e. Emmerson Mnangagwa and Nelson Chamisa, to

---

11 'Zim: Framework for national dialogue and the roadblocks', *Zimbabwe Independent*, 22 February 2019.

12 Ibid.

talks after the disputed 30 July 2018 elections. In the statement, the ZCC General Secretary, Reverend Dr Kenneth Mtata, said:

> We also remain committed to proffering solutions which are inclusive, realistic and sustainable. The church, therefore, commits to create a shared space for a collaborative national consensus-building process aimed at creating a space of trust in which all Zimbabweans can shape a new national imagination.[13]

The ZCC further said it would break the political impasse through ND:

> There is need to forge a renewed sense of shared national vision and social cohesion. We find that there is a lack of consensus on fundamental issues affecting the nation. The underlying tensions pit the rich against the poor, the young against the old, ruling party supporters against opposition party supporters. We, therefore, call for a broad-based consultative process to come up with a national economic vision and a fundamental redistribution of wealth for the benefit of all Zimbabweans.[14]

The first week of February 2019 saw the ZCC organising a broad-based meeting that was attended by government ministers, members of the opposition parties, and delegates from industry, the security sector, civil society, human rights groups and trade unions, as well as international observers and ambassadors. Speaking at the meeting, Dr Mtata said the ND was the church's answer to the crisis. He said the ZCC, which hosted the meeting together with the Zimbabwe Catholic Bishops' Conference, the Evangelical Fellowship of Zimbabwe, and the Union for the Development of Apostolic Churches in Zimbabwe Africa had recognised that 'the nation finds itself at the cross-roads', and said 'the churches had made their voices louder regarding the urgency and necessity of a national dialogue'.

## National Peace and Reconciliation Commission (NPRC)

The NPRC made a similar call for such a process in order to resolve the prevailing challenges in the country. In a statement on 21 January 2019, it announced that it would initiate a multi-stakeholder dialogue process since it was concerned by the situation in the country: 'The NPRC calls upon all key stakeholders to come to a national dialogue in order to share

---

13 'National Dialogue, The Zimbabwe Council of Churches Solution to The Nation's Prevailing Crisis', *Hallelujah Mag*, January 2019.
14 Ibid.

views on how to address the situation in our country and foster sustainable peace and development.'[15]

## National Association of Non-Governmental Organisations (NANGO)

From 21 to 23 January 2019, NANGO convened membership meetings in its northern, western, eastern, midlands and southern regions. NANGO noted its concern over the continuous undermining of people's socio-economic rights because of the problems confronting the country. It also expressed a desire to see the country 'emerging from the economic, social and political doldrums and adhering to the fundamental principles, norms and ethos that entrench the drive to a common and shared vision for the nation which is critical for the attainment of sustainable development'.[16]

In its recommendations, NANGO made a plea for a candid, inclusive and open ND and noted that a huge task lies ahead in tackling the problems and 'demands more structured multi-stakeholder collaborations and partnerships between government, business, non-state actors and citizens on actions and activities which are crucial in addressing challenges bedevilling the country'.[17] The organisation urged the President to 'expedite the national dialogue involving key political parties, civil society, churches to resolve a myriad of issues faced by the nation'.[18]

## Zimbabwe Congress of Trade Unions (ZCTU)

In May 2019, ZCTU President Peter Mutasa called upon stakeholders to engage in a national social dialogue. Speaking at a tripartite seminar on 'promoting and reinforcing social dialogue in Zimbabwe', Mutasa underlined the need for a social dialogue:

> We therefore note as labour that national social dialogue is of extreme importance and has a strategic dimension in that deepening consultation between social partners builds consensus on broad issues. This includes currency options that should enable Zimbabwe to navigate this treacherous terrain and crises in a balanced and inclusive way that promotes social justice, fairness and equity.[19]

---

15  'Peace Commission calls for national dialogue', *The Chronicle*, 21 January 2019.
16  'Towards the Zimbabwe people want: A call to inclusive and open national dialogue', *Bulawayo24 News*, 29 January 2019.
17  Ibid.
18  Ibid.
19  'ZCTU calls for National Social Dialogue as Crises Worsen', *Pindula News*, 8 May 2019.

Mutasa also noted that national dialogue was consistent with the national constitution and international statutes that the country has acceded to:

> Continued violation of rights enshrined in the Constitution, bickering, name-calling, animosity and polarisation will only serve to sink this country deeper into crisis and the abyss, further impoverishing the working people we represent. We therefore stand here as labour to re-affirm our commitment to the founding principles and values of social dialogue espoused in our frameworks negotiated in the TNF, and especially the Declaration of Intent and the Kadoma Declaration.[20]

## The Zimbabwe African National Union–Patriotic Front

ZANU-PF has been the primary political party since the country attained nationhood in 1980.[21] Post-election media reports have shown that the ruling party's leader, Mnangagwa, has tried to extend an olive branch to his main political rival Chamisa. For example, in a press statement issued on 3 August 2018, Mnangagwa showed intentions of accommodating MDC-A when he said 'to Nelson Chamisa I want to say, you have a crucial role to play in Zimbabwe's present and its unfolding future, let us both call for peace and unity'.[22] This probably was an acknowledgement by Mnangagwa that his main political adversary was a significant force that he could not afford to ignore in the country's national discourse.

Shaken by the January 2019 shutdown, President Mnangagwa cut short his four-nation European tour, and called for ND among the country's stakeholders:

> I invite leaders of all political parties as well as religious and civil leaders to set aside our differences and come together. What unites us is stronger than what could ever divide us. Let's begin a national dialogue. Let's put the economy first. Let's put the people first.[23]

Mnangagwa repeated his call for ND, but it is difficult to gauge the extent

---

20  Ibid.

21  Formed in 1963 as ZANU, the PF was born out of a political and military alliance with the Zimbabwe African People's Union (ZAPU) in 1976 during the armed liberation struggle.

22  'National Dialogue in Zimbabwe', *Bulawayo 24 News*, 6 February 2019.

23  'Mnangagwa Calls for Dialogue in Zimbabwe After Violent Protests, Army Killings', *VOA News*, 22 January 2019.

of his sincerity. Officially opening the Zimbabwe–Botswana Binational Commission in Harare on 28 February 2019, Mnangagwa underlined his message for dialoguing amongst stakeholders in Zimbabwe:

> Fully aware that a nation at peace with itself is a nation that can achieve socio-economic development. As such, a national dialogue platform has been established to allow a broader section of the political players to express their views and input into the governance discourse of this country. We are therefore committed to dialogue at home, across the entire region and beyond. Together we shall create a new reality for our people.[24]

In the context of renewed discussions on re-engagement with the European Union in June 2019, Mnangagwa has sought to pursue four main streams of ND:[25]

- Political Actors – this dialogue initiative involves seventeen political parties that took part in the 2018 harmonised elections. Most have negligible electoral support and are not represented in Parliament.[26] This initiative has been boycotted by the MDC-A.

- Presidential Advisory Council (PAC) – this advisory council was established in January 2019 to provide ideas and suggestions about key reforms, and measures needed to improve the investment and business climate for economic recovery. It is largely made up of Mnangagwa allies.

- Matabeleland Collective – this is aimed at building consensus and effective social movement in the Matabeleland region to influence national and regional policy in support of healing, peace, and reconciliation.[27]

- The Tripartite Negotiating Forum – this was launched in June 2019, twenty years after it was first suggested by the ZCTU. Its functions are to consult and negotiate over social and economic issues and submit recommendations to Cabinet; negotiate a social contract; and generate and promote a shared national socio-economic vision.[28]

---

24 'President speaks on national dialogue', *The Herald,* 1 March 2019.
25 'In Zimbabwe, neither repression nor dialogue are working', *The Africa Report*, 21 August 2019,
26 Ibid.
27 Ibid.
28 Ibid.

## The Movement for Democratic Change Alliance

The MDC-A is currently the main political opposition in Zimbabwe. It was formed as a coalition of seven parties[29] to challenge ZANU-PF in the run up to the 30 July 2018 harmonised elections. Its leader, Nelson Chamisa, remains adamant that his party won the presidential election and refused to recognise Mnangagwa's presidency while continuing to allege that the incumbent stole the vote.

Chamisa has reiterated this message using social media platforms: 'presidency is disputed' because of 'rigged presidential election result'; 'we need genuine dialogue under a credible convener and mediator to solve this crisis'; 'stop citizens' abuses, beatings and arrests'.[30] One of the MDC-A's key demands is to have the ND facilitated by an independent regional arbiter such as the Southern African Development Community with African Union or UN guarantees – 'I am afraid, my president (Chamisa) is not going to do things just to massage President Mnangagwa.'[31]

## International actors

On the regional front, SADC has also called on all stakeholders in Zimbabwe to participate in the ND process. Chairperson Hage G. Geingob noted that 'the [Zimbabwe] government has dialogue with all stakeholders in the country with a view to strengthening economic transformation, and calls upon all stakeholders to support the process'.[32] Probably in an effort to reinforce this initiative, former South African President Thabo Mbeki visited Zimbabwe in December 2019 and met Mnangagwa and Chamisa. Other leaders who met Mbeki included MDC-T leader Thokozani Khupe and National Constitutional Assembly (NCA) president Lovemore Madhuku. During the visit, SADC Executive Secretary Stergomena Tax tweeted: 'fellow Sadc citizens, let us give space to the mediation and let us

---

29 MDC-Ncube, led by Welshman Ncube, MDC – Tsvangirai (MDC-T), led by Nelson Chamisa, People's Democratic Party, led by Tendai Biti, Transform Zimbabwe, led by Jacob Ngarivhume, Zimbabwe People First, led by Agrippa Mutambara, Zimbabwe African National Union-Ndonga, Multi-Racial Democrats led by Mathias Guchutu who became leader of the party after its original leader, Revd Gerald Mubaiwa left the country.

30 'Zimbabwe opposition boycotts Mnangagwa political dialogue', *The Zimbabwean*, 7 February 2019.

31 'Zimbabwe: Hope of Dialogue Dead After ED Friday Gaffe – Chamisa', *allAfrica*, 15 June 2019.

32 'SADC endorses Mnangagwa's dialogue process', *Bulawayo 24 News*, 11 February 2019.

be supportive'.[33] On the other hand, the EU issued a statement to the effect that it does not recognise Mnangagwa's pet project, the POLAD, as being adequate to resolve the problems in Zimbabwe and said that it would engage SADC and the African Union to put pressure on his administration to have more inclusive talks:

> The EU will seek increased collaboration with international partners, most importantly the African Union, Sadc and its member countries, and international financial institutions, which can play a key role by supporting Zimbabwe in enabling an inclusive dialogue and in accelerating progress in reforms[34]

Table 9.1 below outlines the various types of dialogue and the proposed forms of mediation as well as the key elements of the ideas being promoted.

**Table 9.1: Multiple dialogue permutations in Zimbabwe, post-2018 elections**

| Type of Dialogue | Proposed Mediation | Key proponents |
| --- | --- | --- |
| ZANU-PF/MDC (Chamisa) dialogue | Domestic mediation | ZANU-PF |
| ZANU-PF/MDC (Chamisa) dialogue | International mediation | MDC |
| Multi-party dialogue | Domestic mediation | ZANU-PF |
| Multi-party dialogue | International mediation | MDC and smaller opposition parties, South Africa, USA, the EU |
| All stakeholder dialogue | Domestic mediation | Civil Society Organisations and the Church, USA, the EU |
| All stakeholder dialogue | International mediation | South Africa, EU and the USA |

## Public attitudes towards national dialogue in Zimbabwe

FGDs conducted in April 2019 show that in the main ordinary Zimbabweans view the ND as a positive initiative, though there is a core that disagree with it. Those who endorsed the ND see it as serving two primary purposes: to resolve issues between the two main political parties, which, in its turn, will enable the country to move forward, especially on the economic front. They believe that dialogue is an instrument for resolving conflict and that this is a necessary precondition to the country making meaningful progress.

Some FGD participants were quick to cite the example of the GNU forged in 2009. They believe that the country's problems can be addressed if Chamisa and Mnangagwa similarly pool their energies towards achieving the same national goal. The quotations below demonstrate the level of support that ordinary citizens have for ND in Zimbabwe:

> If we are to look back, a similar event happened between Mugabe and Tsvangirai. Through a dialogue, Mugabe agreed to make Tsvangirai a Prime Minister and our livelihoods improved; we could get cash in the banks. So, if these two are to have dialogue and agree, then Chamisa will bring the USD he promised us and this, combined with Mnangagwa's plans for the country, our lives can improve. (Matabeleland South Rural Male, 18-24 years)

> It's not going to be helpful for us to kill each other as a people irrespective of whether you are Shona, Ndebele or Nambya or whatever tribe. You know there is another term… in fact there is a Bible verse that says a house divided against itself will not stand. We will not stand as a nation economically, socially and otherwise, as long as we have these demarcations that still exist between political parties, because those political parties are the ones that can speak to people at grassroots level, so for me dialogue is the way to go. (Bulawayo Urban Male, 25-49 years)

> Personally, I see it as good to address interests of the majority of the country. There is no need for selfishness in this time that we are in. What is needed is for us to build the country so it can move forward. If the MDC party refuses, you cannot force a donkey to drink water when it doesn't want to, they can stay behind while we move on our own. (Mashonaland Central Rural Male, 25-49 years)

> I see the idea of national dialogue as something good; I think there is need for inclusivity, so I see that as a good thing. (Masvingo Urban Female, 18-24 years)

> I also say that it's a good idea because if you look back when Mugabe and Tsvangirai met, things got well. But ever since he got in power, their fighting is affecting us. So, I think they should have a dialogue and unite because if the situation continues like

this, nothing will go well. So, if they unite and look for where the problem is stemming from, then they can solve what needs to be solved. (Bulawayo Urban Female, 18-24 years)

I am also in support of that maybe if they have dialogue and stop the fighting and forgive each other and have a peace pact that might lead to resolving of issues. (Matabeleland North Rural Female, 18-24 years)

Participants who said the ND is a bad idea also observed that ZANU-PF and MDC-A have different agendas which neither are prepared to give up. Some even argued that it will worsen the fighting between MDC-A and ZANU-PF and their supporters (Masvingo Urban Female, 18-24 years).

I think it's a bad idea because they are both fighting for power. Who will want to feel inferior to the other one? One thing we know is that we will never have two Presidents. However, they are both ambitious in their own way, they have different ideas, and so for them to meet and form one basic party I doubt that it will be possible because, each one of them has different plans. So, one way or the other, it really won't work because one of them might feel superior, I think we need one head for the country. (Bulawayo Urban Female, 18-24 years)

It's a good idea but a wolf and a sheep can't have a dialogue. Because ED [Mnangagwa] is a trickster – even when he loses the election, he claims that he won. So Chamisa will never be able to deal with Mnangagwa. (Matabeleland South Rural, Female, 25-49 years)

## National dialogue in Zimbabwe, the Mnangagwa way and its uneasy beginning

On 6 February 2019, President Mnangagwa invited over twenty leaders of the political parties that participated in the 2018 harmonised elections to State House for the first 'post-election dialogue'. These included Thokozani Khupe, leader of a breakaway MDC-T faction, Lovemore Madhuku of the NCA and Nkosana Moyo of the Alliance for People's Agenda (APA). The meeting was boycotted by Chamisa.[35] In his opening

---

35 'Zimbabwe opposition boycotts Mnangagwa political dialogue', *The Zimbabwean*, 7

remarks, President Mnangagwa stated that the country has 'lost decades of developing our motherland. It is imperative that we reach out to each other and work out ways of resolving differences through peaceful means and dialogue.'[36]

Using twitter, Mnangagwa stressed that the invitation to the talks was 'without preconditions' urging 'let us all put the people first and politics second'. Chamisa, on the other hand, continues to insist that he won the 30 July 2018 and so tweeted that the 'presidency is disputed' because of 'rigged presidential election result'[37] Going further, he said:

> Mr Mnangagwa and his colleagues are making a mistake of thinking that he is talking to 'just a 41-year-old'. When he is engaging me, he is talking to 2,6 million voices. So, in my voice, there are 2,6 million voices of Zimbabweans and he should not expect to meet with them because they will not, they have sent me.[38]

The first session of the post-election meeting saw the establishment of four committees, to focus on: the institutional framework for dialogue; agenda items; the convenor of the dialogue; monitoring and evaluating the implementation of the agreed issues.[39]

As anticipated, teething problems emerged during the meeting on 22 February 2019 at State House when some of the losing presidential candidates, who had attended the first session, snubbed the event. In a statement, the United Democratic Alliance (UDA) under the leadership of Daniel Shumba said they were withdrawing and attacking the initiative as an 'insincere, choreographed, and a highly compromised process'.[40] The UDA stressed that it disagreed with the process, purpose, issues and the level of engagement because, 'clearly, no outcomes can be expected from this facade. The process starts with a predetermined agenda even before agreeing on the moderator, issues, or milestones. It's inconsequential and of no effect.'[41]

Build Zimbabwe Alliance also chose not to attend the second session.

February 2019.

36  Ibid.

37  Ibid.

38  'Chamisa snubs ED talks', *NewsDay*, 7 February 2019.

39  'Zim political parties walk out of post-election dialogue – and some snub it entirely', *Sunday Times*, 22 February 2019.

40  Ibid.

41  Ibid.

Its leader Noah Manyika said, 'It is my position that any dialogue that does not include the MDC Alliance and other critical stakeholders will not pass the credibility test locally and globally.' [42]

Not unexpectedly, ZANU-PF's Energy Mutodi, Deputy Minister of Information, Publicity & Broadcasting Services, claimed everything was smooth sailing without the MDC-A in attendance. He noted that 'representatives of various political parties established committees to facilitate national dialogue. The national dialogue will go on without MDC Alliance who have refused to accept defeat in last July's elections.'[43]

The leader of the The Alliance for the People's Agenda (APA), Nkosana Moyo, also announced that they were opting out of the talks because of statements made by President Mnangagwa at a ZANU-PF rally in Masvingo. He also stated that unless ZANU-PF and MDC Alliance agreed to dialogue, the talks would not yield anything:

> ZANU-PF and MDC-A must be present. Let us recall the official voting statistics at presidential level, ED 50.6%, NC 44.3% (and the) rest 4.9%. If the idea of national dialogue is to try and bring the nation to a place of cohesion, then it should be self-evident that a platform that excludes either ZANU-PF or MDC-A cannot be considered as a serious undertaking.[44]

The People's Progressive Party of Zimbabwe, led by Timothy Chiguvare followed suit. Nonetheless, ZANU-PF's Legal Affairs Secretary, Munyaradzi Paul Mangwana, said the ruling party was not worried about the withdrawals as the parties were exercising their democratic right not to participate. Mangwana remarked:

> … we are not worried. We were given the mandate to run this country. We are simply saying come and join the club of rulers. If you are called to the club of rulers, you should feel honoured to be in the club of rulers, but if you don't want, you can go to the club of cattle herders, that is the freedom of association [45]

In a bold message to signify the irreversibility of the ND process and challenge the MDC Alliance Mnangagwa launched the 'Political Actors Dialogue' on 17 May 2019. A total of seventeen political parties attended

---

42 Ibid.
43 Ibid.
44 'National dialogue in disarray', *Newsday*, 7 March 2019.
45 Ibid.

with media reports suggesting that close to 10,000 people had supported the launch at the Harare International Conference Centre. They included political party leaders, service chiefs, captains of industry, parliamentarians, government ministers, NGOs, media, the UN and the Islamic Society of Zimbabwe. In his keynote address, President Mnangagwa emphasised the need for positive engagement, and mutual agreement, regarding the values of social cohesion, unity and togetherness. He said:

> The dialogue we are launching today will undoubtedly leave a lasting imprint on our country's political landscape and help to contribute to the turnaround of the country's socio-economic fortunes… this journey we are embarking on must ultimately lead us towards improving our democratic practices and culture. It must ultimately lead us towards improving our democratic practices and culture. It must also lead us to a stage where we can compete and cooperate, always informed and guided by our national interests.[46]

## National dialogue in peril: competing agendas and challenging issues

While stakeholders are of the same mind about the need for ND, they differ about the agenda for dialogue. For example, MDC-A would want an agenda that includes discussions around the legitimacy of the presidency, the constitution and the economic crisis. The NPRC stated that:

> In an effort to come up with a framework for national dialogue, conversations were centred around the following key questions; Why are Zimbabweans not talking? What are the key pillars of national dialogue? Who should participate, how and at what level? How should a dialogue process be structured? What does a successful dialogue look like?[47]

In the meantime, ZANU-PF Secretary for Legal Affairs, Munyaradzi Paul Mangwana, said that every Zimbabwean had an obligation to recognise the result of an election, which was pronounced by the Zimbabwe Electoral Commission (ZEC) before endorsement by the Constitutional Court.

He reiterated that the dialogue process that was ongoing had nothing to do with power-sharing, saying 'ZANU-PF received the mandate to run this country for the next five years, if they want to share the power it received

---

46 'Political party leaders must be exemplary', *The Herald*, 18 May 2019.
47 'NPRC initiates national dialogue', *The Herald*, 1 February 2019.

from the people they have to go back to the electorate'.[48] Mangwana's sentiments were echoed by the Minister of Information, Publicity and Broadcasting Services, Monica Mutsvangwa, in a meeting with editors of various media houses, made it unequivocally clear that 'dialogue is not the same thing with power-sharing negotiations. Every time we go for elections to elect a government, losers selectively choose components of the election results to accept and reject.'[49]

The MDC Alliance has also laid down conditions for political dialogue with the government. Responding to President Mnangagwa's invitation to the POLAD, Chamisa's Chief of Staff, Sessel Zvizvai, stressed that the opposition party believes in 'genuine and sincere dialogue that ultimately must benefit the people of Zimbabwe'.[50] The statement was posted after Chamisa turned down the invitation to join the ND. According to the MDC, any genuine ND has to be facilitated by an independent regional arbiter such as SADC or the AU with UN guarantees.[51] The MDC's ten conditions for dialogue include the immediate cessation of all forms of violence, as well as a genuine and transparent process to bring to book those responsible. Ironically, presidential spokesman George Charamba made the same call, stating that that dialogue 'predicated on violence or coercion would not be accommodated'.[52] The main opposition formation also wants to see the restoration and guaranteeing of the security of all citizens, and the immediate cessation of arbitrary arrests, mass trials and violation of the rule of law. A key demand was that of independence of the judiciary, with guarantees barring executive interference with judicial processes.

Another important precondition for dialogue raised by the MDC-A relates to the release of all political detainees and prisoners of conscience, and respect for human rights, particularly political freedoms. It says that it wants to see all military personnel returned to barracks as the country is not at war, plus a guarantee of freedom of association, expression and movement. Last but not least, it required 'the decriminalisation of the MDC, including an end to the harassment and persecution of its party

---

48 'Power-sharing not on the agenda: Mangwana', T*he Herald*, 23 February 2019.
49 'Political dialogue not a power sharing deal', *The Chronicle*, 13 June 2019.
50 'MDC lays down conditions for political dialogue with Zim government', *African News Agency*, 8 February 2019.
51 Ibid.
52 'Zimbabwe's Presidential Spokesman Relays Conditions for Dialogue', *VOA Zimbabwe*, 6 February 2019.

leadership and their families, and the unbanning of civilian politics'.[53]

Despite what might be called an engagement of smoke and mirrors, Mnangagwa and Chamisa continue their stand-off. The former did not arrive for a discussion with church leaders aimed at working out ways by which he might meet the opposition leader; and as previously stated the latter refused to attend the meeting initiated by the President. However, despite the positions of the two main political players, a number of other proposals have been put forward: Brian Kagoro, a former civil society leader and activist, assessed a number of proposals that have been floated:

(a) Surrender of power by Mnangagwa and return to legitimacy either through an election re-run, recount or nomination of a third party (neutral administrator). The opposite is the unconditional recognition of Mnangagwa as Head of State duly elected for a five-year term in exchange for inclusion of the opposition in government or alternatively irreversible commitment to specific constitutional, institutional and state reforms;

(b) Legal and institutional changes to guarantee a credible, free and fair 2023 election;

(c) Guarantees to ensure that the 2023 elections are presided over by a truly independent electoral commission and, by implication, the dissolution of the current Zimbabwe Electoral Commission (ZEC);

(d) Establishment of a transitional administration or authority or some form of inclusive government (as opposed to government of national unity), with the specific task of undertaking comprehensive state reforms and aligning all laws with the 2013 Zimbabwean constitution. This includes repeal of repressive legislation such as the Public Order and Security Act and the Access to Information and Protection of Privacy Act;

(e) Ensuring civilian control of the military, non-partisan prosecution of corruption in high places, independence of the judiciary and the media (including state media compliance with the constitution);

---

53  Ibid.

(f)   Repeal of the United States law, the Zimbabwe Democracy and Economic Recovery Act and any other restrictive measures and sanctions against Zimbabwe; and

(g)   A national all-stakeholders' dialogue aimed at evolving an inclusive social contract with participation from political parties, civil society, faith-based organisations, labour, government, private sector and diasporas/citizens, etc.[54]

However, the chances of any of these proposals being enacted are very slim as essentially they are a direct threat to the survival and power base of ZANU-PF. This essentially means that even before the launch of any serious dialogue there is a stalemate.

## Wrangling over choice of mediator

The choice of a facilitator for the ND process has been one of the main bones of contention between ZANU-PF and the MDC-A. Chamisa insists on the need for 'a credible convener and mediator to solve this crisis'.[55] Hence, as stated above, he wants the talks to be independently mediated:

> I am working flat out to have dialogue in order to save lives rather than lose lives to have dialogue and a solution. I have written letters without a reply before and after elections. I have met with potential mediators in the church. I have engaged leaders in SADC and AU. I made a public statement of invitation[56]

In addition, Sessel Zvizvai spelt out the opposition party's demands with regards to the choice of the facilitator for the national dialogue.

> It is our considered view that at the core of the crisis in Zimbabwe is the disputed presidential election result and the associated governance issues. In view of this, the MDC's position is that the dialogue process must be convened by an independent mediator and not one of the disputants... in this respect, the MDC believes that genuine dialogue can only take place if regionally facilitated and mediated by SADC and guaranteed by the AU and the UN. It is also our view and position that genuine dialogue can only

---

54   'What are the realistic chances for political dialogue in Zim?', *Zimbabwe Independent*, 7 December 2018.

55   'Zimbabwe opposition boycotts Mnangagwa political dialogue', *The Zimbabwean*, 7 February 2019.

56   'Zimbabwe: Chamisa Heightens Call for Dialogue', *allAfrica*, 9 January 2019.

take place when a conducive environment has been created for the same.[57]

As expected, ZANU-PF has rejected calls for the appointment of a foreign mediator. Indeed, in April 2019, Mnangagwa stated that after the failure by party negotiators to agree on a convenor, 'we took time discussing this issue until we agreed to have the National Peace and Reconciliation Commission chairperson Sello Masole Nare, and the Gender Commission chairperson Margaret Mukahanana-Sangarwe. They will co-chair the process.'[58]

The Crisis in Zimbabwe Coalition (CiZC) is also concerned about the choice of facilitator. It considers that the commissioners from the NPRC are already presidential appointees and therefore heavily compromised. Moreover, the civic body has misgivings about the NPRC because of its failure to rollout tangible national reconciliation initiatives. It argues that the issues at stake require an accepted and un-conflicted party to play the mediator role and a continental or international guarantor.

Regarding the contentious role of SADC mediation, a key unresolved issue between ZANU-PF and the MDC-A, is that the church considers the process would be best solved locally:

> ... we are not insulated from the different regional and international structures. But ... if we can as much as possible deal with the processes ourselves while the other actors from the region and globally are also supporting it from behind. You can't start by thinking that there is need for outside mediation if you have not exhausted local processes and possibilities. I think it is too early to think about external help at the moment. I think there is a possibility for Zimbabweans to find themselves.[59]

While the two main political players haggle over who should mediate, South Africa and the USA have also weighed in, making their position clear that mediation should be managed by a neutral, independent person from beyond the country's borders.[60] Speaking at the launch of the

---

57 'MDC responds to Mr. Mnangagwa's invite to national dialogue', *MDC Media*, 6 February 2019.

58 'National dialogue latest: President Emmerson Mnangagwa rejects foreign, neutral mediator', My Zimbabwe News, *1 April 2019*.

59 Ibid.

60 'South Africa Urges Zimbabwe to Seek External Mediator for Mnangagwa, Opposition Talks', *VOA Zimbabwe*, 17 May 2019.

POLAD on 17 May 2019, Mphakama Mbete, South Africa's Ambassador to Zimbabwe said:

> ... for credibility the leadership of Zimbabwe wishes to consider a facilitator outside Zimbabwe. We as a region we will be ready to propose names from the African continent. At this point we would like to appeal to the political formations, to the political leaders who are not yet part of the political dialogue to join the national dialogue[61]

In a statement released on 12 February 2019 by the US Department of State, Deputy Spokesperson Robert Palladino expressed concern about excessive use of force by the security forces and urged parties to embrace national dialogue.[62] It also called upon the Zimbabwe government to end intimidation and release people arrested during the January 2019 shutdown, and it underlined the need for a neutral mediator:

> The United States calls on all sides to come together immediately in national dialogue. The dialogue process must be credible, inclusive, and mediated by a neutral third party. In order for such a dialogue to succeed, the Government of Zimbabwe should end its excessive violence and intimidation, immediately release the civil society activists who have been arbitrarily detained, and hold security force members responsible for human rights violations and abuses accountable. We also reiterate our call for the Government of Zimbabwe to enact promised political and economic reforms.[63]

## Is national dialogue in Zimbabwe doomed from birth?

There are a number of critical factors that make or break NDs, and Zimbabwe is not insulated from some of these. First, the two main political antagonists, ZANU-PF and the MDC A, are worlds apart in terms of their demands for dialogue. The MDC-A's conditions for dialogue and Chamisa's refusal to attend the POLAD launch are clear indications that ND may proceed without the participation of the main opposition political party. The question is: should it do so? Could the outcome be deemed national in character if a key stakeholder has been excluded? And, under

---

61  Ibid.
62  'United States Speaks on Zim Situation, Calls for Dialogue', *Pindula News*, 12 February 2019.
63  Ibid.

these circumstances would the outcome be accepted by the populace?

In addition, the preconditions for dialogue between the two main political players are by and large 'exclusionary'. This is evident in the meetings convened thus far. Third, to compound matters, the leaders of the parties appear disinterested in compromise. Mnangagwa's statement broadcast on ZBC that he was not going to treat Chamisa as 'the special one' aptly captures this political standoff: 'I am not going to take a tractor or bulldozer to pull him out of his house [for talks]. I do not believe anyone is special. We are having dialogue where everyone is free and the table is still open to anyone who wants to come. Why should he be treated differently?'[64]

Moreover, speaking at Unity Day celebrations in December 2019, Mnangagwa stressed that POLAD is the only platform where political leaders will seek to unite Zimbabwe and map a way forward, hence he will continue the discussion with committed political players: 'Zimbabwe's political issue is one and it must be discussed at one platform and that is POLAD and I am not moving away from that.'[65]

On the other hand, Chamisa's demands for face-to-face meetings with Mnangagwa and his dismissal of other POLAD members as 'useless praise-singers who have no dispute' with the ZANU-PF leader illustrate the MDC-A's exclusionary agenda. Thus, arguably, both protagonists are concerned with narrowing the range of stakeholders to themselves. Such a limited agenda cannot be construed as a 'national' dialogue.

For instance, on 22 January 2019, the Heads of Civil Society Coalitions (HCSC) issued a press statement on the deteriorating political and socio-economic situation in Zimbabwe in which they embraced the call for dialogue by many actors including President Mnangagwa. The coalition emphasised the need for lasting and meaningful solutions to the many crises confronting the nation.[66] According to the HCSC, the ND processes should 'include political and religious leaders, civil society, diaspora community, and most importantly the victims and families being haunted by the structural and direct violence that is currently afflicting the country'.[67] The Coalition further noted that 'the proposed dialogue must acknowledge and chart sustainable solutions to the deep-seated problems for Zimbabwe which are rooted in politics and economy. These are problems whose resolution must not only be left to politicians but must include all sectors of Zimbabwe.'[68]

The Crisis in Zimbabwe Coalition (CiZC), concerned about President

Mnangagwa's restricted call for dialogue with only the political parties which participated in the 2018 national elections, was categorical in its call for 'an inclusive process ... that brings all stakeholders together beyond political boundaries'.[69] For the CiZC, the ND is 'not predicated on creating another version of a Global Political Agreement or an elite power sharing deal', but rather 'a reform process that seeks to safeguard the interest of citizens by restoring the Social Contract between the citizens and those that govern'.[70] It thus envisions an ND with a 'cross section of stakeholders that include civic society, labour, women, youth, persons living with disabilities, farmers, media, students, the diaspora, religious groups and business among other critical stakeholders'.[71] A key imperative is for Mnangagwa to prove his sincerity by ensuring that there is a conducive environment for holding an inclusive dialogue in the wake of state-sponsored terror that has increased fear levels amongst citizens.[72] The Citizens Manifesto,[73] a civic convergence platform, is also an advocate of an inclusive bottom-up process for a:

> national conversation [that prioritises] political, economic and social issues that are holding us back ... as a country rather ... we view national dialogue as a convergence of multiple sub-processes seeking to build cohesion within particular sectors and communities (e.g. political actors dialogue and community level dialogue initiatives).[74]

> ... The repository for solutions goes beyond political parties requiring the participation of all relevant constituencies, including business, churches, women, youth, civil society and indeed political parties to enable co-creation of solutions that work for all.[75]

Church leaders are also part of the movement, wanting to see a broader inclusive national dialogue process. In an interview, ZCC general secretary Revd Dr Kenneth Mtata said:

> ...what we don't want in this national dialogue process is to fuse individual interest groups to shape the whole agenda of the dialogue. For example, the process that the President is having now with political leaders, it is relevant and important, but for us it is not the national dialogue. The national dialogue is bigger, and it involves more actors and it asks all citizens to participate. It is not an elite process. It is a process that must encompass everyone and,

therefore, it raises the broader question, not the specific questions that are being raised at these conversations.[76]

What about the question of legitimacy? Does the church consider that the issue of Mnangagwa's legitimacy should be an agenda item under the ND process?

No, I think what we should talk about is the legitimacy of processes, because the legitimacy of President Mnangagwa is a symptom. The real question is, why is it after elections someone questions the legitimacy of the President? Because, today we can question the legitimacy of President Mnangagwa, tomorrow we will ask the same question when someone comes. For us, as the Church, the question we must ask is: how do we make sure that no one's Presidential legitimacy is ever questioned? This is the pertinent question.[77]

As Brian Kagoro notes, 'in the absence of good faith, mutual trust [and] dedicated, truly impartial and strong interlocutors, the probability of any productive inter-party dialogue is almost zero'.[78] He adds that 'ZANU-PF and MDC Alliance fears and prejudices do not represent the exhaustive national aspiration. Zimbabwe is much bigger than the political parties and those affected by the current political, economic and social crises are not just the members of the two contending parties'.[79]

Kagoro also identifies a number of important challenges: (a) legitimacy or legality question', (b) internal processes and mechanisms to guarantee comprehensive state and legal reforms, (c) issue of executive authority during the period of transition or negotiation and administrative arrangements to ensure that any agreement reached is actually implemented and not wantonly cast aside, and (d) the question of acceptable external guarantors of the non-reversal of the agreements reached consensually.[80] Dialogue without an agenda or menu of comprehensive state reforms in the current context is likely to be an exercise in futility. An unreformed military sympathetic to ZANU-PF, a parliament with a ZANU-PF majority, and the absence of strong human rights guarantees and guarantor, does not

---

76 'Legitimacy of national political processes the real issue: Mtata', *Zimbabwe Independent*, 1 March 2019.

77 Ibid.

78 'What are the realistic chances for political dialogue in Zim?', *Zimbabwe Independent*, 7 December 2018.

79 Ibid.

80 Ibid.

inspire confidence, nor does a militant opposition unwilling to make any concessions.

FGDs conducted in April 2019 reveal that while most participants feel that the ND process is a desirable and possible way forward, its chances of success are limited because of the irreconcilable differences between Mnangagwa and Chamisa. Some participants blamed ZANU-PF as party, which it accused of believing that only liberation war veterans deserve to lead the country. Others felt that as long as major political parties continue to fight about who won the 30 July 2018 presidential elections, then dialogue will not succeed (Midlands Urban, Male, 18-24 years). One participant observed that both parties have selfish interests such as ensuring that their members secure positions in any new arrangement emanating from the ND. Another participant from the Midlands female group (25-49 years) argued that the ND would be a good idea if the President was prepared to genuinely listen to and deliver on the will of the people.

> I think it will only be successful if the two leaders do away with their pride, because the leader of MDC Alliance claims that he won the elections and their victory was stolen and the same is with ZANU-PF, they claim to have won the election and they are in power. So, they all need to humble themselves for the dialogue to be a success and I see it can result in a GNU-government of national unity. (Masvingo Rural Male, 18-24 years)

> I think it's not going to yield anything because this other party is claiming that they won the election and so is the other party claiming the same. So, what I see, is that the dialogue will be a difficult one. (Midlands Rural Female, 25-49 years)

> I do not see the chances of success because Chamisa was given an opportunity for that dialogue and he turned it down and that to me will lead to more fighting and reducing the chances of success. (Matabeleland South Rural Female, 25-49 years)

> What I think will be the problem with the dialogue is, for example, Chamisa has people that he had promised positions when he got in office and yet the dialogue will only accommodate him alone. So, Chamisa has realized that his team will not be accommodated in any unity government that might result from the national dialogue. It would appear therefore that Chamisa has sold out on his friends

that stood with him during campaigns. (Mashonaland East Rural Male, 25-49 years)

Overall, there was a realisation among FGD participants that the major political parties that are critical to the success of the dialogue are also its stumbling blocks. Participants who said ND is a bad idea also observed that ZANU-PF and the MDC-A have different agendas on which they are not prepared to compromise:

I think it's a bad idea because they are both fighting for power. Who will want to feel inferior to the other one? One thing we know is that we will never have two Presidents. However, they are both ambitious in their own way, they have different ideas. (Bulawayo Urban Female, 18-24 years)

I think the dialogue can be tricky to work towards inclusivity because the two political parties have bigger differences. One is claiming to have won and the other party has lost. So, it will be difficult for them to find a common ground to agree, but if they agree and it becomes a success, it will go a long way in helping our country. (Masvingo Urban Female, 18-24 years)

## Ripeness theory and its application in Zimbabwe

What then are the prospects for a successful ND process in Zimbabwe? Two schools of thought presently prevail, one pessimistic, the other more optimistic. The ripeness thesis gives rise to the optimistic prognosis.

The Pessimistic View: this rests on the argument that whereas both state and non-state actors recognise the need for an ND, the process has been undermined from the beginning. The non-participation of the MDC-A and withdrawal of several smaller parties speaks volumes of a process beset by challenges and in need of honest political will to push it forward. Does this exist? It seems unlikely within a heavily polarised environment where the president's camp insists that acceptance of legitimacy is a precondition for any form of engagement,[81] claiming 'ticharamba tichingotonga' (we will continue to rule), to which the MDC-A retaliates with 'jecha!' (we will be spoilers).[82] Observers also note that the ND framework is deficient in terms of 'conceptual clarity around practicalities of what national

---

81 'A framework for dialogue', *The Standard*, 10 November 2019.
82 Ibid.

dialogue entails' why we need it, and how it should be employed'.[83] There is consensus, particularly from non-state actors, that a national dialogue should not be 'confined to frontline political players ...' but should include 'Zimbabweans across the breadth and length of the political and non-political spectrums'.[84] Mandikwaza (2019) aptly summarises this:

> The government's national dialogue facilitation conceptualised the Zimbabwean crises in the context of post-election negotiation, rather than a popular national crisis requiring broad-based consultative content. While the government of Zimbabwe called for inter-party dialogues based on the 2018 election conflict, urgent national issues requiring redress include the economic crisis, unemployment, constitutional reforms and continuing human rights violations. More broadly, there is lack of clarity on the mandate of the national dialogue designed, hence the need to spell out what this intended dialogue seeks to achieve.

Political analyst Eldred Masunungure is of the view that the Zimbabwe crisis is deeply rooted and he contends that a full solution 'lies internally because the crisis is multi-faceted'.[85] Indeed, it looks as if the multi-dimensional crisis will continue to undermine the country. It is only through compromise that the impasse can be broken, but alas the key players have shown no sign that they are willing to go this route.

The Optimistic Perspective: This begins with the recognition that Mnangagwa and ZANU-PF and Chamisa and the MDC have been locked in a stalemate since the July 2018 elections, each party believing that they will eventually prevail. For instance, Chamisa was confident that he would have Mnangagwa's victory nullified in the Constitutional Court and that the court would declare him the winner. When they ruled against him, his reaction was to reject the ruling, and refuse either to accept Mnangagwa's electoral legitimacy or to negotiate with someone who he alleged had stolen his victory. (He has since mellowed and is prepared to seek ND with Mnangagwa though he still insists that the legitimacy question must be on the agenda.)

Meanwhile, Chamisa is increasingly caught in the middle of his own party with two major factions emerging. He stands between the soft-liners who are advocating robust dialogue with ZANU-PF and the hardliners

83 Ibid.
84 Ibid.
85 'Give dialogue a chance: SADC', *NewsDay*, 18 December 2019.

who are viscerally opposed to talking with the 'electoral thief'. The tension between these two opposing tendencies is not sustainable and may easily explode into violence and even result in the party fragmenting. Chamisa is also under tremendous pressure from powerful forces outside the party who are strongly advocating negotiations. These include church organisations – and he is a pastor in the Living Waters denomination of the Apostolic Faith Mission. The Western international community is also pushing for dialogue. Hardliners will have none of this; they are insisting on confronting the 'illegitimate' regime and doing so through street protests and demonstrations – whether sanctioned by the police or not – and other forms of militant action.

Further, one of his three deputies, Tendai Biti, plus the vice-chair of the party, Job Sikhala, are capturing the imagination of the youth wing of the party as well as the militant elements in and outside the party who now find life unbearable and believe that the country has reached a cul-de-sac. This puts party leader Chamisa in an untenable position. In short, the situation is now hurting him as well as his party.

On the other side is Mnangagwa, who finds himself in an equally untenable situation. The Political Actors Dialogue is proving to be an empty shell rather than a forum for dialogue. There is no significant social group on which he can count for support. Even the military, a former bulwark, is now reportedly disillusioned with Mnangagwa's 'new dispensation'. Moreover, intra-party factionalism is back with a vengeance, threatening the continued viability of the long-ruling party. In short, Mnangagwa and his party find themselves trapped in a vicious cycle from which they cannot easily escape. Zimbabwe is more rather than less ripe for ND.

## Conclusion

Socio-economic and political developments before and after the 2018 harmonised elections point to a desperate need for political and civic actors players to find a way to pull the country out of the crisis. However, the ND process, still in its infancy, is unlikely to develop. This is partly because the process, which is supposed to be national in outlook and broad-based in nature, is primarily being driven by a few political actors, the leaders of ZANU-PF and the MDC. While it is true that both parties enjoy strong political support, the crisis engulfing the country transcends political party affiliations and affects every citizen. In addition, there remains a lack of consensus on the choice of facilitators, which means the potential for moving forward is currently close to zero.

# References

Blunck, M., L. Vimalarajah, O. Wils, C. von Burg, D. Lanz and M. Mubashir (2017) *National dialogue handbook: A guide for practitioners*. Berlin: Berghof Foundation.

Bomba, B. and T.L. Chisaira (2019) 'Towards a framework for Inclusive National Dialogue'. Harare: Citizens Manifesto.

Inclusive Peace and Transition Initiative (IPTI) Briefing Note, 'What Makes or Breaks National Dialogues?' April 2017, Available at: https://www.inclusivepeace.org/sites/default/files/IPTI-What-Makes-Breaks-National-Dialogues.pdf

Mandikwaza, E. (2019) 'Constructive national dialogue in Zimbabwe: Design and Challenges', Conflict Trends, 2019/1.

Paffenholz, T., A. Zachariassen and C. Helfer (2017) 'What Makes or Breaks National Dialogues?' Geneva: Inclusive Peace and Transition Initiative.

Zartman, I. William (2008) '"Ripeness": the importance of timing in negotiation and conflict resolution', *E-International Relations*, 20 December.

Zartman, I. William (2013) 'Ripeness', in Guy Burgess and Heidi Burgess (eds) *Beyond Intractability*. Boulder: University of Colorado Conflict Information Consortium.

# 10

# Zimbabwe's Constitutional Framework

## Greg Linington

## Introduction

The purpose of this chapter is to outline and discuss some of the important features of Zimbabwe's constitutional framework, in particular the changes brought about by the 2013 Constitution, the provisions of which are compared with those in the old Constitution. The judiciary receives the most attention, because the courts have a vital role to play in establishing a culture of constitutionalism and respect for the rule of law. The rule of law and the concept of good governance are in fact two of the 'founding values and principles' in section 3 of the 2013 Constitution.

## The President

### Introduction

Zimbabwe's Constitution provides for an executive presidency. He or she is '… the Head of State and Government and the Commander in Chief of the Defence Forces' (section 89 of the 2013 Constitution). The duties of the President are set out in section 90, a progressive provision that promotes respect for the rule of law. Subsection (1) stipulates that 'the President must uphold, defend, obey and respect this Constitution as the supreme law of the nation and must ensure that this Constitution and all other laws are faithfully observed.' The President must also promote unity and peace (section 90 (2) (a)). Although this language is rather vague, it is not meaningless. Thus presidential action that *blatantly* undermines unity and peace will be inconsistent with this provision. In addition, he or she is also under a *positive* duty to 'ensure protection of the fundamental human rights and freedoms and the Rule of Law' (section 90 (1) (c)).

In order to qualify for election as President, a person must be a citizen by birth or descent and have attained the age of 40. In addition, he or she must be a registered voter and ordinarily resident in Zimbabwe (section 91 (1)). A President is limited to a maximum of two five-year terms (section 95 (2)).

What follows below is a discussion of certain features of Zimbabwe's presidency and the changes that have been brought about by the 2013 Constitution. It is not a comprehensive review of the office, but seeks to examine aspects that are of particular interest.

## Presidential law-making power

In 1986 Parliament passed the Presidential Powers Temporary Measures Act [Chapter 10:20]. The purpose of the Act is to enable the President to make regulations to deal with emergency situations. Regulations made by the President are temporary in nature and automatically expire after 180 days (section 6 (1) of the Act). The constitutional controversy surrounding the Act is centred on the fact that presidential regulations have the status of *primary* legislation. In other words, such regulations are equivalent in status to an Act of Parliament. Section 5 of the Act actually states that if there is a conflict between a regulation and an Act of Parliament, the regulation will take precedence. (The only exception is the Emergency Powers Act, but the latter will only be operative if a public emergency is in force.)

Parliament is the body entrusted with the power to create primary legislation. If the President can also create primary legislation, this would be contrary to the doctrine of separation of powers. The constitutionality of the Temporary Measures Act was doubtful even under the old Constitution. However, the High Court held in *S v Gatsi and Rufaro Hotel (Pvt) Ltd* 1994 (1) ZLR 7 (H) that the Act was consistent with the old Constitution. Parliament had not abrogated its law-making powers when it passed the Act. This was because presidential regulations expire after six months and also because of the 'tabling procedure' established by the Act. According to section 4 (1) of the Act, '... copies of all regulations made ... shall be laid before Parliament no later than the eighth day on which Parliament sits next after the regulations were made.' If Parliament resolves that a regulation should be repealed, the President must do so (section 4 (2)). A failure to lay a regulation before Parliament within the specified period will result in the invalidity of the regulation concerned. This meant, according to the court, that the President's law-making powers are still under parliamentary control. Thus, in the opinion of the court, Parliament had not abrogated its legislative responsibilities.

The South African Constitutional Court has taken a different view of the matter. In *Executive Council of the Western Cape Legislature and Others v President of the Republic of South Africa and Others* 1995 (10) BCLR 1289 (CC), the Constitutional Court of South Africa said at 1311-1312:

> There is ... a difference between delegating authority to make subordinate legislation within the framework of a statute under which the delegation is made, and assigning plenary legislative power to another body, including ... the power to amend the Act under which the assignment is made.

The Court held that Parliament cannot abdicate its responsibility to create primary legislation. Delegating such a power to the executive would constitute such an abdication.

The 2013 Constitution states that 'observance of the principle of Separation of Powers' is one of its founding values and principles (section 3 (2) (3)). It is therefore not surprising that section 134 (a) stipulates that 'Parliament's primary law-making power must not be delegated.' This must surely mean that the Presidential Powers (Temporary Measures) Act is now unconstitutional.

## Removing the President from office

As with the old Constitution, the 2013 Constitution provides for the removal of the President from office on certain grounds. According to section 97 (1), the President can be removed for: 'serious misconduct; failure to obey, uphold or defend the Constitution; wilful violation of the Constitution; or inability to perform the functions of the office because of physical or mental incapacity.' Three of these grounds also appeared in section 29 (3) of the old Constitution. The new additional ground is 'failure to obey, uphold or defend the Constitution'. At first sight, this ground could be regarded as a duplication of the 'wilful violation of the Constitution' ground. In fact, it is broader. 'Failure to obey' embraces more than 'wilful violation', since it probably includes negligence and laziness. In addition, the President is now under a *positive* obligation to '... uphold or defend the Constitution.' The words 'serious misconduct' probably include not only criminal activity but also actions and omissions constituting gross negligence. A failure to perform presidential functions properly may also be covered by the phrase.

The removal procedure is activated by a joint resolution of the Senate and the National Assembly which must be 'passed by at least one-half of their total membership' (section 97 (1)). Under the old Constitution (section 29 (3)) the resolution only required the support of at least one third of Parliament's members. Once this has been done, the Parliamentary Committee on Standing Rules and Orders will appoint a joint committee of the Senate and the National Assembly to investigate whether the President should be removed. This Committee must consist of nine members, reflecting the political composition of Parliament (section 97 (2)). The Constitution does not stipulate the procedure to be followed by the committee. However, one of the founding values of the Constitution is the rule of law (section 3 (1) (b)), a concept that generally incorporates the principles of natural justice which include the right to a fair hearing. In addition, section 69 (2) says: 'In the determination of civil rights and obligations, every person has a right to a fair, speedy and public hearing within a reasonable time before [a] ... tribunal or other forum established by law.' Read together, these provisions seem to mean that the committee must give the President a fair hearing before arriving at a decision. The committee is surely a type of 'tribunal' or 'forum.' The decision of the committee must be based on information placed before it.

If the committee recommends the removal of the President, the issue will then be returned to Parliament. Thereafter, the President will cease to hold office if '... the Senate and the National Assembly, by a joint resolution passed by at least two-thirds of their total membership, resolve that the President ... should be removed from office' (section 97 (3) (b)). The role of the committee is vital. Even if two-thirds of parliamentarians want to remove the President, they will not be able to do so unless there is a recommendation to that effect by the committee. The fact that the committee must reflect the political composition of Parliament is an improvement on the position under the old Constitution, which gave the Speaker discretion to determine both the size and composition of the Committee. In 2017, it appeared that President Mugabe would be removed from office through the use of section 27. However, he resigned once it was clear that Parliament was serious about removing him.

# Parliament

## *The structure of Parliament*

Zimbabwe has a bicameral legislative system made up of a National Assembly and a Senate. The National Assembly consists of two hundred and ten members elected by secret ballot in a constituency system (section 124 (1) (a) of the 2013 Constitution) and a further sixty women members, six from each of the ten provinces into which Zimbabwe is divided (section 124 (1) (b)). The latter are elected on a party list system of proportional representation (ibid.). These sixty women members are a temporary phenomenon since their seats will cease to exist when the life of the second Parliament after the 2013 election comes to an end (ibid.).

The Senate has eighty senators (section 120 (1)). Six are elected from each of Zimbabwe's ten provinces, while a further sixteen are chiefs elected by Provincial Councils of Chiefs (section 120 (1) (a) and (b)). In addition, the President and Deputy President of the National Council of Chiefs are automatically senators (section 120 (1) (c)). Finally, two senators are selected to represent persons with disabilities (section 120 (1) (d)).

## *The legislative process*

The focus here is on the power relationship between the two Houses of Parliament in the legislative process and the extent to which the President has the power to block legislation. The first point to note is that all ordinary Bills (i.e. all Bills except Constitutional Amendment Bills) require only a simple majority of votes in each House in order to pass. Once a Bill has been passed by Parliament, it must be sent without delay to the President for his assent (section 131 (5)). The President then has 21 days within which to decide whether to assent to the Bill (section 131 (6) (a)). If the President declines to do so, because he or she thinks the Bill is unconstitutional or has other reservations about it, he or she must refer the Bill back to Parliament '… together with detailed written reasons for those reservations and a request that the Bill be reconsidered' (section 131 (6) (b)). The provision is slightly misleading when it speaks of the Bill being returned to Parliament. In fact, it is sent only to the National Assembly, which may either amend the Bill to accommodate the President's concerns or pass the Bill again in its original form (section 131 (7)). If the National Assembly does decide to pass the Bill again it will now have to do so '… by a two-thirds majority of [its] total membership' (section 131 (7) (b)). If the President is still unwilling to assent to the returned Bill, he or she must within twenty-one days '… refer the Bill to the Constitutional Court for advice on its constitutionality' (section 131 (8) (b)). But if the Constitutional Court rules that the Bill is constitutional, 'the President must assent to it' (section 131 (9)).

So, the President has the power to veto a Bill, but any such veto can be overcome by the National Assembly – though only through a super majority vote – and the Constitutional Court. The fact that the support of legislative and judicial bodies is needed to overcome presidential opposition to a Bill means that in practice the views of the President will normally prevail. The right of the President to ask for an opinion on a Bill before its passage – as a means of preventing the Bill from becoming law – is rather unusual. In many countries the role of the judiciary is limited to hearing challenges to laws already in force.

When a Bill is introduced into Parliament it must be sent to the Parliamentary Legal Committee, which consists of at least three Members of Parliament, a majority of whom should normally be legal practitioners (section 152 (2) of the 2013 Constitution). The purpose of the Committee is to examine Bills (other than Constitutional Bills) and to report on whether any provision in them is inconsistent with the Constitution (section 152 (3)). If the Committee issues an adverse report the House of Parliament concerned must consider the report and decide whether to accept or reject it. Before making a decision, the House must allow the person in charge of the Bill – usually a Minister – to respond to the report (paragraph 8 (5) of the Fifth Schedule to the 2013 Constitution). If the House agrees with the adverse report, the House will be precluded from proceeding with the Bill until its unconstitutional provisions have been removed (paragraph 8 (4)). The House is, of course, free to reject the report, in which case it may proceed with the Bill. If the House does decide to accept the adverse report, the person in charge of the Bill may, within fourteen days, apply to the Constitutional Court for a declaration that the Bill is constitutional. If the Court issues a declaration that the Bill is constitutional, the House may proceed with the Bill (paragraph 8 (6)).

What is clear form all this is that the Parliamentary Legal Committee exercises influence, rather than power, over Parliament. As has been seen, Parliament will only be bound by an adverse report if it chooses to be bound by it. Of course, it will be foolish of Parliament to ignore an adverse report, since once the Bill becomes an Act it may be subject to challenge in the courts. The Legal Committee was also a feature of the old Constitution and there too Parliament had a discretion to accept or reject its reports. What is new under the 2013 Constitution is the possibility of approaching the Constitutional Court as a means of challenging an adverse Legal Committee report.

With regard to the power relationship between the National Assembly and the Senate, the 2013 Constitution has established a legislative system that makes the National Assembly the dominant House. In the event of a disagreement between the two Houses, the National Assembly is entitled to send the Bill to the President in the form in which it was passed by that House, after the expiry of a ninety-day period (paragraph 6 (1)). So the power of the Senate is limited to delaying the passage of legislation if the National Assembly disapproves of amendments made to a Bill by the Senate. If the Bill concerned is a money Bill, the Senate cannot amend the Bill but is limited to *recommending* that the National Assembly amend it (paragraph 7 (1)). In fact, unlike all other Bills, which can originate in either House, money Bills must commence in the National Assembly (paragraph 2 (2)). If the Senate does not pass a money Bill within eight days of its introduction into that House, the National Assembly has the power to send the Bill directly to the President for his assent (paragraph 7 (4)).

## Amendment of the Constitution

Zimbabwe is a constitutional democracy. This means that the Constitution is sovereign. Section 2 (1) of the 2013 Constitution says: 'This Constitution is the supreme law of Zimbabwe and any law, practice, custom or conduct inconsistent with it is invalid to the extent of the inconsistency.' A similar provision was contained in the old Constitution (section 3). Although Parliament has the power to amend the Constitution, this power has to be exercised in accordance with the procedure established in section 328 of the 2013 Constitution. Thus the power to amend is subject to – and under the control of – the Constitution.

Constitutional Bills may be presented in either House of Parliament, but only after the Speaker 'has given at least ninety days' notice in the *Government Gazette* of the precise terms of the Bill' (section 328 (3)). This is in order to facilitate public discussion of the Bill. Changing the supreme law of the land is not something to be done lightly. Indeed, Parliament has an obligation to invite members of the public to express their views on the Bill. This may be through written submissions or in public meetings (section 328 (4)). Parliament would appear to be under an implied obligation to at least consider the views expressed by the public.

Constitutional Amendment Bills require the affirmative votes of at least two-thirds of the membership of each House of Parliament in order to pass (section 328 (5)). This was a feature of the old Constitution too (section 32). The need for a super majority distinguishes Constitutional Bills from ordinary Bills which only need a simple majority. Procedures involving special majorities are of course a feature of constitutional amendment provisions in many constitutions. This is because it is felt that mere simple majorities should not have the power to change the supreme law, and there ought to be broader support for any change before enacting it. But this leads to the problem of the counter-majoritarian dilemma: the tension between democracy – conceived as rule by a simple majority – and a supreme law that can only be changed by a super majority. Can this be justified in the context of Zimbabwe? It certainly can. A super majority requirement imposes a check on a government that has a long history of abusing power. However, it will not amount to much if the ruling party controls two-thirds of the seats in the two Houses of Parliament, which has often been the case in Zimbabwe's history.

If a Constitutional Bill seeks to amend the Declaration of Rights or Chapter 16 (dealing with agricultural land), then it must also be submitted to a national referendum (section 327 (6) (a)). If it receives a majority of the votes cast, the Speaker will send the Bill to the President who must assent to it. This extra procedure in relation to Constitutional Bills dealing with the special topics referred to will help to ensure their political legitimacy. This is particularly important in the area of human rights. The old Constitution did not require a referendum when seeking to amend the Constitution.

## Judicial independence

### Introduction

How do the old and new Constitutions compare in relation to judicial independence? I have taken a broad view of judicial independence, and have examined not only the *structure* of the courts, but also the issue of *access* to the courts. A legal system whose judiciary is structurally independent but which imposes a high *locus standi in judicio* (the legal right or capacity to bring an action before the court) threshold on litigants cannot be said to have a truly independent judiciary.

Both Constitutions address the issue of judicial independence expressly. The relevant provision in the old Constitution is section 79B, a short and succinct provision which says: 'In the exercise of his judicial authority, a member of the judiciary shall not be subject to the direction or control of any person or authority, except to the extent that a written law may place him under the direction or control of another member of the judiciary.' The equivalent provision in the 2013 Constitution – section 164 – is more comprehensive. It states in subsection (1) that 'the courts are independent and are subject only to this Constitution and the law, which they must apply impartially, expeditiously and without fear, favour or prejudice'. The next subsection links judicial independence, impartiality and effectiveness with the concepts of the rule of law and democratic governance. This is a natural progression given the organic relationship that subsists between these concepts. State institutions and agencies are expressly prohibited from interfering with the functioning of the courts (section 164 (2) (a)). In addition, the State is now under a positive obligation to enact legislation to assist and promote judicial independence (section 164 (2) (b)). By recognising the relationship between judicial independence and the rule of law the 2013 Constitution has taken a significant step forward in promoting the independence of the courts. But more is required than just fine words in a Constitution. The development of a culture of constitutionalism is also necessary to ensure that judicial independence becomes a reality.

*Judicial independence defined*

An American scholar, Peter Russel, has defined judicial independence as '… the *autonomy* of judges – collectively and individually – from other individuals and institutions' (Russel, 2001: 6; my emphasis). 'Autonomy' is of course one of the fundamental pillars underpinning the concept of judicial independence. Former Zimbabwean Chief Justice Enoch Dumbutshena has stressed that it includes not only independence from the legislature and the executive but also from political influence exerted by the public (Dumbutshena, 1989: 314). Moreover, '… unless the judiciary is given a special sphere, clearly separated from that of the legislature and the executive and so protected against political, economic and other influences, the value of the qualities of detachment and impartiality, which are the prerequisites for the proper performance of the judicial functions, will be substantially endangered' (ibid.: 313). Where this 'special sphere' is not violated, the judiciary will be able to exercise its adjudicative functions properly, interpreting and applying the law free from external pressure. But interference from the executive can undermine the work of the judiciary. Former Vice President Phelekezela Mphoko is alleged to have interfered with a pending criminal case by instructing officers to release two accused persons from the cells at Avondale Police Station. At the time of writing, Mr Mphoko is about to be tried for criminal abuse of office (*The Herald*, 11 October 2019).

Dumbutshena's successor as Chief Justice, Anthony Gubbay, has said that the judicial office demands of its incumbents 'not merely a sound knowledge of the law but conscience and insight – a sense of balance and proportion' (Gubbay, 2002). Judicial independence requires 'that there never be the motivation to appoint someone ... because of avowed political affiliations' (ibid.). In addition, there must be 'a guarantee of security of tenure during good behaviour and ability to perform the necessary function' (ibid.). Thus, a government must not be able to remove a judge simply because it dislikes a decision he or she has handed down. This does not mean that judges will never be accountable for their actions. As will be seen later, a judge who engages in 'misbehaviour' may be disciplined or removed from office. However, this may only be done through a special procedure set out in the Constitution.

Without an independent judiciary important constitutional principles such as the rule of law and the separation of powers cannot operate effectively. If we say that the rule of law operates in a particular state this means that not only do laws exist there but that the laws have attained a certain standard or quality. More specifically, the rule of law postulates that a legal system ought to provide for equality before the law, the protection of basic human rights and laws that are drafted in clear and precise language. This last characteristic of the rule of law is important because it reduces the danger of arbitrary rule by ensuring legal certainty: laws that are vague do not enable citizens to foresee what the consequences of their actions will be.[1] In *Chimakure and Others vs Attorney General* 2013 (2) ZLR 466 (S), Mlaba DCJ said at 498: 'It is essential in a free and democratic society that people should be able within reasonable certainty to foresee the consequences of their conduct in order to act lawfully.' He added at 499: 'A vague law impermissibly delegates basic policy matters to policemen, prosecutors and judges for resolution on an ad hoc and subjective basis,

---

1  See also *S v Mpofu & Anor*, CC-5-2016.

with the attendant dangers of arbitrary and discriminary application. So the legislature is prevented from passing arbitrary and vindictive laws.' The task of the courts in a modern constitutional state is to ensure that the rule of law is upheld. But if the judiciary is not separate from the executive and the legislature, it will not be able to do this, since it will then be simply a creature of the other state organs, subject to their direction and control.

Zimbabwe's old and new Constitutions both contain provisions designed to protect judicial independence. However, provisions in a constitution do not tell the full story. In deciding whether Zimbabwe's judiciary is in fact independent and able to exhibit the fairness and impartiality that is associated with proper judicial independence, it is necessary to consider the situation on the ground. As Charles Goredema observes, 'the working conditions of the judiciary make incumbents vulnerable to illegitimate direct and subtle influence from government and other sources' (Goredema, 2004: 106). It is a fact that most Zimbabwean judges have been put in possession of farms taken from commercial farmers as part of the 'land reform' programme. Naturally, a reasonable onlooker might be inclined to question the independence of the judiciary in relation to cases dealing with land.

*International law and judicial independence in Zimbabwe*

Zimbabwe is a party to a number of international instruments dealing with aspects of judicial independence. Article 14 (1) of the International Covenant on Civil and Political Rights provides that '[I]n the determination of any criminal charge against him, or of his rights and obligations in a suit at law, everyone shall be entitled to a fair and public hearing by a competent, independent and impartial tribunal established by law.' Article 7 (1) of the African Charter on Human and Peoples Rights (1981) is similar in effect since it establishes the right to be tried before 'competent' and 'impartial' courts. The concept of judicial independence is implicit in both these terms. On 20 October 1991, Zimbabwe signed the Harare Commonwealth Declaration. The document commits signatory States to uphold the rule of law and the independence of the judiciary. Judicial independence is also provided for in article 10 of the Universal Declaration of Human Rights.

A detailed statement of what judicial independence is all about is contained in the 'Basic Principles of the Judiciary', adopted by the United Nations in 1985. The 'Basic Principles' oblige '… all governmental and other institutions to respect and observe the independence of the judiciary'

(Principle 1). Courts must be allowed to '… decide matters before them … without any restrictions, improper influences, inducements, pressures, threats or interferences, direct or indirect, from any quarter or for any reason' (Principle 2). It is for the courts alone '… to decide whether an issue submitted for [their] decision is within [their] competence as defined by law' (Principle 3). Of particular importance is Principle 4 which says: 'There shall not be any inappropriate or unwarranted interference with the judicial process, nor shall judicial decisions by the courts be subject to revision.'[2] According to Principle 6, judicial independence '… entitles and requires the judiciary to ensure that judicial proceedings are conducted fairly and that the rights of the parties are respected.' The other principles (there are twenty altogether) concern issues such as: judicial freedom of expression and association; qualifications, selection and training of judges; conditions of service and tenure; professional secrecy and immunity; and discipline, suspension and removal.

In 1998 Zimbabwe was one of 20 Commonwealth countries that participated in a colloquium on parliamentary supremacy and judicial independence at Latimer House in the United Kingdom. This led, eventually, in late 2002, to the emergence of the Latimer House Guidelines on Judicial Independence. These stipulate that '[j]urisdictions should have an appropriate independent process in place for judicial appointments.'[3] If no such process is in place, '… appointments should be made by a Judicial Services Commission (established by the Constitution or by statute) or by an appropriate officer of state acting on the recommendation of such a commission' (Guideline 1). Moreover, '[t]he appointment process … should be designed to guarantee the quality and independence of mind of those selected for appointment at all levels of the judiciary' (Guideline 1). Appointments must be made on merit (Guideline 1). However, the need for '… the progressive removal of gender imbalance and of other historic factors of discrimination' (Guideline 1) must be taken into account when making appointments. Members of the judiciary ought to be appointed on a permanent basis: contract appointments must '… be subject to appropriate security of tenure' (Guideline 1). The remaining guidelines deal with the funding, salaries and training of judges.

Finally, mention must also be made of the International Bar Association

---

2   However, Principle 4 also states that '[t]his principle is without prejudice to judicial review or to mitigation or commutation by competent authorities of sentences imposed by the judiciary, in accordance with the law.'

3   Guideline 1.

Minimum Standards of Judicial Independence.4 These are important, firstly, because they are very detailed and comprehensive and, secondly, because they were actually used by the IBA when that body undertook an investigation of the judiciary and the rule of law in Zimbabwe in March 2001. As might be expected, many of the IBA's 'standards' overlap with those contained in the other instruments referred to above. Others are however either unique to the IBA document or elaborate on the standards and principles found elsewhere. For example, the IBA standards distinguish between 'personal' and 'substantive' independence. The former '... means that the terms and conditions of judicial service are adequately secured so as to ensure that individual judges are not subject to executive control' (IBA, Standards, Article 1 (b)). 'Substantive' independence indicates '... that in the discharge of his judicial function a judge is subject to nothing but the law and the commands of his conscience' (Article 1 (c)). The standards also state that 'in the decision-making process, a judge must be independent vis-à-vis his judicial colleagues and supporters' (Article 46). The courts must have exclusive responsibility for all judicial matters' (Article 8). In addition, the power to transfer judges from one court to another must '... be vested in a judicial authority' (Article 12).

## Appointment of judges to the superior courts

### Appointment of judges to the superior courts under the old Constitution

Section 84 (1) of the old Constitution stipulated that the power to appoint Supreme Court and High Court judges – including the Chief Justice – was vested in the President. The same provision stated that the President could only exercise this power '... after consultation with the Judicial Service Commission'. Because the President needed only 'consult' the Commission, he was not under any obligation to follow its recommendations.[5] However,

---

4  Adopted at the IBA's nineteenth biennial conference held in New Delhi in October 1982.

5  Section 84 of the original Lancaster House Independence Constitution stipulated that, with the exception of the Chief Justice, judges were to be appointed by the President '... on the advice of the Judicial Services Commission.' This meant in effect that the decision was made by the Commission. The same section also provided that the Chief Justice was to be appointed by the President '... on the advice of the Prime Minister.' However, '... before tendering his advice...' the Prime Minister had to consult the Commission and consider any recommendations it might make. According to section 84 (1) (b), 'if the advice that he proposes to tender is not consistent with any such recommendations, *Parliament shall be informed before the appointment is made*' (my emphasis). Lovemore Madhuku (2005: 126) writes: 'The requirement to inform Parliament before an appointment was made meant ... that the President had to take

if he appointed as a judge someone not recommended by the Commission, the Senate[6] had to '… be informed as soon as is practicable' (section 84 (2)). The old Constitution did not confer any specific powers on the Senate in respect of judicial appointments. However, at the Lancaster House Independence Conference, Lord Carrington said that informing Parliament would 'give an opportunity for debate if members so desire.'[7] If the Senate were to decide that the President had abused his judicial appointment power, Parliament could pass a vote of no confidence in the government (Section 31), or even remove the President from office (section 29 (3)). Given the ruling ZANU (PF) party's domination of Parliament, it was highly unlikely that any developments of this sort would have occurred (Linington 2001: 170, paragraph 445).[8]

The only real limitation on the President's judicial appointment power was to be found in section 82 of the old Constitution. This provision stipulated that a person would not be qualified for appointment to the bench of a superior court unless he or she satisfied the requirements set out therein. A candidate had to be, or had to have been, a judge in a country where the common law is Roman- Dutch or English, and English is an official language (Section 82 (1) (a)). Alternatively, a candidate would also have been appointable if for at least seven years he or she had been qualified to practise as a legal practitioner in Zimbabwe or a country in which the common law is Roman-Dutch and English is an official language (Section 82 (1) (b) (i) and (ii)). If the candidate held Zimbabwean citizenship, an entitlement to practise law in a country where the common law is English and English is an official language would have sufficed (Section 82 (b) (iii)). It is important to note that the 'seven years' requirement refers to the period that had elapsed since the candidate became qualified to practise; the candidate need not have actually practised law for seven years. So a person, who, on registering as a legal practitioner, spent the next seven years working in a bottle store, could have been made a judge!

---

into account the views of Parliament before accepting the Prime Minister's advice. It was competent, under the framework, for the President to decline the Prime Minister's proposed appointee on the grounds of disapproval by Parliament.'

6  Prior to the re-establishment of the Senate it was the House of Assembly of the then unicameral Parliament that had to be informed.

7  Lord Carrington (1979), 'Opening Speech to the Plenary Session of the Lancaster House Conference', paragraph 20. See also Linington (2001: 170, paragraph 445).

8  The opposition Movement for Democratic Change (MDC) failed to secure even a meeting of the Committee appointed by the Speaker in October 2000 to consider whether the President ought to be removed.

From what has been said in the previous paragraph it can be seen that persons appointed to the bench did not normally need to be citizens. It was only if the sole ground for appointment they could satisfy was the one stipulating an entitlement to practise law in a country where the common law is English and English is an official language that they needed to be citizens. In June 2000 President Mugabe threatened to force into retirement judges who failed to renounce their British citizenship.[9] The President's threat was quite unlawful, since none of the judges concerned had been appointed to the bench on grounds requiring citizenship.

Provided that the President chose from amongst persons qualified in terms of section 82, his discretion to appoint whom he liked was unlimited. Accordingly, as Karla Saller notes, 'the appointment of judges is exposed to significant political interference' (Saller, 2004: 18). She rightly adds that 'there is nothing in the constitutional text to prevent a decision that is entirely politically motivated' (Saller, 2004: 18). Since 2001, the Supreme Court and High Court benches have been restructured. Judicial appointments since then have been limited to persons perceived to be sympathetic to the political establishment.

When High Court justices Cheda, Ziyambi, and Malaba were promoted to the Supreme Court in 2001, the Minister of Justice Patrick Chinamasa said they were being appointed to 'handle litigation by white farmers who are contesting and indeed frustrating the government's land reform programme' (Goredema, 2004: 109). Commenting on this development, Charles Goredema says: 'As if to confirm the mandate, the judges joined new Chief Justice Chidyausiku in reversing a decision by the Supreme Court under [previous Chief Justice] Gubbay on the legality of land seizures. The court has since made other questionable rulings' (ibid.: 117). These – and other – promotions have been made without regard to seniority, which ought to be an important consideration. Judge President Chidyausiku (as he then was) was promoted to Acting Chief Justice following the departure of Chief Justice Gubbay, even though he was not a member of the Supreme Court and was therefore junior to the existing Supreme Court judges. Section 85 (1) of the old Constitution said that the President could appoint any Supreme Court judge or the Judge President (the judge in charge of the High Court) to the position of Acting Chief Justice. A substantive appointment to the office of Chief Justice was not limited to the above range of persons – any judge could have been appointed.

---

9  *Sunday Mirror,* 16 June 2000.

No white judges have been appointed since 1999 (ibid.: 104). Previously, judges were chosen from amongst different parts of the legal profession, including the bar and private legal practice. For several years after 2001, new appointees were recruited almost exclusively from amongst lawyers in government service. In respect of the High Court, what happened in practice was that the Minister of Justice chose a candidate and submitted the name to the President. If the President accepted the name put forward the Judicial Service Commission was '... faced with a *fait accompli*' (ibid.: 108). When exercising its consultative function, the Commission did 'not carry out any background or competence checks on the appointee, or interview them' (ibid.: 108).

The structure of the Judicial Service Commission was dealt with by section 90 of the old Constitution, which stated that the Commission consisted of the Chief Justice (or, if not available, the most senior Supreme Court judge who was available; section 90 (1) (a) of the old Constitution); the chairman of the Public Service Commission (Section 90 (1) (b)); the Attorney-General (Section 90 (1) (c)); and 'no less than two or more than three other members appointed ... by the President' (Section 90 (1) (d)). Of these 'other members', one had to be or had to have been a Supreme Court or High Court judge, or had to have been qualified as a legal practitioner for at least five years (Section 90 (2) (a) and (b)). Alternatively, he or she had to 'possess such legal qualifications and ... legal experience as the President consider[ed] suitable and adequate for ... appointment to the Judicial Service Commission' (Section 90 (2) (c)). The other members were to ' be chosen for their ability and experience in administration or their professional qualifications or their suitability otherwise for appointment' (Section 90). Members of Parliament (i.e. members of the National Assembly and Senators) and members of any local authority were not eligible for membership of the Commission (Section 109 (10)). Since the Chief Justice, the chairman of the Public Service Commission (Section 74 (1)), and the Attorney-General (Section 76 (2)) were *all* appointed by the President, all the members of the Commission were chosen by him. Accordingly, the Commission was not in any structural sense an independent body.

A number of suggestions were made concerning how the Judicial Service Commission could be restructured. Clearly, it was inappropriate for the President to have the sole responsibility for appointing members. The independence of the judiciary would have been enhanced if other persons and bodies had been involved, such as Parliament, the Law Society, human rights organisations and civil society groups. Obviously, senior judges such as the Chief Justice and the Judge President deserved to have been members. The presence of other Supreme Court and High Court judges would also have been welcome. At a workshop organised by Zimbabwe Lawyers for Human Rights[10] it was proposed that the membership of the Commission should also include: the Attorney-General; the President of the Law Society; two academics from the law faculties of Zimbabwean universities; two members of the Law Society; two persons representing civil society organisations; and two persons representing trade and industry (ibid., at 2). Broadening the membership of the Commission would, it was argued, enhance its independence (ibid.). The workshop also recommended that the chairman of the Public Service Commission cease to be a member of the Judicial Service Commission (ibid.). This recommendation makes sense since the Public Service Commission ought not to exercise any influence over the Judicial Service Commission. The whole point behind distinguishing between the Judicial Service and the Public Service is to ensure the independence of the former from the latter, and therefore from the government.

A genuinely independent Judicial Service Commission ought to play a significant role in the appointment and promotion of judges. In Namibia the President is required to appoint judges 'on the recommendation of the Judicial Service Commission' (Section 82 (1) of the Namibian Constitution). Lovemore Madhuku believes the Namibian example is the best Southern African model for maintaining judicial independence '… in that purely political appointments are, at least on the face of it, avoided' (Madhuku, 2002: 238). Although section 109 (1) of Zimbabwe's old Constitution said that the '… Commission shall not, in the exercise of its functions, be subject to the direction or control of any person or authority,' the absence of *structural* independence meant that the Commission was not able to play a role similar to its Namibian counterpart, even if it had been given the power to decide judicial appointments.[11]

---

10 'Should the process of appointing judges and removing judges in Zimbabwe be more transparent?' Report on a workshop held on 30 March 2001.

11 Section 111 of the Draft Constitution produced by the National Constitutional Assembly would, like the Namibian Constitution, also confer the judicial appointment power on the Judicial Service Commission.

*Appointment of judges to the superior courts under the 2013 Constitution*

The qualifications needed for appointment as a High Court judge are set out in section 179 of the 2013 Constitution. They are virtually identical to those contained in the old Constitution, with the exception that now candidates for the bench must be at least 40 years old. No age requirement was specified in the old Constitution. High Court judges do not need to be Zimbabwean citizens. However, Supreme Court and Constitutional Court judges *do* need to be Zimbabwean citizens (sections 177 (1) and 178 (1) of the new Constitution). In addition, a person must have been in legal practice 'whether continuously or not' for at least ten years in order to qualify for appointment to the Supreme Court bench (section 178 (1) (h)). In respect of the Constitutional Court, the period is twelve years (section 177 (1) (b)). Candidates for appointment to the Constitutional Court must also possess 'a sound knowledge of constitutional law' (section 177 (1)). However, no means for determining whether a potential Constitutional Court judge has such knowledge is specified.

The procedure for appointing judges is however different from that established by the old Constitution. The original 2013 Constitution stipulated that all judges were appointed by the President in the same way and following the same procedure (section 180). At that time, section 180 (2) said:

> Whenever it is necessary to appoint a judge, the Judicial Service Commission must –
>
> (a)   Advertise the position;
>
> (b)   Invite the President and the public to make nominations;
>
> (c)   Conduct public interviews of prospective candidates;
>
> (d)   Prepare a list of three qualified persons as nominees for office; and
>
> (e)   Submit the list to the President.

Once the list had been submitted to the President, he had to appoint one of the nominees unless he considered that none of the nominees was suitable, in which case he was entitled to require the Judicial Service Commission to submit a second list. Where this occurred the President had to appoint one of the nominees in the second list; he could not ask for a third list (Section 180 (3)). Thus, the position was that the President's discretion was limited to choosing from the names contained in – at most – two lists prepared by the Judicial Service Commission.

The judicial appointment procedure was largely inspired by the procedure contained in the South African Constitution. The South African President is limited to choosing names from two lists prepared by the Judicial Service Commission (Section 124 (4) of the South African Constitution). However, in South Africa the 'list' requirement only applies to the appointment of judges to the Constitutional Court; judges of the lower courts are appointed by the President on the advice of the Judicial Service Commission (Section 174 (6)). This means that the South African President must appoint the candidate put forward by the Commission; he has no discretion.

In 2017, section 180 of Zimbabwe's Constitution was amended, and the position now is that the Chief Justice, Deputy Chief Justice and the Judge President are no longer appointed on the basis of the 'list' procedure. Instead, they are simply appointed by the President 'after consultation with the Judicial Service Commission' (amended section 180 (2)). The words 'after consultation' simply mean that the President must hear the recommendation made by the Judicial Service Commission but is not obliged to comply with it. However, if a judicial appointment is not consistent with a recommendation, the President must inform the Senate 'as soon as is practicable' (amended section 180 (3)). The purpose of the latter requirement – at least in theory – may be to allow the Senate to consider whether the President has abused his appointment power. Parliament might then decide to investigate whether the President ought to be removed from office. However, the possibility of this happening is undercut by the fact that the subsection requiring the President to inform the Senate ends with the words 'provided that, for the avoidance of doubt, it is declared that the decision of the President as to such appointment shall be final.' This language makes it harder – but not impossible – for Parliament to question the President's decision. The fact that the President alone now appoints the three most senior posts in the judiciary obviously undermines judicial independence. Judges who hand down decisions that the government dislikes may find themselves being passed over for promotion.

The 'list' procedure still applies in relation to the appointment of all other judges and is certainly an improvement on that contained in the old constitution. Nevertheless, aspects of the new procedure give rise to concern and are not consistent with orthodox understandings of separation of powers theory. For example, the President is involved in the nomination of candidates. It will be interesting to see, over time, whether the Judicial Service Commission gives preference to presidential nominations over those from the public. Secondly, it will be appreciated from what has already been said that the role of the Judicial Service Commission is vital in the appointment procedure. That being the case it is essential to examine the structure of the Judicial Service Commission under the new Constitution. Is it now, unlike its predecessor, an independent body? As far as its structure is concerned, the answer must unfortunately be no, because so many of its members are appointed – directly or indirectly – by the President. These include the Chief Justice; Deputy Chief Justice; Judge President; Attorney-General and the Chair of the Civil Service Commission (section 189 (1) of the New Constitution). A member having at least seven years' experience in human resources management is also appointed by the President (section 189 (1) (k)). However, there are some independent members. Three members are designated by the Law Society (section 189 (1) (n)). One member is a legal academic designated by 'an association representing the majority of the teachers of law at Zimbabwean universities' (section 189 (1) (i)). In the absence of such an association, the President will appoint that member (ibid.). Another member is a public accountant or auditor 'designated by an association constituted under an Act of Parliament, which represents such persons' (section 189 (1) (j)). Finally, one member must be a judge nominated by the judges of the superior courts (section 189 (1) (d)).

All of the 'independent' members serve for a single non-renewable term of six years (section 189 (3)). This obviously enhances their 'operational' independence since they will not be under pressure to ingratiate themselves with the President in order to secure a second term. The 'operational' independence of the Judicial Service Commission is strengthened by section 190 (2), which says: 'The Judicial Service Commission must promote and facilitate the *independence* and accountability of the judiciary and the efficient, effective and transparent administration of justice in Zimbabwe, and has all the powers needed for this purpose' (my emphasis). This provision is a positive development; the old Constitution did not contain an equivalent provision. Now the Commission is under an *active duty* to support judicial independence. Thus when exercising its role in the judicial appointment process the Commission must do so in a way that is consistent with upholding judicial independence. So the Commission would be acting improperly if, when preparing a list of candidates to present to the President, it based its selection on political considerations. Notwithstanding this, the danger of the Commission failing to act in an entirely impartial manner remains a real one, given the extent of the presidential input into its structure.

Judicial appointments must be published in the *Government Gazette* (section 180 (6)). Finally, note must be taken of section 184, which stipulates that 'appointments to the judiciary must reflect broadly the diversity and gender composition of Zimbabwe.' Appointments to the bench may thus be unlawful if they do not reflect Zimbabwe's ethnic diversity and respect gender balance.

On the 31st of December 2019, Constitution of Zimbabwe Amendment (no. 2) Bill was published in the *Government Gazette*. Publication was repeated on 17 January 2020. The Bill seeks to amend section 180 of the Constitution to enable the President to appoint sitting Supreme or High Court judges to be judges of a higher court when vacancies arise, without having to be interviewed by the Judicial Service Commission. In addition, the Commission would not have to interview other candidates. The Bill also seeks to amend section 186 to allow Constitutional Court and Supreme Court judges to continue in office beyond the retirement age of 70, for periods of one year at a time. The power to grant such extensions would vest in the President who would only need to consult the Commission. As has been shown, this is no constraint on the President's discretion.

These proposed changes are disturbing. They are obviously designed to increase the President's control over the judiciary and undermine judicial independence. However, it may be that the government has overlooked section 328 (7) of the Constitution. That provision states that no amendments extending term limits provisions will apply to persons holding office immediately before the amendment. So, no judge currently in office will be able to benefit from the proposed change and will still have to retire on reaching the age of 70. It remains to be seen whether parliament will enact the Amendment Bill into law in the form in which it was introduced, or whether Parliament will amend the Bill.

## Removal of judges from office

### Removal of judges from office under the old Constitution

Supreme Court and High Court judges could only be lawfully removed from office in accordance with the procedure set out in section 87 of the old Constitution. In respect of the Chief Justice, the removal process had to be initiated by the President. Thus section 87 (2) said: 'If the President considers that the question of the removal from office of the Chief Justice ought to be investigated, the President shall appoint a tribunal to inquire into the matter.' In respect of all other Supreme Court and High Court judges, the President could only appoint a tribunal if advised to do so by the Chief Justice. In *Paradza v Minister of Justice, Legal and Parliamentary Affairs and Others* 2003 S 46/03, Sandura JA said: 'If the Chief Justice advises the President that the question of a judge's removal from office ought to be investigated, the President is obliged to appoint a tribunal to inquire into the matter. [Thus] ... the President does not have any discretion in the matter' (*Paradza*, 2003: 13). This meant the President would be acting unconstitutionally if he declined to act in accordance with the advice of the Chief Justice.

Such a tribunal could consist of not less than three members, all of whom were appointed by the President (Section 87 (4) of the old Constitution). In exercising his discretion to appoint members he had to choose from amongst:

(a)   persons who ... held office as a judge of the Supreme Court or the High Court;

(b)   persons who [held] or [had] held office as a judge of a court having unlimited jurisdiction in civil or criminal matters in a country in which the common law is Roman-Dutch or English and English is an official language;

(c)   legal practitioners of not less than seven years' standing who [had] been nominated [by the Law Society].[12]

If the President decided to appoint all the members of the tribunal from just one of those three categories, he would not have been acting unconstitutionally (Madhuku, 2005: 130).

It was held (*Paradza*, 2003: 14-15, per Sandura JA) that the structure of the Tribunal was designed to conform to the requirements of section 79 B of the old Constitution. That provision stated that members of the judiciary 'shall not be subject to the direction or control of any person or authority' when exercising their judicial authority 'except to the extent that a written law may place [them] under the direction or control of *another member*

---

12  Section 87 (4) of the old Constitution. Subsection (5) said that the Law Society was under a duty '... to nominate a panel containing the names of not less than three duly qualified legal practitioners...'

*of the judiciary'* (my emphasis). Sandura JA said in the *Paradza* case that the Tribunal 'consists of judges, former judges and lawyers qualified for appointment as judges. In other words, only judges may inquire into the misconduct of other judges and report thereon' (*Paradza*, 2003: 14-15). To a large extent his comment was correct. However, any members of the Tribunal sitting by virtue of being legal practitioners qualified for appointment to the bench did not fall within the list of persons constituting the judiciary contained in section 79 A of the old Constitution. That section only referred to Supreme Court and High Court judges and to 'persons presiding over other courts subordinate to the Supreme Court and High Court that [were] established by or under an Act of Parliament'.

On completion of its investigation the Tribunal had to submit a report to the President. The report had to contain a recommendation as to whether or not he should refer the question of the removal of the judge to the Judicial Service Commission (Section 87 (6) of the old Constitution). The President was obliged to comply with such a recommendation (Section 87 (6)). In *Paradza*, Sandura JA said: 'The President has no discretion, but is obliged to act in accordance with the Tribunal's recommendation.' (*Paradza*, 2003:13). Thereafter, if the Judicial Service Commission advised the President to remove the judge concerned, the President had to do so (Section 87 (9)). The Commission would appear to have had a discretion as to whether or not to adopt the views of the Tribunal as its own.[13] Thus, the 'Commission [could], notwithstanding the recommendations of the Tribunal, advise against removal and recommend that the suspension [of the judge] be revoked' (Madhuku, 2005: 131). If the Tribunal decided not to recommend submission of the matter to the Commission, it could instead ask the President to revoke the judge's suspension (Section 87 (8)). (Judges were automatically suspended when a tribunal was established.)

According to section 87 (1), a judge could only be removed from office for 'inability to discharge the functions of [the] office, whether arising from infirmity of body or mind or any other cause, or for misbehaviour'. No other grounds for removal were provided. The words 'any other cause' as they appeared in the section probably referred to other medical causes or to causes not relating to the moral blameworthiness of the judge in question.

What was the meaning and ambit of the word 'misbehaviour' as it

---

13 This was implied by the language used in section 87 (8) of the old Constitution. See Madhuku (2005: 131), and Linington (2001: 168).

appeared in section 87 (1)? In 1995 a Tribunal was established to consider the possible removal of Justice Blackie from office. In considering the meaning of 'misbehaviour', the Tribunal held that its 'presence in the Constitution is in relation to the independence of the judiciary. It cannot therefore be argued that a judge should be removed from office for any type of "misbehaviour"' (Blackie Tribunal Report 1995: 25). Thus errors of law or procedure, or exercises of bad judgement, did not constitute misbehaviour (ibid). It was in order to cater for problems of this sort that there existed a right of appeal from the High Court to the Supreme Court (ibid). For this reason, the Tribunal decided that 'misbehaviour' must mean that a person is 'unfit to remain in the office of a judge' (ibid). The improper exercise of judicial functions, wilful neglect of duty or non-attendance, or 'a conviction for any infamous offence by which although it be not connected with the duties of his office, the offender is rendered unfit to exercise any office of public franchise' (Blackie Tribunal Report 1995: 25, quoting Quick and Garran, 1901: 731), would fall into that category. The criminal conduct concerned had to be relatively serious. Thus, for example, minor traffic offences would probably have fallen outside the ambit of 'misbehaviour' as a ground for removal from office (Hogan and Whyte, 2003: 1009, paragraph 6.4.39).

In *Paradza v Minister of Justice, Legal and Parliamentary Affairs and Others* the Supreme Court accepted that 'misbehaviour' includes criminal misconduct. Sandura JA said: 'I have no doubt ... that [misbehaviour] includes criminal misconduct. If that were not the case, there would be an obvious absurdity because it would mean that a judge could be removed from office for ethical transgressions but could not be removed ... if he committed a criminal offence, no matter how serious the offence may be. That could hardly have been the intention of the framers of the Constitution' (*Paradza*, 2003: 11). Concurring on this particular point, Malaba JA held that 'misbehaviour includes *serious* criminal offences' (*Paradza*, 2003:30; my emphasis).

### The Blackie Tribunal

Two tribunals were established under the old Constitution. The first was in 1995 to investigate an allegation of misbehaviour made against Justice Blackie, a High Court judge. The allegation was that he had improperly granted bail to four accused persons at a police station on a Sunday evening and in the absence of a state prosecutor. He defended himself by saying that though what he had done was unusual it was not illegal. He said that the police had recently adopted an undesirable habit of arresting persons prematurely, before having undertaken proper investigation. In addition, the police often deliberately arrested suspects on a Friday, so that they would have to spend the weekend in custody, before being able to apply for bail on Monday.[14]

The Tribunal concluded that the judge had not acted improperly, since a judge is on duty twenty-four hours a day. However, the Tribunal felt that Justice Blackie had shown poor judgement in travelling to the police station in the same car as the defence lawyer. For this reason, the Tribunal recommended that Justice Blackie be reprimanded. It would appear that in doing this the Tribunal acted unconstitutionally, since the old Constitution did not authorise it to make any recommendations not connected to the issue of removal from office (Linington, 2001: 170, paragraph 444).

### The Paradza Tribunal

On 17 February 2003 Benjamin Paradza, a High Court judge, was arrested by the police. It was alleged that he had attempted to defeat or obstruct the course of justice[15] by attempting to persuade two other judges to release the passport of his business partner. The latter, who was being tried for murder, wanted to make a business trip overseas. Paradza brought a constitutional application in terms of section 24 (1) of the old Constitution, in which he challenged the constitutionality of his arrest and detention as well as the criminal proceedings initiated against him. The Supreme Court unanimously held that Paradza's arrest and detention violated his right to personal liberty as contained in section 13 (1) of the old Constitution. Sandura JA held that the decision to arrest Paradza was not reasonable, since 'there was no likelihood that [Paradza] would abscond, interfere with state witnesses, or commit further offences' (*Paradza*, 2003: 7).

In the same application, Paradza also argued that it was unlawful for criminal proceedings to be instituted against him prior to the establishment of a section 87 tribunal. In *Paradza v Minister of Justice, Legal and Parliamentary Affairs and Others* (2003: 7) the majority of the Supreme Court rejected this argument. Malaba JA denied that any provision of the old Constitution 'expressly secured primacy of the procedure for

---

14 *Blackie Tribunal Report* (1995) at 13. See also Linington (2001: 168, paragraph 441).

15 In the alternative, it was alleged that he had contravened section 360 (2) (b) of the Criminal Procedure and Evidence Act by inciting the two judges concerned to contravene section 4 (9) of the Prevention of Corruption Act.

the removal of an errant judge from office over the initiation of criminal proceedings by the Attorney-General' (ibid.: 32). He added: 'If the makers of the Constitution intended to make the removal of a judge from office a condition precedent to the institution of criminal proceedings against him, they would have provided for it in clear terms' (ibid.).

In arriving at his decision Malaba JA invoked (ibid.: 29) section 76 (4) (a) of the old Constitution. That provision said: 'The Attorney-General shall have power in any case in which he considers it desirable so to do … to institute and undertake criminal proceedings before any court ....' He also noted (ibid.) that section 76 (7) stipulated that 'in the exercise of his powers under subsection (4) … the Attorney-General shall not be subject to the direction or control of any person or authority'. On the basis of these provisions Malaba JA held that 'no limitations on the exercise of [the Attorney-General's] discretion' (ibid.: 35) to institute criminal proceedings existed. He said: 'It would therefore be a clear violation of the provisions of section 76 (7) … were this court to declare that the Attorney-General cannot institute criminal proceedings against [a judge] for criminal offences charged against him before the procedure for his removal from office had been gone through' (ibid.). He rejected the idea that the principle of judicial independence enshrined in section 79 B of the Constitution restricted the power given to the Attorney-General by section 76 (4) (a). Section 79 B was concerned with the 'individual independence of a judge when discharging judicial functions. [Thus] … it cannot be argued that when a judge commits a criminal offence at a time when he is not involved in the adjudication of a case he cannot be arrested and charged with that offence on account of the principle of judicial independence' (ibid.: 36).

The majority view, as enunciated by Malaba JA,[16] is extremely difficult to support. It does not fit well with either the text of the Constitution or the approach to constitutional interpretation adopted by the Supreme Court since independence. Accordingly, the excellent dissenting judgment of Sandura JA is to be preferred. The reasoning of Sandura JA must be understood against the background of his adherence to the generous and purposive approach to constitutional interpretation (ibid.: 9) that has formed a fundamental pillar of Zimbabwe's constitutional jurisprudence for so many years. In *Paradza*, Sandura JA referred with approval to the Supreme Court's earlier decision in *Rattigan and Others v. Chief*

---

16  Ziyambi JA, Gwaunza JA, and Uchena AJA concurred with Malaba JA.

*Immigration Officer and Another* 1995 (1) BCLR 1 (ZS) where Gubbay CJ said at 4 that, 'where rights and freedoms are conferred on persons, derogations therefrom, as far as the language permits, should be narrowly or strictly construed' (referred to by Sandura JA in *Paradza*, 2003:10).

Sandura JA stressed the importance of reading sections 79 B and 87 of the old Constitution together (ibid.: 11). He noted that arresting and detaining a judge effectively places the judge concerned 'under the direction or control of persons who are not members of the judiciary, which is not permitted by section 79 B' (ibid.: 10). The purpose of section 79 B went beyond simply protecting the independence of the judiciary. It was also concerned with ensuring 'that the judiciary, which plays a pivotal role in the protection and enforcement of the Constitution, continues to function effectively' (ibid.: 11, per Sandura JA). Sandura JA therefore held that, when construed in the light of section 79 B, the section 87 (1) prohibition on removing judges otherwise than in accordance with section 87 (1) meant that the tribunal procedure must be followed before a judge can be made the subject of criminal proceedings. He said: 'It was never the intention of the framers of the Constitution that a judge could be prosecuted, convicted and sentenced before he was either suspended from performing the functions of his office or removed from office' (ibid.: 25). Any other interpretation would lead to the absurd result that a judge could be imprisoned while still remaining a member of the bench (ibid.: 24-25). Thus, by necessary implication, the power of the Attorney-General to institute criminal proceedings in any case did not include the power to proceed against sitting judges, until after such judges had been dealt with in terms of section 87. Powers conferred by the old Constitution had to be exercised in a way that was consistent with other constitutional provisions. If the powers of the Attorney-General had included the power to proceed against judges, this would have rendered section 87 meaningless and therefore redundant.

The existence of section 87 meant, in the opinion of Sandura JA, that 'judges ought to be treated differently' (ibid.: 17) from other persons – such as, for example, Members of Parliament – who are not covered by a special constitutional provision setting out how they are to be dealt with in the event of an allegation of misbehaviour arising. 'In my view, it could not have been the intention of the framers of the Constitution that a peace officer could arrest a judge and trigger the prosecution, indictment and trial of the judge before the Chief Justice has had the opportunity to consider whether to advise the President that the question of the judge's removal from office should be investigated. They must have intended that the allegations would first be investigated and the facts ascertained by a high-powered judicial tribunal ... before the police were involved in the investigations' (ibid. : 17).

In his judgement, Sandura JA referred with approval to a joint statement on the arrest and detention of judge Paradza issued on 5 March 2003 by the Chief Justices of Botswana, Malawi, Mauritius, Namibia, South Africa, Swaziland, Tanzania, Uganda and Zambia. In their statement the Chief Justices said:

> Like everyone else judges are not above the law. Their position as judges in a democratic state, however, requires that they must be and must be seen to be independent and not subject to direct or indirect pressure from the executive. For this reason the investigation of criminal charges against them needs to be conducted with sensitivity to their status, their role in society and their relationship with the executive. Procedures should be followed to avoid as far as possible any suggestion that a particular judge is being victimised by the executive for his or her views or decisions. For this reason special procedures are usually followed in democratic societies where allegations of serious criminal conduct are made against a judge. Such procedures ordinarily involve the holding of an independent enquiry into whether or not the judge should be impeached. If the allegations are then found to have substance, and the judge is impeached, a criminal prosecution may follow. The Constitution of Zimbabwe makes provision for such a procedure to be followed in respect of the impeachment of judges. It is regrettable that this procedure, rather than arrest, detention and prosecution, has not been followed in respect of the allegations against Mr Justice Paradza (ibid.: 17-18).[17]

Thus, in the opinion of the Chief Justices, the correct sequence of events is that a special independent enquiry ought to *precede* the institution of

---

17 See also Saller (2004: 44). She notes that ten Zimbabwe High Court judges signed a letter on 5 March 2004 condemning the way in which judge Paradza was arrested. The judges 'drew attention to section 87 of the Constitution as laying down the correct and exclusive procedure for acting against a judge alleged to have committed misconduct. They [also stated] that any other procedure, and particularly any procedure that allows a police official to arrest an active judge on mere suspicion of illegal action, has the effect of intimidating judges and severely undermining the rule of law.'

criminal proceedings against a judge.

In *Paradza* neither Sandura JA nor Malaba JA discussed the meaning of the word 'removal' in any detail. Sandura JA did however say that, in his opinion, 'removal' includes *temporary* removal (ibid.: 13). It would appear that the word clearly encompasses more than just 'formal'[18] removal. In fact, it includes within its ambit *de facto* removal as well. Thus, a judge will have been removed if he is incarcerated, detained or otherwise prevented from performing his functions, regardless of whether he continues formally to remain a judge. The decisive consideration is a factual one: Has the judge concerned been prevented from 'exercis[ing] his judicial authority?' (Section 79 B of the old Constitution). If the answer is yes, then the judge will have been effectively removed.

The fact that there is little likelihood of a prison sentence being imposed does not change the position.[19] A criminal prosecution of any kind would make it impossible for a judge to perform his judicial functions properly and effectively. Persons appealing before such a judge would be entitled to doubt whether he was a person capable of properly upholding and giving effect to their rights under sections 18 (1), (2) and (9) of the old Constitution. In other words, the public would probably regard a judge undergoing criminal prosecution as incapable of affording persons the protection of the law and a fair and impartial hearing, as required by those provisions. The proper functioning of sections 18 (1), (2) and (9) presupposed, and was dependent upon, implementation by judges whose integrity was not in doubt. This problem did not arise where the section 87 procedure was adhered to, because the establishment of a tribunal to investigate whether a judge ought to be removed resulted in the suspension of the judge.

A tribunal was finally established in February 2004 consisting of Justice Denis Chirwa of Zambia (who was appointed chairman of the Tribunal), Justice Isaac Mtambo of Malawi and Justice John Mroso of Tanzania. The Tribunal began its proceedings on 5 April. Counsel representing Justice Paradza immediately raised some preliminary issues. Firstly, it

---

18 *Formal* removal refers to a situation where the person concerned has ceased to be a judge in any sense whatsoever. *De facto* removal on the other hand, describes a situation in which, although the person nominally remains a judge, he has been factually removed in that he has been prevented, in fact, from exercising his judicial functions.

19 Malaba JA and the majority in Paradza would not, of course, agree with the author on this point.

was argued that the public ought to be allowed to attend the Tribunal's proceedings. (The notice in the *Government Gazette* establishing the Tribunal had stipulated that its hearings were to be held in camera.) As Chipo Hama and Arnold Tsunga (2004) note, this gave rise to 'suspicion and protests from Human Rights groups' that the Tribunal would not operate fairly. The second issue raised related to the appointment of the members of the Tribunal. It was argued that, by allowing the Minister of Justice, Legal and Parliamentary Affairs to make the appointments, the President had acted unlawfully. In terms of the old Constitution, it was the President himself who had to make the appointments.[20] Also raised was the issue of whether a taped telephone conversation between Justice Paradza and another judge was admissible as evidence. (This was because the Supreme Court had ruled in *Law Society of Zimbabwe* v. *Minister of Transport and Communications* that sections 98 (2) and 103 of the Postal and Telecommunications Act were unconstitutional.) Finally, counsel for Paradza also informed the Tribunal that these issues had also been raised in a constitutional application to the Supreme Court made in terms of section 24 of the old Constitution. Until the Supreme Court had ruled on these issues, it would be inappropriate, so it was argued, to proceed with the hearing.[21]

On the 15 April 2004 the Tribunal issued a ruling. This began by noting that since hearing argument, the Tribunal's terms of reference had been changed, so as to allow the proceedings to be held in public (*Paradza Tribunal*, 2). However, this point was then rendered somewhat academic by the Tribunal's decision to '... stand down the proceedings until the matters before the Supreme Court are determined' (ibid., 6). In arriving at

---

20  In his replying Heads of Argument, President Mugabe argued that section 31 H (1) of the old Constitution authorised the President to act through the Cabinet, Vice Presidents, Ministers and Deputy Ministers when carrying out functions conferred upon him by the Constitution. However, section 31 H (1) did not in fact refer to presidential functions, but rather to the 'executive authority of Zimbabwe' which is not quite the same thing. Moreover, even if 'executive authority' is synonymous with 'presidential function', section 31 H (1) stated that 'subject to the provisions of this Constitution', executive authority could be exercised by persons other than the President. This qualifying language is important. In the context of section 87 (4) it meant that the President had to personally select the persons to serve on the tribunal.

21  Paradza applied to the High Court for an interdict restraining the tribunal from continuing with its work until the constitutional issues had been determined by the Supreme Court. This application was rejected. Paradza then appealed to the Supreme Court. However, the hearing of the appeal was adjourned sine die.

this conclusion the Tribunal referred to *PTC* v. *Mahachi* as authority for the proposition 'that under the Roman-Dutch law, the noting of an appeal was sufficient for this tribunal to stop its proceedings' (ibid., 5).[22] The Tribunal made it clear though that this point was a subsidiary consideration. The main factors taken into account were the possible prejudice and inconvenience the parties might have suffered had the inquiry continued (ibid., 5). The Tribunal said:

> We have no control over the Supreme Court; they can sit and determine the matter any time depending on their calendar and also how they look at the urgency of the matter before them. Further, we have no control over our appointing authority as to when our recommendations should be acted on: it may be before the Supreme Court has the chance to decide on the matters raised by [Paradza]. But the cardinal point is the possibility that [the] … recommendations [of the tribunal] … may be declared a nullity. We have therefore reluctantly come to the conclusion that it is advisable that we stand down the proceedings until the matters before the Supreme Court are determined. (ibid., 6)

In *Paradza v Chirwa and Others* the Supreme Court decided by a majority that the members of the Tribunal to inquire into the removal of Justice Paradza had been validly appointed by the President. Paradza had argued that 'the President did not consciously apply his mind to the question of the suitability of [the three foreign judges] for selection as members of the Tribunal because he had no information on their personal attributes' (*Paradza v Chirwa*, 2005: 7). He further argued that 'the Minister usurped the powers of the President to select members of the Tribunal by communicating with the Chief Justices of the three countries through their respective High Commissions as if he was the repository of the power to appoint the tribunal' (ibid.: 8). Moreover, 'in the letters of request the Minister expressed it as being his own desire that the Tribunal should consist of judges from foreign countries' (ibid.). The Minister had unlawfully delegated to the Chief Justices of Zambia, Tanzania and Malawi the President's power to select members of the Tribunal (ibid.).

---

22 In fact that is not exactly what was decided in the PTC case. What Chatikobo J actually said was '… that the noting of an appeal to the Supreme Court has the effect of suspending the *decision* of the tribunal' (author's emphasis). A decision is not the same thing as proceedings. (Note: the tribunal referred to in the PTC case was a Labour Relations Tribunal, not a tribunal established under section 87 of the Constitution.)

This meant in effect that the President did not select the members of the Tribunal (ibid.). If Paradza had to appear before a tribunal whose members were not lawfully appointed, it would amount to a violation of his right to the protection of law contained in section 18 (1) of the old Constitution.

In a rather confusing majority judgement, Malaba JA began by insisting – rightly – that 'the power to select members ... in terms of s 87 (4) of the Constitution, must be exercised by the President *personally*' (*Paradza v Chirwa*, 2005:14; my emphasis). He also referred (ibid.) to section 31 H (1) of the old Constitution which said: 'The executive authority of Zimbabwe shall vest in the President and, subject to the provisions of this Constitution, may be exercised by him directly or through the Cabinet, a Vice-President, a Minister or a Deputy Minister.' He said that while some executive powers – like the Tribunal membership appointment power – had to be exercised personally by the President, others could be exercised through ministers, on the basis of section 31 H (1) (ibid.). The Minister's letters to the three Chief Justices fell within the parameters of section 31 H (1) (ibid.). Malaba JA said: 'When a Minister performs an act in his or her capacity as a Minister it must be presumed, in the absence of proof of formal assignment, that he or she is exercising the executive authority vested in the President under administrative agency' (ibid.).

But Malaba JA failed to deal adequately with the argument put forward by Paradza's counsel concerning the meaning of the word 'selected' as it appears in section 87 (4). Counsel cited the *Shorter Oxford Dictionary* which says the word means 'to choose or pick out in preference to others.' The *choosing in preference to others* was done by the foreign Chief Justices, who therefore effectively selected the members. Malaba JA, however, said: 'The fact that the President chose the same persons whose names were submitted does not detract from the fact that he had the right to reject any or all of the nominees if, for any reason, he considered them unsuitable for selection as members of the tribunal' (*Paradza v Chirwa*, 2005:20). The Judge of Appeal's comment appears to be disingenuous. There is *nothing* to show that the President actually did any *choosing*. Simply accepting the names put forward by the foreign Chief Justices did *not* amount to *selecting* the members of the Tribunal. In a dissenting judgement, Sandura JA said: 'the [members] ... were not selected by the President but by [the foreign] Chief Justices' (ibid.). The decisive fact was 'that each Chief Justice was requested to nominate *only one judge* of his Court, and *not two or more* from whom the President might select a member or members of the tribunal' (ibid.; my emphasis). In their correspondence with the Minister the Chief Justices did not provide 'any information as to why the judge concerned should be selected as a member of the tribunal' (*Paradza v Chirwa*, 2005:20). Thus 'the selections made by the three Chief Justices were intended by the President to conclusively determine the three members of the tribunal' (*Paradza v Chirwa*, 2005:28). What the President did, Sandura JA said, 'was an impermissible delegation of the President's power of selecting the members of the tribunal' (ibid.). He concluded therefore that the Tribunal had not been lawfully constituted.

It is difficult to disagree with Sandura JA. The failure of the majority of the Court to accord the word 'selected' the meaning so obviously demanded by the context is cause for concern. It is a well-established legal principle that when a constitution or legislation confers a decision-making power upon a specified person, that person cannot delegate the power to decide to someone else but must himself address his mind to the issues involved in arriving at a decision.

*Removal of judges from office under the 2013 Constitution*

Under the 2013 Constitution judges may only be removed from office for: '(a) inability to perform the functions of his or her office, due to mental or physical incapacity; (b) gross incompetence; or gross misconduct' (section 187 (1) of the 2013 Constitution). The word 'misbehaviour' does not appear in the 2013 Constitution's removal mechanism. However, its import is clearly subsumed by the words 'gross incompetence' and 'gross misconduct'. If the mental or physical capacity of a judge is an issue, the Judicial Service Commission or a tribunal established to investigate whether the judge concerned ought to be removed, has the power to require that the matter be referred to a medical board. However, this is subject to an enabling Act of Parliament authorising the exercise of this power. It is not permitted to remove a judge otherwise than through the procedure set out in section 187. As is the case under the old Constitution, the 2013 Constitution stipulates that the President has the power to decide whether the question of removing the Chief Justice ought to be considered (section 187 (2)). However, unlike the position under the old Constitution, this power can also be exercised by the Judicial Service Commission (section 187 (3)). In other words, both the President and the Commission have the power to appoint investigative tribunals in respect of the Chief Justice.

With respect to all other judges, the decision as to whether to establish an investigative tribunal vests in the Judicial Service Commission (section 187 (3)). This is a change from the position under the old Constitution, which stated that only the Chief Justice had the power to make such a decision. This change is an unfortunate development. In view of what has been said in this chapter about the structure of the new Judicial Service Commission, it is submitted that the change is likely to work against judicial independence. As has been seen, many members of the Commission are not judges. Yet, under the new dispensation, they will be involved in deciding whether judges should be investigated. It would have been much better had this power remained in the hands of the judiciary.

The structure of the tribunal is similar to that under the old Constitution, and the President must act in accordance with its recommendation (section 187 (4) and (8)). Once a tribunal has been established, the judge concerned will be suspended until the President – who must act on the recommendation of the tribunal – has revoked the suspension or removed the judge from office (section 187 (10)).

### Changing the size of the Supreme Court and Constitutional Court benches

Until 2002, Zimbabwe's Supreme Court was normally made up of five judges. Thus, when the court sat as a full bench in constitutional cases, the same five judges would hear the matter. However, the size of the court was then raised to six judges: Chidyausiku CJ; Sandura JA; Cheda JA; Ziyambi JA; Malaba JA and Gwaunza JA. In 2006, the number rose to seven with the promotion of Justice Garwe from Judge President to Judge of Appeal. Justice Minister Chinamasa attempted to justify the expansion of the bench by asserting that the Supreme Court's increasingly heavy workload meant that it needed more judges. In fact, however, in the period leading up to the new appointments, the Supreme Court's workload was less heavy than it had been for some time.[23] It would appear that the real reason for the expansion was to sideline Sandura JA, the only survivor from the old 'Gubbay bench'. His dissenting judgements in a number of important constitutional cases clearly embarrassed the government. When Gwaunza J (as she then was) was elevated to the Supreme Court bench (at first in an acting capacity), Chief Justice Chidyausiku was then able to decide which judges would sit with him to constitute a five-judge bench in constitutional cases. As a result, Sandura JA was not involved in some of

---

23 Confidential source.

the constitutional cases subsequently dealt with by the court.[24]

Zimbabwe's old Constitution did not contain a provision prohibiting the expansion of the Supreme Court bench. However, article 24 of the International Bar Association's Minimum Standards of Judicial Independence stipulates that '[t]he number of the members of the highest court should be rigid and should not be subject to change except by legislation'. Clearly, the move from five judges to seven was not consistent with article 24. The fact that the number of Supreme Court justices could be expanded without limit was cause for concern. The absence of a ceiling figure clearly facilitated the manipulation of the bench, and was not consistent with judicial independence.

The 2013 Constitution does not impose a limit on the number of judges that may sit on the Supreme Court bench. The relevant provision, section 168, simply establishes a minimum of four Justices. The size of the Constitutional Court, on the other hand, is fixed at seven Justices (section 166 (1)). Moreover, section 166 (3) (a) stipulates that cases concerning infringements of fundamental human rights or freedoms must be heard by the full bench. This is a satisfactory arrangement and will hopefully prevent the manipulation of the composition of the bench in particular cases.

## *A fair and independent judiciary must base its decisions on cases and authorities cited in argument by the parties during the hearing*

A judicial decision will only be fair if it is based on cases and arguments raised by the parties before the court. In a number of constitutional decisions in recent years the courts have relied on cases and legal authorities that were not put forward by either side in the proceedings concerned.[25] This is disturbing because the parties are denied any opportunity to comment on or argue against such material. It is doubtful whether such decisions complied with the requirements of section 18 (9) of the old Constitution, which said: 'Subject to the provisions of this Constitution, every person is entitled to be afforded a fair hearing within a reasonable time by an

---

24  Where other Judges of Appeal have been away or have had to recuse themselves, Sandura JA has been able to participate in the proceedings.

25  See for example the judgements of Chidyausiku CJ in *Associated Newspapers of Zimbabwe (Private) Limited v Minister of State for Information and Publicity in the President's Office and Others; Malaba JA in Quinnell v Minister of Lands, Agriculture and Rural Resettlement and Others, and Biti and Another v Minister of Justice, Legal and Parliamentary Affairs and Another.*

independent and impartial court or other adjudicating authority established by law in the determination of the existence or extent of his civil rights or obligations.' Similarly, section 69 (2) of the 2013 Constitutions says: 'In the determination of civil rights and obligations, every person has a right to a fair, speedy and public hearing within a reasonable time before an independent and impartial court, tribunal, or other forum established by law.'

In *Kauesa v Minister of Home Affairs, Namibia and Others* 1995 (11) BCLR 1540 (NMS), a decision of the Supreme Court of Namibia, Dumbutshena[26] AJA said:

> It is the litigants who must be heard and not the judicial officer. It would be wrong for judicial officers to rely for their decisions on matters not put before them by litigants neither in evidence nor oral or written submissions. Now and again a judge comes across a point not argued before him by counsel but which he thinks material to the resolution of the case. It is his duty in such a circumstance to inform counsel on both sides and to invite them to submit arguments either for or against the judge's point. It is undesirable for a court to deliver a judgement with a substantial portion containing issues never canvassed or relied on by counsel (*Kauesa*, at 1545).

This is surely the approach that ought to be adopted by Zimbabwe's own judiciary. The failure of some judges to limit themselves to cases and authorities raised by the parties calls into question their impartiality. The solution is surely the insertion of a provision into the Constitution obliging judges to act in accordance with the dictum enunciated by Dumbutshena in the *Kauesa* case.

## Access to the courts

### Access to the courts under the old Constitution

Judicial independence is concerned not only with the *structure* of the courts but also with *access* to the courts. This is understandable since denying potential litigants access to the courts effectively undermines the whole concept of judicial independence. Under the old Constitution, access in respect of human rights litigation was a particularly contentious issue following the enforced departure of a number of judges in 2001 and the subsequent restructuring of the bench. The new judges often interpreted the

---

26  Formerly the Chief Justice of Zimbabwe. On retiring from the Zimbabwean bench he became a Judge of Appeal in Namibia.

*locus standi* ('right of standing') provision in the old Constitution (section 24) in a restrictive manner. As a result, much human rights litigation was 'nipped in the bud' before the substantive issues raised in the cases could be considered.

According to section 24 (1) of the old Constitution, an applicant was entitled to approach the Supreme Court directly if he was able to allege that the Declaration of Rights had been, was being, or was likely to be contravened in *relation to him or her*. The only exception to this was where an application was brought on behalf of a detained person. It was not possible to bring applications directly to the Supreme Court in the public interest or even when the applicant had a personal interest in the matter. But even when an applicant's rights were contravened in relation to him or her there were times when the language used in section 24 (1) was interpreted so restrictively that the applicant was denied *locus standi*. A good example of this is the Supreme Court's decision in *Tsvangirai v Registrar General and Others* 2002 (1) ZLR 268 (S). The applicant alleged that subordinate legislation enacted by the President acting under a provision of the Electoral Act violated his right to the protection of law, enshrined in section 18 (1) of the old Constitution. It was alleged that the effect of the legislation was to deny the applicant's supporters the right to be registered as voters while affording the President's supporters that right. The applicant argued that according to the Constitution electoral legislation had to be created by Parliament, which could not delegate that power to any other body or person. Because the legislation had not been enacted by the right body it was invalid and the applicant's right to the protection of law – which included due process in law making – had been violated. In other words, section 18 (1) was designed to protect persons adversely affected by invalidly enacted laws.

However, the majority in *Tsvangirai* decided that the applicant did not have *locus standi* to bring the application, even though he was the candidate in the election! Writing the majority judgment, Chidyausiku CJ propounded the view that the impugned legislation affected the rights of potential voters rather than those of the applicant. Much to be preferred is the reasoning of Sandura JA in his dissenting judgment. He said: 'The entitlement of every person to the protection of the law, which is proclaimed in section 18 (1) ... embraces the right to require the legislature ... to pass laws which are consistent with the Constitution. If, therefore, the legislature passes a law which is inconsistent with the

Declaration of Rights, any person who is adversely affected by such a law has the *locus standi* to challenge the constitutionality of that law by bringing an application directly to this court in terms of section 24 (1) of this Constitution' (*Tsvangirai*, 2002: 278).[27]

Under the old Constitution constitutional and human rights litigation could also be commenced in the High Court. Section 81 (1) provided that the High Court 'shall have such jurisdiction and powers as may be conferred upon it by or in terms of this Constitution or any Act of Parliament'. Sections 13 and 23 of the High Court Act gave the High Court full original civil and criminal jurisdiction over all matters in Zimbabwe. According to section 2 of the Act the words 'civil case' mean 'any case or matter which is not a criminal case or matter'. These words obviously include constitutional and human rights issues. Indeed, over the years since independence, the High Court has dealt with a large number of constitutional cases. In spite of this, High Court judge Ndou ruled in *Nyamandlovu Farmers Association v Minister of Lands, Agriculture and Rural Resettlement and Another* 2003 (1) ZLR 185 (H) that the High Court did not have any jurisdiction in constitutional cases! In a subsequent case, *Capital Radio (Private) Limited v Broadcasting Authority of Zimbabwe and Others* 2003 (2) ZLR 236 (S), the Supreme Court made it clear that the High Court *does* have the power to deal with constitutional issues.

In *Minister of Home Affairs v Bickle* 1983 (1) ZLR 99 (S) the Supreme Court made it clear that a person will not be prevented from bringing a constitutional application even if he or she is in contempt of court or has contravened a law prior to instituting the application. This decision rightly recognized the importance of not imposing unacceptable barriers on potential constitutional applications. However, a later Supreme Court judgment – in a case heard after the restructuring of the Supreme Court bench – ignored the approach adopted in *Bickle* and proceeded to apply what is often referred to as the 'dirty hands' doctrine. The case was *Associated Newspapers of Zimbabwe (Pvt) Ltd v Minister of State for Information* 2004 (1) ZLR 538 (S), in which the applicant wished to challenge the constitutionality of a number of provisions in the Access to Information and Protection of Privacy Act, as well as regulations made under the Act. One of the impugned provisions, section 66, stipulated that the applicant had to register with the Media and Information Commission before being allowed

---

27 For a fuller discussion of this issue see Linington (2009).

to publish. However, the applicant did not register, contending that the provision was unconstitutional. It was precisely in order to avoid having to register that the application had been brought. However, the Supreme Court ruled that because the applicant had failed to comply with a legal requirement it had 'dirty hands' and was therefore precluded from proceeding with the application. In other words, the applicant was denied access to the courts.

This decision has been severely criticised (Linington, 2010: 54-56). The Supreme Court made no mention of its earlier approach enunciated in the *Bickle* case. Moreover, the 'dirty hands' doctrine is only applicable in the context of private law, not public law, which of course includes constitutional applications.

*Access to the courts under the 2013 Constitution*

Section 85 (1) of the 2013 Constitution says:

Any of the following persons, namely –

(a)    any person acting in their own interests;

(b)    any person acting on behalf of another person who cannot act for themselves;

(c)    any person acting as a member, or in the interests of, a group or class of persons;

(d)    any person acting in the public interest;

(e)    any association acting in the interests of its members;

is entitled to approach a court, alleging that a fundamental right or freedom enshrined in [the Declaration of Rights] has been, is being or is likely to be infringed.

It is apparent at once that this provision facilitates easy access to the courts in cases concerning constitutional rights. Section 85 is clearly a significant improvement on the equivalent provision in the old Constitution. The key word is 'interests'. It is not necessary to show that one's own rights have been contravened. Applicants will now have *locus standi* even if they have no personal interest in a matter but are simply acting in the public interest. Direct applications to the Constitutional Court are permissible (section 167 (5) of the 2013 Constitution), but the Constitutional Court has been given a discretion as to whether to entertain such applications. In exercising this discretion, the Constitutional Court must consider whether allowing direct access would be in the 'interests of justice' (section 167 (5)). This necessarily involves balancing the interests of the litigants in having the matter finalized speedily against the fact that the quality of a Constitutional Court judgment will usually be improved if the matter has first been considered by lower courts. This will enable Constitutional Court judges to benefit from reading the judgments handed down by the lower courts, rather than considering the matter *de novo*. As Chaskalson P said in a decision of the South African Constitutional Court, *Bruce and Another v Fleecytex Johannesburg CC and Others* 1998 (4) BCLR 415 (CC) at 419:

> It is … not ordinarily in the interests of justice for a court to sit as a court of first and last instance, in which matters are decided without there being any possibility of appealing against the decision given. Experience shows that decisions are more likely to be correct if more than one court has been required to consider the issues raised. In such circumstances the losing party has an opportunity of challenging the reasoning on which the first judgment is based, and of reconsidering and refining arguments previously raised in the light of such judgment.

Generally, if a matter is urgent, direct access may be granted, but where this is not the case, the matter will normally have to be heard by a lower court. This will also be the case where the facts are in dispute, since the Constitutional Court is not a trial court.

The problem of the 'dirty hands' doctrine should have been eliminated by section 85 (2) of the 2013 Constitution. This says that 'the fact that a person has contravened a law does not debar them from approaching a court for relief [in cases concerning fundamental human rights].' However, in spite of the very clear language used in this provision, the doctrine was upheld by the Supreme Court in *Econet Wireless (Pvt) Ltd v Minister of Public Service* 2016 (1) ZLR 268 (S). Surprisingly, the judgment does not even mention section 85. Instead Bhunu JA referred to section 69 (3) of the Constitution which says, 'every person has the right of access to the courts, or to some other tribunal or forum established by law for the resolution of any dispute.' He said at 272 that although that provision 'guarantees the appellant's right to access the courts, it is no license for it to approach the courts with hands dripping with dirt. The appellant is not being denied access to the courts. What it is being asked to do is to cleanse itself by obeying the prevailing laws of the land before approaching the courts.' With respect, this decision is entirely wrong. It is not clear why section 85 (2) was not referred to. The provision is. of course, vital in the context of the dirty hands doctrine. Its purpose is to ensure that a person who has contravened the law will not be precluded from approaching a court in order to allege that a fundamental right or freedom has been infringed.

## International law and the Constitution

### Customary international law

The old Constitution was silent on the question of whether customary international law is part of Zimbabwe's domestic law. However, in *Barker McCormac (Pvt) Ltd v Government of Kenya* 1983 (4) SA 817 (ZS) the Supreme Court answered the question in the affirmative. Georges JA said at 819 that on the basis of a rule of Roman-Dutch common law, the courts will apply rules of customary international law unless they are inconsistent with legislation or the common law. The 2013 Constitution deals with the matter explicitly. Section 326 (1) says: 'Customary international law is part of the law of Zimbabwe, unless it is inconsistent with this Constitution or an Act of Parliament.' Thus rules of customary international law now take precedence over conflicting domestic rules contained in subordinate legislation or the common law. The significance of customary international law is enhanced by its interpretive function. Section 326 (2) says: 'When interpreting legislation, every court and tribunal must adopt any reasonable interpretation of the legislation that is consistent with customary international law applicable in Zimbabwe, in preference to an alternative interpretation inconsistent with that law.' So customary international law will affect the meaning of provisions in Acts of Parliament and the Constitution. In relation to the Declaration of Rights, this interpretative function is strengthened by section 46 (1) (c) of the Constitution which stipulates that 'when interpreting [the Declaration of Rights] a court ... must take into account international law'.

### Treaties

The concept of self-executing treaties is not part of Zimbabwean law. This is not surprising because it would be contrary to the separation of powers system built into the fabric of the Constitution. If the President, simply by assenting to a treaty, could transform its provisions into domestic law, he would be exercising primary legislative powers. But according to section 134 (a) of the 2013 Constitution, only Parliament is entitled to enact primary legislation (i.e. legislation equivalent in status to an Act of Parliament). Accordingly, treaties do not become part of Zimbabwean law unless and until they have been incorporated through an Act of Parliament (section 327 (2) (b)). Zimbabwean courts 'must adopt any reasonable interpretation of ... legislation that is consistent with any international convention, treaty or agreement which is binding on Zimbabwe' (section 327 (6)). Zimbabwe's old Constitution also required treaties to be incorporated through legislation in order to become law in Zimbabwe (section 111B).

Section 327 (3) stipulates that agreements which are not treaties, but which Zimbabwe concludes with 'foreign organizations and entities' and which impose fiscal obligations on Zimbabwe, will not bind Zimbabwe until approved by Parliament. The recent Constitutional Amendment Bill seeks to delete the words 'foreign organizations and entities' and replace them with 'international organizations'. The effect of the change would be to prevent Parliament from vetoing agreements with 'foreign organizations and entities'. Agreements with foreign banks are an example. A change of this type would undermine Parliament's power to control Zimbabwe's fiscal policy. The words 'international organizations' do not cover private banks. In fact, article 2 of the Vienna Convention on the Law of Treaties defines an international organization as 'an inter-governmental organization'.

## Conclusion

The 2013 Constitution is clearly a significant improvement on the old Constitution. There is now more emphasis on the rule of law and the importance of upholding the separation of powers. But it is not a perfect document. For example, the new judicial appointment mechanism could have been improved. But even a very good constitution cannot by itself establish a culture of constitutionalism in Zimbabwe. Society as a whole must absorb the values of the Constitution and – perhaps most important – the government must foster constitutionalism. Sadly, the authorities in Zimbabwe have so far failed to do this.

# References

Dumbutshena, E. (1989) 'The Rule of Law in a Constitutional Democracy with Particular Reference to the Zimbabwean Experience'. *South African Journal on Human Rights*, 5.

Goredema, C. (2004) 'Whither judicial independence in Zimbabwe?', in B. Raftopoulos and T. Savage (eds), *Zimbabwe: Injustice and Political Reconciliation.* Cape Town: Institute for Justice and Reconciliation.

Gubbay, A. (2002) 'The Challenge to Judicial Independence'. Paper presented at the First South Asian Regional Judicial Colloquium on Access to Justice, New Delhi, 1-3 November 2002.

Hama, C. and A. Tsunga (2004) *The Inquiry into the conduct of High Court Judge Justice Benjamin Paradza: A brief interim report on the trial observation.* Harare: Zimbabwe Lawyers for Human Rights.

Hogan, G.W. and G.F. Whyte (2003) *J M Kelly: The Irish Constitution.* 4th ed. Dublin: Butterworths.

Linington, G. (2001) *Constitutional Law of Zimbabwe.* Harare: Legal Resources Foundation.

—— (2009) 'Illegality and Zimbabwe's 2008 Presidential Elections', in E.V. Masunungure (ed.), *Defying the Winds of Change: Zimbabwe's 2008 Elections.* Harare: Weaver Press.

—— (2010) 'Developing a New Bill of Rights for Zimbabwe: Some Issues to Consider', in N. Kersting (ed.), *Constitution in Transition: Academic Inputs for a 2013 Constitution in Zimbabwe.* Harare: Friedrich-Ebert-Stiftung.

Madhuku, L. (2002) 'Constitutional Protection of the Independence of the Judiciary: A Survey of the Position in Southern Africa.' *Journal of African Law*, 46(2).

—— (2005) 'The Appointment Process of Judges in Zimbabwe and Its Implications for the Administration of Justice', *Zimbabwe Human Rights Bulletin*, 12.

Quick, J. and R.R. Garran (1901) *The Annotated Constitution of the Australian Commonwealth.* Sydney: Angus & Robertson.

Russell, P. (2001) 'Toward a General Theory of Judicial Independence', in P.H. Russell and D.M. O'Brien (eds), *Judicial Independence in the Age of Democracy: Critical Perspectives from Around the World.* Charlottesville, VA: University of Virginia Press.

Saller, K. (2004) *The Judicial Institution in Zimbabwe.* Cape Town: Siber Ink.

## Legal Cases cited

*Associated Newspapers of Zimbabwe (Private) Limited v Minister of State for Information and Publicity in the President's Office and Others,* 2004 (1) *ZLR* 538 (S).

*Barker McCormac (Pvt) Ltd v Government of Kenya* 1983 (4) SA 817 (ZS).

*Biti and Another v Minister of Justice, Legal and Parliamentary Affairs and Another,* 2002 (1) ZLR 177 (S).

*Bruce and Another v Fleecytex Johannesburg CC and Others,* 1998 (4) BCLR 415 (CC).

*Capital Radio (Private) Limited v Broadcasting Authority of Zimbabwe and Others,* 2003 (2) ZLR 236 (S).

*Econet Wireless (Pvt) Ltd v Minister of Public Service,* 2016 (1) ZLR 268 (S).

*Executive Council of the Western Cape Legislature and Others v President of the Republic of South Africa and Others,* 1995 (10) BCLR 1289 (CC).

*Kauesa v Minister of Home Affairs, Namibia and Others,* 1995 (11) BCLR 1540 (NMS).

*Law Society of Zimbabwe* v *Minister of Transport and Communications,* 2004 (1) ZLR 257 (S).

*Minister of Home Affairs v Bickle,* 1983 (1) ZLR 99 (S).

*Nyamandlovu Farmers Association v Minister of Lands, Agriculture and Rural Resettlement and Another,* 2003 (1) ZLR 185 (H).

*Paradza v Chirwa and Others,* 2005, not reported, judgement no. S-25-05.

*Paradza v Minister of Justice, Legal and Parliamentary Affairs and Others,* 2003, not reported, judgement no. S-46-03.

*PTC* v *Mahachi,* 1997 (2) ZLR 71 (H).

*Quinnell v Minister of Lands, Agriculture and Rural Resettlement and Others,* 2004 (2) ZLR 293 (S).

*Rattigan and Others v Chief Immigration Officer and Another,* 1995 (1) BCLR 1 (ZS); 1995 (2) *SA* 182 (ZS); 1994 (1) *ZLR* 54 (S).

*S v Gatsi and Rufaro Hotel (Pvt) Ltd 1994 (1) ZLR 7 (H).*

*Tsvangirai v Registrar General and Others,* 2002 (1) *ZLR* 268 (S).

# Abbreviations

| | |
|---|---|
| BCLR | Butterworths Constitutional Law Reports |
| H | High Court |
| IBA | International Bar Association |
| NMS | Namibian Supreme Court |
| S | Supreme Court |
| SA | South African Law Reports |
| SC | Supreme Court |
| ZLR | Zimbabwe Law Reports |
| ZS | Zimbabwe Supreme Court |

# 11

# Dancing Around the Same Spot: The Elusive Quest for Devolution in Zimbabwe's Last Four Decades

Alois Madhekeni

## Introduction

The system of devolving governing power to sub-national entities has gained popularity in several countries across the globe. This is attributed variously from its potential to deepen democracy to its enhancement of development and accommodation of diversity. However, its implementation has been fraught with challenges in both developed and developing nations, African and European countries and small and big states. Western countries such as the United Kingdom, Spain and Italy have seen regional territories that enjoy devolved powers demanding total independence. In some African states such as Namibia, South Sudan, Kenya and South Africa, devolution has fuelled competition for political power at a regional level and renewed ethnic tensions. Nevertheless, devolution remains a popular system of state organisation and a trusted mechanism for equitable sharing of power.

Since devolution is ostensibly a power-sharing mechanism that diversifies centres of power, opposition parties commonly support the policy and advocate for its adoption. However, all ruling parties are driven by the quest for power, its expansion, consolidation and preservation, and so they normally try by all means to avoid devolution. Such avoidance is not always permanent as crisis situations will always arise, necessitating constitutional negotiations that open doors for the accommodation of oppositional interests. Once the crisis has been resolved and a new law enshrining devolution is passed, the previously-held, anti-devolution agenda kicks in resulting in implementation challenges.[1] However, in many cases, legal and political manoeuvring takes over, leading to a stalemate as has been the case in Angola since 1992, Malawi between 2000 and 2014, and Mozambique since 1990. Sometimes devolution provisions within the Constitution are amended or central government clings to powers, functions and resources as has been the case in Namibia since 1990. Some governments have succeeded in recentralising power whilst others like South Africa have failed (Steytler 2014). Zimbabwe is currently experiencing a renewed quest to implement devolution following the ouster of Mugabe from power in 2017. The question that arises is whether this new wave of pressure for devolution signifies a break with the past or not.

As is the trend in most African states, a pattern that is also observable in Zimbabwe, is that devolution is a concept that is more supported in theory than in practice. The devolution conversation in Zimbabwe is not new, it has been around for a century i.e. from section 47 in the 1923 Constitution to section 264 in the 2013 Constitution, devolution has been provided for juridically but denied or undermined empirically. The 1979 Lancaster House Constitution (the framework for the country's independence) made no pretence of devolving power to territorial sub-units of government while its successor, the 2013 Constitution, is full of devolutionary promises.[2] Yet, in practice, the new provisions have come to signify very little. Indeed, the government made two attempts to adopt a controlled system of devolution under the 1999 and 2007 draft Constitutions but both of them suffered a stillbirth.

This chapter discusses the trajectory of devolution in Zimbabwe after independence in 1980. It reveals that irrespective of the juridical devolution framework, there has been more continuity than rupture in practice. The former is reflected through a *longue durée* analysis of three aspects of sub-national autonomy: constitutional protection, local democracy, the powers and functions of provincial and metropolitan councils. The historical background commences with an analysis of the response to the idea of devolution in the colonial era. It proceeds to a period of faith

---

1   This is what happened in Namibia and Malawi after the passing of the 1990 and 1994 Constitutions respectively.

2   See Preamble to Chapter 14 & S 276 (1) Constitution of Zimbabwe Amendment (No. 20) Act 2018.

in deconcentration[3] between 1980 and 1998. It then turns to a long road to devolution commencing with the rejected 1999 draft Constitution, followed by the aborted Kariba draft Constitution of 2007, and concludes with the tedious process of negotiating and drafting the 2013 Constitution. The analysis then moves to a period of *de jure* devolution and *de facto* deconcentration between 2013 and 2017. It then shifts to its departure point, which is a period of devolutionary rhetoric under President Mnangagwa where there is all talk and no walk. This period indicates that despite spirited attempts by the current administration to portray a pro-devolution image, very little has changed in terms of practice, leaving the country stuck in the past. In the main, this chapter demonstrates that whilst the process of devolution in Zimbabwe after (and before) independence has been faltering, an entrenched system of deconcentration has been steadily maintained. This shows the resilience of a centralist ethos remarkably pursued by a regime that has mastered the art of consolidating, monopolising and retaining power at all costs. It also indicates that despite several promises and devolutionary roadshows under the Mnangagwa administration, practice follows the same script of tactfully or blatantly eschewing genuine devolutionary implementation.

## Devolved system of government: a theoretical perspective

To tell the story of devolution in Zimbabwe with clarity, this chapter distinguishes the concept 'devolution' from that of 'deconcentration'. Since the Government of Zimbabwe sometimes loosely conflates the latter with decentralisation, it is also imperative to distinguish between the two concepts. The system of devolved government is anchored on the territorial distribution of power (normally through the Constitution) to smaller entities with political and administrative institutions that have roots within that area (Smith 1985: 1). In detail, the process of devolving governing powers involves fiscal, political and administrative reforms that transfer resources, create newly elected offices and establish autonomous bureaucratic units of decision making and service provision at the sub-national level (Riedl & Dickovick 2014: 323). In short, central to devolution is the establishment, through the law of smaller territorial governments and the transfer of powers and resources that will enable the devolved structures to function with a measure of autonomy. To the contrary, deconcentration does not

---

3  Deconcentration refers to the transfer of government responsibilities to field offices of central government ministries.

involve the establishment of governments but relates to the setting up of field offices of central government at the sub-national level for easy of central government administration (Smoke 2015: 1). The sub-national governments created by the process of devolution vary in terms of levels and types. There are provincial governments, regional governments and local governments. In this chapter, the system of devolved government is analysed in terms of the establishment and conferment of powers and functions to provincial governments.

Tracing and comparing unfolding episodes of devolution and measuring their success or failure is a process that cannot be adequately addressed by analysing the mere mention or not of the term 'devolution' by government officials, laws and policies. More important are the aspects of devolution that confer autonomy to sub-national governments. In this chapter, four such aspects are closely examined over the four decades of independence in Zimbabwe. These are constitutional protection, local democracy, substantive powers and functions of sub-national entities. Constitutional protection entails the provision of sub-national governments in the Constitution. According to Olowu, this recognition of sub-national governments shifts their status from being a creature of the central government to an independent actor that is free from national government impulses (Olowu 2012: 44). Chigwata and Jaap de Visser share the same view, arguing that enshrining the sub-national governments in the Constitution raises their status and guards against arbitrary disestablishment or subversion by the central government (Chigwata & De Visser 2018: 168). Accordingly, part of the devolution question in this chapter is whether the Constitution provides for provincial governments or not and how far it goes with the recognition.

A critical feature of a devolved government that makes the sub-national entities 'governments' and not 'administrative extensions of the centre' is local democracy. Neven provides a comprehensive checklist of questions that need to be answered when determining its existence and scope: Are the sub-national governments elected? Are there multiparty elections? Are ballots secretly cast? Are elections held at regular intervals? Are the elections free and fair? Does the central government have the authority to override local decisions? Is the head of local government elected or appointed? (Neven 2003: 8). In general, the essence of local democracy is that sub-national governments must be made up of members who have roots in the province and are directly elected by its inhabitants, creating downward accountability. This is contrary to deconcentrated institutions whose members are not elected by the people but are appointed by central government officials to whom they should remain accountable.

The existence of elected provincial councils as government structures created by the Constitution will be meaningless without a clear set of functions that are transferred from the central government for discharge at a provincial level. Normally, the functions take two forms – concurrent and exclusive. Exclusive functions are those that can only be discharged by the sub-national government whilst concurrent functions are those that can be discharged at two or more levels. Studies have shown that where functions are shared between central and sub-national governments, the result is the dominance of central government (De Visser 2017: 240; Scharpf 1988: 271). It is therefore imperative that for genuine devolution to prevail, provincial governments must have a share of government functions that are exclusive to them and some that are concurrent. These functions must also be spelt out to avoid ambiguity in the sharing process. Equally important is the need for the functions to be significant enough to make sub-national governance a meaningful enterprise that can cultivate people's respect and participation. Without clarity and meaning, chances are high that people would develop a view that the sub-national governments are 'doing nothing' as is often said about Namibian regional councils or that participating in sub-national governance is a complete waste of time as is often said about Malawi's district councils (Chinsinga 2005: 537; Riruako 2007: 181).

The mere allocation of functions and responsibilities to provincial and local governments will produce a hollow shell if it is not accompanied by powers to pass legislation, appoint and administer personnel and raise and spend revenue in line with local priorities. Thus, for devolution to prevail, provincial governments must be awarded a share of taxing powers, nationally-raised revenue and authority to levy fees on services rendered. Central government control over finances, spending priorities, and appointment and discharge of provincial governments' personnel will turn devolution into deconcentration. As observed by Fessha and Kirkby, the tendency by central governments in Africa to cling to fiscal powers has constituted a back door to centralisation (Fessha & Kirkby 2008: 266).

## Background to devolution in the colonial era – the politics of exclusion

Zimbabwe was colonised by the British in 1890 and administered by Cecil John Rhodes' British South Africa Company for 33 years. In 1923, company rule was replaced with a responsible government of white minorities through the 1923 Constitution of Southern Rhodesia (as Zimbabwe was called then). The 1923 Constitution provided for devolution of governing power to black majorities. This was to be done through the establishment of a Native Council (NC) in any area that is declared a Native Reserve. Section 47 of the 1923 Constitution made provision for the establishment of NCs as platforms where natives would discuss matters of direct interest to them and exercise any other powers conferred to them by the governor (Palley 1966: 659). This provision sought to promote some form of democratic self-government in territorial spaces inhabited by black majorities, resonating with intents and purposes of devolution.

The problem with section 47 was that it did not originate from the settler regime in the colony but was proposed by the British government in London through its High Commissioner for South Africa. To the contrary, the settler regime governing the colony was preoccupied with wealth accumulation and preservation of privileged life for the small white community. To sustain this privilege, the regime understood the importance of maintaining white minority dominance in the politics and governance of the colony. They achieved this goal through the political marginalisation of blacks, who were deftly and sometimes brutally excluded from state power. It is within this context that the implementation of devolution as envisaged by section 47 became problematic. Consequently, the minority regime left the section in abeyance for eight years before a very weak attempt was made to operationalise it through Native Boards (NBs) in 1931. In 1937, section 47 was repealed altogether, paving way for a system of sub-national government whose autonomy was controlled by the settler regime through the use of Ordinances. The regime introduced the NCs in the same year but their composition and powers were so tilted towards central control that they hardly reflected meaningful self-governance. A District Commissioner (DC), representing the white minority regime would be appointed to head the NC whilst the rest of the membership was dominated by ex officio members (especially chiefs and headmen) loyal to the central government. As a result, the NCs started resembling something alien to public expectations – an administrative instrument of central government control. Makumbe observed that in the process, sub-national governance became an elite affair with ordinary people detached from the state, voiceless and permanently pursuing an exit option (Makumbe 1998: 75). The result was a deep and wide legitimacy deficit in the whole process and redundancy of sub-national governance.

## Faith in deconcentration (1980–1998)

Zimbabwe achieved majority rule in 1980 following British mediated negotiations between nationalist movements and the white minority regime. The negotiations held at the Lancaster House in London culminated into a new Constitution (the Lancaster House Constitution) that led to the conduct of democratic elections based on universal adult suffrage. The 1980 elections were resoundingly won by the Zimbabwe African National Union-Patriotic Front (ZANU-PF) but the main opposition party, the Patriotic Front-Zimbabwe African People's Union (PF-ZAPU) had regional dominance. As was the trend with most independence constitutions, brokered by the British government, the Lancaster House Constitution did not provide for devolution. It was mainly viewed as a transitional document facilitating the shift from minority to majority rule.

The fact that the Lancaster House Constitution did not provide for devolution did not automatically mean that the creation of provincial governments was impossible. The United Kingdom's version of devolution is not provided for in a written constitution. Yet, through national legislation, significant autonomy, powers and functions are devolved to the special regions of Northern Ireland, Scotland and Wales. In other words, the ZANU-PF-led government had an opportunity to facilitate devolution through national legislation or to proceed with deconcentration. In the end, it chose the latter. From 1980, the government was on a decentralisation offensive (in terms of rhetoric), stressing its critical role in promoting democracy and development. First was Zimbabwe's ceremonial President, Reverend Canaan Banana, who, in 1980, outlined the government's policy on sub-national governance as focused on the need to democratise councils, deracialise local government, create a unified system of local government and strengthen rural local authorities (Swilling 1996: 39-40). Banana's pronouncements were followed by the then Prime Minister, Robert Mugabe's 1984 Prime Minister's Directive on Decentralisation (Makumbe 1998: 27). The Directive established 'democratic' structures of government that would promote public participation in development from the province to the village. They include Provincial Councils (PCs), District Councils (DCs), Ward Development Committees (WADCOs) and Village Development Committees (VIDCOs) (Makumbe 1998: 27). In 1985, a Provincial Councils and Administration Act was passed giving legal effect to the establishment of PCs as envisioned by Mugabe's decentralisation policy. In many respects, the system fell far short of meeting the basic aspects of devolution; instead, it reflected mere deconcentration.

As already stated, the PCs were not recognised by the Lancaster House Constitution, giving the Mugabe government a free hand in shaping its scope and powers. The composition of PCs itself had very little resemblance of local democracy. They were headed by a Provincial Governor (PG), appointed by the Prime Minister (and by the President since 1988). Other members included a mayor, district chairperson, councillor, chief and three members appointed by the Prime Minister/ President (Section 14, Provincial Councils and Administration Act 1985). In addition to this membership in which the Prime Minister/President had a hand in picking, senior representatives of the Zimbabwe Republic Police (ZRP), Zimbabwe National Army (ZNA) and the feared Central Intelligence Organisation (CIO) in each province were entitled to attend all full council meetings (Makumbe 1996: 42).

Regarding their powers and functions, the PCs were reduced to hollow shells. They merely resembled symbolic structures of governance with no clear mandate. First, the Act awarded them some vague functions in the name of promoting the development of the province, formulating, reviewing and evaluating the implementation of annual development plans and policies (Section 13, Provincial Councils and Administration Act 1985). It was unclear how exactly they were supposed to do this? They were not conferred with any fiscal powers. Their sources of revenue were unknown and neither were their expenditure powers. Besides, the PCs neither had personnel administration powers nor did they have personnel of their own. Rather, the Minister responsible for local government would assign his or her ministry officials to service them subject to the consent of the Public Service Commission (PSC) (Section 33, Provincial Councils and Administration Act 1985).

In sum, the PCs were structures of deconcentration or simply put, they were extensions of the central government meant to assist it in the implementation of its policies. As Makumbe rightly observed, post-independence sub-national governance started revealing striking similarities with the colonial period; an elite affair with ordinary members of the public detached from the state (Makumbe 1998: 75). This practice resonated with the politics of the time as a very ambitious Mugabe and a former liberation movement, ZANU-PF were vigorously pursuing a path to power consolidation. The centralist ethos of the party was inimical to devolution. Practice focused effectively at weeding out any form of competition and creation of a one-party state, centrally controlled by Mugabe himself. By 1988, the grand plan was achieved. PF-ZAPU, the only meaningful opposition at the time was forced into submission and reluctantly joined forces with ZANU-PF under the 1987 Unity Accord.

## The long march to constitutionalised devolution (1999–2013)

### The Constitutional Commission Draft (1999)

In the 1990s, ZANU-PF had consolidated its power to the point of turning Zimbabwe into a *de facto* one-party state. The process of power consolidation had been relentlessly executed, turning the state into a Hobbesian leviathan. It is within this context that increased demands were being made for a new Constitution that would limit executive powers (Vollan 2013: 21). In 1999, holding 147 out of the 150 parliamentary seats in the one-chamber legislature, ZANU-PF commenced a fresh process of drafting a new people-driven Constitution. A Constitutional Commission (CC) led by a former ZANU-PF politician, Justice Godfrey Chidyausiku, published a draft of the Constitution on 1 December 1999, which was to be presented before a referendum in February 2000. Although the draft eschewed the term 'devolution', it contained a whole chapter on local government (*Draft Constitution, 1999* (Zimbabwe) ch. XVI). With several provisions on PCs that resembled a devolved system of government in all but name, a break with the Lancaster House Constitution. With elected PCs and local authorities both entrenched in the draft, the long march towards devolution had begun.

In the CC draft, Zimbabwe was divided into three tiers of government: national government, provincial councils and local authorities (*Draft Constitution 1999* (Zimbabwe), s. 240). However, the security of the PCs existence was not sufficiently protected. This is because first, the names of the provinces were not expressed in the Draft and, second, the Draft provided for provincial boundaries to be altered by an Act of Parliament (*Draft Constitution 1999* (Zimbabwe), s. 244). Aside from these weaknesses, the Draft made other provisions for promoting local democracy with a modicum of powers and functions. Contrary to the deconcentrated system of PCs in the Provincial Councils and Administration Act of 1985, the appointment of members by the President was discontinued. The Draft provided that members of the PC must be democratically elected (*Draft Constitution 1999* (Zimbabwe), s. 241). A limit to this democratic composition was that members were not directly elected for the PCs, but indirectly elected as members of local authorities and senate in the province (*Draft Constitution 1999* (Zimbabwe), s. 244). The Chairperson of the PC was also indirectly elected from the members of senate in the province, a major shift from the appointed Provincial Governors (*Draft Constitution 1999* (Zimbabwe), s. 245 (1)).

Provisions regarding the powers and functions of PCs were shrouded with caution, signifying much hesitation on the part of ZANU-PF but the Draft did mandate central government to transfer some of its functions to the PCs, including co-ordinating government activities, planning and executing policies 'in respect of all matters affecting their communities' (*Draft Constitution 1999* (Zimbabwe), ss. 241 (c); 241 (f) & 244 (3)). A similar vague provision was made on the powers of PCs. First, the Draft provided that PCs 'must be given as much autonomy as is compatible with good governance' (*Draft Constitution 1999* (Zimbabwe), s. 241 (b)). Fiscal and personnel administration powers were not specified, but that PCs must have financial autonomy was intimated by provisions obliging the government to ensure that they have a sound financial base with reliable and adequate sources of revenue (*Draft Constitution 1999* (Zimbabwe), ss. 241 (e) & 242 (1)).

From the foregoing discussion, it can be concluded that the Draft Constitution was a breakthrough in reforming state organisation and power distribution in Zimbabwe. It sought to establish democratically elected PCs with a modicum of powers and functions, a sign that ZANU-PF was warming toward devolution. What explains this major shift from a long-held centralist ethos? In reality, the level of political competition in the country had waned to a point where ZANU-PF had nothing to lose. Thus, given its hegemony, the chances were very limited that devolution would reduce the ruling party's power, it would rather entrench and strengthen the party further. This is simply because at the time it was assured that even if members are subjected to an election, all the PCs would be composed of ZANU-PF members. As shall be seen in the next section, this view was very short-sighted as the politics of the country took a dramatic turn towards cut-throat competition a year later.

When the final draft document was released, it was met with outrage from critics who alleged that it had been substantially altered, so that it no longer reflected the views of the people (Bratton 2014: 75). With a referendum set for February 2000, civil society organisations led by the National Constitutional Assembly (NCA) and a newly-formed opposition party, the Movement for Democratic Change (MDC) led by Morgan Tsvangirai vigorously campaigned for a 'No' vote. ZANU-PF was awarded enormous space in the state-controlled media to campaign for a 'Yes' vote. When the results of the referendum were announced, a majority of 54 % had voted 'No' and the Draft was defeated. Viewed from a competitive interparty perspective, the MDC had proved that it was more popular than ZANU-PF among the electorate. Irked by such an unfamiliar result, ZANU-PF entered into a 'war mode' and the country's politics slid back to the 1980s (when Joshua Nkomo and PF-ZAPU were branded 'cobras in the house'). Mugabe blamed the referendum defeat on the MDC which he branded as a puppet of Western imperialism (Bratton 2014: 75). When the next round of parliamentary/local government and presidential elections was held in 2000 and 2002 respectively, ZANU-PF was ready for combative action. The 2000 referendum became the lynch-pin of multiparty democracy in Zimbabwe, setting the country on a path of increasingly disputed elections.

## The Kariba Draft (2007)

A new draft Constitution emerged in 2007 (Kariba Draft) with provisions on devolution. This draft Constitution was a result of the intervention of SADC following a series of violent and disputed elections that eroded the legitimacy of the ZANU-PF government. A major feature of the Kariba Draft, compared to the 1999 draft, was that it did not derive from public consultations. Rather, it was a product of clandestine meetings in the resort town of Kariba between representatives of the ZANU-PF government and two opposition political parties (MDC-T and MDC-M).[4] South African President and close ally of Mugabe, Thabo Mbeki (as a SADC representative) played a critical mediation role. The meetings were driven by SADC's desperate (but failed) attempt to avoid another disputed election in 2008.

---

4   The MDC had split into two separate political parties, one led by Morgan Tsvangirai (MDC-T) and another one led by Arthur Mutambara (MDC-M).

The drafting process was conducted in a political environment that was different from the one experienced by the Chidyausiku Commission in 1999. ZANU-PF was still clinging to power, but precariously so as the MDC posed an existential threat to the regime. In the 2000 parliamentary election, ZANU-PF had won a historically unprecedented low number of seats (62 of the 120) whilst the MDC closely followed with 57 seats (Vollan 2013: 22). In the 2005 election, international observer missions, which had criticised the 2000 election on account of it being violent were not invited. According to the results, which the MDC rejected as flawed, ZANU-PF increased its seat share to 78 against the MDC's 41 (Vollan 2013: 22). It is within this environment that the parties secretly negotiated the Kariba Draft.

Contrary to the progressive 1999 Draft, devolution provisions in the Kariba Draft were heavily diluted, containing both slight improvements and a huge erosion of autonomy. Whilst very few new provisions were added, several provisions from the 1985 Provincial Councils Act were pasted into the new Draft, taking the process back to deconcentration, with a slight improvement regarding constitutional protection. First, unlike the 1999 Draft that eschewed the term devolution, the Kariba Draft expressly mentioned 'devolution' as one of the fundamental principles guiding state policies (*Draft Constitution 2007* (Zimbabwe), Herein after called *Kariba Draft*, s. 11 (4)). Secondly, PCs were not only mentioned as a tier of government but the ten provinces were each expressly listed, giving them improved security of existence (*Kariba Draft*, s. 244 (1)).

However, in a sharp break with the promising Draft of 1999, the democratic status of PCs was severely diluted. First, the PG appointed by the President was brought back to assume the chairmanship of council, a dramatic return to the 1980s (*Kariba Draft*, ss 245 (2) (a) & 247 (1)). Secondly, membership of PCs was listed but, disappointingly, its exclusive composition was very similar to that of the 1985 Act: members were an assortment of Members of Parliament, senators and councillors. Similar to the 1985 composition, public service officials were also allocated seats, albeit without voting powers (*Kariba Draft*, s 245 (3)). Provisions regarding the functions of PCs resembled a give and take scenario and elaborated beyond co-ordination of government activities to include development planning, management of natural resources, conservation and tourism (*Kariba Draft*, s 246 (1)). However, another provision was inserted to empower the central government with discretion to withdraw those functions and discharge them concurrently with certain PCs or exclusively go it alone as before (*Kariba Draft*, s 246 (2)). The powers of PCs were not specified but, similar to the provisions of the 1999 Draft, they were implied in principle only, leaving the actual determination to an Act of Parliament.

The vague nature of provisions regarding the powers and functions of PCs signalled the making of provincial structures incapable of generating any meaningful legitimacy. What explains this retreat towards more deconcentration than devolution? It is clear from the above discussion that the political environment had shifted such that implementation of genuine devolution would have meant the loss of a significant amount of power by the ZANU-PF-controlled central government. It was also feared that this would give the opposition MDC certain regional footholds of power. In short, the retreat on devolution was simply a sign of ZANU-PF clinging to power in the context of a robust opposition. The Kariba draft was never brought before a referendum as it was overtaken by events around the 2008 election. Similar to the 1999 Draft, the Kariba Draft was another false start on the path to devolution.

## COPAC Drafts (2009-2013)

In 2008, the bitter rivals, ZANU-PF and the two MDC formations faced off again in a hotly contested election. The effectiveness of SADC's efforts to avoid another disputed election through Mbeki's 'quiet diplomacy' faced a litmus test. The pith of the electoral contest was the presidential election where for the first time in the country's post-independence history, Mugabe was defeated by Tsvangirai. The latter emerged the leader (but not winner) with 47.9% of the vote whilst Mugabe came second with 43.2% of the vote (Zimbabwe Election Support Network 2008: 48) Since Tsvangirai had not attained 50% plus one vote, the election was set for a run-off between the two candidates. Tsvangirai later pulled out citing state-sponsored violent reprisals on his supporters, which included arrests, murders, torture, home invasions, abductions and politically motivated beatings directed at opposition members and supporters. The election left about 200 MDC officials and supporters dead, thousands injured and about 200,000 people displaced (Bratton 2014: 87). As aptly observed by Masunungure, the political process of democratic elections was overtaken by a militarised process in which the military elite came to the aid of their political counterparts (Masunungure 2008: 97). Mugabe proceeded with the run-off election where he was the only participating candidate. He was declared the winner by a discredited Electoral Commission but obtained no legitimacy beyond his allies in the ruling party. Soon, the SADC was back to the negotiating table with the three parties that had participated in the Kariba Draft.

After a lengthy period of 'talks', the negotiations culminated into the Global Political Agreement (GPA), a pact that established a Government of National Unity (GNU) for the period 2009 to 2013. The GPA had two major provisions that influenced the 2013 constitutional protection of local government. The GPA established an inclusive government where Mugabe remained President, Tsvangirai became the new Prime Minister and Arthur Mutambara of MDC-M became the Deputy Prime Minister (*Global Political Agreement*, hereinafter referred to as *GPA*, art. XX (20)). In addition, 31 cabinet posts were shared amongst the three main political parties as follows: fifteen posts were allocated to ZANU-PF, thirteen to MDC-T and three to MDC-M (*GPA*, art. XX (20)). A spirit of 'great sensitivity, flexibility and willingness to compromise' underpinned the operations of the GNU (*GPA*, art. XX (20)). The effect of this arrangement was that it greatly diminished ZANU-PF's control of the government, creating room for other political parties to advance their interests. Further, the GPA recognised that the Lancaster House Constitution was meant primarily for the transfer of power from the colonial authority to the people of Zimbabwe hence, it cannot be recognised as the people of Zimbabwe's Constitution (*GPA*, art. VI (6)). To that effect, the GPA tasked the inclusive government to facilitate 'the fundamental right and duty of the Zimbabwean people to make a Constitution by themselves and for themselves; Aware that the process of making this Constitution must be owned and driven by the people and must be inclusive and democratic' (*GPA*, art VI (6)). This provision meant that contrary to the CC Draft, ZANU-PF did not have unfettered control over the Constitution-making process. Further, unlike the Kariba Draft of political parties, the new process had to include public consultations.

In April 2009, a Constitution Parliamentary Committee (COPAC) was established in line with Article VI of the GPA. The composition of COPAC was inclusive, with three co-chairpersons drawn from parliamentary representatives of the three political parties to the GNU. The other 22 members of COPAC were equally selected from the three political parties. The composition of COPAC itself meant that the Constitution-making process was going to be a partisan process driven (and contested) by the three political parties in the GNU. During the outreach meetings, the three parties would mobilise their supporters to attend, such that half the time most of them would simply support or criticise according to their party affiliations rather than as independent voices (Zimbabwe Independent Constitution Monitoring Project (ZICOMP) 2010: 8).[5] In the end, constitutional provisions were more a reflection of political party positions than the preferences of the ordinary Zimbabweans.

During the outreach meetings, opinion was divided over the appropriate system of government. Public views sharply followed the two contrasting positions – ZANU-PF on one hand and the two MDC parties on the other. The former vigorously campaigned for a unitary system of government that would maintain the status quo, whilst the two MDC formations publicly campaigned for a devolved system. Out of the ten provinces, five, including Harare, had majorities that preferred maintenance of status quo – ZANU-PF position – whilst five, including all the three Matabele-dominated provinces preferred devolution – the MDC position (ZICOMP 2010: 26-45). To the contrary, an independent national survey of Zimbabweans' views by Afrobarometer indicated overwhelming support for devolution in eight out of the country's ten provinces (Mass Public Opinion Institute (MPOI) 2012: 53). The telling disparity of results of the two reports is a testament of how politically polarised the constitution-making process was. Indeed, as rightly observed by the Zimbabwe Independent Constitution Monitoring Project (ZICOMP), 'in the main, outreach consultations appear to have been reduced to a contest between the ideological positions of ZANU PF and the MDC T', with the former dominating (ZICOMP 2010: 47).

The debate on devolution became so hotly contested that at some point ZANU-PF threatened to abandon the whole constitution-making process.[6] In May 2012, it pulled out of COPAC citing the need to consult over 'parked' issues (devolution included), crippling the whole process which abruptly came to a halt before resuming months later.[7] What frustrated ZANU-PF was the unfamiliar territory where it had to seek the mutual consent of the two former opposition parties before a draft of the

---

5   The project reported an omnipresence of coaching by the two main partners to the GNU – ZANU-PF and MDC-T.

6   'Zanu PF threat to sink constitution over devolution', *NewZimbabwe*, 7 March 2012

7   'Zanu-PF takes indefinite break from Zim constitution making', *Bulawayo24 News*, 7 May 2012.

Constitution could be finalised. In total, COPAC released three drafts – 2011, 2012 and 2013. The first one was meant for internal discussion by COPAC members only and had no agreement on devolution.

The second draft had a whole chapter on provincial and local government (Chapter 14) where both the term 'devolution' and PCs were expressly provided for. Constitutional protection of the PCs was guaranteed as the provinces were listed (*Constitution of Zimbabwe (Draft 17 July 2012*), hereinafter referred to as *Draft 2012*, s. 14.4),). Similar to the Kariba Draft, local democracy was not sufficiently guaranteed. First, the composition of the PC was dominated by *ex officio* members elected for other purposes – members of the national assembly and senate, mayors and chairpersons of local authorities and a paltry ten members elected on proportional representation (*Draft 2012*, s. 14.5). Secondly, the PG (President's man) was retained as the chairperson of the PC. The two wholly urban provinces of Harare and Bulawayo (Metropolitan Councils) were an exception as they were headed by the cities' mayors. The powers and functions of the PCs were not expressly provided for but were left to the determination by an Act of Parliament.

The 2012 Draft was met with outrage by ZANU-PF elites who demanded that changes be made on several provisions before presentation at the stakeholders' conference. One of the areas where the party had objections was 'devolution'. In the main, ZANU-PF wanted the term 'devolution' to be extinguished from the Constitution and be replaced by a lighter one – decentralisation, as follows:

**Table 11.1: ZANU-PF's response to COPAC's Second Draft**

| section | COPAC's position based on Draft Constitution 17 July 2012 | ZANU PF's position in response to COPAC Draft Constitution |
|---------|-----------------------------------------------------------|------------------------------------------------------------|
| 14.1 | Devolution of governmental powers and responsibilities | Decentralisation of governmental powers and responsibilities |
| 14.1(1) | Governmental powers and responsibilities must be devolved to provincial and metropolitan councils and local authorities | Governmental powers and responsibilities must be decentralised to provincial and local authorities |

| section | COPAC's position based on Draft Constitution 17 July 2012 | ZANU PF's position in response to COPAC Draft Constitution |
| --- | --- | --- |
| 14.1(2) | The objectives of the devolution of governmental powers and responsibilities to provincial and metropolitan councils and local authorities | The objectives of the decentralization of governmental powers and responsibilities to provincial councils and local authorities |
| 14.2(c) | Exercise their functions in a manner that does not encroach on the geographical, functional or institutional integrity of another tier of government | Exercise their functions in a manner that does not encroach on the geographical, functional or institutional integrity of another structure of government |
| Sect 5 | Tiers of government | Structures of government |

**Source: Adopted from Muchadenyika (2015:14).**

Following some resistance from the MDC parties to effect the changes, an agreement was reached to present two documents – the COPAC Draft and a report of ZANU-PF's objections – at a stakeholders' conference. Thereafter, COPAC compiled a list of issues discussed and their outcomes. This was divided into three categories – issues not commented on, recommendations agreed upon and recommendations with no agreement. Devolution predictably emerged on the 'no-agreement' list and the debate continued. The deadlock was later resolved after meetings of an appointed seven-member cabinet committee and the three principals i.e. Mugabe, Tsvangirai and Mutambara yielded some concessions. These paved the way for the preparation of a final draft which was released in 2013. Within this, devolution was adopted and the PGs were replaced by Provincial Chairpersons elected by members of the PC. A set of general functions transplanted from the Kariba Draft was added. Also included was provision for the allocation of an annual share of nationally-raised revenue (not less than 5%) to the PCs, Metropolitan Councils (MCs) and local authorities (*Constitution of Zimbabwe Amendment (No. 20) Act 2013*, s. 301 (3)). The deal-breaker was a strange addition of a preamble under Chapter 14, clarifying what devolution did not mean – disunity, secessionism and inequitable allocation of national resources. On 16 March 2013, the final draft was presented before a referendum where an overwhelming majority (94.5%) voted in favour. When the Constitution of Zimbabwe Amendment (No.20) Act 2013 was published, it appeared as if the curtain had finally come down on the country's long march to devolution. Alas, it was only the beginning. Unbeknown to many, ZANU-PF was down but certainly not out. It had lost the battle but not the war.

## The power play: *de jure* devolution meets *de facto* deconcentration (2013 – 2017)

Following the passing of the 2013 Constitution into law, a debate emerged about whether the country should immediately hold elections or whether they should be delayed to pave the way for reforms in line with the new constitutional order. ZANU-PF, now both irritated and impatient with the GNU's checks and balances, pressed for an immediate election whilst the MDC formations preferred to wait for reforms. In the famous *Mawarire vs Mugabe and others* court case of May 2013, the Constitutional Court ordered Mugabe to proclaim a date for elections, which should be no later than 31 July 2013. The elections were duly held as per this ruling and the results shocked many. They were resoundingly won by ZANU-PF with a two-thirds majority in parliament (73% of seats) and Mugabe with 62% of the presidential vote. The MDC-T denounced the election as a sham but did not appear to know what had hit them. This context had serious implications on the future of devolution. ZANU-PF's two-thirds majority meant that the party could amend the Constitution and remove what it does not like. It also meant that it could pass any laws, block or delay the passing of laws including alignment of local government laws to the new Constitution.

Now left to their own means, Mugabe and ZANU-PF's response to devolution was a severe indictment of constitutionalism. They simply ignored the constitutional obligation to establish the PCs and MCs as if oblivious of its existence. The process of selecting ten members of the PC on the basis of their parties' proportion of votes in the province was not conducted and for the whole five-year term, not a single national budget provided for the mandatory '5%' share of national revenue to PCs, MCs and local authorities. To show his determination with the continuation of status quo, Mugabe replaced the PGs with a similar version, now christened 'Provincial Affairs Ministers.' Ironically, the silence of the opposition parties and civil society organisations that had vigorously lobbied for devolution during the Constitution-making process was deafening. Devolution lay dead in the water whilst an amendment of the Constitution to complete the demolition job looked ominously certain.

## The amplified rhetoric of devolution (2018-2019)

In November 2017, Mugabe was ousted from power following a carefully executed military intervention. His erstwhile and long-time deputy and right-hand man, Emmerson Mnangagwa, replaced Mugabe as the new President. From the onset, Mnangagwa persistently tried to paint himself as different from Mugabe. He made numerous promises to break with the past, including tolerance of differences, strengthening of the country's democratic pillars, international re-engagement and strict adherence to constitutionalism.[8] For instance, in his 24 November 2017 inauguration speech, the President said, 'I implore you all to declare that NEVER AGAIN should the circumstances that have put Zimbabwe in an unfavourable position be allowed to recur or overshadow its prospects. We must work together, you, me, all of us who make up this Nation'.[9] To supporters of devolution, hopes of its implementation were renewed but soon it was clear that their excitement was premature.

The sad news was delivered by Patrick Chinamasa, Mnangagwa's then Minister of Finance whilst making his 2018 national budget presentation in December 2017. With remarkable consistency, Chinamasa did not provide for the '5%' revenue share to PCs, MCs and local authorities, signifying a continuity of ZANU-PF's defiance against the implementation of devolution. The only difference was that this time the Minister had an explanation. With no hint of irony, the man who held the keys to the fiscal purse thundered: 'Funding of the provincial and metropolitan structures, as set out in Chapter 14, section 264 of the Constitution, is not sustainable and political parties represented in Parliament should in the future give consideration to amending the Constitution to lessen the burden on the fiscus'.[10] Considering that this statement was made at a time when ZANU-PF had two-thirds majority in parliament, it was legitimately feared that devolution would soon be history.

When campaigns for the 2018 election commenced, Chinamasa's

---

8   'President Mnangagwa's inauguration speech in full', *The Chronicle*, 27 November 2017.

9   Ibid.

10  'Govt dumps devolution, plots constitutional amendments', *NewsDay*, 14 December 2017.

statement was vindicated. ZANU-PF did not include devolution in its newly minted manifesto, clearly signalling that it was not on the new administration's agenda. To the contrary, the MDC Alliance[11] (MDC-A) manifesto dedicated substantial space to devolution implementation. Then, as campaign rallies were rolled out, Mnangagwa made a surprise detour from the party's manifesto and followed the MDC-A in trumpeting the implementation of devolution. This surprise turnaround was strategically made whilst addressing a rally in Matabeleland South Province where the following promise was made:

> We must now obey our Constitution. In our Constitution there is a provision which provides for the decentralisation of central government, that we have done. There is another decentralisation of power that has not been done called devolution which is separate from decentralisation. Devolution would require the surrendering of some amount of power to the provinces under the provincial councils in terms of our Constitution...[12]

When the results of the 2018 election were announced, ZANU-PF retained its two-thirds majority in parliament whilst Mnangagwa was declared the winner of the Presidential election by a wafer-thin margin. The MDC Alliance dismissed the election as flawed and appealed to the Constitutional Court but lost. The sitting administration continued with its devolution rhetoric but in practice showed very little commitment to the Constitutional provisions. For the first time, ten members of the PC were elected in each province, but they have since become redundant as the government is taking its time to convene the PCs. After the announcement of his cabinet in early September 2018, Mnangagwa's touted commitment to devolution started to sound hollow. Consistent with Mugabe, the man who had promised to respect the Constitution proceeded to appoint Provincial Affairs ministers, signifying determination to maintain strong central control. His government proceeded to mention that the Provincial Affairs ministers would play a key role in spearheading devolution.[13] There has also been a surprising emphasis on the fact that devolution will be for economic development (not deepening of democracy). Without political autonomy and a serious democratic focus, the risk is that PCs and MCs will end up operating as administrative extensions of the central government, taking the country back to deconcentration in everything but name.

In spite of its pursuit of deconcentration in terms of practice, the Mnangagwa administration has proceeded to churn out more devolution rhetoric with each public event. For instance, when the independence celebrations were held in April 2019, the main theme was 'Embracing Devolution for Vision 2030'. In his speech read at the national sports stadium, President Mnangagwa repeated his commitment to the implementation of devolution, with the words, 'Fellow Zimbabweans; Recognising that we are a unitary but diverse State, the Second Republic will seek to facilitate the development of marginalised communities in all our activities. We are steadfast in our commitment to fully implement the devolution system. Treasury has so far allocated a total of $310 million to facilitate the devolution programme' (Office of the President and Cabinet (OPC) (2019).

When the 2019 national budget was presented, the '5%' share was provided for the first time since 2013. However, although the Constitution states that this allocation must be shared amongst PCs, MCs and local authorities, in practice, the Ministry responsible for local government has parcelled the money to local authorities only (Chauke & Nyakuru 2019). Why PCs and MCs have not been given their share remains unexplained. This practice exposes the variance between the political statements made by ZANU-PF elites and the practical implementation of devolution. The Ministry responsible for local government and other government departments have been active in facilitating and participating (in partnership with civil society organisations) in policy dialogues and workshops on devolution country-wide. Examples include a series of devolution conferences conducted in the country's ten provinces by the Government of Zimbabwe in partnership with Citizens Lab Zimbabwe and the Chartered Institute of Project Managers Zimbabwe from late 2018 to early 2019. However, progress on the most important part of devolution implementation (amendment of provincial councils and local government laws in line with the 2013 Constitution) has been very slow. The absence of enabling legislation to interpret the constitutional provisions on devolution has stalled implementation. In the absence of visible progress with implementation, the Mnangagwa administration's commitment to devolution continues to sound hollow.

## Conclusion

The comparative historical analysis above generates important observations and lessons about the practical workings of devolution and each ruling elite's pattern of engagement with it. First, an overall observation is that every ruling party, be it dominated by whites or blacks, is principally concerned with consolidating its power and protecting it against encroachment by opposition parties. This resolve automatically makes devolution problematic, leading governments to find ways of avoiding, neutralising or reversing the process at the very first opportunity. Secondly, given the inevitable resistance of ruling elites, it is important to constitutionally protect devolution. However, constitutional protection will come to nothing when the ruling party undertakes its demolition – constitutional provisions can be amended, ignored or completely abrogated. This realisation brings the discussion to a third lesson – the importance of constitutionalism. There is a need for all state and society actors to play an active role in demanding and defending devolution. These include parliament, opposition parties, civil society organisations, media, international development agencies, academia, organised local government, PCs, MCs and local authorities, traditional leaders and the judiciary. As long as these institutions are weak, the quest for devolution is elusive. The story of Zimbabwe's experience with devolution across decades corroborates this argument. The analysis reveals the fits and starts of the process of devolution. It teeters on the verge of deconcentration as political economy factors and associated imperatives of power drive ruling elites towards central control. The hostility towards devolution becomes more entrenched in the case of former liberation movements such as ZANU-PF whose centralist, command and control ethos are unyielding. The Mnangagwa government may brand itself as *sui generis* but practice certainly indicates more continuities than discontinuities. Indeed, we continue dancing on the same spot as power politics takes precedence over democratisation and constitutionalism.

## References

Bratton, M. (2014) *Power Politics in Zimbabwe*. Boulder: Lynne Rienner.

Chauke, J. and N. Nyakuru (2019) 'Implementation of Intergovernmental

Fiscal Transfer'. Paper Presented at the Ministry of Local Government Public Works and National Housing and Silveira House Workshop Programme. 'The Implementation of the Intergovernmental Fiscal Transfer Framework', 30 August, Rainbow Towers Hotel, Harare.

Chigwata, T.C. and J. de Visser (2018) 'Local Government in the 2013 Constitution of Zimbabwe: Defining the Boundaries of Local Autonomy', *Hague Journal on the Rule of Law*, 10, 165-185.

Chinsinga, B. (2005) 'District Assemblies in a Fix: The Perils of the Politics of Capacity in the Political and Administrative Reforms in Malawi', *Development Southern Africa*, 22/4, 529-548.

de Visser, J. (2017) 'Concurrent Powers in South Africa', in N. Steytler (ed.), *Concurrent Powers in Federal Systems: Meaning, Making, Managing*. Leiden: Brill.

Fessha, Y. and C. Kirkby (2008) 'A Critical Survey of Subnational Autonomy in African States', *Publius: The Journal of Federalism*, 38/2, 248-271.

Makumbe, J. M. (1998) *Democracy and Development in Zimbabwe: Constraints of Decentralisation*. Harare: SAPES Books.

————— (1996) *Participatory Development: The Case of Zimbabwe*. Harare: University of Zimbabwe Publications.

Mass Public Opinion Institute (MPOI) (2012) 'Summary of Results: Afrobarometer Round 5 Survey in Zimbabwe'. Harare: MPOI.

Masunungure, E.V. (2009) 'A Militarised Election: The 27 June Presidential Run-off', in E.V. Masunungure (ed.), *Defying the Winds of Change: Zimbabwe's 2008 Elections*. Harare: Weaver Press.

Muchadenyika, D. (2015) 'The Inevitable: Devolution in Zimbabwe: From Constitution-Making to the Future', in J. de Visser, N. Steytler, D. Powell and E. Durojaye (eds), *Constitution Building in Africa*. Baden-Baden: Nomos.

Neven, I. (2003) 'Background Paper on "Decentralisation"'. Contribution to Cost-Action E 19 National Forest Programmes in the European Context, September, Vienna.

Office of the President and Cabinet (OPC) (2019) 'Forward ever, backward never!' Independence Speech by President E.D. Mnangagwa, 18 April. Available: <http://www.theopc.gov.zw/index.php/398-forward-ever-backward-never-independence-speech-by-president-e-d-mnangagwa>.

Olowu, D. (2012) 'The Constitutionalization of Local Government in

Developing Countries: Analysis of African experiences in Global Perspective', *Beijing Law Review*, 3, 42-50.

Palley, C. (1966) *The Constitutional History and Law of Southern Rhodesia 1888-1965*. Oxford: Clarendon Press.

Riedl, R.B. and J.T. Dickovick (2014) 'Party Systems and Decentralization in Africa', *Studies in Comparative International Development*, 49/3, 321-342.

Riruako, H. (2007) 'The Paradox of Decentralisation in Namibia'. Unpublished PhD thesis, University of the Western Cape.

Scharpf, F.W. (1988) 'The Joint-Decision Trap: Lessons from German Federalism and European Integration', *Public Administration*, 66/3, 239-278.

Smith, B.C. (1985) *Decentralisation: The Territorial Dimension of the State*. London: Allen & Unwin.

Smoke, P. (2015) 'Decentralisation', Professional Development Reading Pack No.9.

Steytler, N. (2014) 'The Politics of Provinces and Provincialisation of Politics', in T. Maluwa (ed.), *Law, Politics and Rights: Essays in Memory of Kader Asmal*. Leiden: Martinus Nijhoff.

Swilling, M.A. (1996) 'Review of Local Government and Development in the Southern African Region', in P. S. Reddy (ed.), *Readings in Local Government Management: A Southern African Perspective*. Cape Town: Juta.

Vollan, K. (2013) 'The Constitutional History and the 2013 Referendum of Zimbabwe'. A Nordem Special Report 2013, Norwegian Centre for Human Rights, University of Oslo.

Zimbabwe Independent Constitution Monitoring Project (ZICOMP) (2010) Final Report Shadowing the Outreach Process November 2010. Harare: ZICOMP.

Zimbabwe Election Support Network (2008) Report on the Zimbabwe 29 March 2008 Harmonized Elections and 27 June Presidential Run-off. Harare: ZESN.

# Legislation

Constitution of Zimbabwe Amendment (No. 20) Act 2013 (Government of Zimbabwe).

Global Political Agreement, 2009 (Government of Zimbabwe).

Draft Constitution of Zimbabwe, 2007 (Government of Zimbabwe).

Provincial Councils and Administration Act, 1985 (Government of Zimbabwe).

# 12

# The Southern African Development Community (SADC), the African Union (AU) and the Zimbabwe Political Question: Policy Continuity beyond Mugabe

## Lawrence Mhandara

## Introduction

Since the end of the Cold War, the 'new regionalism' seems to confirm the centrality of regional and sub-regional organisations in complementing the United Nations (UN) (Wulf and Debiel 2010), and acquiring ever-expanding relevance in international relations, particularly regarding peace, security, development, and mitigation of conflict (Joshua 2017: 455; Castillo, et al. 2016: 11). The developments come in the midst of arguments of the liberal peace theory that membership in such organisations promotes and reinforce democracy (Donno 2010: 593). As a general observation, rigid emphasis on non-interference and respect for absolute national sovereignty has gradually yielded to the principle that regional organisations should also provide mechanisms to guarantee democracy and human rights in member states, thus enabling the link between former and regional integration common in the frameworks of most existing organisations. International and regional scrutiny of possible breakdowns or erosions of democratic regimes is becoming a norm rather than an exception. The correlation is stronger when the organisation is committed to democratic principles. Respecting democracy and the rule of law among member states may also serve as a guarantee of commitment to the objectives of the regional organisation concerned. The SADC and the AU have similar commitments which are represented by their respective charters and several protocols.

The political transition that followed the sudden demise of Robert Mugabe's long political career and the ascension of Emmerson Mnangagwa to power provided an opportunity for both the SADC and the AU to strengthen their commitment to democratic norm enforcement in order to complement Zimbabwe's desire for a new trajectory. Indeed, the post-Mugabe era, had wrought hopes of reform and political liberalisation, promising a new trajectory or a 'new dispensation' from the country that would be distinct from Mugabe's vituperative politics. To confirm this commitment, Mnangagwa's government was credited for a political environment that was different in every sense from the 'old dispensation' in so far as political freedoms, peace and robust competition among all contestants were guaranteed. Certainly, the perceptions that Mnangagwa was serious about laying the foundation for a new direction were common even among those who had opposed his ruling party, locally and internationally. Two events changed the perception of Mnangagwa as a reformer: the 1 August 2018 post-election violence and the 14 January 2019 protests, both of which resulted in at least six[1] and 172 deaths respectively. For many, the symptoms of authoritarian leadership were apparent and the hope of a new trajectory remained a chimera. With memories of the past haunting the population, the fear of regression into the authoritarian abyss, overstated or real, led to calls for international response to Mnangagwa's government to resolve the resilient political question. It was natural that such calls were primarily targeted at the SADC and then at the AU to force Mnangagwa to honour his commitment to a more principled way of conducting politics. In response, the SADC and the AU responded, and continue to respond, in a manner that has been criticised by anti-Mnangagwa voices, both locally and internationally. The anticipated 'strong response' has not been forthcoming, marking a continuity in approach from Mugabe's days. What explains this shared attitude towards Zimbabwe despite a seemingly strong normative framework for the promotion of democracy and the protection of human

---

1    'Post-election Violence Monitoring Report', Zimbabwe Human Rights NGO Forum, 24 September 2018.

2    'Zimbabwe: Excessive Force Used Against Protesters', *Human Rights Watch*, 3 March 2019.

rights at both levels? How does such a continuum encourage a new political trajectory in Zimbabwe? To answer these questions, this chapter applies the securitisation framework to explain the policy continuity. I argue that the shared SADC and the AU positions on Zimbabwe are better comprehended from the securitisation of the liberal ideology – a process marked by the construction of an ideology as a threat because of its fundamentalist demands and representation by the anti-Zimbabwe African National Union (ZANU-PF) bloc. This securitisation has in turn inspired a robust but non-hostile SADC/AU resistance to support for democratic consolidation in Zimbabwe. Consequently, it has the potential to undermine the pledged new political trajectory.

The chapter has three major sections: the first provides a synopsis of what can be considered as the resilient political question that has outlived Mugabe's rule. This sets the context for understanding the voices or pleas for the SADC and the AU to respond in the subsequent section. In order to establish a pattern of continuity, this section traces the SADC and the AU approaches from Mugabe to Mnangagwa's rule. Thereafter, the chapter attempts to account for the policy continuity by applying the securitisation framework and the attendant implication on the new political trajectory in Zimbabwe before the conclusion is reached.

## The resilient political question: developmental repression in Zimbabwe

While the detail regarding the challenges in Zimbabwe are best treated elsewhere (Rutherford 2018; Mhandara and Murwira 2017; Mlambo 2017; Moore 2014; Raftopoulos 2014; Ncube 2013; Masunungure 2013; 2011; 2009; Sachikonye 2011; Alden 2002 among others), it is important to provide a summary of the main issues that have brought the country on the international agenda. The political question in Zimbabwe is related to the hard issue of ZANU-PF rule as it relates to the weak institutionalisation of competitive politics giving rise to contested legitimacy, electoral misconduct (Mhandara and Pooe 2013; Masunugure 2011), and weak economic development (Mhandara and Murwira 2017; Mlambo 2017). Ultimately, the question is one of a multi-centred crisis, namely a crisis of legitimacy as a result of the erosion of the post-colonial consensus built during the course of the liberation struggle; a crisis of expectations arising out of the deteriorating economic situation and the failure of structural adjustment measures to halt the erosion of social and economic gains of the early years of independence; and a crisis of confidence in the institutions of the state, inspired by the actions of the security forces and intimidation of the judiciary (Alden 2002: 8-9).

The challenges in Zimbabwe have been associated with two polarising rights' claims, pitting the hegemonic bloc, ZANU-PF and pro-ruling party movements – best described as a military-economic elite, a capitalist class at the inchoate stage (Raftopoulos 2013 cited in Moore 2013: 104), and the counter-hegemonic bloc (Movement for Democratic Change (MDC) and pro-opposition movements). The former accords primacy to self-determination, anti-colonialism, anti-imperialism and therefore anti-Western constructions. Its main narrative has been based on the long-term structural political-economic legacies of colonial rule, combined with the legacies of African nationalist politics (Mlambo and Raftopoulos 2010 cited in Mhandara and Pooe 2013: 10). The latter emphasises liberal democracy in a manner that challenges the hegemonic bloc. ZANU-PF assumed an oppositional stance to the counter-hegemonic group which it treats as a Trojan horse for Western hegemony,[3] justifying violation of their considered civil and political rights. This primarily played out in the implementation of what Donelly (1989: 187-188 cited in Ncube 2013: 102) calls *developmental repression*, whose key ingredients include a radical racial discourse (Chan 2010: 10), 'purging the judiciary, passing repressive legislation, distributing humanitarian aid along partisan lines, arresting opposition leaders on treason charges, unilaterally withdrawing Zimbabwe from the Commonwealth, implementing the indigenisation policy ... and use of military and paramilitary strategies to maintain hold on power' (Ncube 2013: 103), and 'privatisation' of history and politics (Moore 2013: 110), such that engaging in meaningful competition with ZANU-PF has been difficult or sometimes fatal (Raftopoulos and Savage 2005; Sachikonye et al. 2007; Masunungure 2011; Sachikonye 2011). The ruling party became more agitated with every attempt by the counter-hegemonic group to undermine its claims to power, by which their narrative prioritised civil and political rights (rule of law, voting

---

3   Mhandara and Pooe (2013: 9) argue that ZANU-PF's position was easy to justify given the public pronouncements by British government officials declaring their direct contact with the MDC on how to proceed on Zimbabwe. The authors cite how the former British Foreign Secretary, Robin Cook, during an address to the House of Commons in January 2010, indicated that Britain's policy on Zimbabwe was 'guided by what the MDC says to us...'

rights, freedoms of assembly, speech and association) more than the significance of historical colonial wrongs related to key policies like land and indigenisation (Raftopoulos 2010: 709; Sachikonye 2004). ZANU-PF, in particular Mugabe, saw the human rights discourse as the new form of imperialism that had to be suppressed at any cost, marking the triumph of coercive politics constructed through a radical nationalist discourse (Raftopoulos 2014: 91). The ruling party's resolve to defend its power was renewed each time the anti-government groups discredited its government as illegitimate and when they successfully lobbied the European Union and the United States of America to isolate and sanction the government.

The crisis is commonly traced from the 2000s, although it started in the 1990s, mainly as a direct consequence of 'policy blunders' (Mlambo 2017: 106, 112) – the unbudgeted pay-outs to the fidgety veterans of the liberation struggle in 1997, The Democratic Republic of Congo war in 1998, the repressive response to the formation of the MDC in 1999 and the land reclamation process beginning in 2000, the partisan indigenisation and empowerment policies, tainted electoral processes since the June 2000 general election, with the exception of a few,[4] making elections a farcical ritual (Mandaza 2013; Masunungure 2009). By the time the June 27 run-off election was held, the contradictions among the key political actors had degenerated into a double crisis of legitimacy and efficacy for the ruling party (Masunungure 2009), forcing it into a coalition government on the back of pressure from the SADC and the AU to negotiate with the opposition. Although some modicum of stability and sanity prevailed during the four-year tenure of the inclusive government (Mlambo 2017), the political question persisted as ZANU-PF prematurely announced the date of the 2013 election before the full set of electoral reforms were implemented, setting the stage for contested outcomes in future elections. The 2013 elections, just like the 2018 polls, were peaceful and less prominent in respect of human rights abuses that had become common in elections since 2000. However, allegations of heavy manipulation emerged (Ncube 2013), sounding democracy's death knell (Moore 2013: 101), or signalling a farewell to democracy (Bracking 2013 cited in Moore 2013: 102).

A combination of coercive politics and weak economic indicators yielded a human security deficit in terms of both deprivation and

---

4    The 2013 and 2008 harmonised elections were peaceful with insignificant incidences of the usual inter-party violence being reported.

vulnerability of citizens (Busumutwi-Sam 2008: 16). Key landmarks of the symptoms of a crisis included how the economy tumbled from being the second most industrialised economy after South Africa in 1980 to being one of the poorest in the SADC region, with the formal structures of the economy facing near collapse and citizens increasingly turning into vending (Mlambo 2017: 99). Instantaneously, the socio-economic situation in the country was marked by negative indicators, smacking of a humanitarian crisis. For instance, by 2008, poverty levels shot to 70% from 42% in 1995, unemployment reached 80% and inflation hit a world record (Africa Development Bank cited in Mlambo 2017: 106). The well-being, dignity, welfare and safety of citizens was under siege. And there were calls from the counter-hegemonic group, primarily the MDC-Tsvangirai (MDC-T), civil society, and their international supporters, prominently the EU and the USA, for the SADC and the AU to intervene and 'stop the dying democracy' (Moore 2014: 104), and the 'mutating crisis' (Ndlovu-Gatsheni 2006: 5). Both the SADC and the AU responded to the call for action, albeit in a manner that they saw as fit at the time; and Mugabe departed from the political theatre leaving the question largely unaddressed.

The 'new dispensation', a period that began on 24 November 2017 when Mnangagwa was sworn in as the second president of Zimbabwe, has differed in many respects with the 'old' in as far as political freedoms have been recognised. Outside the technical aspects of the electoral management process, the long-standing questions of legitimacy and credibility were closer to their solution under the 2018 election environment. The four procedural, most important, minimal conditions for uncontested legitimacy were discernible:

- Constitutionalism – respect for not only the Constitution but human rights, social justice and rule of law (legal possibilities of complaint were guaranteed).
- Individuals and political organisations were involved in a competitive struggle for the people's vote.
- Participation and inclusivity – every eligible citizen who wanted to participate in the elections by either voting or running for office was not unreasonably obstructed.
- Freedom – speech, expression and association were guaranteed and protected as required by the Bill of Rights.

However, the post-election violence in August 2018 and the January

2019 disturbances seem to have obliterated the earlier gains. Even the progressive amendments to the two symbols of the repugnant politics of his predecessor, namely, the Public Order and Security Act (POSA) and the Access to Information and Protection of Privacy Act (AIPPA), have missed the attention of Mnangagwa's critics. Despite the post-Mugabe dispensation, the same issues that Mugabe had grappled with are galvanising the counter-hegemonic bloc. Key among these is the view that the 2018 elections were not in line with the AU and the SADC guidelines on democratic elections, and therefore produced an illegitimate winner. The ruling of the Constitutional Court upholding the results of the Presidential election has failed to diffuse the opposition stance that Zimbabwe is still beset by the unresolved political question. The counter-hegemonic bloc insists that the crisis of legitimacy still lingers. Equally, the calls for national dialogue by Mnangagwa to foster unity among all political actors have been ignored by the MDC-Alliance (MDC-A), arguing that the important question is the legitimacy of the president whom they see as imposed by the judiciary. It appears Nelson Chamisa's strategy is predicated on the push for dialogue that results in power-sharing and nothing else. Mnangagwa has however insisted that he is the legitimate president and any dialogue with Chamisa must proceed from that material fact. The result has been a mutually hurting stalemate, pushing the country to a precipice where implosion is just but a matter of time.

Several accounts are emerging to liken Mnangagwa with his predecessor's politics. He has been described as Mugabe's shadow (Rutherford 2018: 53), further describing his government as 'the same bus but different driver' (Rutherford 2018: 63), or 'a new driver in the same old taxi' (Pigou 2019). The likeness of Mnangagwa to Mugabe implies not only resemblance but also a connection, a proximity, an equivalence, even an identity' (Ferguson 2006: 17 cited in Rutherford 2018: 53), to Mugabe. Mnangagwa is seen as an 'attached twin', deeply entrenched to the old ZANU-PF and has been a key player in many of its shadowy and violent practices (Rutherford 2018: 62). Zimbabwe is thus bedevilled by the 'continued insecurity and precariousness' of the enduring political economy (Hammar 2017: 95), inherited from Mugabe. The hope of a new trajectory is thus unreal and the view that Mnangagwa's rule marks a new dispensation has been robustly discredited (Solidarity Peace Trust 2019: 2) as demonstrated in the frustrations of one critic: 'No one ever expected that a government that calls itself a new dispensation could go on the streets and shoot people while the leader is in Europe asking for investments, it's a contradiction ...'[5] The violence that occurred on 1 August and the government response to the January 2019 protests have been used as examples of how Mnangagwa is attached to the old politics (Solidarity Peace Trust 2019: 6-7). The government argued that both incidences of violence were justified on the basis that the protesters were violently seeking to unseat government. The Deputy Chief Secretary to the President and Cabinet, George Charamba, pointedly stated that while the face of protests was local, the politics were external, and intended to brush aside the outcome of electoral process in favour of a preferred candidate.[6] A Government of Zimbabwe Report entitled 'Brief on the Political and Security Situation in Zimbabwe in the aftermath of the 14-16 January, 2019 violent protests', released on 30 January 2019 accused the MDC and 'other local merchants of regime change' in order to, 'cause foreign intervention under the responsibility to protect Principle'. In an interview with a French news agency at an AU summit in Addis Ababa in February 2019, Mnangagwa formally re-stated this position. He claimed that the protests were part of a 'predetermined and pre-planned' regime-change action 'well-oiled by both local NGOs who are well funded and also the opposition MDC Alliance'.[7] Mnangagwa further claimed that the accusations of rape were 'just a make-up by some organisations' in Zimbabwe.[8] Nonetheless, the post-Mugabe government has been perceived as struggling to establish its legitimacy while being as authoritarian as its predecessor.[9]

And again, notwithstanding the political and economic reformist language of international re-engagement of the Mnangagwa government, the shadow of Mugabe's authoritarian nationalist politics has been emphasised, and blamed, for the resurgent economic challenges that deepened immediately after the July 2018 elections and into 2019. Inflation is currently threatening to wreak havoc in the same manner as it did in 2008 with price increases recorded on a daily basis, a shortage

---

5    'Human Rights Groups Urge South Africa, SADC And AU to Stop Bloodshed in Zimbabwe', *Voice of America*, 17 January 2019.

6    'Shutdown a regime change attempt: ED', *The Herald*, 12 February 2019.

7    'Zim demos part of an African plot', *The Herald*, 23 January 2019.

8    'SADC backs Zim against onslaught', *The Herald*, 12 February 2019.

9    'Responses to Zimbabwe highlight gulf between the region and the West,' *The Conversation*, 6 June 2019.

of fuel, a restive civil service, sporadic strikes in the health service and worsening unemployment (Solidarity Peace Trust 2019: 2). Amidst these developments, the SADC and the AU have once again been implored by the same voices that called for action against Mugabe to intervene and assist in the resolution of the political question; a question that borders on perceptions of authoritarianism. How have the organisations responded to this call? How different is their response now from previous responses to the challenging issues raised against Mugabe's government? The next sections attempt to respond to these questions.

## The SADC and the AU Responses to the plea

### Key regional and sub-regional Instruments on democracy and human rights norms

In order to understand the *locus standi* of the SADC and the AU on alleged democratic and human rights deficits in Zimbabwe, a brief overview of the normative framework on the same is instructive. The creation of supranational commitments to democracy brings about an obligation for member states to increase the costs for those who may be accused of violating established norms or contemplating a return to undemocratic regimes. Mechanisms for the promotion of democracy are the rules and procedures which regional organisations employ among member states such as electoral missions, treaties and protocols (democracy clauses). Such mechanisms define the framework for implementation, and the sanctions to be imposed in cases of deviance..

At the turn of the millennium, African heads of state reformed, in a manner that demonstrated the depreciating value of absolute sovereignty and set the continent's institutions and policies on a trajectory that respects democracy and human rights. At the AU level, new continental institutions and normative frameworks emerged with the transformation of the Organisation of African Unity (OAU) into the AU with a mandate to address conflict, including the challenges related to the democratic deficit, rule of law, and protection of human rights. The AU has adopted initiatives such as the New Partnership for Africa's Development and the Conference on Security, Stability, Development and Co-operation in Africa, adopted at the OAU 36th Session of the Assembly in Lome in 2000, to provide a means for African states that are committed to furthering respect for human rights and acting to pre-empt conflict and apply pressure to governments that abuse their power (Nowrojee 2004: 2).

In contrast to the OAU, the AU was established by the Constitutive Act that envisages a more integrated level of continental governance that was eventually intended to follow the EU model. Under the OAU, state sovereignty was paramount: utmost adherence to the principle of absolute sovereignty and non-interference in the internal affairs of member states was its canonical injunction. Regional or sub-regional interventions like those by the Economic Community of West African States (ECOWAS) in conflicts in Liberia and Sierra Leone were the exception, not the rule (Wulf and Debiel 2010).

The AU's Constitutive Act commits to 'promote and protect human and peoples' rights,' and it specifies that 'governments which shall come to power through unconstitutional means shall not be allowed to participate in the activities of the Union' (AU Constitutive Act 2000). It also provides for a Peace and Security Council (PSC) that was established in 2004 with a mandate to facilitate the AU's response to crises and 'promote and encourage democratic practices, good governance and the rule of law, protect human rights and fundamental freedoms, respect the sanctity of human life and international humanitarian law...' (AU, Protocol Relating to the Establishment of the Peace and Security Council 2002). The AU Constitutive Act, as read with the Protocol on Peace and Security, authorises the AU to intervene in a member state in respect of grave circumstances, namely: war crimes, genocide and crimes against humanity. The transformation of the OAU to the AU thus demonstrated the commitment of African heads of state to promote peace, security, and stability on the continent; to promote democracy and good governance, due process, the rule of law and human rights; and to engage in effective intervention under grave circumstances while upholding and defending the sovereignty and territorial integrity of its members (Ibrahim 2012; Wulf and Debiel 2010; Norwojee 2004). Further commitments to democracy and human rights are centred on the African Charter on Human and Peoples' Rights (African Charter) which is supplemented by the African Charter on Democracy, Elections and Good Governance several protocols on women, child and refugee rights. The African Commission on Human and Peoples' Rights and the African Court on Human and Peoples' Rights are the main human rights organs of the region.

The SADC, just like the AU, is a security complex that has also developed a range of mechanisms and responses to deal with peace and security challenges in the sub-region. The principles of the SADC Treaty (as amended in 2001) include peace, security, democracy, human rights and rule of law (constitutionalism). SADC's commitment to democracy is nonetheless clear in the SADC Treaty and the Strategic Indicative Plan for the Organ. This is supported by the SADC Principles and Guidelines Governing Democratic Elections, which compliments the AU framework on the same. Nonetheless, the norm of free and fair elections at SADC level complements the Universal Declaration of Human Rights, the International Covenant on Civil and Political Rights and several AU protocols. The frameworks for the conduct of credible and peaceful democratic elections at the SADC level includes the SADC Parliamentary Forum Norms and Standards (2001), the Electoral Institute of Southern Africa Electoral Commissions' Forum (2003) and the SADC Principles and Guidelines Governing Democratic Elections. These regional guidelines commit SADC member states to follow agreed best election practices. SADC Guidelines on the Conduct of Elections, also known as the Mauritian Protocol, was adopted on 17 August 2004 during the SADC Summit in Mauritius. The Protocol is a governance framework attempting to legitimise the conduct of elections within SADC. As such, it contains principles that member states are obligated to respect. However, the guidelines also call for the resolution of election-related disputes in accordance with members' own national laws. This means that SADC is hamstrung in this crucial area since it can only encourage member states to adhere to the SADC principles. It cannot enforce their compliance (Odour 2019).

In terms of the norm implementation modalities, responsibility is exercised based on the formula of subsidiarity (Moller 2009). This decentralisation has basis in international law. It is implicitly enshrined in Chapter VIII of the UN Charter, which makes reference to regional arrangements as instances of first resort in confronting challenges to peace and security. This suggests that authority and responsibility is hierarchical from the UN, through to regional organisations down to sub-regional organisations and states. Since the AU has no capacity to respond to all peace and security-related challenges on the continent on its own, it outsources the responsibility to sub-regional organisations such as the SADC to implement its architecture. Probably this explains the resonance in the AU and SADC approaches to the Zimbabwe question.

## Benevolent Diplomacy

*Mugabe's tenure: the over-avocation of suasion and engagement*

One central issue to the legitimacy question in Zimbabwe was how Mugabe and the ruling party retained power since its first defeat in the 2000 Constitutional referendum. The counter-hegemonic bloc made allegations of electoral misconduct against the party and appealed to the SADC and the AU to intervene to ensure minimum standards for credible, free and fair elections were guaranteed. Electoral misconduct was related to violation of these fundamental principles, specifically, the presence of one or more of the following patterns: restrictions on the freedom of opposition parties or voters; a biased campaign environment that favoured the ruling party; or flaws in the casting, counting, or tabulation of ballots. The ruling party has increasingly been accused of using these tools in an attempt to limit political competition while still maintaining the appearance of electoral democracy. While electoral misconduct clearly constitutes a violation of democratic norms, the question of whether (and how) international actors should respond is often a contested one. Even within densely democratic regional organisations whose member states have created formal commitments to protect democracy, enforcement is by no means guaranteed (Donno 2010: 599). One source of challenge for the SADC and the AU to act on Zimbabwe is that the two organisations require consensus among their member states to act, creating a tendency toward lowest-common-denominator outcomes that adhere to the preferences of those that least favour enforcement. Less punitive tools were considered more fitting when misconduct was reported. Local and international election observer reports exposed electoral misconduct. Observation missions gathered and revealed information about Mugabe's electoral misconduct. However, concern was raised that both the SADC and the AU brushed aside reports which the organisations could have easily used to pressure Mugabe. Ultimately, the SADC and the AU failed to censure electoral misconduct (Moore 2014), applauding outcomes of successive elections that lacked transparency and integrity. Both organisations preferred a softer approach and congratulated the ruling party for 'winning' the elections despite allegations and disputes around the legitimacy of outcomes.

This opposes the liberal doctrine that insists on diplomacy proceeding frankly and in the public view. The AU did not consider the Zimbabwe question as an opportunity to implement its instruments given its cautious approach. For example, after Operation Restore Order (Murambatsvina) in 2005, the AU sent Commissioner Bahame Nyanduga, in charge of Refugees, Asylum Seekers and Internally-Displaced Persons on a fact-finding mission from 30 June to 4 July 2005 (Ibrahim 2012). Unlike the UN, the AU did not condemn the displacements. Instead, it appointed former Mozambique President, Joachim Chissano, to initiate dialogue by encouraging Mugabe to engage the opposition, primarily the MDC. Mugabe however resisted the AU calls insisting that the MDC was not a bona fide opposition party but merely a regime-change plot instigated by the West against his government (Murithi and Mawadza 2011). The relations between Mugabe and the opposition further deteriorated as the former's defiance deepened demonstrated by the beatings of the opposition leaders at the Save Zimbabwe Campaign meeting on 11 March 2007. Regional and international condemnation of the event forced the AU to mandate SADC to facilitate dialogue in Zimbabwe. The tepid response from the AU was also displayed just before the 2008 run-off election when it ignored the Pan-African Parliament Observer Mission Report which had encouraged the AU and the SADC to facilitate a negotiated settlement as the election could not promote free and fair elections. The AU ignored the recommendation and allowed the election to proceed. After the heavily discredited election, the AU relegated responsibility to the SADC and consistently stood by its decisions on Zimbabwe. This is despite the emergence of isolated voices from Botswana, Ghana, Kenya and to some extent Zambia calling for strong action to punish Mugabe.

Prior to this stage when SADC formally engaged with the Zimbabwe question, there were a few earlier efforts to address the situation (Hove and Ndawana 2016: 70; Mhandara and Pooe 2013: 6; Mufamadi 2010):

- In 2000, the SADC assembled a taskforce of six states, Angola, Botswana, Malawi, Mozambique, Namibia, and South Africa. It went to Zimbabwe in August 2001 in an attempt to ensure the restoration of law and order, and dialogue between Mugabe and the opposition.
- The 2002 Extraordinary SADC Summit in Blantyre, Zimbabwe was called upon to respect human rights and freedom of opinion and association, and the summit called for the transfer of occupiers of non-designated farms to legally acquired land.
- Zimbabwe was removed from deputising the chairmanship of the SADC at the Summit held in Luanda in October 2002.

As these initiatives were underway, the lead mediator in Zimbabwe, Thabo Mbeki, hailed Mugabe for fully supporting the SADC efforts and blamed the 'world powers' for failing to honour the commitments made at the 1998 donor conference on the Zimbabwe land question (Chikane 2013). The SADC's efforts were never directed at the hard core issues of democracy and human rights as had been expected by the opposition, the EU and the USA. Nonetheless, the events of 11 March 2007 broadened the scope of regional efforts from a focus on the historical economic issues to politics. The mood of the two regional organs was to contain the effects of the political question by working for a political solution to roll back the wrong turn of events (Mhandara and Pooe 2013: 6). The mediator had to '... begin the process leading to the normalisation of the situation in Zimbabwe and the resumption of its development and reconstruction process intended to achieve a better life for all Zimbabweans on a sustainable basis' (former president Thabo Mbeki cited in Mlambo and Raftopoulos 2010: 8). The mediator had three immediate tasks: to get the parties to endorse the idea that elections would resolve the political question; to help the parties to agree to electoral reforms that would yield uncontested outcomes; and to help parties to agree on measures that would facilitate the acceptance of outcomes. The SADC succeeded in this respect as demonstrated by the generally accepted conditions of the March 2008 elections, even though the results were not conclusive. But the incidences of violence that occurred during the presidential run-off reversed the gains of its efforts while fracturing the unity among members, with Botswana and Zambia calling for a forceful stance against Mugabe. Thereafter, it became clear to the SADC, also representing the AU, that it was necessary to work on creating conditions that would allow political parties in Zimbabweto close ranks and pave the way for a compromise solution while avoiding the temptation of openly confronting Mugabe. Consequently, the inclusive government to which the contesting parties in Zimbabwe agreed upon and implemented in 2009, following the signing of the Global Political Agreement (GPA) appeared to be consistent with Mbeki's aim for a mutually acceptable outcome that would curtail the deepening political crisis and the associated socio-economic catastrophe. The formation of an inclusive government may also have been influenced by Mbeki's experience in South Africa's transition talks, which resulted in a Government of National Unity (GNU) between the African National Congress and the National Party (Mhandara and Poore 2013: 12).

At this point, the SADC intervention was based on two considerations: an understanding of the existence of a genuine historical wrong that Mugabe was trying to correct, especially his land reform programme: although this wrong was a *fait accompli*, its solution as represented in Mugabe's policies had also resulted in economic dysfunction. The second, which logically arose from the land reform programme and a detest for the opposition political challenge, related to human rights violations The effects of the two created a regional problem, as Zimbabweans were migrating to neighbouring countries in search of a more stable environments. The SADC approach was to find a solution that would balance these issues such that neither the counter-hegemonic group and their supporters (primarily the USA and the EU – more especially the UK, a former colonial power, whose interests were intrinsically linked to the white commercial farmers in Zimbabwe) nor the hegemonic group and their backers would feel alienated. Consequently, the SADC mediation under Mbeki was fixated on 'quiet diplomacy'. Throughout its involvement, the SADC and the AU frustrated the opposition, and the joint EU and USA calls for a stronger stance against Mugabe (including scuttling the attempt to impose UN sanctions on Zimbabwe after the 27 June 2008 run-off election). Soon after the facilitation had led to the parties signing the GPA, the USA made its frustration known. 'We think the facilitation is over, it led to [a] power sharing agreement that is flawed' (USA Assistant Secretary for African Affairs, Jendayi Frazer cited in Chikane 2012: 137).

Former President Zuma succeeded Mbeki as the president of South Africa in 2009 and took over the mediation role in Zimbabwe. He attempted to walk a different path from his predecessor as the SADC and the AU point man in Zimbabwe. Zuma's task was to facilitate the drawing up and implementation of an election roadmap, as required by the GPA to ensure the implementation of key reforms which would pave the way for elections. He took an assertive and forceful stance and thereby became acceptable to the counter-hegemonic bloc, and its backers. In June 2013, former President of the USA, Barack Obama, praised Zuma's efforts for having presented 'an opportunity... to move into a new phase where perhaps Zimbabwe can finally achieve all its promises' (Kaarhus, et al. 2013: 16). The opportunity referred to by Obama related to how Zuma was perceived as steering the process in a direction that his predecessor had rejected, that is, pressuring Mugabe and ZANU-PF to accede to the electoral reforms demanded by the opposition. However, the task ahead grew Herculean as the mediation team appeared to contradict majority opinion in both the SADC and the AU. The SADC meetings that discussed the Zimbabwe question during Zuma's tenure all pointed to a departure from the soft stance on Mugabe as they insisted on the full implementation of the GPA and electoral reforms among all the parties (Mhandara and Poore 2013: 25-26):

- At Zuma's first summit in Kinshasa, DRC in 2009, Zimbabwe's leaders were urged to fully implement the GPA.
- The SADC Troika meeting on 18 March 2010 set 31 March 2010 as the deadline for full implementation of outstanding GPA issues.
- At the Troika summit meetings held in Livingstone, Zambia on 31 March 2011 and Sandton, South Africa on 11 and 12 June, the SADC resolved to appoint additional officials to work on the Joint Monitoring and Implementation Committee (JOMIC) to monitor, evaluate and implement the GPA. The group also initiated a draft roadmap for holding of free and fair elections in line with the SADC guidelines governing the conduct of elections.
- At its December 2012 summit held in Dar es Salaam, Tanzania, the regional grouping expressed its displeasure with delays in implementing the GPA.
- At the summit held in Maputo, Mozambique in June 2013, the SADC endorsed Zuma's call for more reforms before elections and recommended that the political parties petition the court for more time beyond the 31 July 2013 deadline for holding the harmonised elections. This was the same position pushed by the MDC formations.

Nonetheless, the implementation of the GPA remained a challenge as Zuma failed to convince the bloc to support his diplomatic pressure. Outstanding issues such as senior civil service appointments and power-sharing between the Prime Minister and the President caused MDC-T to opt for temporary disengagement from the government in October 2009, followed by a cabinet walk-out in October 2010. The implementation challenges have been interpreted from two perspectives: either Mugabe failed to convince his party on the idea of real power-sharing or he wilfully deviated from his obligation to act in good faith (Odour 2019; Bratton and Masunungure 2011: 35). In both instances, and several others, the opposition turned to the SADC and the AU, the guarantors of the arrangement, to intervene but these organs would not be pushed to change their engagement and approach. They never contemplated coercive diplomacy against Mugabe despite Zuma's assertiveness.

As Zuma became more insistent on the implementation of an election roadmap, Mugabe retreated into the cocoon of brinkmanship by unilaterally setting the date for the harmonised elections and disregarding the mediator's opinion. Subsequently, he threatened to pull out of the sub-regional organisation if the mediation team continued on a path of 'interference' in the affairs of Zimbabwe. Ironically, instead of the SADC coercing Mugabe, the opposite happened. The mediation came to an abrupt halt as the election results were announced and the SADC and the AU did not act beyond embracing the unfolding events in Zimbabwe. Amidst these developments, the joint SADC/AU objective to lead Zimbabwe to an uncontested election collapsed monumentally. The 2013 elections were peaceful and both the SADC and the AU election observer missions declared the elections as free and fair despite the non-implementation of a number of reforms as required by the GPA. Yet allegations of technical manipulation emerged and the resilient question, which was closer to resolution with the SADC and the AU involvement, persisted in the eyes of the counter-hegemonic bloc and its backers.

The term 'quiet diplomacy' is a crisis containment strategy describing (a) the overall framework is traditional diplomacy, rather than coercive diplomacy; and (b) the style of diplomatic engagement, that is respectful of all parties, perceived as wrong or right. In conclusion, throughout Mugabe's tenure a 'soft' approach was used in response to all pleas for strong action, indicating that the regional and sub-regional organisations preferred suasion and engagement over coercive diplomacy advocated by the counter hegemonic bloc. The SADC and the AU responded to complaints against Mugabe mainly through 'quiet diplomacy' (Moller 2009), or constructive engagement, consensus building among primary parties to the conflict and members in the two organisations (Alden 2002: 1 & 6) while refraining from anything more muscular. Both organisations were perceived as aiding and abetting the ruling party (Hove and Ndawana 2016: 63; International Crisis Group 2007 cited in Moller 2009: 10).

## Mnangagwa's tenure: magnanimity continues

While sharing the desire for peace and conflict-free Zimbabwe with the rest of the world, the SADC and the AU have continued to shun coercive diplomacy and confrontation in favour of the suasion and engagement that characterised their response to 'deal' with Mugabe. The SADC and the

AU seem to understand the complicated political situation in Zimbabwe and the limits of coercive diplomacy, while the counter-hegemonic bloc is convinced that the organisations should coerce Mnangagwa's government to address their grievances. Key among their concerns is the view that the 2018 elections were not in line with the AU and the SADC guidelines on democratic elections, and therefore produced an illegitimate winner. Thus despite the ruling of the Constitutional Court upholding the results of the Presidential election, the opposition stance is that Zimbabwe is still beset by the unresolved political question and the organisations must intervene. Some have even wished for an 'ECOWAS moment' in Zimbabwe, encouraging the SADC to emulate the ECOWAS when it managed to restore democracy in the Gambia through coercive diplomacy against the sitting president in 2016 (Christof 2017: 85). Such calls became more pronounced after the post-election and protests violence recorded in 2018 and early 2019.

Contrary to the reservations held by the EU and the USA on the outcome of the 2018 presidential elections and the open condemnation of the post-election violence, the SADC and the AU have again been ambivalent. The AU, through its Election Observer Mission to the 2018 elections, did not only pass the election as peaceful, free and fair but after the 1 August 2018 post-election violence, the Mission issued a statement expressing concern with the unfolding post-election developments, and called on all stakeholders, particularly political leaders and their supporters, to exercise restraint and avoid violent confrontation. Calling on security agencies to equally exercise restraint and ensure the safety of all citizens, it did not use confrontational or coercive language as was expected by the anti-Mnangagwa bloc. The AU also encouraged the aggrieved opposition party, the MDC-A, to utilise the available national legal channels while insisting that the elections were highly competitive and that the opposition claims of vote buying, intimidation by state agents and bias by traditional leaders were not confirmed. In the Communique of the PSC issued on 26 September 2018, the AU welcomed the successful organisation and conduct of the harmonised elections in Zimbabwe and commended the government of Zimbabwe for their commitment to continue deepening and consolidating democracy in the country (Communiqué of the 797th meeting of the PSC, 26 September 2018). Again, a Communique issued after the visit of the AU Chairperson to Zimbabwe on 18 to 22 February 2018, the AU commended Zimbabwe on the peaceful transition that had occurred in November 2017; and expressed support for the efforts to revive the economy, creating an environment conducive for business, deepening political reforms and organising free and fair elections, and undertook to lobby for the early lifting of the EU and the USA sanctions.

After the violence on 14 to 16 January, some international human rights organisations appealed to the South African government, the SADC and the AU to intervene in Zimbabwe where state security agents allegedly used excessive force to stop public protests over the economic problems in the country. The SADC came out in support of the government in the face of allegations of state brutality against its citizens[10], often sensationalised by the anti-government bloc.[11] The SADC, through its Chairperson, President Geingob, instead condemned the continuing illegal sanctions against Zimbabwe and some internal players backed by international actors for fuelling instability in Zimbabwe. The SADC statement points to one conclusion that the regional group's position will not change any time soon. Pigou rhetorically questioned the SADC Chairman's position: 'Must SADC remain a perennial disappointment on Zimbabwe? Geingob echoing an unsubstantiated rumour and allegation. Why must SADC insists on shaming itself?'[12] As per established tradition, and contrary to misplaced hopes that the situation in Zimbabwe would prominently feature at the 32nd ordinary session of the AU held in Addis Ababa from 10 to 13 February, and following the January 2019 disturbances, the Assembly did not see a crisis and chose to ignore the events. Experience shows that the AU has never openly contradicted the SADC on Zimbabwe and contrariwise, the SADC has never done so to the AU. Once again, there was a crisis of expectation for the regional body to censure Mnangagwa. The positions were no different from the standard response of both organisations: the Zimbabwe question is not about governance but about imperial scheming and therefore not resolvable through discussion of democracy and human rights issues.[13] South Africa, whose opinion is considered weightier on Zimbabwe than any other international actor because of its economic

---

10  'Zimbabwe inquiry finds army, police killed 6 during protest', *AP News,* 18 December 2018. Also see 'SADC backs Mnangagwa despite Zimbabwe crisis, calls for end to crisis', *News Africa,* 12 February 2019.

11  Most of the reported cases of abduction and torture which were claimed by the opposition political parties were investigated by the government which reported through the Minister of Justice, Legal and Parliamentary Affairs that most of the reports were fake. See 'People faking abductions', *NewsDay,* 30 August 2019.

12  'Ramaphosa angers Zimbabweans', *Daily News,* 24 January 2019.

13  'SADC backs Zim against onslaught', *The Herald,* 12 February 2019.

power, threw its full weight behind Mnangagwa soon after the January 2019 disturbances, arguing that sanctions on Zimbabwe had to go since the new government had embarked on democratic reforms (Kamhungira 2019). Any expectation of a change in the SADC and AU shared conviction on Zimbabwe is misplaced. If any change is to come, it is the counter-hegemonic bloc and their supporters, the EU and USA that have to bend to suit the SADC narrative. In short, for both the SADC and the AU, the threat to its democracy and human rights norms emanating from Zimbabwe has not reached a threshold warranting their action. The same policy that benefited Mugabe is being generously extended to Mnangagwa.

The experience of Zimbabwe suggests that in respect of a number of conflicts in Africa,[14] the position of the SADC and the AU is mostly associated with a defence of sitting governments. Nonetheless, even if there has been a commitment to humanitarianism in some cases as represented by the attempt to intervene in the 2015 political crisis in Burundi after the incumbent signalled his intention to stay in power beyond the constitutional limit, the democracy and human rights components remains a challenge. Ending impunity for past and on-going human rights violations is an area where the SADC and the AU have not been as strong as they purport to be. Thus despite the commitments on paper, the AU, through its sub-regional organisations like SADC, is yet to decisively act on the commitments made in its Constitutive Act to ensure respect for democracy, human rights, and the rule of law in its member states. Some of the reasons for the weak performance include a failure to exploit an early warning and response mechanism (Wulf and Debiel 2010: 531); the politics of norm enforcement as represented by eclectic governments that do not share similar ideas about what constitutes a violation or how to respond to it (Ibrahim 2012; Donno 2010: 594). In Zimbabwe, both the SADC and the AU have depended on declarations devoid of robust action to address the political question in a sustainable manner. The SADC, like the AU, has a weak record of strong norm enforcement in states where democracy, rule of law and stability are threatened (Benson 2017). The AU has a strong anti-coup norm which has been institutionalised but just like the SADC, it has not taken the ECOWAS approach to embrace coercive diplomacy to restore constitutional order or punish violations of democracy. A cumulative reading of Articles 4(p) and 30 of the AU Constitutive Act give the impression that the AU is more interested in preventing the overthrow of existing governments through unconstitutional means rather than in prohibiting the retention of power by the ruling elites through less than democratic means. What explains this seemingly weak norm enforcement by both the SADC and the AU on Zimbabwe which has continued from Mugabe to Mnangagwa's tenure?

Various analyses have been given to account for the policy stance:

- A contributing factor to the SADC approach may be the tradition of post-independence African leaders offering solidarity to each other, a cardinal principle of African inter-state relations (Alden 2002: 6).
- Africa, primarily the SADC, is dominated by 'brother presidents and sister movements' (Ndlovu-Gatsheni 2011: 3), who act in solidarity with ruling parties.
- Anti-neo-imperialism (Mhandara and Pooe 2013; Nyamunda 2014; Ndlovu-Gatsheni 2011; 2006).
- Weak implementation of norms within the existing conflict prevention, management and resolution frameworks.\

Common among the existing explanations is the focus on *symptoms or effects* of the SADC and the AU actions which then overlook one of the underlying causes of such actions – securitisation of ideology. Indeed, the disempowering realities of liberal fundamentalism are considerably more devastating, but relatively little has been written about the growing tensions between the liberal democratic language of rights, democracy, and the rule of law and the threat construction in developing countries (Robins 2005: 4 cited in Ndlovu-Gatsheni 2006: 10). The next section attempts a nuanced account of the regional and sub-regional organisations' policy continuity on Zimbabwe by utilising the securitisation framework.

# The securitisation[15] of the liberal ideology and the demise of a new trajectory for Zimbabwe

The counter-hegemonic bloc and their sympathisers seeking the SADC and the AU to intervene in Zimbabwe have always based their arguments on a human rights approach with emphasis on liberal and formal conceptions of democracy. They have insisted on the compliance with the four procedural, most important, minimal conditions: constitutionalism; competitive politics; participation and inclusivity; and civil and political freedoms. There is no objection to the value of these norms in African politics but there is contestation on implementation of the same, with the West insisting on their own prescription as the only acceptable exit strategy

---

15 By 'securitisation' we mean malevolent, alien, and threatening to African culture.

to the problems in Zimbabwe; a fanatical way of conducting politics. This is what the SADC and the AU have perceived as the fundamentalism of the ideology, one that they have ultimately securitised, that is, declaring it as an existential threat to their members. Thus while the liberal ideology has taken the form of fundamentalism, it has also successfully provoked the resurgence of nationalist sentiments among the people living in former colonies and one outcome has been a securitisation response. The fundamentalism of the liberal ideology has three major streams: it glorifies coercive diplomacy, including aggressive 'disciplining' of any challenger to the triumphant liberal status quo; it is hegemonic, seeking to keep African states in a subservient position in relation to their Western counterparts (Odour 2019: 114); it is thoroughly intolerant to rival views and annihilatory in its rejection of alternative cultures and ways of approaching and understanding the Zimbabwe question. Indeed 'the neo-liberal perspective wrongly reduces the crisis in Zimbabwe to a mere problem of governance and traces the genesis of that crisis to the year 2000, ignoring earlier antecedents that are equally significant' (Ndlovu-Gatsheni 2006: 3). Its focus has been on the symptoms of the problem such as shrinking democratic spaces, electoral misconduct and economic dysfunction.

As a result, attempts to understand the SADC and the AU responses to Zimbabwe should not miss the securitisation of a threatening ideology which has produced the many effects that have often been the focus in extant literature. The threat of liberal fundamentalism is represented by a construction of Western governments and their ideology as malevolent, alien, and threatening to African culture. Using Zimbabwe as the ideological battle-ground, the view that the fundamentalism of the Western ideology is a threat to Africa and ought to be resisted is strong. The result has been a construction of a threatening Western identity, foreign to that of Africa, triggering a form of resistance against its intrusion. The discursive construction of otherness brings about a situation where liberal ideology is fashioned as 'threatening, absolute other' (Song 2015: 146), opposing anything African. My aim in this section is however not seeking to determine whether the Western threat is real, but simply to examine the articulation and performance of the Western threat discourse in Africa, represented by the SADC and the AU responses to the Zimbabwe political question. I argue that the AU and the SADC are 'securitisors' through their communication and subsequent resistance to conform to the demands that validate a fundamentalist liberal ideology on Zimbabwe.

Securitisation processes take interest in gaining precise understanding of who securitises, on what issues (threats), for whom (referent objects), why and with what result (Buzan and Waever 1998: 32). According to this view, the securitisation theory has two key components: the securitising actor and the referent object. The former refers to an actor who securitises an issue by 'declaring a referent object existentially threatened' (Ibid: 36). The latter refers to the object perceived to be 'existentially threatened' and at the same time to have 'a legitimate claim to survive'. In the case of Zimbabwe, the threat is the fundamental ideology and the referent object to be secured is the Zimbabwe government, and by extension the African identity. Securitisation process is about 'a specific series of representations and practices ... a process in which meanings are produced, identities constituted, social relations established' (Song 2015: 147). This makes it possible to understand the cause, as opposed to the effects, of the SADC and the AU responses to Zimbabwe in which they assigned security to the events, demands and activities of the counter-hegemonic bloc and its sympathisers. Securitisation should then be treated as a conscious attempt by the SADC and the AU to transcend the degrading and denigrating forces and events wrought by a fundamentalist ideology. This has given birth to non-violent resistance to the Western definition and solutions to the Zimbabwe question 'as a [predominantly] unifying centre of Africans' desire to know themselves, to recapture their destiny, agency, and to belong to themselves in the world' (Mbembe 2006: 242). The subsequent sections highlight the prominent ways through which securitisation has been implemented and its associated effects.

*In defence of a neo-imperial bulwark*

Zimbabwe's political question occupies special space in the SADC and the AU discourses where it is presented as the battle-front for neo-imperial resistance. Zimbabwe has articulated discourses of indigenisation and African empowerment, which resonated well with regional perceptions of the colonial legacy and the continuing influence of Western politics in Africa, even as the latter was becoming more authoritarian, suppressing its people through 'the nationality of power and its tools of subjectivation' (Nyamunda 2014: 114; Moore 2014). In the eyes of the majority of the SADC leaders, indeed the AU, Zimbabwe is a priority for the defence of African countries' right to self-determination and for resistance against a Western imperialist policy of ousting odious regimes. No wonder the 2003 SADC Summit in Tanzania opened with a standing ovation for Mugabe despite reports of human rights abuses and the SADC urged the West to remove sanctions against Mugabe and sounded a warning to the EU to keep its aid after threats that it would not fund the SADC projects in which Mugabe was involved (Sirota 2004: 344). At its 2019 Summit, the SADC made a resolution to declare 25 October as the anti-sanctions day in solidarity with Zimbabwe. The liberation party governments share a common anti-imperialist ethos and sense of obligation to safeguard the region from outside interference (Aeby 2017: 274), and have successfully galvanised the majority in Africa to support the ruling party in Zimbabwe. Mbeki was the chief architect of the African Solutions to peace and security challenges and saw the problems in Zimbabwe as emanating from without: 'we, as Africans, don't know enough about ourselves and continue to be enslaved by a narrative about ourselves told by other people' (Mbeki 2013 cited by Moore 2013: 109). Linked to Mbeki's agitation was 'The West's refusal to appreciate the deep emotions and sensitivities of the land issue which set the stage for antagonism with the SADC on the Zimbabwe question. The EU and the US governments ...opted to push for regime change' (Mhandara and Pooe 2013: 16). Indeed, from this analysis, the Zimbabwean crisis is a reflection of the risks involved in any African attempt to defy the 'disciplining' forces of globalisation and neo-liberalism and is located within the broader context of African responses to globalisation, neo-liberalism and cosmopolitanism (Ndlovu-Gatsheni 2006: 8). The forces have no sympathy for any form of radical defiance of the post-Cold War neo-liberalist ideology hence the insistence on 'Mugabe must go' policy. Whereas Hardt and Negri (2000: 113 cited in Nyamunda 2014: 18) suggest that modernity, which is related to discourses of human rights, democracy and good governance represents the Western path to African development, the West's depiction of Africa as characterised by a catalogue of deficits such as lacking democracy (Ndlovu-Gatsheni cited in Nyamunda 2014: 18), is considered as part of a broader neo-imperial scheme that Africa must collectively resist. From Mugabe to Mnangagwa, the counter-hegemonic bloc has sought an approach that forecloses any room for a negotiated solution in Zimbabwe by insisting on a discourse that analyses the problem in dichotomising tropes (Mugabe and Mnangagwa are wrong and the opposition is always right). The anti-ZANU-PF bloc has also been emboldened, rather than embarrassed, to see the EU and the

USA, not SADC and the AU, as their 'knighted saviour with unfettered capacity to bring about a solution' (Mufumadi 2010: 628). The SADC and the AU have nothing but contempt on this flawed thinking of an opposition undermining their joint capacity to resolve the question. The efforts to assert African agency on the Zimbabwe question is part of the commitment by the SADC and the AU not to be contend with the 'flag and anthem independence' (Nyamunda 2014: 115), while being implementing conduits of the political processes decided by 'others'.

The hostile position of the Western bloc based on the belief that getting rid of ZANU-PF would resolve the Zimbabwe question may have pushed the SADC and the AU to sympathise with ZANU-PF and less with the opposition. The same posture has been exported to the post-Mugabe epoch. For the SADC and the AU, losing the Zimbabwe battle to the West would send a wrong message elsewhere that Africa was amenable to neo-imperial designs and would set a bad precedent for similar Western action in future. It becomes easier to understand the solidarity that has permeated the SADC and AU positions on Zimbabwe from Mugabe to Mnangagwa, in particular the weak enforcement in response to allegations of flawed elections, which will likely continue on the same trajectory, considering that Zimbabwe is a country perceived to be of high geopolitical importance *vis-à-vis* neo-imperial resistance. The SADC continues to see Mnangagwa as unfairly criticised by the counter-hegemonic bloc and its Western backers. Speaking immediately after the January 2019 violence in Zimbabwe, President Ramaphosa insisted that Zimbabwe was being unfairly criticised because it had started implementing democratic reforms. In this case, it may be argued that norm enforcement in Zimbabwe will continue to be weak because Mnangagwa's government is perceived as representing an improvement from Mugabe's combative policies. Thus the SADC and the AU are more likely to continue privileging 'other' goals rather than protecting democracy even in the presence of reports exposing resurgent authoritarianism.

A fundamentalist ideology lays excessive emphasis on civil and political rights, especially those related to property ownership, at the expense of socio-economic and cultural rights. The political strategy of the counter-hegemonic bloc has been based on a human rights discourse to challenge ZANU-PF and delegitimise its rule. However, it has resonated with the pleas of the former commercial farmers and Western powers while ignoring the plight of the poor majority in Zimbabwe. This has provided the SADC and the AU with a basis for its policy of seemingly siding with a government that was responding to historical injustice, and in the process obstructing the neo-imperial agenda beyond the veil of liberal democracy. Both organs have remained convinced by the ZANU-PF definition of the political question as being a result of the legacies of imperialism rather than a result of authoritarianism as claimed by the opposition and the Western powers. The open vilification of ZANU-PF is seen as an aberration to the historical role played by the party in the fight against colonialism and white domination; a role which has earned some of its leaders like the Mugabe a special place among the downtrodden people of the third world. As far as the SADC and the AU have been concerned, at the core of ZANU-PF's land reform programme were efforts to address the large-scale white ownership of land at the expense of the majority; a right more fundamental than civil and political liberties. The SADC and the AU, with more people seeking to achieve what ZANU-PF has achieved in Zimbabwe, continue to find it difficult to openly denigrate Mnangagwa's policies just as they did to Mugabe.

## Diffusing cultural imperialism

In the discourse on Africa's democratisation, African states are, more often than not, viewed as inferior to Western ones. Chweya (2002 cited in Odour 2019: 114) blames the repeated failure of liberal democracy in Africa on the Euro-centricity of the liberal democratic structures and values that are introduced into Africa in disregard of the peculiar local situation. Liberal fundamentalists who distinguish between 'advanced' and 'backward' people, and insist that the liberal polity is the only one suited to the former, are motivated by an ideology of 'white' supremacy rather than acknowledgement of cultural differences (Ibid). Hegel declared that what he called 'Africa proper', that is, Africa south of the Sahara, was devoid of reason, and therefore without history, and incapable of "civilised" political organisation characteristic of liberal democracy (cited in Odour 2019: 114). The intentions and values of the cradle of liberal democracy is then imposed to improve 'barbarians' (Mill 2001: 14 cited in Odour 2019: 114), by imposing solutions that they cannot think better. This is despite the fact that Africa has its own peculiar culture which informs its conflict handling approaches.

The Eurocentric conceptual framework has also made the distinction between 'developed democracies' and 'underdeveloped democracies', with the presumption that the ideal is the Western social, economic and political trajectory. Likewise, that their recommendations on African conflicts should be blindly and uncritically adopted. Two features of the imperialist nature of the fundamentalist liberal ideology are thus the Westernisation of everything, that is, the solutions to problems in Africa should adopt Western values for them to be acceptable; and the distinction between the 'liberal' and the 'illiberal' follows that the latter has no better solution under any circumstance. Inherent in this philosophy is a presumption that the intelligence of the people who lack craft competence to import a perfectly Western liberal democracy is constrained. There is the spirit of victimisation that forms part of the present state of Africa. Africans and Africa's realities are said to be proceeding directly from the legacy of a long history of subjugation and cultural imperialism. Therefore, securitisation of liberal fundamentalism must present itself through a consistent and systematic refutation of Western definitions of African problems and the prescribed solutions (Mbembe 2006).

Therein lays the determination by the SADC and the AU to debunk the fictitious cultural and genetic argument by demonstrating sturdy resistance to the objectives of the EU and the USA in Zimbabwe. Mbeki's speech, *I am an African*, in the South African parliament in 1996 when he was still the Deputy President defined how he steered the SADC process in Zimbabwe. This came against a background of the ruling African National Congress's African Renaissance project in which Mbeki was central in articulating and implementing. He became sensitive that a solution to the Zimbabwean problem needed to come out of a process of consultation with fellow African leaders, including Mugabe himself, rather than a capitulation to Western pressure. He resisted the pressure for the SADC to be instrumentalised into a destabilising force in Zimbabwe by frustrating Western unilateralism in favour of multilateralism, often relying on the African solutions arguments to weaken the counter-hegemonic bloc, and its backers. Mbeki had a 'perception of the "white community" as having stubborn and arrogant mind-sets that sought to dictate the outcome of everything' (Mbeki 2002 cited in Mhandara and Poore 2013: 19), further stating that '…as patriots who occupied the same trench of struggle with the people of Zimbabwe ... we together, battled to end white minority rule in the region and continent...' (Mbeki cited McKinley (2006: 96). For Mbeki, representing the SADC and the AU, was a patriotic duty to safeguard Zimbabwe's sovereignty against unwarranted encroachment by the excesses of a liberal ideology. After all, the African Renaissance vision was for Africa to reassert its sovereignty and capacity to make its own decisions about its future without the dictates of other ideologies. 'African countries had to stop being "client states" that govern in the interests of powerful groups and not in the interest of the people of Africa or their countries' (Chikane 2013: 56). Similar sentiments were expressed by Mbeki's successor, Kgalema Mothlante, who refused to denounce Mugabe publicly, in the process contradicting the precepts of the liberal approach: 'They go on as if we have the authority and right to tell Zimbabweans what we want them to do in their own country. After all is said and done, it is only the Zimbabweans themselves who can resolve the crisis there. All we can do at the best of times is to play a facilitative role and try and share our views on problems in their country' (Harvey 2012: 136 cited in Mhandara and Poore 2013: 20). The positions taken by the two SADC mediators augured well with Mugabe's assertive policy which was based on pan-Africanism; hence SADC and AU were more likely to find common ground, compared to the positions pushed by the faces of liberal ideology in the counter-hegemonic bloc.

The SADC has demonstrated non-cooperation while at the same time driving a point to the counter-hegemonic group that Africa has its own model of addressing conflicts that is sensitive to its cultural idiosyncrasies. After all, the mortar of change in society is culture not ideology, politics or economics (Huntington 1993). A solution that is more suited to the cultural context in Zimbabwe and Africa is viewed as better than a solution that is suited to the intolerant liberal ideology, underlined by the nuances of a Western culture. Unless the Western countries shift their position and respect the African conflict prevention, management and resolution culture, I predict a persistent frustration of the Western objectives on the Zimbabwe question. Understanding that Zimbabwe's question will remain anchored by the SADC and the AU rather than 'foreign actors' will promote an inter-cultural solution to the problem. Both the AU and the SADC have been consistent in opposing sanctions on Zimbabwe. Even as South Africa was the President of the UN Security Council it did not dither on its position on Zimbabwe and again frustrated Britain and the USA proposal for punitive sanctions against Mugabe in 2008. The same position has been carried into the post-Mugabe era where both the SADC and the AU have frustrated the call for liberal reforms and protection of human rights by lobbying for the removal of sanctions instead.

## *Challenging the limpidness of liberalism*

The basis of resisting liberal ideology on Zimbabwe has also been pragmatism, making it clear that the merit of the Western ideology should be demonstrated by its usefulness. It is therefore from a pragmatic point of view that the SADC and the AU have been resisting the uncompromising liberal solutions to the Zimbabwe question. While the motif of the dignity of all human beings is central to liberal democracy, the actions of the EU and the USA have been inconsistent or ambivalent in their treatment of the Zimbabwe question and the African initiatives. Colonialism did not only flourish under the watch of liberal governments but historical wrongs persisted with their active encouragement in failing to restrain a race from disregarding the right to the dignity of another. Indeed, colonialism and post-colonial realities in Zimbabwe, and Africa in general, have evidence of the way in which they diminished the dignity of Africans, and exploited their natural resources with impunity, the kind of activity one expects the EU and the USA, with their liberal democratic credentials, to forcefully reject as they have done with Mugabe and Mnangagwa's governments. Why, we should ask, would Western governments, in particular the USA, which lent support to dictatorial governments that repressed and exploited their citizens in both Uganda under Idi Amin, and Zaire under Mobuto Sese Seko, be concerned about the repression in another? (Odour 2019). The perfidy of the USA and Britain in propping illiberalism in Africa through support of apartheid rule in South Africa has been frequently cited by African leaders as a case of duplicity and to discredit the Western concerns on Zimbabwe. Based on such inconsistencies, it is easier for SADC and the AU to question the veracity of the ideology as a reliable tool to emancipate Zimbabweans from the perceived authoritarianism of the ruling party. The responses from the SADC and the AU may be suggesting that the Western political interest in Zimbabwe, indeed Africa, is far from their capitalist conspiracy on the continent. This conclusion is validated in the fears of African scholars like Ndlovu-Gatsheni who insists that the international political economy is built upon a 'real existing empire' since imperialism never ended but merely transformed and continues to 'impose, reproduce and maintain Euro-American hegemony over the world' (cited in Nyamunda 2014: 113-114). This partly explains the SADC's cautious approach in engagement of ZANU-PF governments on alleged human rights abuses and incidences of political repression. Superficially, this approach suggests an endorsement of ZANU-PF but in a fundamental way, it represents resistance to a supercilious ideology.

The polarisation of the old has resurfaced not only within Zimbabwe but also internationally as the SADC and the AU continue with their securitisation narratives. The SADC and the AU policy is one of reverence to the nationalist narrative: i.e. that the Zimbabwe government remains a victim of the neo-imperial scheme that overlooks the positives brought by Mnangagwa, and sensationalise his mistakes to validate the regime change objective, which will benefit a pro-Western post-nationalist arrangement. The continuity in policy by both SADC and the AU strengthens the resolve of the ruling party to cling to coercive politics from the old dispensation in the absence of strong response from the two organisations. Therefore, the new political trajectory remains aspirational and fantasised if the regional and sub-regional organisations are not cajoled to shift their positions.

## Conclusion

The SADC and the AU policy on Zimbabwe remain unchanged. From Mugabe to Mnangagwa, the organisations have eschewed 'muscular' involvement much to the disappointment of the counter-hegemonic bloc and their backers, the EU and the USA. Emphasis has been on quiet diplomacy, constructive engagement and accommodation, all executed within the frameworks of multilateralism and the African approaches. The policy is predicated on the securitisation of a fundamentalist liberal ideology, which emphasises coercive diplomacy, unilateralism and subjective definition of the Zimbabwe problem and its solutions. Resistance against intrusion by a fundamentalist ideology translates into resistance to pleas for regional and sub-regional action that encourages democracy promotion in Zimbabwe as such action is considered as aiding Western agendas. The securitisation approach – challenging the limpidness of liberalism, diffusing cultural imperialism, representing ZANU-PF as the bulwark against neo-imperialism – represents a soft rejection of the full implementation of the democratic norms provided in the existing frameworks at the regional and sub-regional level. Therefore, the continuity of the SADC and the AU policy beyond Mugabe's rule embodies an anti-thesis to a new political trajectory in Zimbabwe that had promised so much prior to the 2018 post-election violence.

# References

African Union Protocol Relating to the Establishment of the Peace and Security Council. (2002) Available: https://au.int/sites/default/files/treaties/37293-treaty-0024_-_protocol_relating_to_the_establishment_of_the_peace_and_security_council_of_the_african_union_e.pdf (Accessed 15 January 2020).

Aeby, M. (2017) 'Stability and Sovereignty at the Expense of Democracy? The SADC Mediation Mandate on Zimbabwe, 2007-2013', *African Security* 10/3-4, 272-291.

Alden, C. (2002) 'South Africa's Quiet Diplomacy and the Crisis in Zimbabwe', *Cadernos de Estudos Africanos* 2, 1-22.

Benson, J. (2017) 'The Region's Role in shaping post-Coup Zimbabwe'. Available: https://oefresearch.org/news/regions-role-shaping-post-coup-zimbabwe (Accessed 29 May 2019).

Busumutwi-Sam, J. (2008) 'Contextualising Human Security: A 'Deprivation-Vulnerability' Approach', *Policy and Society* 27/1, 15-28.

Buzan, B., O. Waever and J. de Wilde (1998) *Security: A New Framework for Analysis*. Boulder: Lynne Rienner.

Castillo Ortiz, P.J., C. Closa and S. Palestini (2016) *Regional Organisations and Mechanisms for Democracy Protection in Latin America, the Caribbean and the European Union*. Sheffield: EU-LAC foundation.

Chan, S. (2010) *Citizen of Zimbabwe: Conversations with Morgan Tsvangirai*. Harare: Weaver Press.

Chikane, F. (2013) *The things that could not be said: From Aids to Zimbabwe*. Johannesburg: Picardo Africa.

Christof, H. (2017) 'ECOWAS and the Restoration of Democracy in the Gambia', *African Spectrum* 52/1, 85-99.

Derso, S. A. (2012) 'The Quest for Pax Africana: The case of the African Union Peace and Security Regime', *African Journal on Conflict Resolution* 12/2, 11–48.

Donno, D. (2010) 'Who is punished? Regional Inter-governmental Organisations and the Enforcement of Democratic Norms', *International Organisation* 64/4, 593-625.

Hammar, A. (2017) 'Urban Displacement and Resettlement in Zimbabwe:

The Paradoxes of Propertied Citizenship', *African Studies Review* 60/3, 81–104.

Hove, M. and E. Ndawana (2016) 'Regional Mediation Strategy: The Case of Zimbabwe', *African Security Review* 25/1, 63-84.

Ibrahim, A. M. (2012) 'Evaluating a decade of the African Union's protection of human rights and democracy: A post-Tahrir assessment', *African Human Rights Law Journal* 12/1, 30-68.

Joshua, S. and F. Orlanrewaju (2017) 'The AU's Progress and Achievements in the Realm of Peace and Security', *India Quarterly*, 73/4, 454-471.

Kaarhus, R., B. Derman and E. Sjaastad (2013) 'Reflections on National Dynamics, Responses and Discourses in a Regional Context', in B. Derman and R. Kaarhus (eds), *In the Shadow of a Conflict: Crisis in Zimbabwe and its Effects in Mozambique, South Africa and Zambia*. Harare: Weaver Press.

Maddox, G. (2018) *The Colonial Epoch in Africa*. London: Routledge.

Masunungure, E.V. (2011) 'Zimbabwe's militarised, electoral authoritarianism', *Journal of International Affairs* 65/1, 47–68.

Masunungure, E.V. (2009) 'Zimbabwe's Power Sharing Agreement'. Paper prepared for a workshop on 'The Consequences of Political Inclusion in Africa', 24-25 April, American University, Washington, DC.

Mbembe, A. (2006) 'The Cultural Politics of South Africa's Foreign Policy: Between Black (Inter) Nationalism and Afropolitanism'. Paper presented at Wits Institute of Social and Economic Research (WISER), University of Witwatersrand, Johannesburg.

Mhandara, L and A. Pooe (2013) 'Mediating a Convoluted Conflict: South Africa's Approach to the Inter-party Dialogue in Zimbabwe', *Occasional Paper Series*. Durban: ACCORD.

Mhandara, L and A. Murwira (2017) 'Factionalism in the ruling Zimbabwe African Union Patriotic Front (ZANU-PF) and the implications on national development' in A.G. Nhema (ed.) Zimbabwe: the search for sustainable development paradigms. Harare: University of Zimbabwe Publications.

Mlambo, A. (2017) 'From an Industrial Powerhouse to a Nation of Vendors: Over Two Decades of Economic Decline and Deindustrialisation in Zimbabwe, 1990-2015', *Journal of Developing Societies*, 33/1, 99-125.

Moller, B. (2009) 'Africa's Sub-regional Organisations: Seamless Web or

Patchwork?', *Crisis States Working Paper*. London: London School of Economics and Political Science.

Moore, D. (2014) 'Death or Dearth of Democracy in Zimbabwe?', *Africa Spectrum* 49/1, 101-114.

Mufumadi, S. (2010) 'Lessons from African Responses to the DRC, Sudan and Zimbabwe', *The Round Table*, 99/411, 621-630.

Murithi, T. and A. Mawadza (2011) 'Voices from Pan-African Society on Zimbabwe: South Africa, the African Union and SADC', in T. Murithi and A. Mawadza (eds), *Zimbabwe in Transition: A View from Within*. Johannesburg: Jacana Media.

Ncube, C. (2013) 'The 2013 Elections in Zimbabwe: End of an Era for the Human Rights Discourse?', *Africa Spectrum*, 48/3, 99-110.

Ndlovu-Gatsheni, S.J. (2011) 'Reconstructing the implications of liberation struggle history on SADC mediation in Zimbabwe', *Occasional Paper* 92. Johannesburg: Institute of International Affairs.

——— (2006) 'The Nativist Revolution and Development Conundrums in Zimbabwe', *Occasional Paper*. Durban: ACCORD.

——— (2003) 'Dynamics of the Zimbabwean crisis in the 21st century'. Paper presented at the 7th Congress of the Organisation of Social Science Research in Eastern and Southern Africa, 14-19 December, Sudan.

Nowrojee, B. (2004) 'Africa on its Own: Regional Intervention and Human Rights', *Human Rights watch Africa*. Available: https://www.hrw.org/legacy/wr2k4/4.htm (Accessed 6 June 2019).

Nyamunda, T. (2014) 'Empire, Global Coloniality and African Subjectivity', *Africa Spectrum*, 2, 113-115.

Odour, R.M.J. (2019) 'Liberal Democracy: An African Critique', *South African Journal of Philosophy*, 38/1, 108-122.

Pigou, P. (2019) 'Revolt and Repression in Zimbabwe'. *International Crisis Group Report*. Available: https://www.crisisgroup.org/africa/southern-africa/zimbabwe/revolt-and-repression-zimbabwe (Accessed 6 June 2019).

Raftopoulos, B. (2014) 'Zimbabwean Politics in the post-2013 Election Period', *Africa Spectrum*, 49/2, 91-103.

——— (2010) 'The Global Political Agreement as a "Passive Revolution":

Notes on Contemporary Politics in Zimbabwe', *The Commonwealth Journal of International Affairs*, 99/411, 705-718.

———— and T. Savage (2005) *Zimbabwe: Injustice and Political Reconciliation*. Harare, Weaver Press.

Rutherford, B. (2018) 'Mugabe's Shadow: Limning the Penumbrae of post-Coup Zimbabwe', *Canadian Journal of African Studies*, 52/1, 53-68.

Sachikonye, L.M. (2011) *When a State turns on its Citizens: Institutionalised Violence and Political Culture*. Johannesburg: Jacana Media.

Sachikonye, L.M., S. Chawatama., C. Mangongera., N. Musekiwa and C. Ndoro (2007) *Consolidating Democratic Governance in Southern Africa: Zimbabwe.* Johannesburg: Electoral Institute for Sustainable Democracy in Africa.

SADC (2000) *Communique of the SADC Heads of State and Government Summit on Zimbabwe*. 6-7 August, Windhoek, Namibia. Available: http://www.sadc.int/files/3913/5292/8384/SADC_SUMMIT_COMMUNIQUES_1980-2006.pdf (Accessed 2 June 2019).

Sirota, B. (2004) 'Sovereignty and the Southern African Development Community', *Chicago Journal of International Law*, 5/1, 343-353.

Solidarity Peace Trust (2019) 'Resurgent Authoritarianism: The Politics of the January 2019 Violence in Zimbabwe'. Available: http://solidaritypeacetrust.org/download/report-files/Resurgent-Authoritarianism-The-Politics-of-the-January-2019-Violence-in-Zimbabwe.pdf (Accessed 6 June 2019).

Song, W. (2015) 'Securitisation of the 'China Threat' Discourse: A post-Structuralist Account', *China Review* 15/1, 145-169.

Wulf, H. and T. Debiel (2010) 'Systemic Disconnects: Why Regional Organisations fail to use Early Warning and Response Mechanisms', *Global Governance* 16, 525-547.

# 13

# Re-engagement under the 'New Dispensation': Dead in the Water?

## Ashton Murwira

## Introduction

The changing of the guard through a military-assisted transition, dubbed Operation Restore Legacy (ORL), marked a significant development to Zimbabwe's body politic. Internally, it culminated in the resignation of Robert Mugabe as the President of the Republic and the elevation of his former vice-president Emmerson Mnangagwa. On the day of the latter's return from a brief exile in South Africa after he had been sacked by Mugabe, he made a speech with a lofty reformist agenda at the ZANU-PF headquarters and maintained the same tone in his inauguration speeches of 24 November 2017 and 26 August 2018. Mnangagwa promised a new paradigm anchored on his new foreign policy thrust, a mantra of re-engagement: 'Zimbabwe is open for business'. Such statements shaped a new policy direction, one that turned its back on the open hostility that had characterised Mugabe's relations with the West i.e. the United Kingdom, Germany, and the United States of America since the turn of the new millennium. However, the new president also sought to consolidate the existing relations with major Look East power-houses, China and Russia.

The ascendancy of Mnangagwa was generally welcomed by the West who saw an opportunity for the country to embark on a new political path based on a new political culture under a new leadership. However, the window for re-engagement began to close with the post-election events of 1 August 2018 followed by the protests and riots witnessed in January 2019. The heavy-handed reaction of the security forces on both occasions cast doubt on whether Zimbabwe had genuinely departed from the old to a 'new' dispensation. Despite these and subsequent events, the doors of re-engagement have remained slightly ajar in the hope that the government might still implement the necessary political and economic reforms.

This chapter examines Zimbabwe's re-engagement thrust, the pillar of Mnangagwa's foreign policy, and interrogates the argument that the new policy drive under the new dispensation is dead in the water. I begin by unpacking the concept of re-engagement within the context of International Relations theory. This will be followed by a background of Zimbabwe's relations with the East and the West. The question on the future of re-engagement will be answered in the section on the Western response to Mnangagwa's nominal reforms.

## The concept of engagement and re-engagement in international relations

Conventional literature has rarely defined engagement or re-engagement but as rather dealt with the utility of engagement in various spheres. Despite this lacuna, Taylor and Kent (2014: 384) define engagement in the context of public relations as part of a dialogue, an orientation that influences interactions and an approach that guides the process of interaction among groups. Of importance is the term 'interaction' which implies verbal communication, action and reaction among the actors. Engagement is understood as a commitment to do which implies that engagement is based upon standards that can govern the interaction of actors or parties. In theory, engagement/re-engagement appears easy yet in reality the process can sometimes be frustrating and bitter. This reality will be exposed in the actions and reactions between Mnangagwa's government and the West.

In the context of International Relations, 'engagement' involves the interaction of two or more actors at different levels; while 're-engagement' can be understood as either a formal or informal process by which states seek to restore, rebuild or normalise their relations. The interconnectedness of states in the contemporary global community makes 'splendid isolation' virtually impossible in the twenty-first century. Murphy (2008: 9) buttresses this view stating that governments need to talk to other governments. They also, however, need to interact with other vital non-state actors or foreign publics to achieve their foreign policy goals. For example, Zimbabwe embarked on engagement and re-engagement with the diaspora communities during the Government of National Unity (GNU) (McGregor and Pasura 2010). Their aim was to attract them to invest in Zimbabwe thereby contributing to economic development[1] (ibid.). However, this chapter departs from the idea of re-engagement with the diaspora and focuses on government to government re-engagement in the 'new' dispensation.

States can engage at political, diplomatic, economic, socio-cultural and technological levels. In some cases, political-diplomatic and economic engagements may be strained but social/humanitarian interactions are maintained. Zimbabwe and the West have had strained political-diplomatic and economic engagement but they have never recalled ambassadors.[2] The West has continuously supported Zimbabwe financially on humanitarian grounds through non-government organisations. Non-engagement has never been an option, rather relations have been characterised by fluctuating tensions; and from 2000, have been decidedly cold and cautiously maintained. Murphy (2008: 11) notes that the success of foreign policy goals depends on co-operation and genuine engagement, not clumsy propaganda. Co-operation occurs when actors' values and interests converge. In the context of Zimbabwe and the West, the levels and depth of co-operation will determine the future of any political engagement. This chapter will discuss the reality of Mnangagwa's re-engagement policy under the 'new' dispensation.

Domestic and international factors constantly drive relations between states, and non-state actors. A change of a government can alter relations for good or bad between two or more actors. For example, the attainment of independence by South Africa in 1994 resulted in its re-admission into the Commonwealth (Makin 2009) and was made possible because Britain wanted to invest in the new South Africa. Britain's interests were not served by the apartheid government or by sanctions and boycotts. This example demonstrates that national interests are key to determining engagement/disengagement in state relations. When national interests are

---

1   Ironically, the Zimbabwean diaspora already contributes to socio-economic development through millions of dollars in remittances every year. For instance, in 2018 personal remittances received by Zimbabweans were USD1,856 million (Bandura et al. 2019).

2   The USA embassy in Zimbabwe is one of the largest in Africa, an indication, perhaps, that once it has overcome its problems, Zimbabwe will have a promising future.

threatened by another state, inter-state relations are disrupted or broken, and the reverse is true. Once relations are broken a call for re-engagement may arise as no state can live in isolation (Keohane and Nye 2008; Farrel and Newman 2016). Mutual dependence remains a constant feature of international relations today and whether formal or informal engagements exist, actors will realise relative gains. Thus, Zimbabwe as a rational actor is seeking to restore normal relations with the West and the latter warmed to possible re-engagement because the expected benefits are both material and ideational. Materially, Zimbabwe is endowed with natural resources such as diamonds, gold, platinum which are essential for Western economies. Ideationally, the need to spread liberal democratic ideology in Zimbabwe is also key to offsetting China's presence in Africa. Hegemonic tensions between China and USA in Africa have been referred to as the 'new' scramble for Africa (Ouma 2012). Such constructions help to explain the politics of re-engagement between Harare and the West under a 'new' government. While the theory of complex interdependence acknowledges the mutual dependence of states, it fails to explain why relations sometimes break down. Its limitations are explored by constructivists such as Wendt (1992) and Hopf (1998) who argue that events in international relations are a product of social and historical constructs by states/individuals. For instance, the perception that the international system is anarchic emerges from what states make of it. States can construct either friends or foes based on real or perceived threats emerging from the actions/inactions of another state/actor.

A constructivist view suggests that Zimbabwe and the West have 'constructed' perceptions about the nature and intent of re-engagement. On the one hand, Western liberal governments view an 'unreformed' Mnangagwa government as a threat to a liberal political ideology/political culture. On the other hand, some sections of Zimbabwe, especially the incumbent party, fear losing power through the implementation of the conditions set out by the West for re-engagement. The government perceives such demands as a cover to neo-imperial schemes and assumes the West is bent on trying to reverse the land reform programme and ultimately the gains of the liberation struggle.[3] Liberal Western ideology has been securitised, that is, declared an existential threat to the survival of the regime, to the extent that full implementation of political reforms

---

3   Security sector reform is viewed as targeting the military commanders, and property rights issues are viewed to be targeting the reversal of the land reform.

under the current government is next to impossible. The West perceive the 'unreformed' incumbent government and 'unprofessional' security as a threat to their material interests in Zimbabwe. The social construction of what constitutes threats to either side's value system has a negative bearing on the future of re-engagement.

## Overview of Zimbabwe's relations with the East

Since independence in 1980, Zimbabwe has adopted a foreign policy guided by the following principles: 'sovereign equality of member states, non-discrimination at home and abroad, non-alignment, non-interference in the domestic affairs of another sovereign state and upholding Pan-African integrity'.[4] These principles were organically shaped by the country's protracted liberation war for independence (1967-79) which was supported, materially and diplomatically, by the Frontline States (Mozambique, Zambia, Tanzania, Angola, Botswana), China, Cuba, and the then Union of Soviet Socialist Republics (USSR) – support which created a bond between the newly independent state and its liberation war allies.

During Mugabe's tenure, and in response to the exigencies of the economic and political situation, he declared a Look East policy in 2003 which strengthened the bond between Zimbabwe and the East and has intensified under the 'new' dispensation. For example, after his inauguration, Mnangagwa visited China on 3 April 2018 to seek financial assistance and enhance trade relations to relieve the country's distressed economy. This visit resulted in the construction of relations by elevating them from that of 'all-weather' friend to strategic comprehensive partnership. The two countries are tied by historical legacies, normative convergences and practical economic gains (Ramani 2016). The historical legacies stem from China's assistance to Zimbabwe's liberation struggle against colonialism and racial discrimination. Zimbabwe-China relations are also a direct response to the deterioration of political relations and economic stability following the bilateral fall-out with the West and the global financial institutions (Ojakorotu and Kamidza 2018: 18). Strategically, Zimbabwe values its relations with the East due to what is perceived as Western hostility since 2000. The engagement is a counter-strategy to Western sanctions. For example in 2008, China and Russia

---

4   Zimbabwe Ministry of Foreign Affairs Strategic Plan 2013-2015, Available at: www. zimfa.gov.zw (Accessed 27 June 2019).

vetoed the United Nations Security Council (UNSC) draft resolution (S/2008/447) which called for an arms embargo and financial restrictions on Zimbabwe.[5] The action further strengthened the political-diplomatic engagement between Harare, Beijing and Moscow.

The East also uses Zimbabwe as a buffer to Western encroachment in southern Africa. Apart from its presumed strategic importance, China regards Zimbabwe as a trading partner in particular in the agriculture and mining sectors which are critical in supporting her growing economy. For example, China imports tobacco, nickel and ferroalloys (Chun 2014). In this case, relations between the two have moved beyond solidarity and the struggle against perceived Western imperialism to commercial and diplomatic relations. Diplomatically, China needs Zimbabwe's support on its 'One China' policy (ibid.: 11) which aims to fulfil China's reunification agenda with Taiwan, which China regards as its re-engage province; thus, in 2005, Zimbabwe supported the adoption of Anti-Secession law by China (ibid.) which was aimed at blocking Taiwan's independence. The political-diplomatic engagements explain the 'unconditional' aid[6] and assistance to Zimbabwe from China. However, the 'unconditionality' is political given that China's support to Zimbabwe will depend on its access to resources such as diamonds, gold, tobacco, etc. Such an exchange is as simple as it is attractive while the reforms demanded by the West are perceived as politically threatening. China believes that domestic affairs are better left to the sovereign state while the West's aid comes with conditionalities, i.e. political and economic reforms (Wang and Ozanne 2010, Stokke 2013) as the West prioritises the rule of law, respect of civil and political liberties, good governance, market-driven economy and respect for property rights (Stokke 2013).

## Zimbabwe's relations with the West: from friends to foes

Bilateral relations between Zimbabwe and the UK are central to defining the former's relations with the rest of the Western international community, largely because Britain was the former coloniser and tended to shape the opinion of Western policy makers; thus, during the first decade of independence, Zimbabwe and the West enjoyed cordial relations.

At independence, Mugabe's policy of racial reconciliation pleased the erstwhile coloniser that had not anticipated such a pragmatic approach

---

5   'China and Russia veto Zimbabwe sanctions', *The Guardian*, 11 July 2008.
6   Unconditional aid is aid or assistance that a country receives without demands for political and economic reforms.

from someone they regarded as a hardened Marxist-Leninist guerrilla. Zimbabwe also became an active member of the Commonwealth. Indeed, Harare was the venue of the twelfth Commonwealth Heads of Government summit in 1991 and the birthplace of the 'Harare Declaration' which is anchored on 'promoting democracy and good governance, human rights and the rule of law, gender equality and sustainable economic and social development'.[7]

During the eighties and early nineties Mugabe was feted by the West whose academic institutions seemed to compete in awarding him honorary doctorates. The British Queen even awarded him an honorary Knight Grand Cross in the Order of the Bath (later rescinded, as were many other honorary degrees), while the country was perceived as a jewel of Africa, despite being tarnished by the Gukurahundi massacres from 1982-87 (see Chapter 2). Unfortunately, such cordial relations could not be sustained. Towards the end of the nineties, the land question and a change in political culture became the centre of the fall-out. Between 1999 and 2000, Zimbabwe embarked on a Fast Track Land Reform Programme (FTLR). ZANU-PF argued that this was designed to rectify the colonial imbalances that the Lancaster House Agreement had failed to solve, and that Britain had failed to honour its promise of paying compensation for the farms. The critics of FTLR saw it as a means by which the ruling party consolidated power in the face of an emerging strong opposition party, the Movement for Democratic Change (MDC) in 1999. The FTLR resulted in the seizure of white commercial farms (where a significant number of the owners were British descendants) which were then parcelled out to the ostensibly landless black majority. These land seizures, were described as the 'Third Chimurenga' (Mawere et al. 2018: 452; Mlambo and Chitando, 2015) and the government deliberately revived the liberation rhetoric of the 'First and Second Chimurenga' when the indigenous people fought against white colonists and a white minority authoritarian system. As a result of the *hondo yeminda*, the war for the land, Zimbabwe-British relations progressively deteriorated and with the involvement of the EU and USA became internationalised.

Internal politics within Zimbabwe further strained the already fractured relations. A systematic violation of human rights targeted members of the opposition MDC and civil society. Melber (2003: 150) observed that the

---

7   See 'Harare Commonwealth Declaration', available at: https://thecommonwealth. org/history-of-the-commonwealth/harare-commonwealth-declaration

'victims-cum-liberators had turned into perpetrators' of the very human rights abuses they fought against during the liberation struggle. Elections from 2002 were described as 'militarised' or exploited with 'electoral authoritarianism' (Masunungure 2011; Masunungure and Shumba 2012). Hove (2017) argues that the military, police, prisons and intelligence organisation disregarded the rule of law before, during and after the elections. The actions made it appear as if power had been transferred from a white authoritarian regime to a black authoritarian regime (Munhande and Nciizah 2013). A climate of fear and intimidation was rampant and it was said that to openly criticise government is to risk your life.[8] At the height of internal strife and antagonism with the West, the then Minister of Information and Publicity, Jonathan Moyo, labelled foreign journalists 'terrorists working to unseat the Mugabe government'.[8] In February 2002, two journalists were expelled from the country on the grounds that their permits had expired (ibid.). The developments signalled the adoption of an illiberal political culture, the very antithesis of Western values and norms. Britain reacted by withdrawing its military advisors who had been training Zimbabwean army under the British Military Advisory and Training Team programme (BMATT) since 1980.[9] Taylor and Williams (2002) posit that delivery of 450 Land Rovers intended for the police were halted by the British government. Such actions were also made in protest at the involvement of Zimbabwe in the war in Democratic Republic of Congo and what the British government called 'ethnic cleansing of the whites' which took place under the land reform programme.[10] Such an outcome negatively impacted on the relations between the ZANU-PF government and the Labour Party in the UK leading to a break in engagement (Tendi 2014).

Zimbabwe's isolation began, with the West enacting punitive measures against the Mugabe regime. For instance, the USA passed the Zimbabwe Democracy and Economic Recovery Act (ZIDERA) in 2001. Section 2 of the ZIDERA, states: '… the policy of the United States is to support the people of Zimbabwe in their struggle to effect peaceful, democratic change, achieve broad-based and equitable economic growth, and restore the rule of law'.[11] The Act resulted in the government being denied international capital from the International Financial Institutions (IFIs), travel bans on the ZANU-PF elite and

---

8   Reporters Without Borders Annual Report 2005, Available at: http://www.refworld. org (Accessed 26 June 2019).

security services, decreased foreign investments from the West, etc. The EU also responded by issuing a travel ban, arms embargo and asset freeze on Mugabe's government.[12] Such measures were intended to persuade or coerce ZANU-PF to improve the quality of its governance. However, the party interpreted ZIDERA and the EU sanctions as part of the Western 'regime change' menu. Mugabe revived ZANU-PF patriotic history, African nationalism and securitised the opposition as 'sell-outs' (i.e. Western puppets) seeking to reverse the gains of the liberation struggle. At one point, the security service chiefs declared that they would not salute any presidential winner without liberation war credentials (Nyakudya 2010; Hove 2017: 425).

In 2002, Mugabe emerged the winner of a presidential election amidst credible claims of election irregularities and human rights abuses. The West reacted by suspending Zimbabwe from the Commonwealth in 2002, and Mugabe decided to unilaterally withdraw from the group in 2003, citing unfair treatment. The then British Prime Minister, Tony Blair once described the seizure of land from white farmers as 'barbaric'.[13] This resulted in a diplomatic stand-off and Mugabe told Tony Blair to keep his England while he kept his Zimbabwe.[14] Election campaign banners carried the message that 'Zimbabwe will never be a colony again'[15] (Banda 2005). The toxic tone was repeated in the 2005 general elections which were trumpeted as 'anti-Blair' elections (ibid.) and mutual demonisation (Tendi 2014) was the order of the day. The USA weighed in, with the then Secretary of State, Condoleeza Rice, branding Zimbabwe as an 'outpost of tyranny'[16] due to the escalation of human rights abuses, and the stand-off between the West and Zimbabwe continued until Mugabe resigned in 2017. Then, on assuming office, Mnangagwa embarked on reversing the isolation of the country by pronouncing his government as ready to re-engage with the West.

## The 'New' Dispensation and a new foreign policy trajectory

The so-called 'New Dispensation' was 'new' in that Mnangagwa promised

---

12 'EU hits Mugabe with sanctions and pulls out monitors', *The Guardian*, 19 February 2002.

13 'Highlights of Mugabe's love-hate affair with the West, *Africanews*, 8 September 2009.

14 'Mugabe's address Word Summit on Sustainable Development', *Zimbabwe Mail*, 2 September 2002.

15 'Hands off Zimbabwe, Mugabe tells Blair', *The Guardian*, 2 September 2002.

16 'Rice targets 6 outposts of tyranny', *The Washington Times*, 19 January 2005.

an end to Mugabe's toxic politics internally and internationally; promising on 22 November 2017 a 'new and unfolding democracy',[17] and even asserting that 'the voice of the people is the voice of God'.[18] In other words, he was offering a new social contract based on the general will. These promises were consistent with the expectations of Western liberal democratic governments with whom he sought to re-engage and they became the favoured audience of Mnangagwa's re-engagement thrust.

Consistent with the emerging reformist agenda, Mnangagwa echoed a reconciliatory message in his first inaugural address as President on 24 November 2017. Unlike his predecessor's predictable verbal salvos, Mnangagwa said:

> Whatever misunderstandings may have subsisted in the past, let these make way to a new beginning which sees us relating to one another in multi-layered, mutually beneficial ways as equal and reciprocally dependent partners...We will take definite steps to re-engage those nations who have had issues with us in the past.[19]

A plea to bury the past and mend relations with Western countries became the drive in the foreign policy trajectory of the 'new' government. As a sign of goodwill, Britain dispatched the UK Minister for Africa, Harriet Baldwin, to Harare on 1 February 2018. In her visit she stressed that 'the UK has a longstanding relationship with Zimbabwe, and we are committed to working with the government of Zimbabwe for a bright, prosperous and hopeful future for all Zimbabweans'.[20] Such statements gave hope and momentum for re-engagement.

Knowing the conditions that would come with the process, Mnangagwa made a promise to initiate reforms. For example, he promised to clear debts with IFIs, compensate former white commercial farmers and protect foreign investment. These statements constructed a view that Mnangagwa was pro-West thereby defining his re-engagement thrust.

From 24 November 2017 to 30 July 2018, Mnangagwa's government was put to the test to fulfil its promises before the harmonised elections. Europe and America remained hopeful of a change in political culture, a key measure for re-admission of the country into the Western community

---

17 'Emmerson Mnangagwa hails "new democracy" in Zimbabwe', *The Guardian, 22 November 2017.*

18 Ibid.

19 'President Mnangagwa's inauguration speech', *The Chronicle*, 24 November 2017.

20 'British Minister for Africa arrives in Zimbabwe', *Zimbabwe Mail,* 1 February 2018.

of nations.

In the eight months leading up to the elections, Mnangagwa walked his talk as a reformer. For the first time since the 2002 elections, the new government invited Western international observers to the July 2018 harmonised elections, a step towards resetting relations and keeping the re-engagement agenda on its intended course. One of the key observer groups that was invited was the European Union Election Observation Mission (EUEOM). On 6 July 2018, the Chief Observer, Elmar Brok, emphasised the centrality the of elections in the re-engagement process, saying, '… the July elections were a critical test for Zimbabwe's reform process… the successful conduct of the plebiscite would influence the attitude towards Zimbabwe and unlock investment opportunities…'[21] The future of re-engagement would be determined by the quality of the elections.

Amplifying his re-engagement drive, Mnangagwa applied for Zimbabwe's re-admission into the Commonwealth on 18 May 2018. His government believed that the prevailing pre-election environment was relatively consistent with the Commonwealth ideals which include the rule of law, free and fair elections and respect of human rights. Moreover, Zimbabwe's invitation to international observers was in keeping with the Commonwealth governance standards. Re-joining this group would mark a major breakthrough towards normalising relations with the West.

Cognisant of the ZIDERA provisions, Mnangagwa's government promised to conduct peaceful elections and to institute internal reforms that would enhance its re-engagement drive. For instance, political parties pledged to uphold paragraph 5 of the Electoral Act which prohibits parties from using violence and intimidation against anyone holding different political opinions. For the first time since 2000, opposition political parties were able to campaign in traditional 'no-go' areas previously considered ZANU-PF strongholds. Indeed, incidences of intra-party violence were higher than inter-party clashes.[22] Civil and political rights were generally respected though calls for electoral reforms were constantly made by the opposition. For example, the MDC Alliance presidential candidate Nelson Chamisa, became popular with his 'No Reforms, No Elections' slogan.

---

21  'EUEOM 6 July 2018 report', Available at: http://eeas.europa.eu (Accessed 20 June 2019).

22  According to the Zimbabwe Peace Project 2018 report, 24 cases of intra-party violence in MDC were recorded in May while two cases were on inter-party violence between ZANU PF and MDC.

Part of the call was to 'demilitarise' the Zimbabwe Electoral Commission (ZEC), the format of ballot papers and timely provision of the voters' roll. Despite these concerns, the country was set for 30 July 2018 harmonised elections. In short, in the pre-election phase, the re-engagement strategy was still alive and on track.

## The aftermath of 30 July elections and the implications on re-engagement

The promise of re-engagement depended on the outcome of the July elections. Did the Mnangagwa government live up to the expectations of the election observers, in particular, those from the West? Did the government support a credible electoral process that would warrant re-admission in the Western family of nations? Such questions were addressed in the post-election observer reports. Once the election day was over and counting processes began, the nation anxiously waited for the announcement of the results by ZEC. Before long, social media began to circulate emotive messages that the delay was the result of ZEC rigging the count of the presidential results. A rumour that Chamisa had won the presidency emerged, and a group of youths began to protest outside the ZEC command centre in Harare. The crowd grew, apparently becoming violent enough to overwhelm the police. This justified the intervention of the military who beat and shot protestors resulting in the injury of 35 people and six deaths.[23] Suddenly, what had seemed a promising electoral environment was engulfed by a dark cloud. Widespread condemnation followed. The overreactions by the security forces tarnished what had appeared a peaceful democratic transition fulfilling the ZIDERA criteria and expectations of the Western international observer missions. The authoritarian political culture that had resulted in the rupture in relations between Harare and Western countries was repeating itself under the 'new' dispensation. Re-engagement seemed a forlorn hope.

The Southern African Development Community (SADC) and the African Union (AU) responded cautiously to the overreaction by the military while the East stuck to their trademark non-interference policy. The Western international community, however, reacted strongly to the 1 August events.

United Kingdom foreign minister Harriet Baldwin said that

---

23 GoZ 2018. See also Crisis in Zimbabwe Coalition, 'Darkness at Noon: Inside Mnangagwa's "New" Dispensation', February 2019 report.

they were 'deeply concerned... political leadership should take responsibility for ensuring calm and restraint at this critical moment'. The USA embassy noted that they were 'deeply concerned by the events unfolding in Harare... urged the military to use restraint in dispersing the protesters'.[24] EU through its ambassador to Zimbabwe Timo Olkkonen stated that:

> 'Again the events in August were a setback because during the elections there were a number of flaws and I am not saying they were perfect, but had gone quite easily and the violence was a setback'.[25]

From this juncture, the Western bloc was dubious of the Mnangagwa government's ability to change ZANU-PF's political culture. The concept of a 'new' dispensation was subjected to deeper scrutiny, although the doors of re-engagement were not shut. The army's excessive use of force reinvoked calls by the West for security sector reform as one of the pre-conditions to the normalisation of relations.

Soon after the 1 August shooting, ZEC announced the presidential election results with Mnangagwa being declared the winner. ZANU-PF managed to retain a two-thirds majority in parliament. This presidential result was immediately contested by Chamisa who alleged that the elections had been rigged. His challenge was taken to the Constitutional Court which dismissed it and ruled that Mnangagwa was the duly elected president.[26] Despite, the declaration, the leader of the main opposition MDC continued to dispute the ruling and this created a legitimacy crisis in the newly minted presidency. Again, a call for electoral reform became part of the menu of Zimbabwe's re-engagement agenda.

Notwithstanding the 1 August events, Mnangagwa maintained his rhetorical commitment to political and economic reforms and this was expressed in his inauguration speech on 26 August 2018. In response to the post-election military intervention, the new president regretted the event and promised to set up a commission of inquiry.[27] He further expressed

---

24 'Zimbabwe election unreststurns deadly as army opens fire on protestors', *The Guardian*, 2 August 2018.

25 'EU won't ignore Zimbabwe's rights abuses', *Newsday*, 27 March 2019.

26 Nelson Chamisa versus Emmerson, D Mnangagwa and others Constitutional Court Judgement number CCZ 21/19, 24 August 2018.

27 'President Mnangagwa's Inauguration Speech 26 August 2018,' Available at: www. zbc.org (Accessed 20 June 2019).

commitment to constitutionalism, rule of law, separation of powers and independence of the judiciary.[28] Such calls were a signal of his continued desperate appeal to mend relations with the international community and the tone of his speech renewed hopes for the 'new' government's commitment to transform the toxic political culture of the past regime.

In walking the talk, Mnangagwa set up a Commission of Inquiry (also known as the Motlanthe Commission into the August shootings on 25 September 2018). Its mandate was to unearth the facts about what happened on 1 August 2018. It was hoped that its findings would enable a process of national healing.[29] As with the harmonised elections, the Commission was acting as a re-engagement tool. This stems from its composition which had four foreign against three local Commissioners including Kgalema Motlanthe (Chair of the Commission of South Africa), Chief Emeka Anyoku (Former Commonwealth Secretary-General, Federal Republic of Nigeria), Rodney Dixon (UK) and General Davis Mwamunyange former Chief of Tanzania Defence Forces).[30] The inclusion of a UK national and former Commonwealth secretary general was meant to bolster Mnangagwa's re-engagement policy. Firstly, Zimbabwe's president wanted to normalise relations with the UK and secondly, he sought to enhance the country's chances of being re-admitted into the Commonwealth. To this end, repairing communication with the UK was vital as it was seen to be key to the way in which the West would interact with the Zimbabwe government.

The Motlanthe Commission held hearings which were streamed live on the national broadcasting television and radio. It reported that the MDC-A supporters were responsible for the violent demonstrations that occurred on 1 August.[31] Such behaviour resulted in the failure of the police to respond adequately. This warranted the deployment of the military to assist the police in dealing with the rowdy protesters. Unfortunately, there was excessive use of force that led to the deaths and injuries.[32] From this, the Commission recommended that: the police should undergo retraining in order to deal effectively with the protests in a manner that does not risk the lives of the citizens, the Public Order and Security Act (POSA) should be amended to provide clarity with regard to military intervention, the use

28 Ibid.
29 GoZ 2018.
30 Ibid.
31 Ibid.
32 Ibid.

of force should only be used as a last resort, and use of live ammunition was discouraged except in limited circumstances.[33] These recommendations became a part of the reforms that the Mnangagwa government was expected to implement in pursuit of re-engagement.

In his inauguration speech, Mnangagwa had also promised to carry out sweeping neo-liberal market-driven economic reforms, a departure from Mugabe's command, populist economic policies. In October 2018, the government embarked on a Transitional Stabilisation Programme (TSP), marking the return of austerity. The 'Zimbabwe is Open for Business' mantra was further reinforced. Together with the Finance Minister, Mthuli Ncube, Mnangagwa claimed that the economic reforms would bring short-term pain for long-term benefits. However, by early January 2019, the economy had nose-dived, prices of goods escalated, long fuel queues were the norm, and salaries paid in the local currency fast lost value. Paradoxically, the government responded by hiking the price of fuel by up to 150%.[34] The fuel increases, and the general economic hardships, were resisted through street protests which erupted from 12 January 2019.

News of the harsh security operations and attendant human rights abuses led to condemnation by the international community, particularly from the West. Britain's Minister of State in the Foreign and Commonwealth Office, Lord Tariq Mahmood Ahmad, condemned the attacks on protestors. He stated that, 'the events that have unfolded recently put Zimbabwe's quest to re-join the Commonwealth into question... it is a matter not for the UK but for the Commonwealth as whole'.[35] While the statement appears not to be conclusive, Britain has the power to influence other Commonwealth member states. The UK's Minister of State for Africa, Baldwin, who had been optimistic about the 'new' dispensation, also began to think otherwise:

> As of today, the UK would not be able to support this application because we don't believe that the kinds of human rights violations that we are seeing from security forces in Zimbabwe are the kind of behaviour that you would expect to see from a Commonwealth country.[36]

---

33  Ibid.
34  At this time the USD and Zimbabwe dollar were at par; the latter was referred to as bond currency.
35  'ED's Commonwealth bid hits snag', *Newsday*, 25 January 2019.
36  'Britain's minister for Africa calls for more sanctions against Zimbabwe', *The Zimbabwean*, 6 February 2019.

So the spirit of re-engagement was dampened for the second time in five months. Again, questions of an entrenched political culture were raised. Had the nation migrated from the old to a new era? Evidence of a blocked democratic transition were visible in backsliding on the rule of law and the excessive use of force by the government. The thaw in relations that Mnangagwa had experienced from November 2017 to the 2018 election began to chill. Chances of Zimbabwe's re-entry into the Commonwealth are slim, signalling the death of its re-engagement policy with the West.

However, presidential spokesperson, George Charamba claimed that, '…it is the British government that wanted Zimbabwe back in the Commonwealth… this coincided with Zimbabwe's re-engagement policy'.[37] While Charamba's statement may be true in the context of mutual dependence, it is Zimbabwe which desperately needs the UK and membership of the Commonwealth. Its status as a pariah has not led to re-investment in the country. Mnangagwa, on the defensive, claimed that the 'UK's stance is not the position of the Commonwealth as a whole,'[38] thus he remained hopeful of Zimbabwe re-joining the group. Nonetheless the test for re-admission rests on a country's compliance with Commonwealth values and principles such as rule of law and respect of human rights, which the current regime has repeatedly violated.[39] Meantime, Mnangagwa's re-engagement policy hangs in the air and the next section discusses the political and economic reforms that Mnangagwa has undertaken and reactions from the West.

## Western reactions to Mnangagwa's nominal reforms

Mnangagwa reacted to the tragic events of 12 January by calling for an investigation into the conduct of the security forces in dealing with the protests. His aim was to steer re-engagement back on track. This time, he did not promise a Commission of Inquiry rather he made a bold statement that heads would roll in the security sector. Mnangagwa posted that '… violence or misconduct by our security forces is unacceptable and a betrayal of the new Zimbabwe. Chaos and insubordination will not be tolerated. Misconduct will be investigated. If required, heads will roll'.[40]

---

37 Ibid.
38 'Mnangagwa lashes out over UK's stance on Commonwealth re-entry', *Times Live*, 11 February 2019.
39 'Ex-UN boss savages Mnangagwa govt', *The Standard,* 1 March 2020.
40 Ibid.

The message acknowledges that the security sector was undermining his re-engagement policy and so the West waited to see how he would attempt to bring it to heel.

It should be noted that reform of the security sector lies at the heart of political reform. Given this reality, could Mnangagwa walk the talk without losing power? Could he achieve reform without alienating the security sector? Can the 'new' government change its political culture without losing power and the spoils of power? From a realist viewpoint, this is not possible, in fact, it would be suicidal to embark on such a path. This explains the debate between pro-reformers and anti-reformers of the security sector (Hove 2017: 426). The former (MDC and CSOs in the democracy and governance cluster) believes the sector should be reformed before democracy and sustainable peace can be realised while the latter (ZANU-PF) resist reform arguing that it as a Western regime-change agenda tailored to reverse the gains of the liberation struggle (ibid.). Power is both an end and a means. It is instrumental in the amassing of wealth and wealth is used in turn to corruptly protect and expand its political reach. Dealing with endemic corruption has thus become central to the demands in the re-engagement agenda with the West [41] while the anti-reformers seek to preserve power at all costs: this can only undermine any possibility of re-engagement with the West.

Chitiyo (2009) describes the military as either spoilers or enablers of Zimbabwe's renaissance and Mnangagwa is well aware how security sector reform could affect the survival of his government as the military has always played a key role in shaping the country's political and economic trajectory. Mnangagwa, like President Mugabe, will not embark on security sector reforms just for the sake of normalising relations with the West. At a ZANU-PF Congress, Mugabe declared, 'May I state clearly and categorically, as ZANU (PF) the defence of our sovereignty rests with us and with no other. Any manoeuvres to tamper with the forces will never be entertained by us'.[42] To this end, security sector reform is close to a non-negotiable issue with the current government. Thus, the promise of security sector reform, turned out to be more of a conjuring trick. On 18 February 2019, Mnangagwa retired four army generals: Major General Anselen Sanyatwe, Major General Douglas Nyikayaramba, Air Vice-

---

41 USA Ambassador to Zimbabwe Brian Nichols noted that American companies are deterred to invest by the massive levels of corruption and economic uncertainty...

42 'Mugabe will resist reforming security forces', *Reuters*, 12 December 2009.

Marshal Shebba Shumbayawonda and Major General Martin Chedondo.[43] Appearances were deceptive, actually the retrenchment was demotion by promotion. The generals were effectively appointed as ambassadors of the 'new' government.

Realising, moreover, that security sector reform is a complex if not prohibited area, Mnangagwa opted for soft political and economic reforms. Politically, he repealed the draconian Public Order and Security Act (POSA) and replaced it with Maintenance of Peace and Order (MOPA) Bill. A Political Actors Dialogue (POLAD) platform was initiated for the purposes of political dialogue among the 2018 July presidential candidates. On the land question, assurances have been made about compensation for former dispossessed white commercial farmers and a commitment to upholding property rights. However, the compensation process has been marred by policy inconsistences and inflation. The 'new' government also embarked on labour reforms by coming up with a Tripartite Negotiating Forum (TNF) between the government, business and the employees. Most of these apparent reforms are seen by the critical populace (elite in the opposition, civil society and academia) as window dressing.

Lack of 'genuine' reform by the Mnangagwa administration continues to impair its relations with the West: the USA renewed targeted sanctions on 6 March 2019 and in March 2020. The extension was driven by the continued deterioration of the rule of law and human rights abuses following the two incidents in August 2018 and January 2019 which suggested to them that nothing had changed. Mnangagwa's policy was essentially 'Mugabeism without Mugabe'. President Trump posted on the White House website that:

> The actions and policies of these persons continue to pose an unusual and extraordinary threat to the foreign policy of the United States. For this reason, the national emergency declared on 6 March 2003, and the measures adopted on that date, on 22 November 2005, and on 25 July 2008, to deal with that emergency, must continue in effect beyond March 6, 2019. Therefore, in accordance with section 202(d) of the National Emergencies Act (50 U.S.C. 1622(d), I am continuing for 1 year the national emergency declared in Executive Order 13288.[44]

---

43 'Four Zimbabwe generals retired in Mnangagwa's first purge of military', *Reuters*, 18 February 2019.
44 'Trump renews Zimbabwe sanctions', *Zimbabwe Mail*, 4 March 2019.

Trump emphasised that the government of Zimbabwe remained with a political culture and system of governance that contradicted the USA's political principles and values. While the website post appears somewhat toned down, its effect is similar to the 'axis of evil' or 'rogue state' characterisations that the Mugabe government attracted in 2003. Clearly there is little hope of re-engagement with the USA unless genuine political reforms are made within the year. No reform means a continuation of targeted US sanctions on Zimbabwe.

While little hope of re-engagement remains, the EU and the Mnangagwa government managed to launch a formal political dialogue on 5 June 2019. This was based on Article 8 of the Cotonou Partnership Agreement which governs relations between member states of the African Caribbean-Pacific regions and the EU.[45] Though the launch is a welcome development, its success will be determined by the implementation of political and economic reforms in Zimbabwe. The EU, like the USA, stressed the need for liberal political reforms such as rule of law, respect for human rights and good governance. It is very unlikely that the dialogue will bring material benefit to the country as the ZANU-PF government will not embark on political reforms that could lead to its demise. For instance, Stefan Oswald, the director-general for sub-Saharan Africa in the Economic Cooperation and Development forum noted that: 'The lyrics of the new Zimbabwe government are perfect, but what counts is to move from lyrics to action, otherwise I cannot convince anybody over here [Europe] to re-engage and that is also something, which is really important'.[46] Clearly there has been more talk than action on the much-needed reforms that the government is expected to make and only action will determine the pace or fate of the political re-engagement. I argue that soft or apparent reforms will be undertaken but not those that matter to all the parties in the re-engagement process.

Another non-event, though celebrated officially as part of the re-engagement success, was Mnangagwa's attendance of the US-Africa's business summit in Mozambique on 18 June 2019. The multilateral stakeholder summit was composed of African heads of state, private sector executives, and international investors. The fruits of the summit can only be realised if the government implements key reforms as stipulated by the USA and Europe. As it stands, investment commitments will only be made

---

45 'Zimbabwe-European Union in historic talks', *The Herald*, 6 June 2019.
46 'Germany sceptical about ED's reforms', *The Standard*, 10 June 2019.

after good governance and property rights reforms are implemented, as we see from Tibor Nagy, Assistant Secretary of State for African Affairs, who on 20 June posted on his twitter account that:

> I met with Zimbabwean President Mnangagwa today. I stressed the urgent need to hold security forces accountable for acts of violence committed against Zimbabweans in August 2018 and January 2019 and the importance of real political and economic reforms.

This indicates that the USA interpret Mnangagwa's talk of reform as no more than rhetoric. Nagy's statement was echoed by Oswald of Germany who said, 'You can write nice papers, but if the political will is not there to really make it happen then the president has to go into a discussion with those ones who brought him into power [because] the military is having a strong role and they are not reform-minded'.[47]

No amount of talk without action will yield positive results in the Mnangagwa's re-engagement drive. The West will continue to channel funds through NGOs and development partners for humanitarian purposes. For example, on 25 October 2019, the EU provided USD$43 million to support public health delivery, USD$18 million for food and nutrition stocks while on 16 January 2020 USD$18.7 million was channelled towards emergency food aid for the vulnerable.[48] Social and humanitarian engagements will remain but the much-needed government-to-government funding will not materialise under the current status quo, as a Germany official told me, our taxpayer's money will not be channelled into a corrupt government.

In addition, apart from nominal reforms, re-engagement is threatened by the internal contradictions within government as officials appear to be pulling the agenda in different directions. The new foreign policy thrust seems not to be endorsed by everyone (elite in the government and ZANU-PF). Two camps have emerged. One appears to favour the East, in particular China, while the other favours the West.[49] Mnangagwa has not pursued the Look East policy as vigorously as Mugabe did. Nonetheless, despite the perceived intra-executive tensions, the Chinese

---

47 Ibid.

48 'EU releases 18.7 million USD in humanitarian aid to Zimbabwe', EEAS, 16 January 2020.

49 Mnangagwa's ascendancy to power in November 2017 was accepted by the West who perceived him as a soft person compared to Mugabe. Chiwenga is assumed to be pro-East due to his official visit to China and his medical treatment in China during his illness.

have maintained their contacts with Zimbabwe as its perceived ally. For example, on his visit to Zimbabwe, the Chinese Foreign Affairs Minister Wang Yi described China-Zimbabwe relations as unbreakable[50] and his words resulted in the submission of five projects by the Zimbabwe government to China for consideration. Arguably, the Chinese factor is another a key factor in Zimbabwe's re-engagement (or not) with the West who are well aware that China does not interfere in the internal affairs of a nation, does not impose the same standards, and will turn a blind eye to abuses. It could be argued, for example, that Zimbabwe's relationship with China may have resulted in Zimbabwe not being invited to UK-Africa business summit held in February 2020. Whether or not this is the case, the absence of an invitation signals the UK's low confidence on the 'new' government's reform path. Charamba, the presidential spokesperson, reacted to the snub on his twitter account, '...The UK is no longer an investing global power, long ceased to be thus!' A petulant statement that appears to contradict the re-engagement thrust that his principal is pursuing. Different approaches within the government[51] also inevitably threaten the future of re-engagement between Zimbabwe and the West while both China and the UK will play a wait and see game.

Of the three major Western actors (i.e. the UK, EU and USA), the EU had appeared to be the softest and most patient in its (re-) engagement with Zimbabwe. It has continuously supported the country with economic partnerships and humanitarian assistance.[52] However, even the EU has been frustrated at the slow pace of political and security sector reform. This was registered in its annual sanctions review when it renewed an arms embargo and asset freeze on the Zimbabwe Defence Industry for a period of one year.[53] The renewal was necessitated by Mnangagwa's failure to investigate the role of the security forces in human rights abuses. Sanctions are therefore meant to push the government to implement substantial reforms that include inclusive political dialogue, the recommendations of the Motlanthe Commission of Inquiry and inclusive national dialogue.

---

50 'President meets Chinese foreign minister', *The Herald*, 13 January 2020.

51 'Chiwenga feud escalates', *The Standard*, 10 March 2019.

52 EU provided 10 million Euro in January 2020 for the Zimbabwe Economic Partnership support programme aimed at boosting trade. In April 2019, EU gave Zimbabwe 4 million Euro as humanitarian aid for Cyclone Idai.

53 Council of the European Union; Zimbabwe Council Conclusions, Brussels, 17 February 2020

The EU has shown that the 'new' government still cleaves to the idea of power by coercion and, thus, persistent human rights abuses by the security sector.

The EU, however, suspended sanctions on Grace Mugabe, Vice-President Chiwenga, Zimbabwe Defence Forces Commander Valerio Sibanda and Minister of Agriculture Perence Shiri. However, this gesture has little effect in determining the future of the re-engagement drive. This is shown in the reaction of the Mnangagwa's administration which acknowledged the partial lifting while condemning the maintenance of sanctions on the Defence Force Industry.[54] Arguably, renewed sanctions will frustrate reform efforts and in the long term, further harden the government against political reforms lest it loses power. Sanctions on Zimbabwe have caused debate about their intention, targets and effect. On one hand, they have allowed ZANU-PF and the government to use them as a scapegoat for the country's economic woes voiding their own responsibility[55]while arguing that are also an imperialist regime change strategy. The West, on the other hand, maintains that sanctions are targeted against specific individuals and companies, not the country as a whole, and are intended to restore democracy, upholding human rights and good governance. They further argue that sanctions have little impact on the national economy of the country and the suffering of the ordinary citizen.[56] The perceptions created around the maintenance of sanctions on Zimbabwe and the conditions leading to their removal will continuously stall the re-engagement agenda under the 'new' dispensation.

## Conclusion

For the first eight months, December 2017 to July 2018, Mnangagwa's re-engagement efforts with the West and the attendant policies demonstrated a movement towards a new trajectory. However, from August 2018 up to the time of this writing, his reformist stance under the 'new' dispensation remains at the level of rhetoric. It is action alone that will shape the

---

54 'EU renews Zimbabwe arms embargo, freeze on defence company', *Bloomberg News*, 17 February 2020.

55 Mnangagwa describes sanctions as a cancer sapping the economy.

56 US Ambassador Nichols argues that sanctions are a lame excuse by the government, rather it is corruption that is affecting the economy. Only 141 Zimbabweans are on the sanctions list out of a population of 16 million. Furthermore, there is no trade embargo imposed on Zimbabwe by the USA.

future re-engagement agenda with the West because the gap between the expected and actual has caused frustration. Similarly, the renewal of sanctions by the West has frustrated Mnangagwa's government's foreign policy. The stalemate that existed under the Mugabe regime has resurfaced. Mnangagwa is not prepared to make what he regards as suicidal reforms, so the land and security sector questions remain stumbling blocks in the re-engagement process. ZANU-PF's illiberal political culture has gained new momentum under the Mnangagwa government.

Relations between Zimbabwe and the West will not experience a complete rupture, they will simply remain tense. While the East will continue as the political and economic pillar of Mnangagwa's government, the death of Western re-engagement means the country and its people will continue to suffer under the 'new' dispensation.

## References

Banda, C. (2005) 'Mugabe sets for ugly campaign'. Institute for War and Peace, Africa reports: Zimbabwe elections, 12 February.

Bandura, W. N., J. Zivanomoyo and K. Tsaura (2019) 'Remittances, Financial Developmewnt and Economic Growth: A Case of Southern African Development Community', *Œconomica*, 15/4, pp. 67-82.

Chitiyo, K. (2009) 'The case for security sector reform in Zimbabwe', Occasional Paper, Royal United Services Institute.

Chun, Z. (2014). 'China-Zimbabwe relations: A model for China-Africa relations?' Occasional paper 205, Southern African Institute for International Affairs.

Farrel, H. and A. Newman (2016) 'The new interdependence approach: theoretical development and empirical demonstration', *Review of International Political Economy*, 23/5, pp. 713-736.

Government of Zimbabwe (GoZ) (2018) 'Report of the Commission of Enquiry into the 1st of August post-election violence'. Harare: Government of Zimbabwe.

Hopf, T. (1998) 'The Promise of Constructivism in International Relations Theory', International Security, 23/1, pp.171-200.

Hove, M. (2017) 'The necessity of security sector reform in Zimbabwe', Politikon, 44/3, pp. 425-445.

Keohane, R.O. and J. Nye (2008) 'Power and interdependence', *Survival*, 15/4, pp. 158-165.

Latek, M. (2018) Zimbabwe's post-electoral challenges, Available, (online): www.europarl.europa.eu (Accessed 23 June 2019).

Makin, M. (2009) 'The prodigal returns: South Africa's re-admission to the Commonwealth of Nations June 1994', *South African Journal of International Affairs*, 4/1, pp. 100-117.

Mawere, M., N. Marongwe and F.P.T. Duri (2018) `The end of an era? Robert Mugabe and a Conflicting Legacy*. Bameda: Langaa Research and Publishing Common Initiative Group.

Masunungure E.V. (2011) 'Zimbabwe's militarised electoral authoritarianism', *Journal of International Affairs*, 65/1, pp. 47-64.

Masunungure E.V. and J.M. Shumba (2012) 'Exorcising the spectre of electoral authoritarianism in Zimbabwe's political transition', in E.V. Masunungure and J.M. Shumba, *Zimbabwe: Mired in Transition*. Harare: Weaver Press.

McGregor, J. and D. Pasura, (2010) 'Diasporic Repositioning and the Politics of Re-engagement: Developmentalising Zimbabwe's Diaspora'. *The Round Table*, 99/411, pp. 687-703.

Melber, H. (2003) 'Liberation and Democracy: Cases from Southern Africa', *Journal of Contemporary African Studies*, 21/2, pp. 149-153.

Mlambo, O.B. and E. Chitando (2015) '"Blair keep your England and let me keep my Zimbabwe": Examining the relationship of physical space and political order in Zimbabwe's land redistribution programme 2000-2008', *Journal of Pan African Studies*, 8/8.

Munhande, C. and Nciizah, E. (2013) 'Perpetuating colonial legacies: Reflections on post-colonial African State's development trajectories; Observation from Zimbabwe'. Gweru: Midlands State University.

Murphy, J. (2008) 'Engagement', in J. Welsh and D. Fearn, *Engagement: public diplomacy in a globalised world*. London: Foreign and Commonwealth Office.

Nyakudya, M. (2010) 'Security Sector Reform in Zimbabwe: Prospects and Challenges'. Harare: Solidarity Peace Trust.

Ojakorotu, V. and R. Kamidza (2018) 'Look East Policy: The Case of Zimbabwe-China Political and Economic Relations Since 2000', *A Journal of International Affairs*, 74/1, pp. 17-41.

Ouma, S. (2012) 'The New Scramble for Africa', *Regional Studies*, 46/6, pp. 836-838.

Ramani, S. (2016) 'Zimbabwe: China's "All-Weather" Friend in Africa', *The Diplomat*. January. Available at: https://thediplomat.com/2016/01/zimbabwe-chinas-all-weather-friend-in-africa/

Stokke, O. (2013) *Aid and Political Conditionality*. London: Routledge.

Taylor, M. and M.L. Kent (2014) 'Dialogic engagement: Clarifying foundational concepts', *Journal of Public Relations Research*, 26/5, pp. 384-398.

Taylor, I. and P. Williams (2002) 'The limits of engagement British foreign policy and the crisis in Zimbabwe', *International Affairs*, 78/3, pp. 547-565.

Tendi, B.M. (2014) 'The Origins and Functions of Demonisation Discourses in Britain-Zimbabwe relations (2000–)', *Journal of Southern African Studies* 40/6, pp. 1251-1269.

Wang, X. and A. Ozanne (2010) 'Two Approaches to Aid in Africa: China and the West'. Paper prepared for the International Conference, 'Ten years of War against poverty', University of Manchester, 8-10 September.

Wendt, A. (1992) 'Anarchy is what states make of it: The Social Construction of Power Politics', *International Organization,* 46/2, pp. 391-425.

# 14

# Conclusion:
# Zimbabwe's Unrelenting Fragility

In 1979, a year before Julius Nyerere warned Robert Mugabe, the newly inaugurated Zimbabwe Prime Minister, to judiciously nurture the jewel he had inherited from the settler-colonial regime, Professor Ali Mazrui delivered the Reith Lectures[1] in which he lamented the African Condition, as the 'Garden of Eden in Decay'. At the time, Mazrui anticipated that 'the agony of Zimbabwe' would soon be over, and indeed, within a year, the country's independence was achieved to ecstatic celebration. Today, 40 years on, Zimbabwe's trajectory continues to fall with about a quarter of its population having flown to more habitable conditions in and outside Africa. Those who remain continue to suffer but now under a black authoritarian regime. This is Zimbabwe's condition.

## Contours of Zimbabwe's fragile governance

From the foregoing chapters on Zimbabwe's fragile independence, several patterns are discernible a few of which are prominent. These include: the supremacy of politics in the hierarchy of values held and practised at the level of the party-military elites; the now towering role of the military in particular and the security sector in general in the country's governance system and political economy, giving rise to the 'deep state' phenomenon; and a schizophrenic and risk-averse citizenry.

## Primacy of politics

One of the defining contours of the country's governance is the primacy of politics as a guide to public decision making and action by the governing elites. Virtually everything is interpreted in political (read, partisan) terms

1    Mazrui, 1979.

in the Machiavellian sense of power politics i.e. the relentless pursuit of power for its own sake and for the benefits it brings to the power-wielder and his close associates. The public interest is of secondary importance. This is unlike the Aristotelian conception of politics as the 'Master Science' in pursuit of the public good or 'human happiness' as Aristotle called it. In this positive conception, politics is a virtuous activity in search of higher order, socially-desirable goals.

Sadly in Zimbabwe, politics is a vicious activity that takes a zero-sum character; what one side gains, the other loses. Until the country's politics assumes the character of a positive-sum game – i.e. each of two sides gets an advantage – Zimbabwe will have difficulty in escaping from the vicious circle in which it is presently trapped. To be fair, politics in its developmental sense seemed to have been the guiding principle in the first independence decade but this had unravelled by the end of that decade, displaced by the predatory imperative. This has contaminated all politics and almost all those who practice it, including those in the opposition. Thus, it is only a slight exaggeration to assert as a general rule that, today, virtually everything in Zimbabwe vibrates with the rhythm of politics.

## The towering role of the military

The second defining feature is the increasingly commanding if not hegemonic role of the military in the governance of the country through the security-sector's embeddedness within the state and via its historically-rooted symbiotic relationship with the ruling ZANU-PF party. More than ever before, Zimbabwe is now a party-military state under a party-military coalition. In the first twenty years of independence, the military initially played a covert, below-the-political radar role which was doubtless because ZANU-PF was firmly ensconced in power with only tepid competition from a fragmented and fragile opposition, particularly after the absorption of the rival PF-ZAPU into the ruling party in 1987.

With the onset of the twin economic and governance crisis at the end of the 1990s, the military increasingly encroached into partisan politics culminating in the November 2017 'Operation Restore Legacy' whereby the military became the arbiter of the deep, internecine and long-running succession-driven factionalism in 'their' party. With that giant intrusive step, the military had become fully politicised just as politics had become fully militarised. Today, the military is not only a kingmaker but part of the kingship with its former commander – General Constantino Chiwenga – at the heart of both the government and the ruling party as Vice-President. From this vantage point, it is a small step for one of the men with the gun to become the King. And, history teaches us that once the military has intruded into the politics of the country, it will be virtually impossible to reverse this tendency; once in, always in. This means the twin processes of militarisation of politics and the politicisation of the military are likely to be a feature of Zimbabwe politics and civil-military relations beyond the foreseeable future.

Moreover, and based on the historical fusion of the liberation war soldier, war veteran and politician in ZANU-PF, it is likely that the military will continue to see itself as a defender of the ruling party. This is notwithstanding the national aspirations that are unambiguously expressed in the country's 2013 Constitution (Sections 206 and 208) whereby the military's role is defined as 'protecting national security' with 'the utmost respect for the fundamental rights and freedoms and democratic values and principles, and the rule of law'. Additionally, according to the supreme law, members of the security forces should not further the interests of any political party or cause.

Given the legacy of the 1970s liberation war, it is unlikely that the military, while it is still dominated at its apex by the veterans of that war, will be amenable to subordinating itself to democratic civilian oversight other than that of ZANU-PF. In other words, it is difficult to envisage the war veteran-dominated military leadership subordinating itself to a political leadership other than that arising from ZANU-PF. November 2017 proved beyond reasonable doubt that the military can decide who, within ZANU-PF, will be its commander-in-chief. In any case, Mugabe himself had been enthroned by ZANLA – ZANU's military wing – at Mgagao in October 1975. Whoever the military can enthrone, it can dethrone, as it did 42 years later. This is a lesson that must not be forgotten by any current and future political leadership.

The war veteran's generation is not psychologically open to the possibility that anyone outside ZANU-PF be entitled to rule the country and be their commander in chief. It also exposes as a fallacy the principle – long held and stressed by Mugabe during and after the war – that 'politics controls the gun'; it holds true only when there is a convergence of interests between the ruler (the commander-in-chief) and the military. When they diverge, as they did by November 2017, the gun trumps politics.

In short, there are serious psycho-historical impediments to the kind of security-sector reforms envisaged by and in the national constitution. The hard reality is that at this critical juncture, the military exercises veto power over what kind of security sector reforms can be undertaken, by who, when and why. Democratic reform promoters should bear this in mind, putting this front and centre. Constitutional engineering, as reflected in the 2013 national Constitution, cannot easily change this reality.

The umbilical cord between the two – the apex of the military and ZANU-PF – is still intact and it may well take another generation for the ties between the two to be loosened. Until then, those who wield the gun will continue to defend their party. The democratisation of the military and the security sector more broadly should be regarded as a long-term project. Until then, the travails of the opposition – individually and collectively, big or small – will continue and even intensify for the foreseeable future.

## Resilient fragility

A unifying thread in Zimbabwe's often tumultuous four decades of *uhuru* is resilient fragility which, over the last two decades, has been unrelenting and manifests itself along multiple dimensions that, cumulatively, have eroded the robustness of the state and the viability of the economy while tearing apart the fabric of society. Zimbabwe now stands out in the region and the continent as a country plagued by chronic fragility. It is a tragic case of a country that, at independence, proudly stepped forward with its tail firmly up but which, within one-and-a-half decades, was precipitously sliding backwards with its tail dangling between its legs. A bread basket that was overflowing, with enough food for domestic consumption and for export, was later replaced by a begging bowl held by an ever-outstretched hand for fatigued donors and humanitarian agencies to fill which they have been generously doing since the turn of the new millennium. This, in the context of and alongside systemic, grand corruption that has sapped the energy of the nation and been elevated to a 'national religion', as the main opposition leader recently described the scale of the scourge.[2]

A syndrome of crises is a more befitting description of the now-chronic and multifaceted problems in the country. The thirteen preceding

---

2  Nelson Chamisa, the MDC-Alliance leader, was commenting on the combustible situation in Zimbabwe as of June 2020 in a critique of the repression wrought by the regime against the opposition party: 'Mnangagwa is forgetting real issues on the ground that include a collapsing economy, the economy is in the doldrums and corruption has become the new national religion'. See 'We can't breathe: Chamisa', *NewsDay*. June 8, 2020.

chapters in this book have outlined the contours of the vicious syndrome, demonstrating that none of the facets of the complex crisis shows any signs of abating. Indeed, the situation is worsening, more or less relentlessly.

The book is about the country's fragility but when all that can be said has been said, one is struck, not so much by the fragility, but by the durability of that fragility. In fact, it can be asserted that one of the most politically significant facts about Zimbabwe is the resilience of its fragility alongside the staying power of the country's party-military regime. In a private email correspondence to this author, a seasoned observer of Zimbabwe political dynamics puzzled (as many do) over 'the sources of resilience for states that face serious headwinds and, by some people's reckoning, should have already given way'. He suggested that there are some sources of strength that enable such a regime to remain intact. What could be that magical source of that resilience when most other regimes, with less grave problems, have previously been swept away while others are facing the same fate? Could it be that this is a unique, special regime type akin to no other i.e. a *sui generis* regime type?

## Deep State in Zimbabwe?

Most of the chapters, covering a diverse range of topics, all tend to attest to and converge directly or implicitly, on a troubling reality that Zimbabwe resembles what elsewhere is called a 'deep state'. The deep state phenomenon originated in the Mediterranean region and has been associated with a special type of state politics in countries such as Turkey and Egypt. The concept has been extended to cover many other countries in parts of the world with sometimes different and almost always with pejorative meanings.

A dictionary definition of a deep state is that it refers to 'organisations such as military, police, or political groups that are said to work secretly in order to protect particular interests and rule a country without being elected'.[3] According to Wikipedia, 'a deep state, also known as a *state within a state*, is a form of governance made up of networks of power operating independently of a state's political leadership in pursuit of their own agenda and goals'.[4] To the *Politics Dictionary*:

The Deep State is believed to be a clandestine network entrenched

---

3  'Meaning of deep state in English', https://dictionary.cambridge.org/dictionary/english/deep-state

4  'Deep State', https://en.wikipedia.org/wiki/Deep_state (emphasis original)

inside the government, bureaucracy, intelligence agencies, and other governmental entities. The Deep State supposedly controls state policy behind the scenes, while the democratically-elected process and elected officials are merely figureheads. ... Deep State has since come to mean any "shadow government" operating behind the scenes of a democracy. If true, this would mean that the democratic process is a façade.[5]

Nicholas Chan observes that in countries like Pakistan, Thailand and Turkey, 'the term deep state is often used to signify a parallel state consisted of a politically influential military state'.[6] Writing specifically on Malaysia, Lim Tech Ghee points out that one of the characteristics of the deep state is that it is hard to establish or pinpoint 'because it consists of amorphous groups that operate beneath or behind the political radar'.[7] In an earlier article, Ghee had written that: 'In other parts of the world, the deep state has been defined as a body of people, typically influential members of government agencies, the military and other sectors, involved in the secret manipulation or control of government policy'.[8]

At home, Nyamutatanga Makombe, in his 2011 article on security sector reforms during the 2009-13 coalition government, sees a similar tendency in Zimbabwe which originated in the 1970s liberation war. For him, the term 'refers to a situation where an entire nation is held hostage by a group of influential anti-democratic coalitions usually comprising high-level elements within the intelligence services, military and security'.[9] It is vital to note that while in countries such as Malaysia, the deep state consortium has been viewed as operating against the dictates and wishes of the elected governing elites, this is not always the case. Thus, as Ghee argues, when deconstructing the deep state (at least in Malaysia's case), 'it should not be assumed that the deep state is always in opposition to the state *de jure*'.

In Zimbabwe, the deep state phenomenon refers to the pivotal role

---

5   'Deep State', https://www.dictionary.com/e/politics/deep-state/
6   'Unpacking the idea of Malaysia's "deep state"', *new mandala*, 20 February 2020.
7   'Encounters with the deep state', *The Sun Daily*, 20 July 2019.
8   'Current and future position of Malay political dominance', *The Sun Daily*, 16 June 2019.
9   'Security reforms: The need to uproot the "deep state"', Zimbabwe Independent, 29 July 2011. Makombe was writing at the height of the four-year constitution-making process that birthed the 2013 Constitution which futilely tries to clip the wings of the military by subordinating it to civilian authority.

of the security sector – especially the military – in the governance and political economy of the country and concomitant diminution of the role of democratic and constitutional institutions and processes. The military is the decisive stake player especially in most if not all strategic matters in the country.

The most visible and living evidence of this is the existence and role of the Joint Operations Command (JOC), the colonial-era, counter-insurgency but semi-formal, non-statutory security structure at the apex of the security establishment that represents the joint chiefs of staff. It is heavily involved in the governance of the country to a point where Bratton asserts that:

> After 2000, the JOC took charge of key governance functions, effectively sidelining the constitutionally appointed cabinet and parliament, especially on security issues. ... As military men gained control over national security and related policies, the tables of civil-military relations were turned, with the military often controlling civilians. This power inversion was most evident during periodic national elections....[10]

In effect, according to Bratton, the JOC 'became the supreme, but unofficial, decision-making body'[11] which did not only sideline the civilian Cabinet but 'even rivaled the party Politburo'. In sum, when the JOC coughs, the whole country catches the flu. And, in Zimbabwe's case, the deep state is part of and the bulwark to the *de jure* state.

## ZANU-PF is a system

Another conclusion which emerges from the contributions in this book as well as from the accumulated evidence in the last two decades is that ZANU-PF, though classified as a political party among other parties in the country, is in fact more than just a party. It is *a system* and a well-established and fully-fledged one. Therefore, in the game of political competition for state power, other parties are competing, not against the ruling party *qua* party but a system that is intimately connected to the state, the security organs, the legislative and judiciary[12] branches, as well as the business world in which many shadowy cartels play a key role, mainly as primitive capital accumulators. Thus, any party that commits to competing with ZANU-PF should factor into its calculations, the many roles and faces of the ZANU-PF system. Defeating ZANU-PF –

the party – does not translate into defeating ZANU-PF – the system – as the MDC's Morgan Tsvangirai ruefully discovered in the aftermath of the March 2008 presidential elections. As a system, and for that very reason, it cannot easily be changed without changing the other parts of its system. To change a system one must change or replace each of its parts, that is, every cog in the wheel needs to change.

The fact of the ruling party being a system has over the years been consistently displayed in various ways, most visibly in electoral contests (especially since 2000), the judiciary processes, legislative games, local governance (especially in the rural areas), traditional political governance, in dealing with the opposition and civil society organisations, and in policy implementation e.g. Fast Track Land Reform Programme (FTLRP) and within it Operation Tsuro, food/humanitarian aid and agricultural inputs distribution, and in other arenas. The system also extends its tentacles to regional and continental organisations as well as to the Look East countries, notably China, the 'all-weather friend'. In sum, as a system, ZANU-PF is omnipotent and omnipresent and there is no part of the country that does not 'know' the party and feels its commanding presence, allied to the other parts of the system.

## Zimbabwe's chronic fragility: Act of man or act of God?

One of the central lessons arising from this compendium is that neither fragility nor robustness is God-given or necessarily a product of bad luck. In both cases, they are acts of Man ('man' in the generic, genderless sense). Zimbabwe's fragility – initially in small, incremental steps in the first two independence decades – accelerated in the last 22 years. For instance, according to the International Monetary Fund, the country had the fastest shrinking economy in the world by the first half decade of the new millennium with citizens becoming 'one-third poorer in the last five years'.[13] In 2005, Clemens and Moss went further, noting that 'Zimbabwe has experienced a precipitous collapse in its economy over the past five years. The purchasing power of the average Zimbabwean in 2005 has fallen back to the same level as in 1953' (2005, 2). The two authors then concluded that: 'The scale and speed of this income decline is unusual outside a war situation' (2005, 3). Survey findings by Afrobarometer have consistently confirmed the degraded welfare of the majority of Zimbabweans post-2000. Indeed, Martin Meredith, a Mugabe biographer,

---

13 Chikwanha et al., 2004.

claims that: 'By 2000, Zimbabweans were generally poorer than they had been at independence; average wages were lower; unemployment had tripled; and life expectancy was falling. More than two-thirds of the population lived in abject poverty.'[14] This precipitous decline, which has continued, could not have been a result of bad luck but of bad policy i.e. an act of Man. Samantha Power, a former U.S. Ambassador to the United Nations could not have put it more fittingly with her 2003 article aptly entitled: 'How to Kill a Country: Turning a breadbasket into a basket case in ten easy steps – the Robert Mugabe way'.[15]

True, Zimbabwe has suffered from natural calamities in the form of cyclones and droughts, mostly induced by the El-Nino global weather phenomenon which often ravages Zimbabwe, and more frequently in recent years. However, it is also true that Zimbabwe has not been the only victim of such natural disasters, just as it has not been singled out by Covid-19. These are indeed acts of God but their scope and gravity can be either mitigated or aggravated by human intervention. That Zimbabwe became southern Africa's breadbasket was attributed to government's prudent public policy, especially in the first independence decade, widely acknowledged as the country's development decade. Wise and rational leadership accounted for this. In an analysis of the first three decades and the role of leadership, Bratton and Masunungure concluded that:

> Generally speaking … the 1980s were a decade of moderate economic growth and rapid social development in Zimbabwe. The country's gross domestic product expanded at an average rate of 4.5 percent per annum between 1980 and 1989, though droughts in 1982-4 and 1987 caused the growth rate to fluctuate from year to year. …
>
> Indeed, within five years of independence, nearly all children of primary school age were in school and more than 80 percent of eligible students were moving on to secondary school. And the Minister of Health was able to make the landmark announcement that the infant mortality rate had been cut in half (2011, 23-24).

Admittedly, there were auspicious circumstances or good fortune that contributed to the developmental outcomes, e.g. the economy benefited from a peace dividend at the end of the guerrilla war, the removal of trade sanctions against the former settler regime, a generous influx of aid from

14  Meredith, 2018.
15  Power, 2003.

the international community,[16] and pent-up demand for goods and services from a growing population. It needed good leadership to take advantage of these favourable conditions. The fact that the leadership later lost its way does not detract from the reality that Mugabe and his ZANU-PF regime started off on the right path, driving the country in the right direction.[17] During that decade, almost all development indicators were pointing in the right direction. And, though there were already small burning fires of corruption – e.g. the Paweni and 'Willowgate' scandals in 1982 and 1986 respectively – they had not become the raging inferno that corruption has become today. Rational economic management, under the former UN Under Secretary General Bernard Chidzero, tempered some of the radical ideological excesses of the hardliners in the Mugabe regime. Even though there was no large-scale job creation, unemployment in the formal sector was nowhere near the world-setting record of between 80-90%.[18] The honeymoon soon ended, earlier in Matabeleland than in the rest of the country.

Operation Gukurahundi (1983-87), Zimbabwe's darkest moment in its troubled four-decade history, was not an act of God. Neither was the chain of disastrous 'operations' unleashed from the late 1990s – prominent among which were Operation Hondo Yeminda ('War for Land' or the Third Chimurenga), Operation Murambatsvina (2005), Operation Mavhoterapapi (April to June 2008) etc. All of these saw Zimbabwe sliding backwards not only in terms of national development and nation-building but also in the relations between the country and the international community, especially the West, with some of the countries imposing and enforcing targeted sanctions which they have largely maintained in the last eighteen years.

Zimbabwe is a tragic but not inevitable case of a seemingly permanent clash between bad politics and good policies, where the former almost always trumps the latter. The saving grace is that both politics and policies are man-made and when judiciously combined, can produce a virtuous circle but when imprudently conjoined produce the opposite, a vicious

---

16  Meredith (ibid) noted that: 'On the international stage, Zimbabwe was accorded star status. In the first year of independence, Zimbabwe was awarded more than $1 billion in aid, enabling Mugabe to embark on ambitious health and education programs'.

17  As with most human affairs, not everyone agrees with this positive assessment during this period. One early critic was Andre Astrow (1983).

18  'Reality Check: Are 90% of Zimbabweans unemployed?' *BBC News*, 3 December 2017. See also: 'Zimbabwe's unemployment rate at 90%: union', *eNCA*, 2 May 2017.

circle. Zimbabwe's syndrome of crises arise from the conjoining of bad politics and bad policies. There is nothing inescapable about Zimbabwe's trajectory in the last four decades. It is neither necessary nor compulsory for Zimbabwe to be caught in this downward spiral. Until good policy is matched to good politics, Zimbabwe will for the foreseeable future remain deeply mired in its syndrome of crises.

## Are the masses complicit?

It is common wisdom that policies – whether good or bad – are made by leaders, sometimes unilaterally, as is notoriously the case in Zimbabwe. The question, with particular reference to Zimbabwe, is whether leaders are solely to blame or the blame should be shared between the leaders and those they govern. Carl Friedrich's (1937) 'rule of anticipated reactions' teaches us that, in taking decisions, those who rule or lead almost always anticipate how the intended target or audience is going to react to the decisions, whether in praise or condemnation or sometimes a mixture of the two. They then proceed on the basis of that assessment. If leaders rule badly, is it not partly – or even largely – because the populace allow them to do so, or at the very least, acquiesce in the bad governance?

The question of whether the electorate is also blameworthy reminds us of the question that Masipula Sithole (1998) asked with respect to ethnicity. He pondered whether ethnicity resides in the demos or the elite. He found both guilty. Similarly, one can ask: Is poor governance because of the leadership elites or the masses are also culpable? The essays in this book do not acquit the leadership. What Bratton and Masunungure concluded in 2011 in respect of the first three decades of independence is even more valid today than then: the country has been under a predatory rather than developmental leadership. But what about the role of the citizenry? Are they innocent or complicit? Have they abetted or abated the degraded governance?

Was it not the general public that ecstatically and understandably celebrated the achievement of *uhuru* in 1980 but then allowed the liberators to govern without any encumbrances, throwing caution to the wind? The leaders abused the trust and confidence invested in them and what did the masses do; they turned the other cheek. For more than twenty years, from the mid-1990s to 2013, Zimbabweans attributed the increasingly degraded governance to a bad, elite-imposed supreme law, the Lancaster House Constitution. Then they laboured for nearly four years participating in a constitution-making process at the end of which was a people-driven social contract that only a few have faulted and many have praised. Since its enactment in 2013, it has been eviscerated on numerous occasions while the people are watching, again turning the other cheek.

Economic degradation has ravaged the country for the last 22 years and what do the masses do. They withdraw from the state and public affairs, taking an atomistic stance to collective problems instead of organising for collective action against the source of the grievances. The motto seems to be: 'Each one for himself or herself, and God for us all'!

Yet, was it not the Zimbabwe citizens that wildly celebrated the palace coup in November 2017, taking selfies with or hugging the coup executors while throwing caution to the wind? Before long, ecstasy turned to apprehension and then despond, but again, a risk-averse population recoils into its cocoon.

The fact of the matter is that the leadership does what it does because it knows the reactions of the public, in this case quiet anger i.e. *kukuwarire mukati* (suffering in silence). To state this is not to praise it. It is simply to acknowledge this reality for those who want or can do 'something' about it. In other words, the hydra-headed governance problem in Zimbabwe has two sources: the risk-taking, unilateralist leadership and the risk-fearing masses most of whom seem to have either over-internalised the biblical injunction of turning the other cheek or have become fatalistic, finding solace in the Church (especially the Evangelical or 'prosperity' churches) and the idea that God will prevail and deliver. To borrow Mamdani's famous characterisation, the generality of Zimbabweans are subjects rather than citizens. It is also true that those who have claimed their citizenship have been pilloried in many different ways while others have kept quiet because they have benefited from the patronage system.

A more charitable description, offered by Bratton and Logan (2013), is that they are voters but not yet citizens. As such, their maximum level of political participation is going to the voting booth and casting their ballot, once in five years. In between, they withdraw into their shells, but their detachment is not due to satisfaction with their lives but to a deep and sustained despair. Afrobarometer and other surveys consistently show that Zimbabweans are schizophrenic. They are deeply unhappy with the governance of their country and persistently say it is going in the wrong direction and yet, given the opportunity to vote, they vote the same political elites in power, sometimes – as in 2013 and 2018 – with apparently large majorities.

In sum, it is true that Zimbabwe suffers from the historical burden of 90 years of authoritarian settler-colonialism, and 40 years of its post-colonial version which at times has taken malignant forms. Indeed, as adherents of path dependence tell us: history matters. But is Zimbabwe chained to this burden or can we put our hope in Ayi Kwei Armah's suggestion that 'the beautyful ones are not yet born'?[19]

# References

Armah, Ayi Kwei. (1968) *The Beautyful Ones Are Not Yet Born*. Boston: Houghton Mifflin.

Astrow, Andre (1983) *Zimbabwe: A Revolution That Lost Its Way?* London: Zed Books.

Bratton, Michael (1981) 'Development in Zimbabwe: Strategy and Tactics.' *The Journal of Modern African Studies*, 19(3), pp. 447-475.

———— (2014) *Power Politics in Zimbabwe*. Boulder, CO: Lynne Rienner.

———— and Eldred Masunungure (2011) 'The Anatomy of Political Predation: Leaders, Elites and Coalitions in Zimbabwe, 1980-2010'. Paper prepared for The Developmental Leadership Program (DLP). (January).

———— and Carolyn Logan (2013) 'Voters but Not Yet Citizens: The Weak Demand for Vertical Accountability', in *Voting and Democratic Citizenship in Africa*. Boulder, CO: Lynne Rienner.

Chan, Nicholas (2020) 'Unpacking the idea of Malaysia's "deep state"', *new mandala*, 20 February 2020.

Chikwanha, Annie, Tulani Sithole and Michael Bratton (2004) 'The Power of Propaganda: Public Opinion in Zimbabwe, 2004', Afrobarometer Working Paper No. 42.

Clemens, Michael and Todd Moss (2005) 'Costs and Causes of Zimbabwe's Crisis'. Washington, DC: Center for Global Development.

Diamond, L. (2002) 'Elections Without Democracy: Thinking About Hybrid Regimes', *Journal of Democracy*, 13(2), pp. 21-35.

Friedrich, Carl J. (1937) *Constitutional Government and Politics*. New York: Harper

---

19 Armah, 1968.

Mazrui, A. (1979) The African Condition, The Reith Lecturers. Available at: https://www.bbc.co.uk/programmes/p00gq1wn

Meredith, M. (2018) 'Mugabe's Misrule: And How It Will Hold Zimbabwe Back', *Foreign Affairs*, March/April.

Power, Samantha (2003) 'How to Kill a Country: Turning a breadbasket into a basket case in ten easy steps – the Robert Mugabe way', *The Atlantic*, December.

Sithole, M. (1998) 'Tribalism's Base: Leaders or Masses?', in *Zimbabwe's Public Eye: Political Essays*, October 1997-October 1998. Harare: Rujeko Publishers.

# Appendix 1

*President Emmerson Mnangagwa's first Cabinet*

(1 December 2017)

(*indicates ministers who were not in Robert Mugabe's Cabinet
** indicates former members of the armed forces)

Emmerson Mnangagwa - President
Constantino Chiwenga - Vice President & Minister of Defence, Security
    and War Veterans**
Kembo Mohadi - Vice President
Obert Mpofu - Minister of Home Affairs and Culture
Chris Mutsvangwa - Minister of Media, Information and Broadcasting
    Services
Sibusiso Moyo - Minister of Foreign Affairs**
Priscah Mupfumira - Minister of Tourism and Hospitality
Supa Mandiwanzira - Minister for Information and Communications
Ziyambi Ziyambi - Minister of Justice and Legal Affairs,
Amon Murwira - Minister of Higher Education, Science and Technology*
Paul Mavima - Minister of Primary and Secondary Education
David Parirenyatwa - Minister of Health and Child Welfare
Petronella Kagonye - Minister of Labour and Social Welfare*
Winston Chitando - Minister of Mines and Mining Development*
Patrick Chinamasa - Minister of Finance and Economic Planning
Perance Shiri - Minister of Lands, Rural Resettlement and Agriculture**
Michael Bimha - Minister of Industry and Commerce
July Moyo - Local Government and Public Works*
Sithembiso Nyoni - Minister for Youth and Women Affairs
Kazembe Kazembe - Minister of Sport, Arts and Recreation*
Joram Gumbo - Minister of Transport and Infrastructural Development
Oppah Muchinguri - Minister of Environment, Water and Climate
Simon Khaya-Moyo - Minister of Energy and Power Development
Simbarashe Mumbengegwi - Senior Advisor to the President
Christopher Mushohwe - Minister of State for Government Scholarships.

# Appendix 2

## *Splits in the MDC explained*

The acronym MDC stands for Movement for Democratic Change, an opposition political party formed in September 1999. The MDC split in 2005 over disagreements on whether or not to participate in the country's senatorial elections. To distinguish between the two splinter parties, the MDC led by Morgan Tsvangirai was named MDC-T while the other formation led by Welshman Ncube was dubbed MDC-N. In April 2014, the MDC-T suffered yet another split when the secretary-general, Tendai Biti and deputy treasurer-general, Elton Mangoma pulled out of the party to form MDC Renewal. The death of MDC-T leader, Morgan Tsvangirai, on 14 February 2018, triggered a succession row in the main opposition MDC-T party among three rival leaders: Nelson Chamisa, Elias Mudzuri and Thokozani Khupe. Nelson Chamisa, an appointed Vice President of the party, was eventually appointed its acting president and later confirmed as the leader of the party. Thokozani Khupe, challenged Nelson Chamisa for the leadership of the party and was subsequently dismissed from the party and she formed her own faction. A legal dispute arose between Chamisa and Khupe over the use of the party name and symbols. In what is seen as a compromise, Khupe's faction retained the MDC-T name and Chamisa's faction became the MDC-Alliance (alternatively MDC-A). The MDC-A was a coalition of seven opposition parties launched on 5 August, 2017 to challenge ZANU-PF in 2018 harmonised elections. The electoral coalition brought together MDC-T and former MDC breakaway parties Welshman Ncube and Tendai Biti who had left in 2005 and 2014 respectively) together with other parties including Zanu-Ndonga, Transform Zimbabwe and Zimbabwe People First. From the May 2019 Congress, the MDC-A changed its name to the original party name, the MDC. However, it is still known as MDC-Alliance in Parliament and at the Zimbabwe Electoral Commission and has competed under this name in all post-congress by-elections.

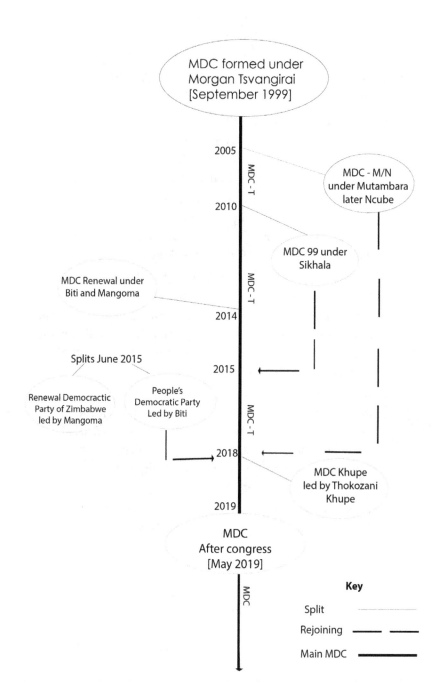

# Appendix 3

*Sections of the Draft ZMC in violation of the Zimbabwean Constitution*

a) Sections of the Draft Bill that bestow wide discretionary powers on the Minister over the Commission should not be allowed to stand in the final Bill or Act. This setup significantly compromises or depletes the independence of the Commission

b) The Bill states that the Commission can initiate investigations on its own. This arguably, is open to abuse and theoretically promotes persecutory type investigations. It is more desirable that the primary basis for investigations to be the filing of a complaint by a specific identifiable complainant.

c) In respect of Section 10 (1) of the Bill, the possibility of closed proceedings should be separated from the requirement for hearings to be public. The starting point should be that in the spirit of transparency and open democracy, proceedings of the Commission shall be public.

d) In respect of Section 10 (2) of the Bill, it is not clear why the representative of entities in proceedings should be the principal officer. Consider adopting the approach taken for instance in the Criminal Procedure and Evidence Act where "a director or employee of [the pertinent] corporate body" would be a competent representative.

e) Under Section 10 (3) of the Bill, sections 9 to 18 of the Commissions of Inquiry Act [Chapter 10:07] are infused into the Zimbabwe Media Commission Bill. The inclusion of these imported sections is problematic *because*:

a. Section 9 of the Commissions of Inquiry Act provides for the possibility of the exclusion of "any particular person or persons" from the Commission's proceedings. This is a worrisomely wide power that could easily be abused, and it violates the principles of natural justice that are enshrined in the Constitution, and

b. Section 12 (c) provides for the swearing in of witnesses. However, the practice of swearing is unacceptable for some individuals on religions, ethical, intellectual, and other convictions, or beliefs.

c. Section 13 of the Commissions of Inquiry Act also refers to the oath. In other jurisdictions the concept of "affirmation" as an alternative to oath taking is now common, and

d. Section 14 (1) of the Commissions of Inquiry Act refers to "insults" on any Commissioner, but the ZMC Bill does not define the term. This term is too broad and must therefore be defined under the interpretation section of the ZMC Bill, if the importation of Section 14 of the Commissions of Inquiries Act is at all necessary.

e. Section 14 (1) of the Commissions of Inquiry Act also refers to "detention in custody until the rising of the commission." All of this language sounds very drastic. Similarly, the possibility of "a fine not exceeding level five or to imprisonment for a period not exceeding six months or to both such fine and such imprisonment" under Section 14. (2) of the Commission of Inquiries Act is also clearly draconian.

f) The possibility of police involvement in investigations of the Commission under Section 10 (4) of the ZMC Bill as well as Section 18 of the Commissions of Inquiry Act could be problematic *because*:

a. This suggests the criminalisation of communication activities, and

b. It might compromise the independence (or even the reputation) of the Commission.

g) That Section 16 of the ZMC Bill entrenches a right of Appeal is positive. It would be even better to have a schedule with attendant Appeal Rules to give full effect to relevant appeal-related constitutional rights.

h) Part IV of the ZMC Bill omits provisions on the establishment of a Media Fund. AIPPA carries provisions for the establishment of such a Fund, and this must be maintained in the new law. The Commission must plough some of the funds it collects back into the media sector.

i) The Declaration on Principles of Freedom of Expression in Africa (adopted by the African Commission on Human and

People's Rights in 2002) is instructive in respect to the issue of self-regulation. Article 9 (3) of the Declaration refers to effective self- regulation as the best system for upholding and promoting high standards in the media. This means Zimbabwe must take every step possible, including recognition of existing self-regulatory mechanisms in the proposed ZMC Bill.

j) ZMC Bill lacks clarity on the relationship between the Voluntary Media Council or any other self-regulatory mechanism with the ZMC.

CPSIA information can be obtained
at www.ICGtesting.com
Printed in the USA
LVHW080535191220
674519LV00005B/125